HONG KONG ENGLISH
AUTONOMY AND CREATIVITY

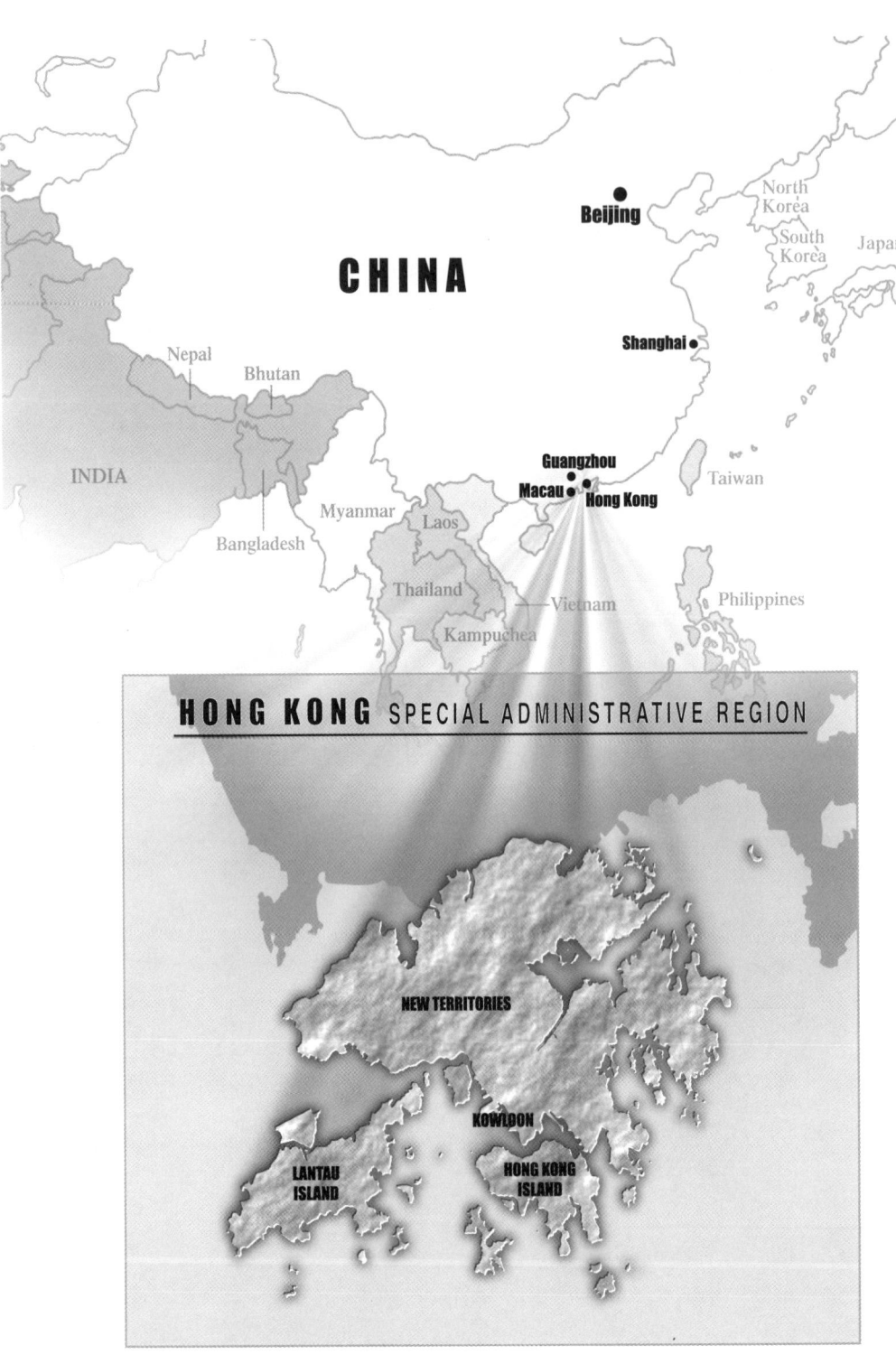

HONG KONG ENGLISH
AUTONOMY AND CREATIVITY

Edited by
Kingsley Bolton

香港大學出版社
HONG KONG UNIVERSITY PRESS

Hong Kong University Press
14/F Hing Wai Centre
7 Tin Wan Praya Road
Aberdeen
Hong Kong

© Hong Kong University Press 2002

First published 2002
Reprinted 2004, 2005

ISBN 962 209 553 4

All rights reserved. No portion of this publication may be reproduced or transmitted in any form or by any means, electronic or mechanical, including photocopy, recording, or any information storage or retrieval system, without prior permission in writing from the publisher.

Chapters 1–12, 15 and 16 were first published in the journal, *World Englishes*, Vol. 19, No. 3. Reproduced here by permission of Blackwell Publishers Ltd.

British Library Cataloguing-in-Publication Data
A catalogue record for this book is available from the British Library.

Secure On-line Ordering
http://www.hkupress.org

Printed and bound by Caritas Printing Training Centre, Hong Kong, China.

Contents

List of Contributors — vii

Introduction — 1
Hong Kong English: Autonomy and creativity
Kingsley Bolton

Part I: Language in Context — 27

1 The sociolinguistics of Hong Kong and the space for Hong Kong English — 29
   Kingsley Bolton

2 The discourse and attitudes of English language teachers in Hong Kong — 57
   Amy B. M. Tsui and David Bunton

3 Cantonese-English code-switching research in Hong Kong: A survey of recent research — 79
   David C. S. Li

4 The English-language media in Hong Kong — 101
   Chan Yuen-ying

Part II: Language Form — 117

5 Towards a phonology of Hong Kong English — 119
   Tony T. N. Hung

6	Relative clauses in Hong Kong English *Nikolas Gisborne*	141
7	Hong Kong words: Variation and context *Phil Benson*	161

Part III: Dimensions of Creativity — 171

8	Hong Kong writing and writing Hong Kong *Louise Ho*	173
9	Defining Hong Kong poetry in English: An answer from linguistics *Agnes Lam*	183
10	Writing between Chinese and English *Leung Ping-kwan*	199
11	From Yinglish to sado-mastication *Nury Vittachi*	207
12	Writing the literature of non-denial *Xu Xi*	219

Part IV: Resources — 239

13	Analysing Hong Kong English: Sample texts from the International Corpus of English *Kingsley Bolton and Gerald Nelson*	241
14	Cultural imagination and English in Hong Kong *Shirley Geok-lin Lim*	265
15	Researching Hong Kong English: Bibliographical Sources *Kingsley Bolton*	281

Part V: Future Directions — 293

16	Futures for Hong Kong English *Kingsley Bolton and Shirley Geok-lin Lim*	295

Index — 315

List of Contributors

Phil Benson is an Assistant Professor in the English Centre, the University of Hong Kong.

Kingsley Bolton is Professor of Linguistics in the Department of English, Stockholm University, and Honorary Professor of English at the University of Hong Kong.

David Bunton is an Associate Professor in the Faculty of Education, the University of Hong Kong.

Chan Yuen-ying is Professor and Director of the Journalism and Media Studies Centre, the University of Hong Kong.

Nikolas Gisborne is a Lecturer in the English Language Department, the University of Edinburgh.

Louise Ho was until recently an Associate Professor in the Department of English, the Chinese University of Hong Kong.

Tong T. N. Hung is an Associate Professor and Head of the Language Centre, Hong Kong Baptist University.

Agnes Lam is an Associate Professor in the English Centre, the University of Hong Kong.

Leung Ping-kwan is Chair Professor of Comparative Literature in the Department of Chinese, Lingnan University.

David C. S. Li is an Associate Professor in the Department of English and Communication, City University of Hong Kong.

Shirley Geok-lin Lim is Honorary Professor of English at the University of Hong Kong, and Professor of English at the University of California, Santa Barbara.

Gerald Nelson is a Lecturer in the Department of English Language and Literature, University College London.

Amy B. M. Tsui is Chair Professor and Director of the Teachers of English Language Education Centre (TELEC) in the Faculty of Education, the University of Hong Kong.

Nury Vittachi is a Hong Kong-based writer, and also a columnist for the *Far Eastern Economic Review*.

Xu Xi is a writer based in both Hong Kong and New York.

Introduction

Hong Kong English: Autonomy and creativity

Kingsley Bolton

Background

Hong Kong is an extraordinary society that has experienced a series of dramatic changes over the last fifty years in almost all aspects of its economic, social and political life.[1] Immediately after the Second World War, the population of Hong Kong exploded as a result of continuous waves of immigration from Guangdong province and other parts of China, with its population almost quadrupling from 1945 to 1951. Since then, its population has continued to increase at an average rate of one million people per decade, to 3.1 million in 1961, 4.1 million in 1971, 5.6 million in 1991 and to around 6.7 million in the year 2001. In the late 1940s, the transfer of Shanghainese industrial expertise and capital helped set up the labour-intensive low-cost industries, such as textiles, garments and plastics, that became the major employers in the period up to the mid-1970s. These Shanghai emigrés brought with them a cosmopolitanism and cultural capital that found expression in the film industry, music, food and entertainment in 1950s Hong Kong. The Shanghainese were soon outnumbered by huge numbers of refugee immigrants from southern China, many of whom came from small towns and pre-modern agricultural communities in the Pearl River Delta and Guangdong province. These immigrants provided the labour force for the low-cost industries of the 1950s and 1960s, and were initially housed in extreme conditions of discomfort and overcrowding.

After the riots and social disturbances of 1966 and 1967, Hong Kong underwent another period of rapid change. In the 1970s, MacLehose's reformist administration began to provide a greatly expanded range of social services, including public housing, health care, public transport and education. The equivalent of the British 1870 Education Act (providing for elementary education for all) took effect in Hong Kong in 1974, and the equivalent of the British 1944 Education Act (providing secondary education) went into effect in 1978. Judged by the usual economic indicators, Hong Kong society became rich extremely quickly in the period of its modern formation, with the per capita GDP rising from US$410 in the 1960s to US$23,000 by 1996, although great disparities of wealth continue to exist. The territory's separation from mainland China meant that Hong Kong also began to develop its own cultural identity. By 1971, a majority of the population (some 56 percent), could claim to be 'Hong Kong-born', and by 1991 this proportion had risen to almost 60 percent. By the early 1980s, it was clear that Hong Kong people (a term that first appeared after the 1967 riots) were no longer 'sojourners', but 'Hong Kong people', *hēung góng yàhn*, with their own distinctive culture in film, television, music, print-media and much else.

The period from the 1960s to the 1990s also witnessed the rise of the modern Hong Kong Cantonese language, and its growing use in a wide range of public domains, including the civil service, the mass media, and the entertainment industry. This also contributed to the specific characteristics of the Hong Kong speech community in the late colonial period. Immigrants and their children from the different dialect areas of Guangdong and Fujian province quickly adapted their speech to meet the norms of urban metropolitan Cantonese in the territory. The use of indigenous dialects, such as Hakka, began to decline rapidly at this time. After the riots and disturbances of the 1960s, language rights and the recognition of Chinese as an official language became a focus of intellectual radicalism in the early 1970s, which led in turn to the recognition of 'Chinese' as a co-official language of government and law in 1974. Nevertheless, the demands of parents in the mid-1970s ensured that English was retained as a language of textbooks and at least at a nominal level of instruction in the vast majority of secondary schools. The use of Cantonese in this period also began to expand into many so-called 'high' domains of use, including government, the law courts, and broadcasting. The fact that English occupied the space of a *de jure* official language in the territory allowed Cantonese to elaborate its functions in Hong Kong in ways that were denied to 'dialects' in Guangzhou and other parts of mainland China, where official policy since 1949 has forcefully promoted the national language, Putonghua.

The pre-eminence of Cantonese in the 1970s and 1980s helped foster among academics and commentators in the media the ideology of Hong Kong as a 'monocultural', 'monoethnic', and 'monolingual' society. The fact that this ideology was at odds with the early history of the society, as well as its contemporary development, seems to have weighed little against the force of such belief. By the 1990s, however, it became clear that Hong Kong's linguistic profile was changing, and this was reflected in the results of language censuses and surveys for this period. The numbers of those claiming a reasonable command of English rose from 6.6 percent in 1983 to around 33.7 percent in 1993 (Bacon-Shone and Bolton, 1998). By 2001, the census results indicated that, overall, 43 percent now claim to speak English, 34.1 percent Putonghua, and 96.1 percent Cantonese (HKSAR Government, 2001: 39). Multilingualism is not only confined to these languages, as there are also minority groups of Chinese dialect speakers, as well as Filipinos, Indonesians, Thais, Japanese, Indians, Malaysians, Parsees and others resident in the territory.

After the Joint Declaration of 1984 had decided Hong Kong's political future, the problematization of English was intensified by a range of language debates in academic circles and the media. The 'falling standards' debate became a focus of commercial, political and ethnic anxieties. Against this political backdrop, there seemed to be little space for a recognition of 'Hong Kong English'. In other Asian societies such as India, Singapore and the Philippines, there was a growing awareness and occasional pride in a local variety of English, as well as a local literature written in that variety. Among the general Hong Kong population, however, there was a tendency to regard Hong Kong English as, if not non-existent, then as 'bad' and 'incompetent' English (Harris, 1989: 40). Among linguists, this attitude took different forms, as it was mediated by a more sophisticated and professional approach that described the English proficiency profile of local speakers in terms of concepts such as 'error analysis', 'approximative systems', 'interference', 'transfer', 'communicative strategies' and 'interlanguage'. Identifiable language contact phenomena included 'code-mixing', 'code-switching', 'language alternation' and 'mixed code', and linguists strove to describe and analyse the linguistics of language contact from a professionally modern perspective. In spite of the anxieties about 'falling standards' and 'monolingualism', knowledge of English in the community continued to spread, as did the use of a localized variety of the language; which drew the interest of journalists if not academics. A 1987 *South China Morning Post* editorial noted:

> The fact is Hongkong English has evolved into an incipient patois, an inevitable process in any colonial setting where the imported tongue cannot avoid absorbing the characteristics of the vernacular, especially one as vibrant as Cantonese (*South China Morning Post*, 1987a: 28)

In the 1990s, the numbers of English speakers increased, particularly among the younger age groups. One result of the popularity of emigration to North America in the late 1980s was that by the mid- and late 1990s, large numbers of Hong Kong residents had been educated abroad. A *Time* magazine article of 1996 noted that, with the exception of Filipino domestics, the 34,000 resident Americans then constituted the largest foreign community, outnumbering the 27,000 British. The authors went on to argue that Hong Kong's style was becoming rapidly Americanized:

> In the streets ... the tempo of American mass culture — from hamburgers to fashion and TV shows — suits Hong Kong's fast-track lifestyle like no other foreign influence. Hong Kong consumers devour anything American. Disney's new stores push everything from T shirts to gold Mickey Mouse earrings.

American retailers such as Timberland, Esprit and Toys 'R' Us have sprouted in American-style malls — which are catching on in a society that had always preferred the small, mom-and-pop store. Cricket is out; basketball is in, overtaking soccer as the preferred sport among teenagers. The National Basketball Association runs a nine-person office in Hong Kong. On television, the Cantonese version of the NBA's 'Inside Stuff' attracts 56 percent of the young male Chinese audience (Elliot and Strasser, 1996: 28).

The same article then discussed Chief Executive Designate Tung Chee-hwa's intention to 'revamp' Hong Kong's education system along US lines in order to promote high-tech industries, and noted that four out of six university vice-chancellors polled had American passports. The prediction that Hong Kong universities would move towards an American unit-credit system has proved substantially correct, and this change now has been made at most tertiary institutions in the territory.

At the same time, just before and after the 1997 Handover, there was a rapid growth in the use of personal computers and the Internet at all Hong Kong universities, and most schools. Hong Kong students have become computer literate in a very short space of time, and much computer communication, particularly website use on the Internet, is conducted in English, as well as e-mails and online chat. Whether all this is evidence of increasing 'Americanization' remains to be seen. Hong Kong's culture, like its language, has a strong hybrid quality, which finds expression in the interface between English and Chinese so that '[i]n the new breed of Hong Kong Chinese, the mediation of languages and cultures is an internal one that takes place inside individual speakers as they interact within the home speech community', so that 'the younger generation of Hong Kong Chinese are creating hybrid identities from a mixed pool of linguistic and cultural resources' (Pennington, 1998: 28).

The origins and development of Hong Kong English

The origins of English in southern China date back to 1637, when the first British trading ships under the command of Captain Weddell reached Macau and Canton. After the restriction by imperial decree of all foreign trade to Canton (Guangzhou) after 1755, this port became the world centre for the tea trade, and a range of other exports including silks and porcelain. The first attestations that are available for Chinese speakers of English date from the 1740s and are cited by pidgin scholars and creolists as early examples of 'Chinese pidgin English'. The term 'pidgin English', however, did not appear 1859, and, throughout the late eighteenth and early nineteenth century, reference was typically made to the 'broken English', 'jargon', or 'mixed dialect' used at Canton. One early glossary of such jargon from Canton includes such items as *chop* ('a seal or stamp'), *face* ('appearance in society, reputation'), *hong* ('a commercial establishment'), and *side* ('a position, place'), and it is interesting to note that these words and expressions are still in use in Hong Kong today (Morrison, 1834).

After the First and Second Opium Wars of 1839–42 and 1856–60, 'Canton-English' (yet another term for the jargon spoken in Guangzhou) spread north with the expansion of compradore system to Shanghai and other treaty ports throughout the country. After the ratification of the Treaty of Tianjin in 1862, numerous other 'ports', including inland enclaves, were opened to Western missionaries, merchants, and colonial officials. By the turn of the century, over forty Chinese cities had been opened to Western powers, and a system of treaty-port 'semi-colonialism' had been established in China. By the early twentieth century, however, there was greatly increased access to educated varieties of English through mission schools and other sources, and some Chinese speakers of English developed a distaste for pidgin. For example, Green (1934) noted that 'hundreds of mission schools have for years past been turning out thousands of Chinese who speak English at least as well as most non-English peoples; even among servants there are those who really resent being addressed in pidgin' (1934: 331). By 1944, Hall noted the 'decline' of pidgin English, which he claimed had begun in the 1890s. After the end of the Second World War, and the formation of the PRC in 1949, conditions in the treaty ports in mainland China changed drastically. According to some accounts, pidgin English continued to be spoken in Hong Kong during the 1950s and 1960s among tradespeople and servants, but most contemporary writers today claim that Chinese pidgin English no longer exists, even in HKSAR.

Elsewhere, I have argued that characterizations of Western 'comic' writers such as Leland (1876) played an iconic role in the creation of a 'Chinese imaginary' in Britain and the USA from the mid-nineteenth century onwards. Leland's 'rhymes and stories' were published during an era of unequalled Western expansion into China through the treaty-port system, and also during a period of mounting Sinophobia against the 'heathen Chinee' in the United States. Leland's book, *Pidgin English Sing-Song*, helped construct an overtly racist anti-Chinese discourse that was spread across all classes of society in both the United States and Britain (Bolton, 2000).

The 'de-pidginization' of English in treaty-port era came about through the system of missionary schools that spread across China in the late nineteenth and early twentieth centuries. The earliest of these missionary schools were established in South China, in Macau and Hong Kong. Prominent amongst these were The Morrison Education Society School (opened at Macau in 1839, and transferred to Hong Kong in 1842), and the Anglo-Chinese College (which moved to Hong Kong from Malacca in 1843). Early mission schools in Hong Kong included St Paul's College (1851), Diocesan Girls' School (1860), Diocesan Boys' School (1869), and St Joseph's (1876). Eventually, the colonial government established the Central School (1862) which later became Queen's College. These schools played a crucial role in the history of Hong Kong as a British colony, by educating a compradore class of merchants who played in the commercial and political development of China in the late Qing period (Smith, 1985).

It was not, however, until the late colonial period that access to English in Hong Kong became available through a mass education system. Following the 1967 riots in the territory, a number of social reforms were initiated by the colonial government, including the educational reforms of 1974 and 1978, which provided for a system of free, compulsory primary and secondary education. Largely because of these reforms, the numbers of English speakers in the territory in recent decades has risen dramatically. In 1960, the proportion of the population claiming to know English was estimated at 9.7%. By 1991, this figure had risen to 31.6%, and by 1996 to 38.1%, and by 2001 (as noted above) this figure had reached 43%, with 39.8% of these respondents identifying themselves as speakers of English 'as another language' (i.e. English-knowing bilinguals).

Post-colonial Hong Kong

At midnight on 30 June 1997, Hong Kong ceased to be a British colony. The Handover ceremony took place at the Convention and Exhibition Centre in Wanchai, on the northern waterfront of Hong Kong Island. The British representatives at the ceremony included Christopher Patten, the last governor of Hong Kong, the Foreign Secretary Robin Cook, Prime Minister Tony Blair and Prince Charles. Chinese government officials included President Jiang Zemin, Prime Minister Li Peng, Vice-Premier Qian Qichen, People's Liberation Army General Zhang Wannian, and Tung Chee-hwa, the first Chief Executive of the HKSAR. In his speech to the 400 guests and assembled world media at the ceremony, President Jiang Zemin commented on the historical significance of the event, declaring in Putonghua that:

> The national flag of the People's Republic of China and the regional flag of the Hong Kong Special Administrative Region of the People's Republic of China have now solemnly risen over this land. The return of Hong Kong to the motherland after going through a century of vicissitudes indicates that from now on, the Hong Kong compatriots have become true masters of this Chinese land and that Hong Kong has now entered a new era of development (Matheson, 1997: 3).

Jiang Zemin concluded his speech by re-stating the commitment of the PRC (People's Republic of China) government to the 'one country, two systems' concept, with its promise of 'a high degree of autonomy' for the executive, legislative and judicial branches of the Hong Kong government. At the end of the ceremony, in the words of the *South China Morning Post*, 'the two groups of principal officials stood, shook hands and descended from the stage into history' (Matheson, 1997: 3).

Some five years on, Hong Kong's history has been less political than economic. By 1998, the recession that hit other Asian economies had begun to bite Hong Kong and the following three years have seen unprecedented budget deficits, increasing unemployment, and the halving of residential property values. Ironically, in the years before 1997, a favourite trope of journalists and other commentators had hinged on the nature of the transition, and whether Hong Kong's economy and lifestyle would 'take over' the mainland, rather than the reverse. In the event, since 1997, most economic indicators for the territory have plunged while those of the PRC, led by the resurgent financial powerhouse of Shanghai, have risen sharply. On 12 October 2001, the World Trade Organization granted full entry to China as an equal member of the world's leading capitalist trade organization. As capitalism 'with Chinese characteristics' spreads throughout mainland China, a number of commentators, both local and international, have voiced concerns that Hong Kong's position as a leading business and financial centre might soon be superseded by Shanghai.

As China's business and trading communities adapt to international markets, the popularity of English in the PRC seems to have reached a new high with government policy-makers, educationalists, and the Chinese public. Last year, the government introduced plans to begin teaching English from the first year of primary schools across the whole nation. In major Chinese cities today, such as Beijing and Shanghai there are now campaigns to promote English among police, restaurant staff, taxi-drivers, and other service personnel in anticipation of an influx of businessmen and tourists in the next few years. Beijing will be hosting the 2008 Olympic Games, and, in the minds of many, English seems inextricably linked to the nation's continued economic growth and the continuation of the 'Open Door' policy towards the West that was introduced by Deng Xiaoping in the late 1970s (Bolton, 2002).

Hong Kong's reunification with mainland China since 1997 has raised a number of issues related to the economic, political and social development of the HKSAR, but linguistic issues obviously are present in this process as well. The Basic Law of Hong Kong broadly stipulated that the Hong Kong way of life would remain largely unaltered through a system of 'one country, two systems' for a period of 50 years, but the 'convergence' of the HKSAR with the People's Republic has already begun. Since the economic recession began to bite in 1998, Hong Kong has begun to re-evaluate its cultural identity as well as its economic fundamentals. Despite the often mixed messages of government spin doctors, part of Hong Kong's postcolonial PR message to the international business community has been its claim to 'world-class' cosmopolitanism. In his October 1999 Policy Address, entitled 'Quality People Quality Home', Mr Tung Chee-hwa, the HKSAR's Chief Executive, launched the re-branding of Hong Kong as a 'world-class city', asserting that 'Hong Kong should not only be a major Chinese city, but could become the most cosmopolitan city in Asia, enjoying a status comparable to that of New York in North America and London in Europe'. As part of this policy statement Tung also announced 'a territory-wide publicity campaign to promote the use of English' to halt 'a decline in the English standards of our younger generation since the early 1990's' (HKSAR Government, 1999).

English since the Handover

Before 1997, there was speculation that the change of sovereignty in Hong Kong would lead to a reduced role for English in the HKSAR, and the parallel promotion of Chinese in various domains of society, including government, the law, and education. In reality, the changes that have taken place in the last five years or so have been less dramatic than many previously imagined.

In government, the official line of the government has been to pursue a 'trilingual, biliterate' language policy that recognizes Cantonese, Putonghua, and English as spoken languages, and written Chinese and English as written languages. However, within the government generally, and within the Legislative Council in particular, there has been a marked shift from English to Cantonese since the Handover. The shift towards Cantonese was already quite noticeable by the early 1990s. Yau (1997: 44–5), for example, notes that in 1995, there were already quite significant numbers of Legco councillors using 'only Cantonese', i.e. 53% of non-directly elected members, and 89% of directly elected members. Smaller percentages of both groups also opted to use 'both English and Cantonese'. It is signficant that no directly elected members in her data chose to use 'English only', compared to 34% of those members who were non-directly elected. Since 1997, English is rarely heard in Legco, although some non-Chinese civil servants continue to present information in English, and some Chinese officials and legislators do occasionally opt for English instead of Cantonese.

Within the civil service, the 'localization' policy of the Hong Kong government in the 1990s led to a decrease in the numbers of 'expatriate' civil servants (i.e. non-Chinese government officers, on 'overseas terms'). In 1999, it was reported that the numbers of such staff had fallen from 1,807 in 1995 to 778, out of a total civil service workforce of 188,000. As a result of such changing demographics and the changed political status of the HKSAR, it is perhaps now more common to conduct internal meetings in Cantonese than in the past. But this is by no means always the case, and whatever the choice of language at the spoken level, English still appears to be firmly entrenched as the *written* language of the civil service, and at present English remains the dominant language of written records ('the files'). At the spoken level, a good deal of Cantonese-English code-mixing (see Li, this volume) takes place in many government departments, despite the efforts of the 'Official Languages Agency' whose stated mission foregrounds 'promoting wider and more effective use of Chinese within the civil service', and 'setting the standards for official writing in Chinese and monitoring its use' (HKSAR Government, 2000).

In the domain of law, various changes took place in the runup to 1997. In 1986, the Hong Kong government launched the 'Bilingual Laws Project', and since then a large proportion of the written laws of Hong Kong have been translated into Chinese. From the late 1980s to the mid-1990s, various amendments to the Official Languages Ordinance have permitted the use of spoken Chinese into the higher courts. In December 1995, the first civil High Court case was heard in Putonghua, and in August 1997 the first criminal High Court case was conducted in Cantonese (Cheung, 1997). Previously, before the late 1980s, so-called 'expatriate' lawyers from the UK, Australia, and New Zealand were heavily represented in the higher ranks of the legal profession, and a system of court interpreters was available to manage the negotiation between English, Chinese, and other languages such as Vietnamese, Filipino, etc. In the last ten years or so, increasing numbers of 'local' Hong Kong Chinese have been appointed as barristers and judges, but, in spite of increasing flexibility towards the use of varieties of spoken Chinese, spoken English is still used, particularly in the higher courts of the HKSAR, and English seems to have retained its *de facto* status as the the dominant language of court records and almost all important legal documents. Given the role of the law courts in bolstering the HKSAR's reputation as a centre for regional and international business, and the importance of contractual law to the international business community, it is likely that the language will retain its importance in the system of law for the foreseeable future.

Within education, the major change in secondary education occurred in March 1997, when the government announced a new 'firm guidance' policy of requiring the majority of secondary schools to teach through the 'mother tongue', Cantonese. According to this, only 100 secondary schools (some 22% of the total of 460) would be allowed to use English as a teaching medium, with stiff penalties prescribed for school principals who did not comply with the government directive (Kwok, 1997). Later the figure of 100 was amended to 114, after applications from a number of schools to retain English were approved. Since then, however, it seems that the government policy on this issue has relaxed somewhat, and significant numbers of schools are now continuing English in the upper forms of secondary schools. A recent report from Hui (2001) claims that 'as many as 134 out of the 294 Chinese-medium secondary schools in Hong Kong are now teaching either all or some of this year's Form Four students in English', and then goes on to explain that:

> These students are the first group affected by the Government's "mother tongue" policy, introduced three years ago when 223 secondary schools were forced to adopt Chinese as the medium of instruction. Many principals said that the decision was made because students educated in Chinese-medium schools needed to be proficient in English both to succeed in the tertiary education system and to meet society's expectations (Hui, 2001: 2).

The apparent confusion in government circles on a language policy for Hong Kong's public schools has been matched by contesting views among educationalists on the same issue. In April 2000, Professor Cheng Kai-ming, a prominent educationalist, took issue with the use of Cantonese as a teaching medium, arguing that Cantonese had no use outside southern China and Chinese immigrant communities worldwide, and that 'Cantonese is leading us nowhere' (Tacey, 2000: 9). Cheng's suggestion to promote the wider use of Putonghua, in preference to Cantonese, was recently echoed by Michael Tien Puk-sun, a prominent businessman and the chair of a government think-tank on language policy, who suggested that 'all secondary school students should be taught in English and Putonghua in the future to make Hong Kong a trilingual city':

> Mr Tien said English was the key language in commerce and Putonghua was becoming more important in the light of economic integration with the mainland. Most students and teachers were not ready for the switch and it might not be achievable even by 2010. He said it was essential to create an English-speaking environment in secondary schools (cited in Cheung and Ng, 2001)

Ironically perhaps, at a time when Hong Kong continues to debate the issue of the teaching medium for schools, it has also been announced that the HKSAR's neighbours in Guangdong schools have now begun to experiment with the use of English as the medium of instruction in senior secondary schools, in a move 'to equip Guangdong students in urban and Pearl Delta areas with the same command of English as their counterparts in Hong Kong and other Southeast Asian countries by 2005' (Yow, 2001: 2). Back in the HKSAR, the current debates on language in education remain unresolved, although a thorough review of language policy has been slated for 2003 (Cheung and Ng, ibid.).

In other domains, such as media and employment, the role of English has also been the subject of scrutiny and criticism. Chan's survey of the media (this volume) highlights a number of limitations on English-language newspapers and print media, including their limited circulation within Hong Kong's Chinese community. In the last year or so, the general situation has deteriorated still further. In September 2001, 140 employees were suddenly dismissed from the *Hong Kong iMail*, including many of the newspaper's international staff. Overnight, the tabloid was transformed from a feisty, irreverent rival of the *South China Morning Post* to a somewhat unreadable digest of local and 'Greater China' business news. In November 2001, *Asiaweek* magazine was shut down by its parent company, Time Inc., on grounds of dwindling profitability. This now leaves the *South China Morning Post* with an uncontested position as the leading voice of HKSAR journalism. The *Post* management now calculates that around 50 percent of its readers are bilingual Chinese, and they are very much concerned to increase their appeal to such an readership in future.

In the electronic media, English continues to find a place in local television and radio stations, despite the limited size of audiences, but the variety of satellite television stations on offer is surprisingly many fewer in other supposedly less developed Asian societies such as the Philippines. At the cinema, by contrast, there has been a marked increase in the popularity of English-language films, particularly Hollywood movies (subtitled in Chinese), since the heyday of the Cantonese cinema in the 1980s. Internet usage has also grown rapidly in the last few years. By June 2001, it was claimed that Hong Kong, South Korea and Singapore were leading the Asian region in terms of home Internet usage, with 58% of Hongkongers regularly surfing the Internet from home computers, compared with 57 percent in Korea and 56 percent in Singapore (Zajc, 2001). Popular local Internet sites include such Chinese-language webpages as *Apple Daily, Netvigator, HongKong.com*, although English sites such as the international *Geocities.com*, and *Microsoft.com* and the locally-based *Icered.com* also enjoy a measure of popularity. At the same time, however, other figures put the degree of 'Internet penetration' in the HKSAR at 43 percent of the adult population, compared with 51 percent for South Korea and 48 percent for Singapore (Chiu, 2001: 8). Nevertheless, many young people in the HKSAR increasingly surf the Internet in both Chinese and English. At university, many students favour English-language email in preference to Chinese, not least because of the relative ease of communication in typing English emails, compared with inputting Chinese characters. For recreation, many students now surf the Web bilingually and multiculturally, accessing popular entertainment sites, music, film sites, and other Web pages in both Chinese and English.

In personal domains such as family, friends, social activities, etc., the use of spoken English is typically superseded by Cantonese or 'mixed code', when Hong Kong Chinese talk to one another. But at the same time, there is also evidence that the HKSAR is becoming increasingly multilingual and multicultural, in a variety of ways. Patterns of emigration to English-speaking countries in the late 1980s and early 1990s, coupled the increased popularity of overseas universities, have helped create a younger generation with an international outlook. 'Returnee' children now account for 70% of the student population in the English Schools Foundation (ESF), which previously mainly taught the children of British families resident in Hong Kong. Even the 'stay-at-home' students who form the majority of the student population in Hong Kong have become increasingly cosmopolitan over the last decade, and that internationalism has been negotiated partly through English and increasingly through electronic media such as the Internet, with which young people in Hong Kong are so skilful.

Precisely how much English Hong Kong people encounter in the personal domain depends on a wide variety of factors, including social class, educational level, and age. The élite (sociologically, 'capitalist') class in Hong Kong has long been multicultural, and for their children an overseas education has been the norm for almost three decades. In local 'dynastic' families that own banks and major Hong Kong companies, a degree of intermarriage with Europeans and Americans has become increasingly acceptable in the last four decades. This is also increasingly true of other social classes in the community as well, to the extent that so-called 'mixed marriages' are by no means uncommon. In such families, overseas education, travel, cosmopolitanism, and fluency in a number of languages is the norm.

In many 'ordinary' families in Hong Kong, English is encountered at home on a daily basis in a number of different ways. Children of all ages devote hours of homework to the study of the language, with older brothers and sisters teaching the language to their siblings. A large proportion of undergraduates at the University of Hong Kong and other universities have part-time jobs as English tutors, and parents themselves often teach their children simple conversational skills. In addition, there are now around 160,000 Filipina domestic helpers or 'amahs' working in the territory, who often mainly use English and who function as unofficial tutors with children. Given that Hong Kong households numbered 1.8 million in 1996, the indication is that English-speaking Filipinas are resident in over 11% of households. In the 1993 survey referred to earlier, a total of 26.9% of the sample reported speaking English with 'foreign friends', while 57% of the sample stated that they had close relatives in an English-speaking country.

Many of the lower-middle class and working-class children at local universities have parents who emigrated from mainland China to Hong Kong twenty or thirty years ago, and have little or no knowledge English themselves. In such families the children often have little chance to speak English, but when they graduate from university and begin work in the business sector, as the majority increasingly do, they find an immediate use for spoken English. This is particularly the case if they manage to secure a job in one of the international companies based in the territory, for whom so many students aspire to work on graduation. In such companies, there is frequently an immediate context for the use of spoken English, often with colleagues from other Asian societies as well as from Hong Kong. Spoken English also serves as a lingua franca between some Hong Kong Cantonese speakers and Putonghua speakers from mainland China, particularly in the professional and academic sectors of society. The fashionable restaurant and bar areas popular among young Hongkongers attract resident British and American youths, ethnic Chinese from local international schools, returnee kids from Canadian and US universities as well as large numbers of 'local' young people, creating a multicultural social mix in the social domain was almost unknown twenty years ago. Thus today, the complete range of purposes that young people 'need' English for may range from work to social life, and from academic study to entertainment and recreation.

Since 1997, a number of competing and often contradictory trends have emerged in the sociolinguistics of Hong Kong society. Official language policies promoting the increased use of the 'mother tongue' have been accompanied by a range of anxieties concerning both the future status of Cantonese as well as the continued use of English within the HKSAR. The blurring of linguistic concerns with political worries also seems to be a recurrent theme in such discussions. For example, Ng (2001) recently penned a scathing assessment of government policies (entitled 'Cosmopolitanism at risk') in which she equated recent linguistic trends with a growing ethnic nationalism:

> A few years ago, the streets of Central teemed with people of every race and colour. Now, the crowd is almost uniformly Chinese and local. Bilingualism used to be the rule in street signs and public notices, now they often are in Chinese only. Although the media has always consisted of more Chinese than English, now a non-Chinese speaker might stay unaware of even major news. [...] In the Legislative Council, English speeches are given little coverage. Subtly but certainly, non-Chinese-speaking people find the Chinese speakers around them less prepared to make allowance for their disability. Their areas of activity and awareness have diminished. Barristers who have no Chinese more frequently find themselves out of work. Patriotism and nationalism are the prerequisite for political advancement. Only Chinese food is politically correct for official functions. The best people swear by Chinese medicine. The only jarring note is that most senior civil servants (all of whom are Chinese) send their children to Britain and the US to be educated (Ng, 2001: 16)

Ng goes on to argue equate such trends with the increasing sinicization of Hong Kong, as well as concerns about the continued autonomy of the HKSAR, culturally and politically, noting that 'The SAR Government is to move towards greater concentration of power in the hands of a few senior officials, and power is to be exercised personally and directly, in imitation of Beijing' (Ng, 2001: 16). Ng's measured yet pessimistic conclusion is that:

> The determination to cleanse Hong Kong of its colonial past and its multiculturalism, and strive for a stronger and purer Chinese identity will do Hong Kong no good. Nor does Hong Kong's situation require such fundamental ethnic cleansing, even if pervasive economic hardship is making people seem stuck in pessimism. Hong Kong's fundamental institutions and values are sound. They have made Hong Kong prosperous. China's recent

success is a story of how the leadership succeeded in steering the nation away from old habits into a modern society – such as Hong Kong. [...] To marginalise what is non-Chinese will not make the SAR a jewel of the ascending China. It will only strip Hong Kong of its cosmopolitan nature and expose its raw centre as no more than second-rate and provincial (Ng, ibid.).

Such concerns perhaps catch the mood of Hong Kong at the time of writing. With the HKSAR stuck in the economic doldrums from early 1998, with budget deficits, salary cuts, and low levels of 'confidence' in the community, political and economic anxieties find expression in a range of discourses, including those on language. In this context, it is perhaps useful to consider Hong Kong's own 'complaint tradition' in language issues, a tradition that mirrors discourses in Britain and other societies where 'language issues' often instantiate a displacement of other concerns, particularly political and social anxieties of various kinds (Milroy and Milroy, 1985).

The Hong Kong complaint tradition

The expression of political and social concerns in commentaries on local language issues is hardly new. One obvious example of this is the discourse on 'falling standards' that has permeated debates about language for at least the last thirty years. As early as the 1970s, a number of articles appeared detailing the weaknesses and shortcomings of Hong Kong students in learning English. (Kwok and Chan, 1972, Kwok and Chan, 1975). Around the same time, Hunter (1974) reported that there was much discussion about 'the poor standard of English spoken and written in Hong Kong by non-native speakers', and suggested that the problem could be seen as symptomatic of the gulf between the Chinese-speaking and English-speaking communities (1974: 15). The use of 'bad English' could thus be seen as 'a successful compromise between the twin necessities of communicating with another community and of remaining an acceptable member of one's own' and a way of 'informing one's interlocutor that one is not trying to become accepted by his community' (1974: 17).

In the early 1980s one local linguist described students as 'cultural eunuchs' who were 'semilingual' in English and Chinese (T'sou, 1985). Another (Gibbons, 1984) lamented the low standards of proficiency, and endorsed Lord's (1974) earlier blistering appraisal of students at the University of Hong Kong:

> For the majority of students entering the University of Hong Kong English is not a viable means of communication at all. About a fifth of them cannot make themselves understood in English, and their comprehension of spoken English is poor in the extreme. Few students can write English which is not bizarre (Lord, 1974, cited in Gibbons, 1984: 66).

The debate on 'low' or 'falling' standards of English has thus run from at least the mid-1970s to the present, although it probably reached a peak in the late 1980s, when a *South China Morning Post* editorial declared that '[t]he decline in the standard of spoken and written English in recent decades is obvious and measurable, and efforts by the Government and the tertiary education institutions have been insufficient to stop the slide' (*South China Morning Post*, 1989: 18). The debate was not confined to academics, but was rehearsed and expressed in the broadcast media and the local press, with editorials on language policy, feature articles, news reports and letters to the editor regularly appearing in the *South China Morning Post*. Many of the arguments also turned on the choice of language for schools between English, Cantonese and Putonghua but, as Lin (1997) notes, one of the strongest arguments in favour of English was economic, expressed through an identification of English with business, trade and prosperity. One 1986 editorial in the *South China Morning Post* made the case for English thus:

> English is pre-eminently the language of international trade, which is, and for the foreseeable future will remain, Hongkong's raison d'etre. There are indications that the territory's role in world commerce, far from diminishing as 1997 approaches, will increase in importance. Southeast and East Asia is widely seen as the growth area of the future and we are ideally placed to take advantage of this. Hongkong, as a stable and sophisticated oasis, is the obvious choice of any overseas company wishing to participate in the boom years ahead. The widespread use of English is an obvious added attraction (*South China Morning Post*, 1986a: 10).

A second editorial appeared in the same newspaper some two months later expressing concern about the possible effects on business and finance of the promotion of Cantonese:

> It is honourable for the people of Hongkong to feel a sense of 'nationalism' as we move towards 1997 and the change of sovereignty which will again make the territory part of China ... Cantonese is and should always be the mother tongue of Hongkong. There is no dispute in this. But it is a fact of life that Hongkong has grown to become a world leader in trade and finance on the back of and assisted by the English language ... It cannot be disputed that the international language in trade and commerce and a plethora of other interactions is English. And so it should be in Hongkong (*South China Morning Post*, 1987b: 8).

The reference to nationalism in the editorial also pointed to another strand in this debate, which was overtly political. In fact, some months earlier, the *Post* had published another editorial in response to a warning from a Chinese Education Ministry official (Mr Yang Xun) that the promotion of Cantonese as the teaching medium ran against the grain of mainland policy and would be 'a step backward for Hongkong'. The *Post*'s response in those pre-Tianmanen days was to endorse such concerns:

> Mr Yang has made an important point. We would recommend a fresh look at the subject. Putonghua and English are the languages which Hongkong should be stressing. English has, because of its adaptability, subtlety and richness, plus historical accident, become the language of international contact. Hongkong's status as a centre of world trade must be maintained, and our children must learn English to prepare them for the role they will one day assume. Putonghua is the official language of the nation to which Hongkong will be irrevocably joined after 1997. Our children will also become citizens of China, and should speak the language of their compatriots as well as English (*South China Morning Post*, 1986b: 16).

The political was to take a number of other forms in the language debates of the era. One news report even suggested that many schoolchildren were beginning to lose the motivation to study English because there was 'a different political atmosphere with Hongkong coming under Chinese rule' (Lau, 1986: 4). Ten years later, the politics of English took a new turn when significant numbers of the Chinese business and political elite started to 'drop' the use of English first names in favour of their Chinese given names. One prominent civil servant explained his decision by saying 'I do not have a Christian name, because I am not and have never been a Christian', adding that 'I have always been an atheist and the name "Brian" is, in fact, a product of colonialism' (*South China Morning Post*, 1996: 11).

From an empirical perspective, very little hard research was conducted on the issue of 'falling' language standards during these years, and what was done was inconclusive at best. King (1987) reported on the results of the Hong Kong Examinations Authority's (HKEA) English language examination for the years 1984 and 1986. After analysing a substantial number of statistics relating to 15,000 students, his conclusion was that there was no 'convincing evidence to suggest that the English standard of the best students coming through the Hongkong system has deteriorated in recent years' (King, 1987: 17). However, he went on to add that '[i]t is clear that the whole of the secondary system is being seriously affected by the presence of large numbers of students whose English language standards are quite inadequate to cope with an education in the medium of English' (ibid), which suggested that the root cause of such perceptions was the rapid expansion of the educational system. Johnson and Cheung researched levels of reading literacy in the mid-1990s as part of the International Association for the Evaluation of Educational Achievement (IEA) World Literacy Project. Their results showed good levels of attainment in Chinese-language reading proficiency, but relatively poor levels of proficiency in English literacy, although the research report suggests that this result might be influenced by the quality of schools as much as the choice of language, as '[g]ood schools produce good results in both Chinese and English and poor schools are equally consistent in producing poor results' (Johnson and Cheung, 1995: 10).

As has been shown in many other societies, ideologies about 'falling standards' are often related to other factors, including social class divisions. Romaine (1994) suggests that '[s]tandards of language use and standard languages are essentially arbitrary conventions which can be learned only by going to school', and that '[t]his is precisely why they are so effective in maintaining barriers between groups' (1994: 202). She also points out that such debates have existed in Britain since the fifteenth century, and continue to the present day, even at Oxford University. In the Hong Kong context, one plausible inference with reference to these 'language standards' debates is that, in large part, they were a reaction to the rapid and unprecedented expansion of education, as well as the pace of political and social change in the society at large. These ideologies continued to be voiced with varying degrees of amplitude up to the 1997 Handover (Boyle, 1997), but now seem to have undergone a definite revival since Hong Kong entered an economic slump in 1998.

In March 1998, for example, a *South China Morning Post* editorial with the rubric 'Standards of English' gave a dismal assessment of the English of HKSAR university students:

> The poor standard of English among students in Hong Kong will continue to cause concern until the right questions are asked. Years of English-language education has failed to produce a bilingual society. Pupils often leave secondary education with only rudimentary knowledge of the tongue in which they were taught. It is surprising that so many go on to higher education with English as the medium of instruction, and emerge with a degree. [...] Hong Kong's educational institutions are failing to produce the goods (*South China Morning Post*, 1998: 18).

By 2000, various government-backed campaigns had begun to raise the standard of English in business and professional sectors in the HKSAR, including the *Workplace English Campaign*, which began in March 2000 by focusing on upgrading the English skills of relatively junior staff in Hong Kong businesses, i.e. secretaries, clerks, frontline service personnel, receptionists, and telephone operators, who collectively account for around a third of the work force. The scheme received substantial financial backing from the Department of Education and Manpower, who were also concerned to 'benchmark' levels of attainment for higher-level employees such as computer operators, engineering technicians, law clerks, and nurses (as well as schoolteachers who have been targeted in a separate and parallel campaign). The chairman of the government's *Workplace English Campaign*, Michael Tien, identified the issue as crucial to the HKSAR's future:

> Hong Kong is at risk of being perceived as just another "mainland city" unless standards of written and spoken English are not improved, a local businessman says. English is essential for the future of Hong Kong and the SAR must improve the language skills of its workforce to be globally competitive. [...] He said the last 10 or so years had seen a decline in English standards, perhaps reflecting the political shift towards the mainland. The perception in the business world is that other Asian capitals are stealing a march on Hong Kong. "We're not making Hong Kong user-friendly enough to attract foreign businessmen. We must make Hong Kong the first choice location of corporate executives and businessmen in Asia," Mr Tien said. (Regan, 2000: 23)

An examination of the record, as noted above, throws some doubt on the reality of a 'decline' in English standards in Hong Kong in the last ten years or so, as it is clear that the discourse on low standards goes back at least to the 1970s. An alternative explanation is that the demands of a rapidly changing economy have vastly increased expectations of the quality of English required, even from relatively low-level employees, particularly in comparison with that found in such Asian societies as Singapore and the Philippines where the sociolinguistic dynamics of society are very different. Which receives support from reports that in the HKSAR, the 'demand for good English speakers was now outstripping supply' (Gould, 2002: 1). Whether the government's *Workplace English Campaign* will be judged a success remains to be seen, but, if nothing else such debates at least testify to the raw tenacity of a complaint tradition that surfaces continually in the expression of ideologies on the decline in 'language standards'. Whether this culture of complaint actually improves the climate for language education in the community is again debatable. One important theme of the present volume is that a paradigm shift, especially at an attitudinal and ideological level, is long overdue in the community.

Hong Kong English: Autonomy and creativity

In the last twenty years or so there has been a forceful attempt by academics from a number of different countries to promote a non-Eurocentric (or 'non-Americentric') approach to the discussion world Englishes (or 'international varieties of English'), and this 'paradigm shift' in the academic world has been seen in the publications of journals like *English Today, English World-Wide*, and *World Englishes*. Braj B. Kachru, the co-editor of *World Englishes*, has argued for a model of global English, in terms of 'three concentric circles', *the inner circle* (societies such as Britain, the USA, Australia, New Zealand, etc. where English is the 'first language' of a majority of the population), *the outer circle* (societies such as India, the Philippines, etc. where English has the status of a 'second language') and *the extending (or 'expanding') circle* (societies such as China or Japan where English has the status of a 'foreign language').

In pioneering a pluricentric approach to the study of world Englishes, Kachru has challenged a range of previously orthodox approaches to English worldwide, particularly those that saw the 'new Englishes' of Asia as linguistically and culturally dependent on the authority of such native-speaker norms as British or American English. In a recent paper, Kachru describes the spread of English in Asia, noting that at present:

- That the estimated total English-using population of Asia adds up to 350 million out of an estimated population of $3\frac{1}{2}$ billion;
- That India, in the Outer Circle, is the third largest English-using country after the USA and the UK;
- That English is the main medium in demand for acquisition of bilingualism/multilingualism in the whole Asian region;
- That in parts of Asia (e.g., in Singapore) English is gradually acquiring the status of the dominant language or the *first* language — whatever we mean by that term (Kachru, 1997: 7)

Kachru argues for the acceptance and utilization of English as an Asian language, and the acculturation of English to sociolinguistic realities, as well as the imaginative needs, of Asian societies such as India, Malaysia, the Philippines and Singapore. The world Englishes approach to Asian varieties of English thus raises a number of questions for Hong Kong. In the case of Hong Kong, the existence of 'Hong Kong English', has received little recognition, despite the long and rich history of the English language in the South China context.

Some years ago, Llamzon (1986) wrote on the 'life cycle' of new Englishes in a paper which attempts to identify and describe the developmental stages of 'outer circle' Englishes. The metaphor of a life cycle for Asian Englishes is an interesting one, and one speculation that might arise from a comparison of Hong Kong and Philippine English is that the two varieties are located at different points in such a cycle. The irony in Hong Kong seems to be that at just that time when the government has felt moved to restrict the use of English in some official domains, bilingualism in English among the general population has reached its highest point ever. As Bacon-Shone and Bolton (1998) put it, the current situation is that 'not only are more and more people speaking English, but also that they are doing so with varying degrees of ability', in other words, 'more people than ever are speaking "good" English, and more people than ever are speaking "bad" English' (1998: 84). In its own specific post-colonial moment, Hong Kong English thus seems caught on a cusp of both 'expansion' and 'restriction' (Llamzon, 1986: 101–2). In this context, the notion of 'autonomy' refers not only to issues of linguistic description with reference to features of accent and vocabulary, but also to the history of the variety, as well as the existence and vitality of creative writing in the HKSAR.

This volume is divided into five Parts, 'Language in Context', 'Language Form', 'Dimensions of Creativity', 'Resources', and 'Future Directions'. Part I includes four chapters that discuss a variety of issues related to the specifics of the Hong Kong sociolinguistic context. Bolton's chapter on the sociolinguistics of English in Hong Kong gives an overview of the sociopolitical background in the late colonial period, and then proceeds to make the case for the recognition of Hong Kong English in terms of both distinctive linguistic features and the growing literary creativity of the variety. The following chapter from Tsui and Bunton presents a detailed account of an investigation into the normative attitudes of English-language teachers in Hong Kong secondary schools. The results of their research indicate that at present there is little support for a notion of 'Hong Kong English' from practising schoolteachers, and that target model of English adopted by teachers is clearly exonormative, usually as represented by British dictionaries and grammars and other sources of 'Standard English'. Li's chapter on Cantonese-English code-switching presents a broad survey of research in this area over the last twenty-five years or so. In his analysis of the motivations for such language switching (and 'mixing') in the written discourse of the Chinese press, Li posits four context-specific motivations, i.e. euphemism, specificity, bilingual punning, and the 'principle of economy'. Chan's chapter on the English-language media is written primarily from the perspective of a professional newspaper writer now working in the field of journalism education. Chan provides a comprehensive survey of the English media in print journalism, radio, and television, and then goes on to argue the case for the training of a new type of bilingual media professional who can contest the assumptions and biases in the English-language news coverage of Hong Kong and China.

Part II, entitled 'Language Form', details research on the linguistic aspects of the description of Hong Kong English. Hung's chapter reviews previous research on the phonology of Hong Kong English (HKE), and also reports on his own original research on the Hong Kong accent. Hung's study of the speech forms of a group of university students suggests that the typical Hong Kong speaker operates with a smaller set of vowel and consonant contrasts than in 'native' varieties of English. Hung postulates an underlying phonemic system for HKE, and also describes a number of allophonic variations. Gisborne's chapter discusses relative clauses in Hong Kong English, and discusses a number of issues concerning the morphosyntactic feature system of the variety, with particular reference to relative constructions in Cantonese. Benson's chapter on Hong Kong words deals with the distinctive vocabulary of Hong Kong English. In his discussion of this, Benson focuses on patterns of semantic and pragmatic relationships internal to the variety, as well as the sociocultural context in which a localized vocabulary is used.

Part III focuses on 'dimensions of creativity' in Hong Kong English with specific reference to literary production in the HKSAR. The five authors in this section are all themselves creative writers and write with some authority on this topic. Louise Ho's contribution considers Hong Kong ('essentially a cosmopolitan city with a rock-hard Chinese core') as a site for works of the imagination, especially poetry. The chapter includes the work of young Hong Kong poets, as well as four poems from Ho herself. Agnes Lam's chapter tackles the issue of defining 'Hong Kong poetry' from a number of perspectives, interrogates both notions of 'poetry' and 'Hong Kong', and suggests that the sociolinguistic concept of 'speech community' may be of relevance in framing an adequate definition. Two poems by Lam are appended to this chapter. Leung Ping-kwan considers the task of writing poetry 'between' Chinese and English, describing the difficulties and excitements of negotiating between two languages and two cultures with reference to his poem, 'A Leaf of Passage'. This poem draws on the mythology of the Haida Gwaii, native Americans from British Columbia as well as the experiences of contemporary Hong Kong 'astronaut' fathers who shuttle between the HKSAR and Vancouver. In the following chapter, Nury Vittachi, an acclaimed columnist and writer of comic Hong Kong fiction, explores the humorous dimensions of 'Chinglish', a broad form of Hong Kong English that might well be dubbed 'basilectal' by the technical linguist. In his contribution, Vittachi affectionately satirizes a range of colloquial styles of this variety, including bar girl patois and taxi-driver talk. In the final chapter of this section, Hong Kong novelist Xu Xi describes both her evolution as a Hong Kong writer, and the schizophrenic identity of Hong Kong itself, a city 'neither both Chinese nor Western'. This chapter also includes an excerpt from Xu Xi's recent (2001) novel of Hong Kong life in the 1990s, *The Unwalled City*.

Part IV of the book carries the rubric 'Resources' and comprises three chapters intended to indicate further resources for those interested both in the linguistic and literary aspects of Hong Kong English. The chapter from Bolton and Nelson dealing with the International Corpus of English project in Hong Kong (HK-ICE) includes examples of a range of non-literary texts in Hong Kong English, including a business talk, popular writing, business and social letters, a broadcast talk, broadcast news, a Legco (Legislative Council) debate, and an informal conversation. The following chapter from Shirley Geok-lin Lim discusses the potential of creative writing in English for developing the 'cultural imagination' of HKSAR university students. Lim recounts insights from her own experience of teaching creative writing at the University of Hong Kong and presents a number of poems and short stories authored by her students, providing an invaluable guide to the work of new voices in Hong Kong English literary production. The final section in this chapter is a guide to bibliographical resources and the academic literature on English in Hong Kong. Part V comprises a single essay from Bolton and

Lim on possible 'futures' for Hong Kong English, which reviews a number of issues, linguistic and literary, relating to the themes of 'autonomy' and 'creativity'. This final chapter expresses the hope that a paradigm shift establishing a new discourse for 'Hong Kong English' will help create the cultural space for a revitalized attitude to the teaching of English as well as for the creative potential of English and Englishes in the HKSAR.

That the potential for such literary creativity is present in Hong Kong has been witnessed by a series of literary initiatives in the last few years, including the establishment of the Hong Kong Literary Festival (now moving into its third year), as well as the setting up of a number of creative writing programmes at local universities. A new anthology of Hong Kong writing spanning five decades, called *City Voices* will be published later this year (Ingham and Xu, 2002). In another development, Shirley Lim (together with Page Richards from the University of Hong Kong) has also been a driving force in the 'Moving Poetry' project to teach creative writing in Hong Kong primary and secondary schools. The quality of the contributions in the first volume of such poems to come out of this project challenges the pessimism of complaint (Lim and Richards, 2001). When a ten-year-old Hong Kong Chinese boy[2] can produce a poem that runs *Among the creatures of the deep,/ I saw a goose,/ in metallic grey,/ diving in the abyss,/ stealthily, neck straight./* something unexpected happens, reminding us of the power of both imagination and literary expression. If the challenge of a paradigm shift is somehow to change a culture of complaint to one of confidence, the children *are* our future. The other half of the equation, we may recall, is to teach them well.

Notes

1. The editor would like to thank all the contributors to this book for their encouragement and support in bringing these papers together in this volume. He would also like to thank Susanna Chow, Emily Lee, Zoe Law, Ian Lok, and Michelle Woo for their help in formatting this book, and checking the text. All errors, of course, remain the editor's. This volume is the first in a new series from Hong Kong University Press entitled *Asian Englishes Today*. The editor is very grateful to Hong University Press for their belief in this project and their solid support throughout. He would also like to thank the members of the *Asian Englishes Today* editorial board, which comprises M.L.A. Bautista (De La Salle, Philippines), Susan Butler (Macquarie Dictionary), Braj Kachru (University of Illinois), Yamuna Kachru (University of Illinois), Shirley Geok-lin Lim (University of California at Santa Barbara), Tom McArthur (editor of *English Today*), Larry Smith (co-editor of *World Englishes*), Anne Pakir (National University of Singapore), and Yasukata Yano (Waseda University). I wish to thank my colleague Page Richards and the reviewer appointed by Hong Kong University Press for their very helpful comments on this introduction. Many also thanks to Cand Lau, who did wonders with the cover design. This volume has been supported by a grant from the Research Grants

Council of the Hong Kong Special Administrative Region, China (Project No. HKU/7174/00H).
2. The writer of this poem is Justin Ho Ching, who wrote it while a Primary 5 student at St Paul's Co-educational Primary School.

References

Bacon-Shone, John and Bolton, Kingsley (1998) Charting multilingualism: Language censuses and language surveys in Hong Kong. In *Language in Hong Kong at Century's End*. Edited by Martha C. Pennington. Hong Kong: Hong Kong University Press, pp. 43–90.
Bolton, Kingsley (2000) Language and hybridisation: Pidgin tales from the China coast. *Interventions* **2**(1), 35–52.
Bolton, Kingsley (2002) Chinese Englishes: From Canton jargon to global English. *World Englishes*, special issue on 'English in China'. In press.
Boyle, Joseph (1997) Native-speaker teachers of English in Hong Kong. *Language and Education* **11**, 163–81.
Cheung, Anne (1997) Language rights and the Hong Kong courts. *Hong Kong Journal of Applied Linguistics*, 2, 49–75.
Cheung, Gary and Ng, Kang-chung (2001) Schools 'should teach in English and Putonghua'. *South China Morning Post*. 18 November. 1.
Chiu, Annette (2001) SAR's Internet growth rate slows. *South China Morning Post*. 28 June. 8.
Elliot, Dorinda and Strasser, Steven (1996) Hong Kong's American Tune. *Time*. 30 December. 27–30.
Gibbons, John (1984) Interpreting the English proficiency profile in Hong Kong. *RELC Journal*, 15, 64–74.
Gould, Vanessa (2002) SAR edge slipping: Survey Low marks on English standards and costs underline extent of investor dissatisfaction. *South China Morning Post*. 30 January. 1.
Green, Owen M. (1934) Pidgin English. *Fortnightly*, 142, 331–9.
Hall, Robert A. (1944) Chinese pidgin English grammar and texts. *Journal of the American Oriental Society*, **64**, 95–113.
Harris, Roy (1989) The worst English in the world? *Supplement to the Gazette* XXXVI, 37–46. Hong Kong: The University of Hong Kong.
HKSAR Government (1999) The 1999 policy address. October 1999. http://www.info.gov.hk/pa99/english/speech.htm. Accessed 22 February, 2000.
HKSAR Government (2000) The Official Languages Agency: Our vision, mission and values. http://www.info.gov.hk/ola/ english/mission/index.htm. Accessed November 2000.
HKSAR Government (2001) *2001 Population Census: Summary Results*. Hong Kong: Census and Statistics Department, HKSAR Government.
Hui, Polly (2001) 'Mother tongue' schools bow to English as best medium. *South China Morning Post*. 29 September. 2.
Hunter, Duncan B. (1974) Bilingualism and Hong Kong English. *The Educationalist*, 5, 15–8.

Ingham, Michael and Xu Xi (eds.) *City Voices: An Anthology of Hong Kong Writing in English.* Hong Kong: Hong Kong University Press. In press.

Johnson, Robert K. and Cheung, Yat-shing (1995) *Reading Literacy in Hong Kong: An IEA World Literacy Project on the Reading Proficiency of Hong Kong Students in Chinese and English.* Hong Kong: Department of Chinese and Bilingual Studies, Hong Kong Polytechnic University.

Kachru, Braj B. (1997) English as an Asian language. In *English is an Asian Language: The Philippine Context.* Edited by M. L. S. Bautista. Manila: The Macquarie Library, pp. 1–23.

King, Rex (1987) Why pupils are facing testing time. *South China Morning Post.* 24 February. 17.

Kwok, Shirley (1997) New rule will halve schools using English. *South China Morning Post.* 22 March. 7.

Kwok, Helen and Chan, Mimi (1972) Where the twain do meet: A preliminary study of the language habits of university undergraduates in Hong Kong. *General Linguistics,* 12, 63–79.

Kwok, Helen and Chan, Mimi (1975) Creative writing in English: Problems faced by undergraduates in the English Department, The University of Hong Kong. *Topic in Culture Learning,* 3, 27–38. Honolulu: East-West Centre, University of Hawaii.

Lau, Chi-kuen (1986) Political excuse for poor studies. *South China Morning Post.* 16 December. 4.

Leland, Charles G. (1876) *Pidgin English Sing-Song.* London: Kegan Paul, Trench, Trubner and Co. Ltd.

Lim, Shirley and Richards, Page (ed.) (2001) *Moving Poetry: Hong Kong Children's Poems.* Hong Kong: Hong Kong University Press.

Lin, Angel Mei Yi (1997) Analyzing the 'language problem' discourses in Hong Kong: How official, academic, and media discourses construct and perpetuate dominant models of language, learning, and education. *Journal of Pragmatics,* 28, 427–40.

Llamzon, Teodoro A. (1986) Life cycle of new Englishes: Restriction phase of Filipino English. *English World-Wide,* 7(1), 101–25.

Lord, Robert (1974) English — How serious a problem for students in Hong Kong? *The English Bulletin,* 4(3), 1–10.

Matheson, Ruth (1997) Dignity reigns as Britain lowers flags. *South China Morning Post.* 1 July. 3.

Milroy, James and Milroy, Lesley (1985) *Authority in Language: Investigating Language Prescription and Standardisation.* London: Routledge and Kegan Paul.

Morrison, John R. (1834) A glossary of words and phrases peculiar to the jargon spoken at Canton. In *A Chinese Commercial Guide Consisting of a Collection of Details Respecting Foreign Trade in China.* Edited by J. R. Morrison. Canton: Albion Press, unnumbered.

Ng, Margaret Ngoi-yee (2001) Cosmopolitanism at risk. *South China Morning Post.* 12 September. 16.

Pennington, Martha C. (1998) The folly of language planning; or, a brief history of the English language in Hong Kong. *English Today,* 54, 25–30.

Regan, Mark (2000) Language 'essential to future of SAR'. *South China Morning Post.* 29 February. 23

Romaine, Susanne (1994) *Language in Society: An Introduction to Sociolinguistics.* Oxford: Oxford University Press.

Smith, Carl T. (1985) The English-educated elite in nineteenth-century Hong Kong.

In *Chinese Christians: Élites, Middlemen, and the Church in Hong Kong*. Edited by C. T. Smith. Hong Kong: Oxford University Press, pp. 139–71.
South China Morning Post (1986a) Language project deserves applause. *South China Morning Post.* 1 November. [Editorial] 10.
South China Morning Post (1986b) Putonghua, not Cantonese in classes. *South China Morning Post.* 22 July. [Editorial] 16.
South China Morning Post (1987a) Magic and wonderment of English must remain. *South China Morning Post.* 11 June. [Editorial] 28.
South China Morning Post (1987b) Need for far-sighted policy on languages. *South China Morning Post.* [Editorial] 25 January. 8.
South China Morning Post (1989) 'Worst' English tag should be eliminated. *South China Morning Post.* 27 February. [Editorial] 18.
South China Morning Post (1996) Ignorant. *South China Morning Post.* 11 February. Letters page. [Letter from Chau Tak-hay] 11.
South China Morning Post (1998) Standards of English. *South China Morning Post.* 9 March. 18.
Tacey, Elisabeth (2000) Lessons of mother tongue learning. *Sunday Morning Post.* 9 April. 9.
T'sou, Benjamin (1985) Chinese and the cultural eunuch syndrome. In *The Language Bomb*. Edited by R. Lord and B. T'sou. Hong Kong: Longman (Far East), pp. 15–9.
Xu Xi (2001) *The Unwalled City*. Hong Kong: Chameleon Press.
Yau, Frances Man Siu (1997) Code switching and language choice in the Hong Kong Legislative Council. *Journal of Multilingual and Multicultural Development*, **18**(1), 40–53.
Yow, Sophia (2001) Guangdong to trial English as medium. *South China Morning Post.* 20 October. 2.
Zajc, Lydia (2001) SAR comes out top in domestic Internet access. *South China Morning Post.* 14 June. 17.

Part I
Language in Context

1

The sociolinguistics of Hong Kong and the space for Hong Kong English

Kingsley Bolton

Introduction

The starting point for this chapter is Kachru's call for a paradigm shift and pluricentric approach to World Englishes. Today it is something of a cliché that English is a global language, no longer the property of Britain or the United States, and that, in McCrum's words, '[t]here is not one English language anymore, but there are many English languages' (McCrum, cited in Iyer 1993: 53). The effects of this paradigm shift have been felt in many societies where English has the status of a second language or 'outer circle' variety, including such Asian societies as India, Malaysia, Philippines, and Singapore. Previously, the notion of Hong Kong English has received more support in the international sociolinguistics literature than it has in the territory itself (see, for example, Todd and Hancock, 1986: 233–5; McArthur, 1992: 483–4). On 30 June 1997, Hong Kong ceased to be a British crown colony and became the HKSAR (the Hong Kong Special Administrative Region, China). The change in sovereignty not only signalled a transition from a colonial to a post-colonial society, but also, marked the transformation of a colonial city to a global city, 'with a form of governance that has no clear historical precedents' (Abbas, 1997: 2). This chapter explores the sociolinguistic background to the recognition of a local and global space for Hong Kong English, in a community that was promised a 'high degree of autonomy' in the negotiations that decided its future.

A paradigm shift for English in Hong Kong

Over the last fifteen years or so, Braj Kachru has suggested a model of global English in terms of 'three concentric circles', *the inner circle* (societies such as Britain, the USA, Australia, New Zealand, etc. where English is the 'first language' of a majority of the population), *the outer circle* (societies such as

India, the Philippines, etc. where English has the status of a 'second language') and *the extending* (or *'expanding') circle* (societies such as China or Japan where English has the status of a 'foreign language'). In a sustained academic campaign for a non-Eurocentric approach to the study of World Englishes, Kachru has challenged a number of assumptions about the study of English as a global language.

In particular he has been eager to kill off such 'sacred cows of English' as the 'native speaker' versus 'non-native' speaker dichotomy, and to argue for a 'pluricentric' approach to the acquisition and use of 'new' varieties of English, or, more precisely, 'world Englishes' in such outer-circle areas as Bangladesh, Kenya, Malaysia, Nigeria, the Philippines, Singapore, etc. This has evolved into a challenge to such 'myths' as the 'native speaker idealization myth', the 'native vs. non-native speaker interaction myth', the 'culture identity (or monoculture) myth', the 'exocentric norm myth', and the 'interlanguage myth' (Kachru, 1997: 10). Kachru has also been concerned to challenge the dominance of the Anglocentric literary canon, to argue for the recognition of bilingual creativity in the 'new literatures' in English that have appeared in Africa, Asia, and the Caribbean, and to illuminate the extent to which these 'contact literatures in English' have undergone *nativization* and *acculturation*. Kachru argues that in West Africa, South Asia and Southeast Asia, these literatures are thus 'both nativized and acculturated' as instanced by the work of Wole Soyinka from Nigeria, and that of Raja Rao of India, and that the issue of the bilingual's creativity is an important area for linguistic, literary and pedagogical research (Kachru, 1990: 159–73). The notion of 'multi-canon' attempts to accommodate the current sociolinguistic reality in world Englishes where speakers of a wide range of first languages communicate with one another through English, so that, 'a speaker of a Bantu language may interact with a speaker of Japanese, a Taiwanese, an Indian, and so on'. As a result English has become acculturated in many 'un-English' sociolinguistic contexts, in many African and Asian societies where there is no shared Judeo-Christian or European cultural heritage, or shared literary canon, and thus the English language has become 'multi-canonical' (Kachru, 1991).

Kachru has further urged a re-think towards the teaching of English worldwide, calling for a two-fold 'paradigm shift' in approaches to English studies:

> First, a paradigm shift in research, teaching, and application of sociolinguistic realities to the functions of English. Second, a shift from frameworks and theories which are essentially appropriate only to monolingual countries. It is indeed essential to recognise that World Englishes represent certain linguistic, cultural and pragmatic realities and pluralism, and that pluralism is now an integral part of World Englishes and literatures written in Englishes. The pluralism of English must be reflected in the approaches, both theoretical and applied, we adopt for understanding this unprecedented linguistic phenomenon. (Kachru, 1992: 11).

In a recent paper on 'English as an Asian Language', Kachru reviews the contemporary spread of English in the region, noting that at present the English-using population of Asia totals 350 million out of an estimated population of 3.5 billion; that India is the third largest English-using nation after the USA and the UK; that English is the language most in demand for acquisition of bilingualism/multilingualism in Asia; and that in some societies, including Singapore, English is assuming the role of first language, 'whatever we mean by that term' (Kachru, 1997: 7). Kachru argues for an acceptance and utilization of 'English on Asian terms', noting that, in Asia, English has a potential as a liberating language, and that '[o]nce a language establishes its autonomy, it is actually liberated, and its "liberated" uses and functions have to be separated from its non-liberated uses'. Again, Kachru notes the importance of literary creativity in this context, and argues for the acculturation of English to the needs and visions of Asian societies, in such societies as India, Malaysia, the Philippines and Singapore:

> The architects of each tradition, each strand, have molded, reshaped, acculturated, redesigned, and – by doing so – enriched what was a Western medium. The result is a liberated English which contains vitality, innovation, linguistic mix, and cultural identity. And, it is not the creativity of the monolingual and the monocultural – this creativity has rejuvenated the medium from 'exhaustion' and has 'liberated' it in many ways. (Kachru, 1997: 23)

In the case of Hong Kong, two related questions arise: First, is it possible to argue that the conditions now exist for a recognition of the autonomy of Hong Kong English, on a par with other Englishes in the Asian region? Second, has the time also come to recognize the creativity of English in Hong Kong, as evidenced by a range of literary initiatives in recent years? These are two of the themes explored in this book.

From Canton English to Hong Kong English

The origins of English in China, and of Hong Kong English itself, may be traced back to the early seventeenth century, when the first British trading ships reached Macau and Canton (Guangzhou). With the development of the Canton trade in the eighteenth and early nineteenth century, a distinct variety of Chinese pidgin English emerged at Canton and Macau. In the early nineteenth century, this was referred to as Canton 'jargon', and it was not until 1859 that the term 'pidgin English' began to be used. With the annexation of Hong Kong during the First Opium War between Britain and China in 1842, and the development of the 'treaty port' system from the 1840s onwards, English began to spread through education, notably through the various mission schools that were established in Hong Kong and throughout China. Early mission schools like St Paul's College (1851), Diocesan Girls' School (1860), Diocesan Boys' School (1869), and St Joseph's (1876), were complemented by the government-run Central School (1862) which later became Queen's College. Such schools played a significant role in the linguistic history of Hong Kong as a British colony, in educating a compradore class of merchants who played a key role in Sino-European and Sino-American trade, as well as the promotion of modernity in late nineteenth-century China (Smith, 1985).

The establishment of the early system of mission schools did not mean that the study of Chinese was typically neglected. Western missionaries who arrived in China from the beginning of the nineteenth century onwards encountered a rich literate culture that, as in the case of India, spoke for an advanced civilization with its own strong literary and philosophical tradition. Many of the largely Protestant educators who set up the first missionary schools had a profoundly orientalist interest in the Mandarin language as well as the dialects of South China, notably Cantonese, Hakka, and Chiu Chau. Consequently, Chinese language and literature was taught at most mission schools, alongside English, thus creating a category of school referred to as 'Anglo-Chinese', a term which survives until today, referring to schools where English is the declared teaching medium and the printed medium for most textbooks. In 1911, the University of Hong Kong was established, and although this increased the demand for English-medium education, large numbers of Chinese-medium schools were established in the 1920s and 1930s (So, 1992: 72). In 1963, the Chinese University of Hong Kong was set up, with the mission of providing Chinese-language university instruction. After the Communist-led riots in 1967, there followed the 'Chinese language campaign' of the 1970s which pressed for greater recognition of Chinese. In 1974, Chinese was first recognized as a co-official language, and in 1974–8, education reforms took place at both the primary and secondary levels, and an era of 'mass education' began to be established. In recent years, other social and political events have contributed to the contemporary history of both English and Chinese. Such events include the rise of a popular Cantonese culture in film and music from the 1960s to the 1990s, the expansion of university education from 1989 onwards and recent policy changes in relation to the use of English as an official language and a teaching medium in schools.

As in other Asian societies such as India, Malaysia, the Philippines, and Singapore the role that English plays in contemporary Hong Kong society has been shaped by specific historical processes, including British colonialism, which in the case of Hong Kong spanned the years from 1842–1997. What distinguishes the Hong Kong experience, however, is the relative longevity of the colonial era in the 'territory', as it was referred to in the era of late British colonialism which lasted from the mid-1960s until the 'Handover' of sovereignty to the People's Republic of China five years ago. This period of 'sixties to nineties' was crucial to the formation of 'modern Hong Kong' in a number of ways, as it saw the economic transformation of Hong Kong from a relatively poor refugee community to a wealthy commercial and entrepreneurial powerhouse. The Hong Kong 'success story' in the postwar period involved a number of factors closely related to the politics and economics of mainland China, including the influx of Shanghainese industry and capital; the UN trade blockade of China from the early 1950s to the 1970s; the growth of the city as a financial centre during the 1970s; and the move of Hong Kong businessmen into China trade throughout the 1980s.

The same period also saw rapid rises in the population of the territory. In 1945, the population was just 600,000; by 1961, because of waves of immigration from the People's Republic of China, it had increased to 3.1 million. This was followed by continued increases over the next three decades; by 1971, the total was 3.9 million; by 1981, 5.1 million; by 1996, 6.2 million, and by 2000, approximately 7 million. From the late 1950s until the 1970s, much of Hong Kong was a refugee immigrant community. Until 1980, the Hong Kong government maintained a 'touchbase' policy which stipulated that once illegal immigrants reached the 'urban areas' of the colony, they would be allowed to settle permanently. This policy ended in 1980, but in the following decades illegal immigration continued, as its does today. In addition to the arrival of 'IIs' (illegal immigrants), there has also been a system of legal immigration from the late 1970s onwards. Legal immigrants in the 1980s were arriving in Hong Kong at the rate of 75 a day, by the mid-1990s this figure had risen to 150. The underside of the officially endorsed economic success story was the social reality of the refugee fight for survival in a rapidly modernizing urban metropolis. This was also a story of living space, as a refugee immigrant community struggled for room to live in a city that was frequently ranked the world's most crowded.

During this era of late British colonialism, Hong Kong people were denied the opportunity of political involvement in the political process until the arrival of Christopher Patten, the last governor of Hong Kong (1992–7), by which time it was largely too late to establish a strong system of democratic representation. During the period of reformism from the 1970s to 1990s, the government did, however, contribute to the social transformation of Hong Kong society in a number of ways, through public housing programmes, the provision of low-cost medical services, the reform of the police force, anti-corruption campaigns, and civic education. From the 1980s, local sociologists were noting the growth of a 'new middle class', whose membership ranged from junior clerical staff and secretaries to the executives of major corporations (Leung, 1996: 12).

In this same era of economic and social transformation, the nature of public education changed dramatically, and this was to have a major impact on the learning of languages, and the degree of multilingualism in Hong Kong society. In the 1960s, typically only the socially privileged were able to provide their children with a complete secondary education, and as far as English was concerned, a system of *elitist bilingualism* existed within education (Bratt-Paulston, 1980: 2). Children progressed from an elite (or 'famous') primary school to an elite secondary school and then to either the Chinese University of Hong Kong or the University of Hong Kong. By the 1980s, the rich had started sending their children overseas for higher education, and, from the 1970s, basic educational reforms providing for compulsory primary and secondary schooling gave all children the opportunity to gain an education, which meant that increasing numbers of children from poorer backgrounds were able to go to university. The earlier system of elite schooling in English and 'elitist bilingualism' began to shift towards a system of *mass bilingualism* (or *folk bilingualism*), which, in spite of great imperfections, gave a large proportion of children at least the opportunity to acquire some English in 'Anglo-Chinese' secondary schools, where English textbooks were used. The proportion of children going to universities increased from around 2–4% at the beginning of the 1980s to something like 17% by 1996. In 1989, the government upgraded a number of post-secondary colleges and financed the establishment of a new university of science and technology, and today there are eight local universities, compared with two at the beginning of the 1980s, where English is widely used as the language of lectures and textbooks. The educational reforms of the 1970s and 1980s have contributed more than any other factor to the spread of a knowledge of English within modern Hong Kong society. The census figures for the period indicate a rise in the proportion of the population claiming a knowledge of English from 9.7% in 1961 to 43.0% in 2001, as illustrated in Figure 1.1.

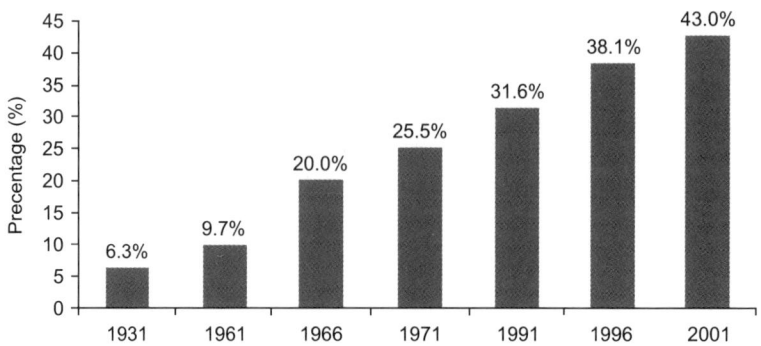

Figure 1.1   Census results for knowledge of English in Hong Kong 1931–1996

In the late colonial era, however, when a knowledge of English was spreading throughout the population at an unprecedented rate, official government language policy began to move in the other direction, towards the promotion of the Chinese language in a number of official domains, as is explained in the following section of this chapter.

Language planning in Hong Kong

The specific history of Hong Kong has helped determine the space allocated to the English language in the current language hierarchy of what is now the Hong Kong Special Administrative Region (HKSAR), as well as the language policies that have recently been formulated by the Hong Kong government. During the period of late British colonialism from the late 1960s to the late 1990s, the colonial government failed to formulate a clear language policy for the community, a lack of will often excused by the government as 'non-interventionism', but described by others as political 'vacillation' (Branegan, 1991: 27).

It was not until 1974 that Chinese was recognized as a co-official language in the territory, and during the period of British colonial rule, the English language had the status of the official language of government, the official language of law, and was *de facto* the most widely used medium of secondary and university education. Its functions included its use as an official language, its use in education, its use in industry, trade, business, finance, and communications. The Official Languages Ordinance of 1974 established that Chinese and English would thenceforth 'enjoy equality of use'. A decade or so later, after the negotiations between Beijing and London determined the arrangements for the 1997 'Handover', the position of Chinese was further strengthened by the publication of the Basic Law of the Hong Kong Special Administrative Region, in which Article 9 stated that: 'In addition to the Chinese language, English may also be used as an official language by the executive authorities, legislative and judicial organs of the Hong Kong Administrative Region' (Chinese Government, 1992).

In 1995, the Hong Kong government announced that its new language policy would be 'to develop a civil service which is biliterate in English and Chinese and trilingual in English, Cantonese and Putonghua' (Lau, 1995), an official policy statement which is still in force. In the years immediately prior to the July 1997 Handover, an increasing proportion of Cantonese was used in Legislative Council speeches, and since July 1997 the Provisional Legislative Council has mainly used Cantonese to conduct its proceedings. Attempts have been made by the government since the early 1990s to provide training courses in Putonghua for Hong Kong civil servants, but, at present, Cantonese, rather than Putonghua, is still the dominant variety in this domain. Similar changes have taken place in the legal system in Hong Kong, and through the 'Bilingual Laws Project', from 1986 onwards, a large proportion of the written laws of

Hong Kong have been translated into Chinese. From the late 1980s to the mid-1990s, amendments to the Official Languages Ordinance extended the use of spoken Chinese into the higher courts. In December 1995, the first civil High Court case was heard in Putonghua, and in August 1997, the first criminal case was conducted in Cantonese in the High Court (Cheung, 1997).

In Hong Kong, many local linguists have been less concerned about a conflict between English and Chinese, and more anxious about the possible tension between the use of Cantonese and that of Putonghua. The use of Cantonese in Hong Kong is obviously out of step with the language policies of the People's Republic of China (PRC), which specifically promote the national language Putonghua, together with the written correlate of simplified Chinese characters instead of the 'full characters' used in Hong Kong and Taiwan. Hong Kong is the Cantonese-speaking capital of the world, and in the HKSAR, Cantonese, a mere 'regional dialect' in the PRC, enjoys a pre-eminent position, not only in intimate domains such as family and friends, but also in employment, public life, social activities, and even in such official and semi-official domains as the government, civil service, and education. It is also the dominant language of Hong Kong popular culture, which finds expression in television, popular music, and films. In many ways, Cantonese can be regarded as *the* language of Hong Kong. Sin and Roebuck thus comment that, given the wide use of the language in education, religion, the print and broadcast media, and the government, 'the status of Cantonese is much higher than is normally thought and cannot be simply brushed aside as the "vernacular"' (Sin and Roebuck, 1996: 252).

The stated official language policy of the PRC is essentially opposed to the use of 'regional dialects' such as Cantonese, Fukien, Shanghainese in government, education, and other official domains of use. Language planning in the PRC since the revolution has been presented in the form of a national 'language reform policy' (Cheng and Pasierbsky, 1988), which attempts to tackle four main issues: (1) illiteracy, (2) the development and promotion of a standard national language, (3) the promotion of simplified Chinese characters, and (4) the promotion of the Latinized alphabetic writing system, 'Pinyin', for certain specialist purposes. A *China Daily* newspaper report on language policy in 1992 emphasized the standardization of language, especially in its written form, noting that: 'The State Council demanded that all departments and local governments support the work of the committee by assuming leadership of the language and Chinese characters' (*China Daily*, 1992). It is thus evident that, in Hong Kong, language planning diverges from that of the PRC in a number of important respects, notably where official policy stipulates the promotion of the national language (*Putonghua*), the use of simplified characters, the use of the Pinyin writing system, and the standardization of written characters. On this last point, it should be noted that in Hong Kong the use of 'written Cantonese' is popular in advertising, newspapers, and comic books, and a number of local linguists have expressed concern about the future 'autonomy' of Cantonese (Bauer and Benedict, 1997: xxxii; Chin, 1997: 88).

The 'medium of instruction' issue in Hong Kong

The policy vacuum that existed before 1997 can be seen most clearly within education, although, in fact, the British colonial administration attempted as early as the mid-1970s to introduce a policy of vernacular language education. In 1973, the government published a 'Green Paper', or policy proposal, in favour of using Chinese as the teaching medium in the lower forms of all secondary schools, explaining its thinking thus:

> The medium of instruction bears significantly upon the quality of education offered at post-primary level. Pupils coming from primary schools where they have been taught in the medium of Cantonese have a grievous burden put on them when required to absorb new subjects through the medium of English. We recommend that Chinese become the usual language of instruction in the lower forms of secondary schools, and that English should be studied as the second language. (Hong Kong Government, 1973: 6, cited in Gibbons, 1982: 117)

Following the publication of the Green Paper, the government met strong opposition from parents and schools, backed down on these early plans to promote Chinese as a teaching medium, and, finally, in the White Paper of 1974, settled for a *laissez-faire* approach, allowing individual school principals to decide the teaching medium in their schools. This aborted policy move by the colonial government was significant in that it occurred at just that point in time when the educational system of modern Hong Kong was being created through the expansion of education. It thus appears that the initial instinct of the colonial government was to opt for Chinese-medium instruction, which, in the vast majority of schools, would have meant Cantonese.

Ironically, this in turn provides evidence that the promotion of Cantonese was a feature of colonial language policy in the territory, just as the use of regional Chinese dialects in religion and education had been a tenet of missionary language policy throughout the nineteenth century. The promotion of 'mother tongue' education in contemporary Hong Kong can thus be seen as both missionary and colonial; the PRC has never had a policy of promoting the 'mother tongue' as a teaching medium. In pre-modern China, classical Chinese was used as the language of the educated or 'Mandarin' class; after the foundation of the Chinese Republic in 1911, a new form of standard written Chinese, *baihua*, was adopted. Later, after the communist government came to power in 1949, the standard written language was further amended through the use of simplified characters, and a form of the spoken language, *Putonghua*, was promoted as a national and official language, for use in domains such as government and education. Despite this historical irony, many of those involved in the Chinese language from the 1970s have been concerned to promote the use of Chinese for a range of sound educational reasons, including the practical necessity of teaching lower-ability groups for whom English is a major obstacle to learning, as well as the desire for greater social equality (Kwok, 1982: 40–3; Pun, 1997: 95–6).

The government's failure to implement a strong policy in favour of *either* Chinese-medium teaching *or* English-medium instruction in the mid-1970s was perhaps symptomatic of the dilemma that it faced. To follow its instinct and implement Chinese-medium education at that time would have incurred the displeasure of the majority of local parents and schools, but to have adopted a vigorous policy of using English would have meant that the government ran the risk of accusations of linguistic and cultural imperialism. By contrast, in Singapore, Lee Kwan Yew, bolstered by the authenticity of his role as the nation's post-colonial leader, had few qualms about the promotion of English as the official language of administration, business, and education. The result of this 'vacillation' in policy led to the continued increase in the proportion of 'Anglo-Chinese' schools, which were secondary schools that advertised themselves as English-medium institutions. In practice, few of these schools provided a total immersion in the English-based education system, and by the late 1980s and early 1990s, the 'English-medium' system in place could be described as a 'continuum'. At one end of the scale were prestigious secondary schools which prided themselves on teaching all subjects through the medium of English (apart from Chinese studies), while at the other end of the scale were the lowest rank of schools that used Cantonese for teaching almost all subjects, even though the majority of textbooks were in English, and students took English-medium examinations. In between these two extremes were the majority of schools, which used both spoken Cantonese and English (together with English textbooks) in a 'mixed mode' practice of teaching. Among other things, this resulted in the extensive use of code-switching and code-mixing in schools among the younger generations of students who were receiving their education in the system (Johnson, 1994: 187–8).

In the 1980s and 1990s, the government began to encourage Chinese-medium education through a number of other measures, including various incentives for secondary school principals to adopt Chinese as a teaching medium, but, given the strong parental demand for English-medium schools, these measures had little effect. In 1994, for example, the statistics showed that over 90% of all secondary schools were at least nominally English-medium (Johnson, 1994: 186–7). Shortly before the change of sovereignty in 1997, the colonial Hong Kong government in its final months suddenly adopted a coercive strengthening of policy, and, on 22 March 1997, it announced that in future approximately only 100 secondary schools (some 22% of the total of 460) would be allowed to use English as a teaching medium and that punitive measures, e.g. a maximum fine of $25,000 and two years in jail, might be used against school principals who did not follow the instructions of the government on this issue (Kwok, 1997). Later the figure of 100 was amended to 114, after protests from schools and parents, but at present the policy remains one of providing 'firm guidance' for secondary schools, and of encouraging the use of Cantonese as a teaching medium.

Why the colonial government in its last few months should have chosen to break with its *laissez-faire* past so dramatically remains something of a mystery. What seems clear, however, is that the announcement of this policy *was* a decision of the colonial government, *not*, as has been the subsequent perception, the decision of the first Beijing-appointed post-colonial Chief Executive, Mr Tung Chee-hwa, and his advisors. There are a number of possible explanations of the policy change. The government may finally have accepted the arguments of those local educationalists who despaired of the inefficiency and wastage of the previous system, particularly with reference to the education of lower-ability children in what are called the 'lower-band' schools in Hong Kong. Alternatively, some in the government may have believed that by promoting an education system based largely on Cantonese that they would also be giving support to a local Cantonese-speaking community faced with a takeover by northern Chinese communists, and that supporting Cantonese would also mean support for a local Hong Kong identity, and the 'high degree of autonomy' promised by the Draft Agreement between Britain and China that had decided Hong Kong's future in 1984.

In the two and a half years since the announcement of this policy, there has been a great deal of government rhetoric in support of its new policy of 'mother tongue' teaching, but it is by no means clear that this policy will continue unaltered into the future. Recent reports in the newspapers suggest that the government itself may be split on the issue of language policy. For example, the Secretary for Education and Manpower was recently quoted as reaffirming his belief in the government's 'mother tongue' policy (Chan, 1999), but a report one week later cited the head of a government-appointed working group on the medium of instruction as stating that senior secondary students 'should have freedom to choose which language to be taught in if the schools believed they have teachers capable of using English to teach' (Cheung, 1999). A newly appointed Director of Education was also reported as calling for a 'radical overhaul' of the education system, adding that the government was 'keeping an open mind' on the teaching medium issue (Moy, 1998). To many in Hong Kong, it seems that the government is again undecided on the issue of a clear language policy for education, all of which moved the *South China Morning Post* to publish a recent editorial on the topic, that noted the apparent confusion in current official thinking:

> Contradictory findings follow one another with bewildering speed ... Even as one government-sponsored working group recommends that secondary schools teaching in Cantonese should be allowed to choose which language to use as a medium of instruction at senior level, fears are being voiced that the government could be planning to make all SAR schools switch to mother-tongue teaching ... It will cause great dismay among the public if the remaining 114 schools teaching in English are made to change. An international city with cyber-world aspirations needs schools that teach in the language of business and modern science. (*South China Morning Post*, 22 November 1999)

Whatever happens in the next few years, it would be surprising if Hong Kong jettisoned English entirely as a medium of school instruction. Despite the reassurances of the government, large numbers of parents remain unconvinced that the language can be effectively taught if its status is relegated to that of a 'foreign' language in schools. The government is also under pressure to maintain and improve the 'standard' of English from the business community, anxious that Hong Kong's economic prosperity, and its status as a centre for international business, already dented by the post-1997 Asian economic crisis, might be further eroded in comparison with its regional rival Singapore, or its rapidly developing mainland competitor, Shanghai.

There is also an important social-class dimension to all this, as many Hong Kong parents feel that access to English for their children is being restricted by these new policy measures, and that, as in other societies, 'the requirement for children to have education in the mother tongue can lead to an apartheid situation which may be socially divisive and/or oppressive' (Gupta, 1995). If the new policy continues in its present form, the worry for many parents is that the English-medium schools will become largely the preserve of children of parents from middle-class or upper-middle-class backgrounds, who are most adept at steering their children through a competitive system of kindergarten and primary school before gaining entry to the more prestigious English-medium schools. In addition, many of the high-ranking civil servants and educationalists who are responsible for formulating language policies often send their own children overseas for education, typically to private schools and universities in Australia, North America and Britain (Postiglione, 1998: 151). The question of language and social class in Hong Kong is one of a number of sociolinguistic issues that have been largely ignored in the past, as Lee (1998) indicates. Other issues include multilingualism and multiculturalism, immigrant education, with specific relevance to immigrants from mainland China, and the problem of 'language standards', a discourse applied even-handedly to 'falling' standards of Chinese and English. The discussion of such issues has also been influenced greatly by the rapid and dramatic political, economic and social changes that have occurred in the HKSAR over the last few decades. As in many other societies experiencing rapid change, the discussion of language has been accompanied by its own ideologies and myths. Two of the most powerful myths in the sociolinguistic description of the society have been what one might dub the 'monolingualism myth' and the ' invisibility myth'.[1]

Hong Kong and the 'monolingual myth'

The 'myth of monolingualism' is persistent in many communities where the sociolinguist sees diversity, variation and multilingualism. It may be true that 'in England they speak English', but they also speak many other languages as well. A recent survey on the languages of London schools reported that 307 languages were spoken by the city's schoolchildren, with Cantonese listed in eleventh place. The degree of multilingualism in Hong Kong, among bilingual and trilingual Chinese, as well as among various linguistic minority groups may be less dramatic, but it does exist. Throughout the 1980s and early 1990s, however, many linguists seemed reluctant to recognize the particular forms that multilingualism takes in Hong Kong, choosing instead to emphasize the dominance of Cantonese in the local community.

Thus Fu (1987: 28) comments that 'Ninety-eight percent of the population speaks Chinese at home' and that 'English continues to remain more a foreign language than a second language to most people'; Yu and Atkinson (1988: 307) state that 'Hong Kong [is] a British colony where 98% of the population are Cantonese-speaking Chinese'; Yau (1989: 179) describes the speech community as 'a virtually monolingual Chinese society'; So (1992: 79) affirms that 'Hong Kong is an essentially monolingual Cantonese-speaking community'; and Yau (1993: 25) claims that 'Hong Kong is basically a monoethnic society'. Few would deny the vitality of Cantonese, but, at the same time, notions of linguistic homogeneity and ethnic purity hardly fits the daily experience of life in a community that has so relatively recently morphed from a *wah kiu* refugee community into a vibrant Asian metropolis. Chako (1995) describes the flavour of this in an essay written in the mid-1990s:

> As a child in Hong Kong, I spoke English with a British-Indonesian-Cantonese accent, and never really knew what my 'mother tongue' was. Today, many Hong Kong Chinese children also find themselves in confusion about their native language. They speak fluent English with a Filipino accent, acquired by daily proximity to their maid, or they rattle on in Canadian English, the fallout of their parents' pre-1997 pursuit of a passport. ... My minibus driver in Kowloon Tong exhibits an admirable command of Tagalog, and is besieged by a flock of willing tutor-passengers who want to know when he's moving to Manila. ... Whether we're talking language (who put the 'putong' in putonghua anyway?) culture (Confucius or Cantopop?) or political ideology (hands up, all you capitalist communists), Hong Kong Chinese can hardly claim to have a clear-cut 'Chinese' identity.

Recently the view of Hong Kong as a 'monolingual' and 'monoethnic' society has been strongly challenged by a number of Hong Kong sociolinguists, including Afendras (1998), Bacon-Shone and Bolton (1998), and Patri and Pennington (1998). Bacon-Shone and Bolton, working from a variety of census and language survey data, point out that empirical results indicate that knowledge of English in the general population expanded greatly during the 1980s and 1990s. For example, the total number of respondents claiming to speak English 'quite well', 'well', and 'very well' rose from 6.6% in 1983 to 33.7% in 1993; conversely the numbers of those stating that they did not speak 'at all' dropped from 33.1% in 1983 to 17.4% in 1993. These results received a strong measure of support from the official by-census that was carried out in 1996, where 3.1% of the population claimed to speak English as 'a usual language/dialect', but another 34.9% reported speaking English as 'another language/dialect' (giving a total of 38% of all those claiming to know English). The dramatic change in the linguistic profile of the society in this time may be related to a number of factors, but it seems certain that the extension of education through the primary and secondary reforms of the 1970s and the university reforms of the late 1980s and early 1990s has played a major role in the spread of English throughout the community.

At the written level, English also plays an important role in formal communications of all kinds, in government, the legal domain, in university textbooks and teaching materials, and as a professional language of business and technical communications in the territory. In the 1993 survey conducted by Bacon-Shone and Bolton, 54.7% of those that wrote notes, memos, etc. at work normally use English, and 59.2% of those who read written materials at work read materials written in English. The pre-eminent language of newspapers and print media is Chinese, and in the popular dailies, a localized variety of 'written Cantonese' is also used for informal styles of newspaper reporting. The dominance of Chinese in the print media is evidenced by the numbers of Chinese-language newspapers, which total around fifty, compared with two main English-language dailies, the *South China Morning Post*, and the *Hong Kong Standard* (see Chan, Chapter 5 in this book).

While acknowledging the strength of Cantonese in the Hong Kong community, Bacon-Shone and Bolton suggest that at present, 'English and Cantonese have an increasingly complex co-existence in government, law, education, and business'. They further note that 'English has also intruded into the private domain of Hong Kong families in unexpected ways', and cite findings from their 1993 survey which reported that: (1) 56% of the population had an English name, with 43% claiming to use that name 'all of the time', and 30% having an English name on their ID cards; (2) 53% used English to write out the words on a cheque; (3) 57% had close relatives in an English-speaking country; (4) 30% either had a close relative who was planning to emigrate to an English-speaking community, or were planning themselves to emigrate; and that (5) the vast majority reported hearing a good deal of code-mixing (English words in Cantonese speech) in various domains: at home, 45%; among friends, 75%; at school, 90%; at work, 79%; and in public, 83% (1998: 84–85; see also Li, Chapter 4 in this book). Very recently, there has been a strong trend among Hong Kong university students, who now all have access to computers either from within their institutions or at home, to use the Internet to 'chat' informally to each other through email and 'ICQ' programmes. In this, they often use a 'mixed' form of written English and Chinese, with Cantonese vocabulary items and conversational particles 'romanized' into a linguistic matrix of written Hong Kong English.

Bacon-Shone and Bolton also note that bilingualism is not confined to Cantonese and English, but that a substantial number of respondents also claim a knowledge of Putonghua (1.1% as a usual language, 25.3% as 'another language' in the 1996 census). From a sociolinguistic perspective, they conclude, the community is far from 'monolingual', and Hong Kong might be more accurately described as 'a multilingual society, where speakers of the majority language, Cantonese, and speakers of minority "dialects" of Chinese also tend to report increasing degrees of fluency in both English and Putonghua (Mandarin)' (1998: 85). In addition, Hong Kong is the adopted home of a number of non-Chinese minorities, who often speak Cantonese and English as well as minority languages. The history of such groups in the society is under-researched, but such communities as the South Asians, Parsees, Portuguese, and Eurasians played a major role in nineteenth-century Hong Kong. Today, significant numbers of Indians, Parsees, and Eurasians still live in the territory, as do Indonesians, Filipinos, Japanese, Malaysians, Nepalis, Pakistanis, and Thais. Of these, by far the largest group is that of Filipinos, predominantly Filipina domestic helpers or 'amahs', whose numbers rose from 72,000 in 1991 to approximately 170,000 in 1999. Not only do such workers make a major contribution to the Hong Kong economy in enabling many middle-class couples with children to both hold full-time employment, but research suggests that they also make a linguistic contribution to the society in providing an opportunity for the children of such families to gain an early facility in spoken English. Afendras notes that 'Hong Kong's "guest" domestic workers may be emerging as the main caregivers and, at the same time, as live-in English tutors for middle-class children', and that 'Filipinas ... may be making a contribution to the ecology of English far greater than has hitherto been recognized' (1998: 136–7).

Hong Kong and the 'invisibility myth'

The apparent reluctance in earlier studies to consider the multilingual character of Hong Kong society has been matched by a similar attitude to the existence of Hong Kong English as an autonomous (or semi-autonomous) variety. For example, Luke and Richards (1982: 55) claim that 'In Hong Kong ... the norm or standard consumed by learners of English is an external one rather than an internal one ...' There is no such thing then as 'Hong Kong English', a judgement echoed by Tay (1991: 327) who asserts that '[t]here is no social motivation for the indigenisation of English in Hong Kong' and that 'English in Hong Kong has been considered either a learner's language, a developmental rather than lectal continuum ... or is described in terms of a cline of bilingualism'. This view is also endorsed by Johnson (1994: 182), who comments that the notion of a Hong Kong variety of English has so far gained 'little support', as '[t]here is no social or cultural role for English to play among Hong Kong Chinese; it only has a role in their relations with expatriates and the outside world'. Perhaps it is now time to re-examine such previous judgements, and one obvious reason for so doing is the passing of British colonial rule. Whatever the future of the HKSAR, which came into being in July 1997, it is now simply a historical fact that Hong Kong is no longer a colony of Great Britain. Given the experience of other Asian societies, it is unavoidable that the post-colonial development of society will impact greatly on its sociolinguistic dynamics. A second reason for re-evaluating the role of English would be the argument that the essential conditions necessary for the emergence of such a variety may be already present in the community.

Criteria for world Englishes

Butler (1997: 106) suggests the following characteristics help define a variety of world English: (1) a 'standard and recognizable pattern of pronunciation handed down from one generation to another' (accent); (2) '[p]articular words and phrases which spring up usually to express key features of the physical and social environment and which are regarded as peculiar to the variety' (vocabulary); (3) '[a] history – a sense that this variety of English is the way it is because of the history of the language community' (a history); (4) '[a] literature written without apology in that variety of English' (literary creativity); and (5) '[r]eference works – dictionaries and style guides – which show that people in that language community look to themselves, not some outside authority, to decide what is right and wrong in terms of how they speak and write their English' (reference works).

The Hong Kong accent

With reference to the first criterion of accent, Bolton and Kwok (1990) provide a description of both segmental and supra-segmental features of the phonology of Hong Kong English, and investigate the reactions of university students to a number of English accents, including RP accents, US accents, and Hong Kong accents through the use of a verbal guise technique. The results of this research indicate that 'Hong Kong English speakers typically share a number of localised features of a Hong Kong accent' (1990: 166). Other results suggested that the respondents 'identified' (Le Page and Tabouret-Keller, 1985) with local speakers in a number of ways: (1) they could recognize a Hong Kong accent relatively easily; (2) they had difficulty in labelling other accents of English; and (3) a substantial number of respondents (particularly male students) stated a preference for that accent of English associated with 'Hong Kong bilinguals' (p. 170). Further research on this issue is presented by Hung (see Chapter 6).

Hong Kong vocabulary

At the level of vocabulary, a number of studies of a distinct Hong Kong vocabulary have been published in recent years. Such work includes Chan and Kwok (1985), a study of 'lexical borrowing from Chinese into English'; Taylor (1989) on the use of English in Hong Kong newspapers; Benson (1994) on 'political vocabulary of Hong Kong English'; Carless (1995) on 'politicised expressions' in local newspapers; and work in this area is continuing (Benson, see Chapter 8). As significant, however, are the studies carried out by Susan Butler and the Australia-based *Macquarie Dictionary*, who, over the last decade, have compiled wordlists for Asian Englishes including Hong Kong English. Examples of Hong Kong words in the *Macquarie* database may be seen below in the form of dictionary entries for a new dictionary that *Macquarie* is now co-publishing with Grolier Publishers, the *Grolier International Dictionary: World English in an Asian Context*, which highlights the use of distinctly local vocabularies in Asian Englishes. Examples of entries for Hong Kong include the following:

> **ABC** *noun* **1.** an Australian-born Chinese **2.** (especially in Hong Kong) an American-born Chinese
> **Ah** *noun Hong Kong English* an informal term of address: *Ah Sam | Ah Chan*
> **almond cream** *noun Hong Kong English* a sweet dessert of crushed almonds in a soup, usually served hot
> **AO** *noun Hong Kong English* a public servant in the most senior career grade in the Hong Kong Civil Service
> **astronaut** *noun* **1.** someone specially trained to travel in a spaceship **2.** *Hong Kong English* a person whose family has emigrated abroad, for example to Australia or Canada, but who remains working in Hong Kong, and then spends a great deal of time flying between his or her family and Hong Kong
> **bak choi** /bʌk ˈtʃɔɪ/ *noun Hong Kong English* a variety of Chinese green and white cabbage ❐ *Other Forms:* Another spelling is **pak choi**

banana *noun* **1.** a long curved fruit with a yellow skin **2.** *Asian English* a westernised Chinese

BBC *noun Hong Kong English Informal* a British-born Chinese

beggar's chicken *noun* in Chinese cuisine, a chicken dish baked in lotus leaves and mud

big brother *noun Asian English* **1.** a Chinese kinship term referring to the eldest male sibling in a family **2.** A recruiter or protector in a Chinese secret society or triad

black hand *noun Hong Kong English* a behind-the-scenes mastermind who plans political or criminal activities

black society *noun Hong Kong English* a Chinese secret society or triad

bo lei /ˈboʊ ˈleɪ/ *noun Hong Kong English* a variety of strong dark tea

Buddha's delight *noun* a vegetarian dish of bean curd, nuts, tiger lilies and a hair-like seaweed which is particularly popular at Chinese New Year, as the Cantonese name of the seaweed (*fat choi* or 'hair vegetable') sounds very similar to the New Year greeting wishing prosperity

cage *noun* **1.** an enclosure made of wires or bars, in which animals or birds can be kept **2.** anything that is like a prison **3.** in Hong Kong, a partitioned bedspace in an apartment, rented by the very poor -*verb* **4.** To put someone or something in, or as if in, a cage: *The prisoner was caged in his cell.* The occupants of **a cage** (definition 3) are known **as cageman, cagewoman, cage dwellers** or **cage people** and it is short for cage house, the translation of the term in Chinese.

Canto- a prefix indicating the influence of the Cantonese language or culture, especially in books, film, television, or pop music: *Canto-drama | Canto-movie*

Canto-speak *noun Hong Kong English Informal* the Cantonese language

Canto star *noun Hong Kong English* a singer of Cantonese pop songs ❐ *Other Forms:* You can also use **Canto-popstar**

char siew /tʃa ˈsju/ *noun* Chinese-style roast pork ❐ *Other Forms:* Other spellings, in Hong Kong English, are **char siu** and **cha siu**

char siew bau /tʃa sju ˈbaʊ/ *noun Hong Kong English* a white bun containing spicy pork, a popular Cantonese snack ❐ *Other Forms:* Another spelling is **char siu bau**

cheeky *adjective* (**cheekier, cheekiest**) **1.** rude or lacking respect, especially in a playful way: *Her cheeky behaviour annoyed the teacher.* **2.** *Asian English Informal* behaving in a way that is overconfident and lacking respect for the opposite sex -*phrase* **3. Get cheeky with someone,** *Hong Kong English* to be insolent towards someone ❐ *Word Family:* **cheekily** *adverb* -**cheekiness** *noun*

chicken *noun* **1.** a young hen or rooster **2.** the meat from this bird: *chicken for dinner* **3.** *Informal* a coward: *He's too much of a chicken to climb that tree.* **4.** *Hong Kong English Informal* a prostitute -*adjective Informal* **5.** Cowardly -*phrase* **6. Chicken out,** *Informal* to back out because you are scared

China doll *noun Hong Kong English* a pretty young Chinese woman of submissive demeanour

Chinese banquet *noun* a dinner consisting of approximately a dozen courses, frequently attended by a large number of guests, as at a Chinese wedding banquet

Chinese broccoli /ˌtʃaɪnɪz ˈbrɒkəli/ *noun* → **kai lan**

Chinese cabbage *noun* → **bak choi**
Chinglish /ˈtʃɪŋglɪʃ/ *noun Informal* **1.** any variety of English strongly influenced by Chinese **2.** any variety of Chinese featuring a high proportion of English loanwords
chit *noun Asian English* **bill**[1] (definition 1)
Chiu Chau /ˈtʃju ˈtʃaʊ/ *adjective Chinese and Hong Kong English* of or relating to people, objects and activities associated with the Chiu Chau dialect areas of Guangdong and Fukien province: *Chiu Chau food | Chiu Chau dialect* ❐ *Other Forms:* Other spellings are **Chiu Chow** and **Teo Chew**
choi sum /ˈtʃɔɪ sʌm/ *noun Asian English* a green leafy vegetable with tender white fleshy stems and yellow flowers ❐ *Other Forms:* Another spelling is **choy sum**
chop[1] *verb* (**chopped, chopping**) **1.** to hit with quick, strong blows using an axe or other sharp tool: *I chopped some wood for the fire. | They chopped the tree down.* **2.** to cut into smaller pieces: *You'd better chop that meat a bit smaller.* **3.** *Asian English* to hit (someone) with a chopper or knife ❐ *Word Family:* **chopper** *noun*
chop[2] *Asian English -noun* **1. a.** a personal seal or stamp, used to approve transactions, show that papers are official, etc. **b.** a design, corresponding to a brand or trademark, stamped on goods to indicate their special quality *-verb* (**chopped, chopping**) **2.** to mark with such a stamp
cocktail /ˈkɒkteɪl/ *noun* **1.** a drink made from a mixture of alcoholic drinks and other ingredients such as fruit juice, cream, crushed ice, soft drink, etc. **2.** *Hong Kong English* a party at which such drinks are served. [etc., etc.]

(*Macquarie* 2000)

The historical dimension

The third criterion in Butler's taxonomy of essential characteristics is that of 'history'. As this has partly been dealt in an earlier section of this chapter, I shall not discuss this issue further, other than to make two additional points. First, that it is quite evident that Hong Kong, and indeed China, has a long history of linguistic contact with English that dates back to the seventeenth century, and that surprisingly little has been hitherto written on this topic, at least from a 'languages in contact' perspective (Bolton, 2000). Second, one needs to reiterate that an account of such a history would also include the period from the late 1960s to the 1990s that saw the recognition of a distinct 'Hong Kong identity', personified and gendered as 'Hong Kong Man' who, by the early 1980s, is 'go-getting and highly competitive, tough for survival, quick-thinking and flexible', and 'speaks English or expects his children to' (Baker, 1983: 478). It might too include discussion of the late colonial period that, almost unexpectedly, saw the transformation of a *colonial* city to a *global* city. As Abbas explains, 'culture in Hong Kong cannot just be related to "colonialism"; it must be related to this changed and changing space, this colonial space of disappearance, which in many respects does not resemble the old colonialisms at all', out of which may emerge a new identification with 'the cosmopolitan' (Abbas, 1997: 3, 13).

Literary creativity

On the fourth issue of literary creativity, past commentaries on the literary history of Hong Kong have focused on the absence of a Hong Kong literary tradition in English. In one essay published in 1994, Chan identifies three possible obstacles to the development of Hong Kong English writing: first, 'the language problem'; and, second, 'the psychological obstacle', and the fact that 'there is no particular general urge to try writing poems, nor any particular prestige attached to the ability to do so'. Third, Chan suggests that there may not only be a lack of creative talent, but also a lack of will to use English as a literary medium, as 'linguistic competence is not necessarily coupled with creative talent', while, additionally, '[e]ven those in whom creativity and linguistic facility meet may have no inclination whatsoever to write in a "borrowed tongue"' (Chan, 1994: 407). Despite Chan's pronounced pessimism, there have been a significant number of creative works published by local writers in recent years. Examples include the poetry of Ho (1994, 1997), Lam (1997), Leung (1992, 1997), Parkin and Wong (1997), as well as novels and short stories by Xu Xi (Sussy Komala/Chako). Most recently, there have been other initiatives, including the appearance of the literary journal *Dim Sum*, and the expansion of creative writing programmes at City University of Hong Kong and the University of Hong Kong. In addition, there are works of fiction by Hong Kong writers in translation, notably *Hong Kong Collage*, edited by Cheung (1998). All this indicates a literary culture with a much greater vitality than previously existed, or recognized, which has much promise for the future creativity of English locally. The contributions from Ho, Leung, Lam, Vittachi, and Xu Xi in this book present a range of creative voices as well as commentaries on contemporary writing in the HKSAR.

Reference works

On the final criterion of reference works, at present, there are few reference works, e.g. dictionaries and style guides, that acknowledge the existence of a local variety of English. In a number of other 'outer circle' societies, some dictionaries and reference works have been published, but even in India, Singapore, and the Philippines, such works have received a mixed reception. Nevertheless, there are developments underway, and it is possible that the Macquarie Dictionary company will publish a dictionary of Hong Kong English in the near future (Susan Butler, personal communication). Bolton, Hung, and Nelson (forthcoming) are also compiling a database of around one million words of English in Hong Kong as part of the worldwide ICE (International Corpus of English) project. At present, the *South China Morning Post* serves as a *de facto* reference point for local usage, particularly vocabulary.

Whether the discussion of 'criteria' set out here is sufficiently persuasive or powerful a signal to render visible a distinct 'variety', is perhaps less important that the desire to create a new space for discussion and discourse on Hong Kong English. Such a space would encompass not only the global and cosmopolitan, but also the local and ludic, not just one variety of localized English, but a number of different voices. For example, as Hong Kong 'moves forward', to cite a much-used phrase in local political speeches, its government is now promoting the vision of the HKSAR as a 'world-class city' and 'cyberport'. Although there is the desire in the business community to improve standards of English in the domains of business and tourism, linguistic creativity also finds expression in other ways. One example of this is explosion in popularity among the territory's computer-savvy young of Internet communication, particularly the use of so-called ICQ ('I seek you') software for online chat. Very often, particularly among university students, the language of ICQ is English, sometimes of a distinctly code-mixed and hybrid variety, as in the example text below, which is an online ICQ conversation between two university students in November 1998. At the time 'Billy' was a twenty-five-year-old postgraduate studying in the Chinese Department of the University of Hong Kong, and 'Amy' was a postgraduate student of around the same age studying linguistics. In the following conversation, Amy is at home using her personal computer, while Billy is working at his part-time job, teaching at a local tutorial centre. Varieties of English, as is often said, are not only created from above, but also bubble up from below.

Bubbling up from below

(ICQ conversation between university students, November 1998)
Billy: knock ... knock ... anyone in??
Amy: yup, what's up?
Billy: No ar!! Just to make u type some words!! hehe
Amy: u r really 'mo liu'[1]
Amy: should find a gf quick ma!
Billy: No. So up till now no one suits me. I am too bad and eye corner high[2] ar!!!
Amy: i don't think u can find them easily. u know, good looking girls are difficult to find nowadays la!
Billy: Haha ... that's true. One day I have to go back to China to find a perfect one ... hehe north mui!!!![3]

Amy: but most of the 'dai luk mui'[4] are materialistic ah! i don't want u to cry in front of me some day!
Billy: Sometimes I think I am a bad man. I cheat women.
Amy: how?
Billy: By words lor ... I am often mouth flower[5] and tell lies to them kar.
Amy: ai ya, how can u say u r a good man then?
Amy: where r u now?
Billy: In my company.
Amy: having lesson now?
Billy: yes
Amy: so when u r teaching the students, how can u play icq ah? they pay money ga, be more responsible la!!!
Amy: u r really very impolite! what's the name of ur tutorial centre? i'll call to 'kam yat tei chun d'[6] n 'sing si chun ging'![7]
Amy: What presents will you buy for my birthday?
Billy: ok lor. I am your servant for one day. U can order me to do anything for u!!
Amy: no ah! i want presents ah!!!!
Billy: Uh ... five time flower six time change[8] kar u!!
Amy: ok thks in advance. take care la!
Amy: how's your girlfriend?
Billy: She stays at her out-home[9] these nights lar ... I feel pretty comfortable these days
Billy: Hey, what do u ususally do on Sundays ?
Amy: y r u so nosy???
Billy: I am nosy cos I have a nose ...
Amy: ha ha ... very funny ... CRAZY!!!
Billy: Yum cha[10] lor ...
Amy: ai ... got no breath[11] to talk to u la! ;-p
Billy: I am going to sleep lar ... zzzzzzz
Amy: ha ha ... go out to wet[12] lor!
Billy: no. I prefer to be dry tonight. ...
Amy: wow, unexpected wor![13]

Key:
1. Mo liu – Cantonese *mòuh lìuh*, 'nonsense'.[2]
2. Eye corner high – Cantonese *ngáahn gok gōu* [eye corners high], 'to be very demanding'.
3. North mui – Cantonese *bāk mūi* [northern sister], 'girl from the PRC'.
4. Dai luk mui – Cantonese *daaihluhk mūi*, 'girl from the PRC'.
5. Mouth flower – Cantonese *háu fāa fāa*, 'sweet talk'.
6. Kam yat tei chun d – Cantonese *gāmyaht tái jāndī*, ATV programme, 'Today's investigative reporting'.
7. Sing si chun ging – Cantonese *sìhngsíh jēui gīk*, TVB programme, 'City news latest'.
8. Five time flower six time change – Cantonese *ńgh sìh fāa luhk sìh bin* [You like flowers at 5 o'clock, but you've changed your mind by 6], 'you're always changing your mind'.

9. Out-home – Cantonese *ngoihgāa* [out home], 'a married woman's parental home'.
10. Yum cha – Cantonese *yámchàh* [drink tea], Hong Kong English, yum cha, 'go to the restaurant for snacks'.
11. No breath – Cantonese *móuh hei*, 'there's no point in going on'.
12. Go out to wet – Cantonese *heui wēt*, 'go out and have fun'.
13. Ah, ar, kar, la, lar, lor, wor – Cantonese particles *aa, aa, gaa, laa, laa, lo, wo*, used for varying degrees of intimacy and expressions of attitude.

Conclusion

The first professor of English in the University of Hong Kong was a Mr Robert K. M. Simpson, whose memory has been somewhat overshadowed by that of his successor, the war poet Edmund Blunden (1896–1974), who taught at Hong Kong from 1953 to 1964, and left to take up the Oxford Professorship of Poetry. Simpson served as Professor of English from the late 1920s until the early 1950s, and spent the war years in the Stanley internment camp as a prisoner of the Japanese. In an essay written on 'The difficulty of English' in 1933, Simpson mused on the problems of Chinese students learning the language, noting that: 'For the British peoples, English is a birthright eagerly inherited. But for other nations it is a difficult acquisition. I sometimes wonder why they are anxious to learn it. I once set the question as an examination essay, and from more than one candidate got the answer because "Americans use it"' (Simpson, 1933: 51). Some sixty-six years on, perhaps, the time may have finally arrived when Hong Kong can move on to create a space for its own use, and discourses, of English, with a place for the language as *one* of Hong Kong's languages in a diverse and pluralistic society. As Kachru himself notes, '[i]n culturally, linguistically, and ideologically pluralistic societies, there is a complex hybridity ... I believe linguistic and cultural hybridity is our identity', and that 'our major strategy is to acculturate the language in our contexts of use, on our terms, Asian terms' (Kachru, 1997: 22). In Hong Kong, it remains to be seen just what the terms for Hong Kong English will be. The Chief Executive of the HKSAR, Tung Chee-hwa, in his October 1999 Policy Address, highlighted the vision of Hong Kong as a 'world-class city', explaining that 'Hong Kong should not only be a major Chinese city, but could become the most cosmopolitan city in Asia, enjoying a status comparable to that of New York in North America and London in Europe'. Tung also restated the effectiveness of mother-tongue instruction, and also announced 'a territory-wide publicity campaign to promote the use of English' to halt 'a decline in the English standards of our younger generation since the early 1990s'. In the long term, he affirmed, 'we will continue to improve the quality of our English teachers and the method of instruction in schools to ensure that students master basic language skills at an early stage of their education' (Hong Kong

Government, 1999). In the meantime, Hong Kong's new 'chattering classes' play with two languages.

Notes

1. Cameron (1990) points out that the task of 'demythologizing' sociolinguistic commentaries involves 'making explicit the hidden assumptions which underlie linguists' models, showing that they are historical constructs ... and subjecting them to critical scrutiny' (pp. 79–80). 'Myths' and ideologies about language are of course not unique to linguists, but find expression in a wide range of discourses.
2. The Yale romanization system used here to transcribe Cantonese recognizes six tones: high (**mān**), mid-rising (**mán**), mid-level (**man**), low-level (**mahn**), low-rising (**máhn**) and low-falling (**màhn**).

References

Abbas, Ackbar (1997) *Hong Kong: Culture and the Politics of Disappearance*. Hong Kong: Hong Kong University Press. (Originally published by the University of Minnesota Press.)

Afendras, Evangelos A. (1998) The onset of bilingualism in Hong Kong: Language choice in the home domain. In *Language in Hong Kong at Century's End*. Edited by M. Pennington. Hong Kong: Hong Kong University Press, pp. 113–41.

Bacon-Shone, John and Bolton, Kingsley (1998) Charting multilingualism: Language censuses and language surveys in Hong Kong. In *Language in Hong Kong at Century's End*. Edited by M. Pennington. Hong Kong: Hong Kong University Press, pp. 43–90.

Baker, Hugh D. (1983) Life in the cities: The emergence of Hong Kong man. *China Quarterly*, **95**, 469–79.

Bauer, Robert and Benedict, Paul K. (1997) *Modern Cantonese Phonology*. Berlin: Mouton de Gruyter.

Benson, Phil (1994) The political vocabulary of Hong Kong English. *Hong Kong Papers in Linguistics and Language Teaching*, **17**, 63–81.

Bolton, Kingsley (2000) Language and hybridization: Pidgin tales from the China Coast. *Interventions*, **2**(1), 35–52.

Bolton, Kingsley and Kwok, Helen (1990) The dynamics of the Hong Kong accent: Social identity and sociolinguistic description. *Journal of Asian Pacific Communication*, **1**, 147–72.

Bolton, Kingsley, Hung, Joseph, and Nelson, Gerald (forthcoming) *The International Corpus of English project in Hong Kong*.

Branegan, Jay (1991) Finding a proper place for English. *Time*. 16 September, p. 27.

Bratt-Paulston, Christina (1980) *Bilingual Education: Theories and Issues*. Rowley, MA: Newbury House.

Butler, Susan (1997) Corpus of English in Southeast Asia: Implications for a regional dictionary. In *English is an Asian Language: The Philippine Context*. Edited by M. L. S. Bautista. Manila: The Macquarie Library, pp. 103–24.

Carless, David R. (1995) Politicised expressions in the *South China Morning Post*. *English Today*, 42, **11**(2), 18–22.
Chako, Sussy [Xu Xi] (1995) Wah Kiu wanderer. *Asia Magazine,* March 1995, p. 30.
Chan, Felix (1999) Students learn more using mother tongue, survey finds. *South China Morning Post*, 29 October, p. 2.
Chan, Mimi (1994) Hong Kong. In *Traveller's Literary Companion to South-east Asia*. Edited by A. Dingwall. Brighton: In Print Publishing, pp. 405–43.
Chan, Mimi and Kwok, Helen (1985) *A Study of Lexical Borrowing from Chinese into English with Special Reference to Hong Kong*. Hong Kong: Centre of Asian Studies, The University of Hong Kong.
Cheng, Tien-mu and Pasierbsky, Fritz (1988) China. In *Sociolinguistics: An International Handbook of the Science of Language and Society*. Edited by U. Ammon, N. Dittmar and K. J. Matteier. Vol. 2. Berlin: Walter de Gruyter, pp. 1274–82.
Cheung, Anne (1997) Language rights and the Hong Kong courts. *Hong Kong Journal of Applied Linguistics*, **2**(2), 49–75.
Cheung, Chi-fai (1999) School language choice urged senior pupils' should have option for English-medium learning. *South China Morning Post*, 2 November, p. 4.
Cheung, Martha P. (ed.) (1998) *Hong Kong Collage: Contemporary Stories and Writing*. Hong Kong: Oxford University Press.
Chin, Wan-kan (1997) From dialect to grapholect: Written Cantonese from a folkloristic point of view. *Hong Kong Journal of Applied Linguistics*, **2**, 77–91.
China Daily (1992) Li: Work to standardize language. *China Daily*. 26 September 1992.
Chinese Government (1992) *The Basic Law of the Hong Kong Special Administrative Region of the People's Republic of China*. Hong Kong: One Country, Two Systems Economic Research Institute.
Fu, Gail Schaefer (1987) The Hong Kong Bilingual. In *Language Education in Hong Kong*. Edited by R. Lord and Helen N. L. Cheng. Hong Kong: The Chinese University Press, pp. 27–50.
Gibbons, John (1982) The issue of the medium of instruction in the lower forms of Hong Kong secondary schools. *Journal of Multilingual and Multicultural Development*, **3**(2), 117–28.
Gupta, Anthea Fraser (1995) Discussion on linguistic human rights. Linguist list. http://www.sfs.nphil.uni-tuebingen.de/linguist/issues/6/6–1381.html. 5 October 1995. Accessed 27 February 2000.
Ho, Louise (1994) *Local Habitation*. Hong Kong: Twilight Books Company.
Ho, Louise (1997) *New Ends Old Beginnings*. Hong Kong: Asia 2000.
Hong Kong Government (1999) The 1999 Policy Address. October 1999. See also http://www.info.gov.hk/pa99/ english/speech.htm. Accessed 22 February 2000.
Iyer, Pico (1993) The empire writes back. *Time*, 8 February, pp. 48–53.
Johnson, Robert Keith (1994) Language policy and planning in Hong Kong. *Annual Review of Applied Linguistics* **14**, 177–99.
Kachru, Braj B. (1990) *The Alchemy of English: The Spread, Functions, and Models of Non-native Englishes*. Urbana and Chicago: University of Illinois Press.
Kachru, Braj B. (1991) Liberation linguistics and the Quirk concern. *English Today*, 25, **7**(1), 3–13.
Kachru, Braj B. (1992) World Englishes: Approaches, issues and resources. *Language Teaching*, **25**(1), 1–14.

Kachru, Braj B. (1997) English as an Asian language. In *English is an Asian Language: The Philippine Context*. Edited by M. L. S. Bautista. Manila: The Macquarie Library, pp. 1–23.
Kwok, Edmond S. T. (1982) From 'the Campaign for Chinese to be an Official Language' to 'the Second Chinese Language Campaign'. In *Hong Kong in the 1980s*. Edited by J. Y. S. Cheng. Hong Kong: Summerson Eastern Publishers Ltd., pp. 32–44.
Kwok, Shirley (1997) New rule will halve schools using English. *South China Morning Post*, 22 March, p. 7.
Lam, Agnes (1997). *Woman to Woman and Other Poems*. Hong Kong: Asia 2000.
Lau, Chi-kuen (1995) Language of the future. *South China Morning Post*, 18 September, 19.
Lee Wing-on (1998) Social class, language and achievement. In *Schooling in Hong Kong*. Edited by G. A. Postiglione and W. O. Lee. Hong Kong: Hong Kong University Press, pp. 155–74.
Le Page, Robert and Tabouret-Keller, Andrée (1985) *Acts of Identity: Creole-based Approaches to Language and Ethnicity*. Cambridge: Cambridge University Press.
Leung, Benjamin K. P. (1996) *Perspectives on Hong Kong Society*. Hong Kong: Oxford University Press.
Leung, Ping-kwan (1992) *City at the End of Time*. With Gordon T. Osing. Hong Kong: Twilight Books Company.
Leung, Ping-kwan (1997) *Foodscape*. With Lee Ka-sing and Martha Cheung. Hong Kong: The Original Photography Club Limited.
Luke, Kang-kwong and Richards, Jack C. (1982) English in Hong Kong: Status and functions. *English World-wide*, 3(1), 47–64.
Macquarie (2000) *Grolier International Dictionary: World English in an Asian Context*. Sydney: Macquarie Dictionary Company Ltd.
McArthur, Tom (ed.) (1992) *The Oxford Companion to the English Language*. Oxford: Oxford University Press.
Moy, Joyce (1998) Education chief wants 'radical' system review. *South China Morning Post*, 25 November, p. 1.
Parkin, Andrew and Wong, Laurence (1997) *Hong Kong Poems*. Vancouver: Ronsdale Press.
Patri, Mrudula and Pennington, Martha C. (1998) Acculturation to English by an ethnic minority: The language attitudes of Indian adolescents in a Hong Kong international school. In *Language in Hong Kong at Century's End*. Edited by M. Pennington. Hong Kong: Hong Kong University Press, pp. 339–62.
Postiglione, Gerald A. (1998) Schooling and social stratification. In *Schooling in Hong Kong*. Edited by G. A. Postiglione and W. O. Lee. Hong Kong: Hong Kong University Press, pp. 137–53.
Pun, Shuk-han (1997) Hegemonic struggles in the language policy development of Hong Kong, 1982–1994. In *Education and Political Transition: Perspectives and Dimensions in East Asia*. Edited by W. O. Lee and M. Bray. Hong Kong: Comparative Education Research Centre, The University of Hong Kong, pp. 81–98.
Simpson, Robert K. M. (1933) *The Student Reader*. Hong Kong.
Sin, King-sui and Roebuck, Derek (1996) Language engineering for legal transplantation: Conceptual problems in creating common law Chinese. *Language and communication*, 16(3), 235–54.

Smith, Carl (1985) *Chinese Christians: Elites, Middlemen, and the Church in Hong Kong.* Hong Kong: Oxford University Press.

So, Daniel (1992) Language-based bifurcation of secondary education in Hong Kong: Past, present and future. In *Into the Twenty First Century: Issues of Language and Education in Hong Kong.* Edited by K. K. Luke. Hong Kong: Linguistic Society of Hong Kong, pp. 69–95.

South China Morning Post (1999) Language lessons. Editorial. 22 November, p. 16.

Tay, Mary W. J. (1991) Southeast Asia and Hongkong. In *English Around the World: Sociolinguistic Perspectives.* Edited by Jenny Cheshire. Cambridge: Cambridge University Press, pp. 319–32.

Taylor, Andrew (1989) Hong Kong's English newspapers. *English Today,* **20**, 18–24.

Todd, Loreto and Hancock, Ian (1986) *International English Usage.* London: Croom Helm.

Yau, Man-siu (1989) The controversy over teaching medium in Hong Kong: An analysis of a language policy. *Journal of Multilingual and Multicultural Development,* **10**(4), 279–95.

Yau, Man-siu (1993) Functions of two codes in Hong Kong Chinese. *World Englishes,* **12**(1), 25–33.

Yu, V. W. S. and Atkinson, P. (1988) An investigation of the language difficulties experienced by Hong Kong secondary school students in English-medium schools: II some causal factors. *Journal of Multilingual and Multicultural Development,* **9**(4), 307–22.

2 The discourse and attitudes of English language teachers in Hong Kong

Amy B. M. Tsui and David Bunton

The language situation in Hong Kong

In Hong Kong, approximately 96% of the population is Chinese.[1] According to a sociolinguistic survey conducted in 1993, 81.6% of the population spoke Cantonese as their mother tongue and 91.9% could speak Cantonese. Only 1.3% were native speakers of English (see Bacon-Shone and Bolton, 1998: 73, 75). Since then, Cantonese has spread even wider. According to the 1996 By-Census, 88.7% of the population indicated that Cantonese is their usual spoken language, and 3.1% indicated English.

For social communication between Cantonese speakers and speakers of other Chinese dialects, for example, immigrants from the People's Republic of China (PRC) mainland, Cantonese is the lingua franca. However, for formal communication with government officials in the PRC, especially since 1997, as well as for formal events at national level in Hong Kong, Putonghua is often the lingua franca. For business communication, the lingua franca is whichever language is shared by both parties, Cantonese or Putonghua. This is unlike the situation in Malaysia, Singapore or India, where English is the main lingua franca between different ethnic and linguistic groups.

On the other hand, the government's policy is that Hong Kong people should become trilingual in spoken Cantonese, Putonghua and English and biliterate in written Chinese and English. The bilingual population has increased considerably, mainly through the introduction of mass education in the 1970s. According to Bacon-Shone and Bolton (1998: 76), the percentage of the population who reported that they knew English quite well, well and very well rose from 6.6% in 1983 to 33.7% in 1993, and to 38.1% in 1996 (see Bolton, Chapter 1). There is more and more demand for knowledge of other languages, especially English, in the employment sector. English is actually used for much written communication among Cantonese speakers, for example, business letters, internal memos and email, even though they would use Cantonese for oral communication (see So's 1998 survey, pp. 163–4). The importation of Filipinas into the labour market as domestic helpers has also created a need to use English as the lingua franca at home.

In Malaysia and Singapore, the need to use English as the lingua franca for multi-ethnic communication led to the emergence of distinctive varieties of English which are different from Standard English in aspects of pronunciation, lexicon and grammar. The local variety is often the preferred choice in informal conversation, even for speakers who are highly proficient in Standard English, as a sign of solidarity and camaraderie (see Crismore et al., 1996).

In Hong Kong, however, although there are identifiable local features of English pronunciation and lexis, such a variety of English does not seem to be accepted by the community. Luke and Richards (1982: 55–6) observed that 'there is no such thing ... as "Hong Kong English". ... There is no equivalent of the mesolectal or basilectal speech styles found, for example, in Singapore ... since there is no equivalent range of English speech varieties in regular use by Hong Kong Chinese.' They pointed out that there was 'no societal need nor opportunity for the development of a stable Cantonese variety of spoken English' despite the fact that Hong Kong Chinese speakers of English did display certain distinctive features. We would suggest that with the dramatic increase in the bilingual population since the early 1980s and the more widespread use of English at work and even at home, Hong Kong English has developed to some extent since Luke and Richards were writing in the early 1980s. However, there has been little change in societal attitudes to Hong Kong English.

Hong Kong falls within what Kachru refers to as Outer Circle countries, many of which were British colonies, in which British English or native-speaker standard was used (Kachru, 1985). During the days of colonial rule, it was the exonormative model that was referred to when making judgements about standards in both education and business communication, the exonormative model being either British English or American English. Deviations from these models were described as indicative of the falling standards of English, which was, and still is, one of the major concerns of the business community and the government. In the late 1980s and early 1990s, some of the biggest and most well-known business enterprises, including the then Hong Kong Telecom[2] and Hongkong Bank, joined hands to launch the Language Campaign in an effort to arrest the falling standards. Native-speaker English teachers were brought in from 1987 to provide models of English to secondary school students.

After the change of sovereignty in 1997, the Hong Kong Special Administrative Region (SAR) government revived the scheme to bring in native-speaker English teachers, referred to as the NET scheme, following the implementation of mother-tongue education in nearly three-quarters of the secondary schools. The scheme is now being extended to primary schools.

Language benchmarks are also being set for English language teachers in schools and the government has stipulated that starting from September 2000, all graduating student-teachers are required to sit English language benchmark tests and practising English teachers are given a period of five years to meet the English language benchmarks. Recently, the government launched an 'English in the Workplace' campaign and employees in the business sector were given incentives to take overseas examinations for employees, such as those run by UCLES (University of Cambridge Local Examination Syndicate) and Pitman. The examination results will be used by employers for reference in recruitment.

We can see from the above account that in the business and government sectors, the model of English has always been exonormative. Any deviations from the model have been considered errors. The term 'Chinglish' is a derogatory term which refers to English sentences containing features of Chinese syntax or lexical items which are directly translated from Chinese. Some of these features can also be found in Singapore English, Malaysian English and even Brunei English, such as the use of 'would' to indicate futurity. However, while they are taken as features of the local variety of English in the respective countries, they are frowned upon by the Hong Kong community as 'errors'.

Giles (1998) pointed out that the attitudes that people hold towards particular language varieties and the social meaning attached to them influence how motivated they are in learning them. Lowenberg (1990: 124) maintained that the acceptance or rejection of norms of standard English 'frequently depends on attitudinal variables, particularly on the relative sociolinguistic status of the sources of an innovation'. Crismore et al. (1996) argue that perceptions and language attitudes play an important part in the growth and decline of language variations in a society. Bamgboṣe (1998) in arguing for the legitimacy of each variety having its own norms, outlined a number of factors which contribute to establishing the status of a linguistic innovation. Among these factors, according to him, 'acceptability is the ultimate test of admission of an innovation' (p. 4) without which all innovations will be labelled errors. Acceptability has to do with the attitude of the users and non-users towards these innovations.

In Hong Kong, there are a number of studies conducted on language attitudes (see for example, Pierson et al., 1980; Pennington and Yue, 1994; Axler et al., 1998). However, very few have been conducted on the language attitudes of teachers (see for exception Hirvela and Law, 1991). As Crismore et al. (1996) point out, teachers' language attitudes are important because they influence the attitudes of their students. Moreover, most of these studies, like most attitudinal studies conducted elsewhere in the world, used questionnaire surveys. Very few have actually analysed language attitudes as revealed in the discourse that people engage in.

This chapter attempts to fill the gap in the language attitudes research literature by investigating the attitudes of English language teachers in Hong Kong as exhibited either implicitly or explicitly in the way they talk about English in electronic messages over a period of two years. The discourses of English teachers who are native speakers and non-native speakers of English were analysed. The results of the analysis show that an exonormative model of English is clearly what both non-native speaker and native speaker English teachers defer to.

Methodology

Data for this study consisted of more than a thousand language-related messages posted over a two-year period on an Internet-based computer network for English language teachers across Hong Kong. The network, known as *TeleNex*, was created by the Teachers of English Language Education Centre (TELEC) in the Department of Curriculum and Educational Studies at the University of Hong Kong. The messaging component of this network consists of a number of conference corners on various topics. Two of the main corners are the *Teaching Ideas Corner* and the *Language Corner*. The former gives teachers a chance to ask questions and share ideas on the teaching of English, while the latter gives them the opportunity to ask and answer questions on grammar, vocabulary and other aspects of English which are important to their teaching. Participating in the discussions in these corners are native and non-native speaker teachers of English, as well as TELEC staff who specialize in English language teaching and English linguistics.

In the two-year period from October 1997 to October 1999, a total of 1,234 messages were sent to the *TeleNex Language Corner*. Of these messages, 850 were from Hong Kong teachers and 384 from TELEC staff. Six of the eight TELEC staff sending messages were native speakers of English (NS). Of the 102 teachers sending messages, a large majority, 85, were non-native speakers of English (NNS), while 17 were native speakers.[3]

Data analysis

All 1,234 messages were searched for the term 'Hong Kong English'. It did not occur at all. This would seem to indicate that the concept of Hong Kong English as a legitimate variety is not a strong one amongst teachers of English in Hong Kong, NNS or NS, nor amongst TELEC staff. The term 'Chinglish', however, was found in two messages but it was used to refer to the students' errors.

Queries and responses

Messages were initially categorized as being 'Queries' (asking a question) or 'Responses' (answering a question) or 'Non-relevant' (acknowledgements, thanks, apologies, news, etc.). Some responses also contained queries, but as long as the message contained some response to another query, it was categorized as a response.

The NNS teachers sent 698 messages, including 307 queries and 313 responses, while the NS teachers sent 152 messages, including 43 queries and 97 responses (see Table 2.1). It was found that NS teachers sent more than twice as many responses as queries (97 vs. 43) while NNS teachers sent a similar number of responses as queries (313 vs. 307). As would be expected, TELEC staff mainly sent responses (303 vs. 13).

Table 2.1 Queries and responses sent by participants in *TeleNex*

	NNS teachers	NS teachers	TELEC staff	Total
Queries	307	43	13	363
Responses	313	97	303	713
Non-relevant*	78	12	68	158
No. of messages	698	152	384	1,234

*acknowledgements, thanks, apologies, news, etc.

Sources of authority

We started off with no preconceived ideas of how the messages should be analysed. As we went through the messages, we noticed that when expressing their views, and even when they were posing questions, teachers tended to cite certain sources to support their views or to provide the basis for their questions. This suggests that teachers defer to these sources as the authority on what should be considered acceptable and not acceptable. Such attitudes were more prevalent in NNS teachers' discourses than those of the NS teachers. We therefore compiled a list of sources that were cited in all messages. Once the list was compiled, we went over the data again and investigated how frequently each source was referred to and by whom. Since some messages were found to give more than one source of authority (e.g. citing native-speaker usage and then a grammar book), we decided that it would be more valid to use the number of times that the sources were cited as supporting evidence, rather than the number of messages.

TELEC staff's discourse

Messages from TELEC staff were not included in the analyses of attitude as they could be seen as reflecting views of the TELEC project rather than those of teachers in schools. Nonetheless, the sources of authority they cited are of interest because of the influence their messages have on teachers using the network.

Staff of TELEC, in responding to questions, made many references to grammar books and dictionaries (13.5%), as well as to the *TeleNex* grammar database (15.8%). Most of all, however, they referred to the 50 million word corpus *Bank of English* to which they have access, and a smaller in-house corpus of 5 million words (33.6% of responses). These NS corpora were used to give authority to their suggestions of 'naturalness' or grammatical or lexical acceptability, as well as to give new insights:

> Message 1/138
> I agree with Matthew[4] that *spoonfuls* sounds more natural — *spoonsful* is traditionally the 'correct' form, but it strikes me as horribly pedantic. I had a look in the *Bank of English* and didn't find even one instance of *spoonsful* in 50 million words, so that is a good indication.

> Message 2/063
> One thing that neither Swan nor any of the dictionaries I checked revealed was the strikingly high number of 'measurement' words collocating with 'large'. Here's a quick sample from our 5 million word corpus:
>
>> this on a large **scale**, the material requirements are so st
>> to a very large **extent**, a subjective thing, people who can
>> o quite a large **degree**, the time when they prepare their n
>> ing for a large **increase** in the public sector (all talking

Non-native speaker English teachers' discourse

Among the 698 messages sent by NNS English teachers, we identified 255 messages in which language attitudes were either explicitly or implicitly expressed when teachers discussed acceptability, corrections and differences between various linguistic forms. We then conducted a detailed analysis of these 255 messages and found that nearly half of them (121 messages) time and again referred to certain sources of authority in the teachers' discussions. The other half (134 messages) were based on the teachers' own judgement.

Let us take one message as an example. In responding to a question from another teacher about whether there is such word as 'shopaholic', an NNS student teacher said, 'I have heard this word used by native speakers, so it must be okay' (Message 3/12).[5] In this message, the deference to NS as a source

The discourse and attitudes of English language teachers in Hong Kong 63

of authority is explicit. Let us take another example. One of the NNS English teachers asked a question on whether one should say 'cheaper' or 'more cheap', and in a subsequent message, she explained why she posted this question.

> Message 4/55
> ... *I was taught* to use 'cheaper' instead of 'more cheap' when I was a student. I think it is absolutely correct. What confuses me is that English is always changing and I have heard of *natives speaking* 'more cheap' instead of 'cheaper'. That's why I would like to find out if the former is widely accepted now and to know what we teachers should do if it is really the case.

In the above message, we can see that there is implicit deference to the NNS English teacher's former teacher as well as to NS usage as sources of authority. It is the conflicting statements that this teacher received from these two sources that led to her turning to *TeleNex* as a third source of authority.

In these messages, there were altogether 300 references made to various sources of authority. Table 2.2 shows the categories of references made by NNS and NS English teachers. We can see from Table 2.2 that the highest frequency of reference by NNS teachers is dictionaries (51 references) followed by books about usage and grammar books (39). Reference to native speakers, the teachers' own colleagues and the media were about the same but they trailed far behind dictionaries and grammar/usage books as sources of authority. Moreover, their attitudes towards these sources were not as unanimous as the first two. In the rest of this section, we shall analyse each of these sources, focusing on the ones with higher frequencies of reference.

Table 2.2 Authorities cited by NNS and NS teachers
(N = 255 and 93 messages respectively)

Authority cited	NNS No. of references	%	NS No. of references	%
Self (own knowledge or judgement)	134	44.7%	44	38.9%
Dictionaries	51	17.0%	7	6.2%
Grammar or usage books	39	13.0%	15	13.3%
Media	14	4.7%	1	0.9%
Native speakers	13	4.3%	21	18.6%
Colleagues	13	4.3%	0	0.0%
Own teacher	9	3.0%	7	6.2%
Textbooks	7	2.3%	3	2.7%
Hong Kong Examinations Authority	7	2.3%	2	1.8%
Corpus	1	0.3%	10	8.8%
Others	12	4.0%	3	2.7%
Total	300	100.0%	113	100.0%

Dictionaries

There were 51 references made to dictionaries. In all cases, the dictionary was looked upon as a source of authority. There were 36 instances where the dictionary was cited as the voice of authority or as supporting the statements NNS teachers made about the language form or use in question. For example, the following message is from an NNS teacher in a series of discussions about the grammatical correctness of 'she need know':

> Message 5/416
> I was also shocked when I saw the sentence 'she need know' *but since the example is given in a prestigious dictionary*, I can't just ignore it.

Another example is from an NNS teacher, in response to a question asking whether 'dawn' could be used as a verb, who wrote as follows, 'Maybe it's not common to use "dawn" as a verb; *but the dictionary says ...*'. He then quoted the dictionary entry which showed that 'dawn' could be used as a verb, as in 'The morning dawned fresh and clear after the storm' (Longman Interactive English Dictionary) (Message 6/1029).

Some teachers cited the dictionary in support of their responses to other teachers' questions. For example, in response to a question about the use of 'as well as', an NNS English teacher wrote:

> Message 7/219
> I've checked the *Collins Cobuild Dictionary*, and it says,
> '... if you refer to a second thing AS WELL AS a first thing, you refer to the second thing in addition to the first.'
> ...
> Therefore, though AS WELL AS is a preposition, it does not mean that it has to be followed by a gerund, but by noun or adjective as well.

In message 7, the teacher prefaced her own response with a citation from the dictionary. This kind of sequencing is commonly found in messages where the dictionary was cited as supporting evidence: it is almost as if the teacher felt that citation from the dictionary would give more weight to his/her response. There were also cases where the teacher explicitly stated that they actually checked their own understanding with the dictionary before responding. For example, in response to a teacher's question about whether 'in the sale' or 'on sale' should be used, an NNS teacher wrote, 'I've also got the impression that "on sale" should be used. Then, I checked from the dictionary and found that it's correct' (Message 8/767).

Of the other 15 messages, 7 were about information not found in the dictionary, 5 sought further clarification on definitions that teachers found in the dictionary and 3 found conflicting evidence in dictionaries or textbooks.

What is interesting is that in all of these messages, there was not a single instance in which the NNS teacher expressed any doubts about the authority of the dictionary.

The dictionary was treated as more authoritative than the native speaker of English. Take the following message for example.

> Message 9/46
> When I was in primary school, I was taught to use 'sporty' to describe people. Recently I've heard a native speaker use 'sportive' to describe a kid. *I checked the dictionary*, but 'sportive' isn't in it. I wonder if anyone can help?

In the above message, there were conflicting messages between what the NNS teacher's former teacher said and what the NS said. The NNS teacher therefore consulted the dictionary for a verdict. Although she failed to get the answer from the dictionary, the message shows that the NNS teacher did turn to the dictionary for a verdict in the first instance and failing that she turned to *TeleNex* as an alternative source of authority.

Grammar and usage books

There were 39 references to grammar and usage books. Among them, 33 references cited usage and grammar books as sources of authority or as supporting evidence. The books referred to were mostly British and the books with the highest number of references were *Collins Cobuild Grammar* and Swan's *Practical English Usage*. Very often, in response to a teacher's question, an NNS teacher would either refer the teacher to a specific grammar or usage book, or simply quote what it said without any personal comments.

When the statements made by these sources contradicted what the teacher believed in, they were taken as voices of authority. For example, in response to a teacher's question about the difference between 'one another' and 'each other', an NNS teacher wrote:

> Message 10/78
> Traditional wisdom says 'each other' is used for two people or things while 'one another' for three. However, grammarian Michael Swan pointed out in his book 'Practical English Usage' that this is not the case. He said that there is little or no difference in meaning between the two expressions. ...

The NNS teacher who wrote this message signed off after citing Michael Swan. The implication is that he took what Michael Swan said as the voice of authority.

There were 5 references in which the teacher sought clarification about statements made in grammar and usage books. Similar to their attitudes towards dictionaries, they simply accepted the statements made as correct. For example,

> Message 11/271
> What is the major difference between 'if I were a lion' and 'if I was a lion?' Some grammar books say that the former one is more formal. Which one is more commonly used?

The question posed by the teacher implied that she accepted what 'some grammar books' said about the former being more formal.

Native speakers of English

There were 13 references to native speakers of English. The majority of them either explicitly or implicitly accepted the NS as a source of authority (11 references). However, we can see a cline in terms of teachers' deference to NS as a source of authority. At one extreme, there is absolute deference to the NS as the norm. For example, Message 1 cited above. There is also a reference to NS English as 'natural', as in Message 12 below.

> Message 12/979
> Could you give me some comments on the following answers? Which answers are both grammatically correct and belong to *natural language*, i.e. *commonly used by native speakers* in contexts?

There are cases in which the NNS teachers' own teachers were treated as an equal source of authority as the NS, like Message 4 cited above. This is followed by teachers who felt that what NSs said should not be taken as necessarily grammatical, but who would take it as acceptable, as in the following message which responds to Message 4 above.

> Message 13/56
> I absolutely agree that 'cheaper' is grammatical. But I just wonder if 'more cheap' is acceptable or not? And if yes, to what extent? I want to quote another e.g. 'More easy'. I have heard *many native speakers* saying it. *It does not mean that it is grammatical automatically.* But I just want to draw attention to the dynamics of English. I think it is not a matter of grammaticality but *a matter of acceptability.*

However, there are two messages where teachers cast doubt on what NSs said. For example,

> Message 14/166
> I wanna know which of the following is 'more' correct:
> a) but enough

> b) but sufficient
> The NET[6] of my school insisted that they natives speakers (do) not say 'but enough', yet she did not explain why.
> Is she correct? I doubt.

> Message 15/488
> Please advise if the following sentences mean the same. One of my colleagues, (*herself a native speaker!*) said so.
> 1. He put his customer in a special barbers chair.
> 2. He put his customer in a special barber's chair.
> Sentence 1 appears on the oral exam paper which was set by her.
> Initially, I and some teachers thought there should be an apostrophe, like sentence 2. Then she found an article in *SCMP*[7] ... which said apostrophe should be omitted even if it is talking about possession. She insisted that it was acceptable to add 's' to show either plurals and possession. We are quite confused. Please help.

In both Messages 14 and 15 above, the NNS teachers had doubts about what the NS teachers in their schools said. It is interesting to note that in both cases despite the fact that both NS teachers 'insisted' that they were correct, the NNS teachers did not take them as a source of authority. Yet, they did not take themselves as a source of authority either. Therefore, they turned to another source of authority, *TeleNex*.

Media

There were 14 references to the media, which includes local newspapers and television programmes and movies. Although there were 8 references which either explicitly cited or implicitly acknowledged the media as a source of authority, there were 4 references which actually questioned their authority. For example,

> Message 16/540
> This Sunday, I watched a RTHK[8] TV program of which topic is about the difference between American English and British English. I found an interesting point and want to confirm whether it is true or not. ...

In the above message, the NNS teacher did not take what the television programme said as correct and wished to seek the views of staff and users of *TeleNex*.

Textbooks

There were 7 references to textbooks in the messages. It is interesting that except for one, all references were questions regarding conflicting evidence that they found in different textbooks, or conflicting statements made in textbooks and by the NNS teachers' former teachers. One actually queried the authority of the textbook:

> Message 17/810
> ... The reason for me to raise this question is that in (name of textbook in Hong Kong), *there's an expression saying 'Robot Teacher is a comedy film.' which is rather odd to me.* I discussed it with my colleagues but we have no answer.

In this message, the NNS teacher explicitly expressed her doubts about the acceptability of the expression. This kind of statement was not found in the NNS teachers' discourse when they referred to usage and grammar books or dictionaries. It is also noteworthy that none of the messages cited textbooks in Hong Kong as a source of authority when responding to teachers' questions.

Hong Kong Examinations Authority

There were only 7 references to the Hong Kong Examinations Authority. However, from the NNS teachers' discourse, we can see that it has a powerful influence on their attitudes towards the correctness and acceptability of linguistic forms and usage. For example, in response to a question about salutations and signing off in letter writing.

> Message 18/224
> I prefer to stick to "Yours faithfully" after "Dear Principal", "Dear Editor" and "Dear Customers". The *Exams Authority* remains quite strict with this rule and so does the business world.

Teachers are keen to stick the rules laid down by the Hong Kong Examinations Authority because they do not want their students to be penalized in public examinations rather than because they defer to its expertise. The following message made this point explicit in response to a teacher's question about whether British or American English should be used.

> Message 19/737
> ... Personally I would go for American English, since it sounds better to me and it's more popular, I think.
> But unless the Exam Authority formally states that American English is also acceptable, I think we should stick to British for the benefit of our students.

NNS teachers' colleagues and former teachers

There are altogether 9 references to the NNS teachers' own former teachers and 13 references to their own colleagues. In the former, 4 out of 9 references explicitly cited what their former teachers said as a source of authority and the rest asked for clarification in the face of conflicting evidence from other sources without challenging their authority. For example,

> Message 20/527
> When I studied grammar in school, my teacher told me that the question tag with "I am" should be "am I not?" Some textbooks said that it should be "aren't I?" Which one is better?

By contrast, in the references made to their own colleagues, only one out of 13 cited what their colleagues said as a source of authority. The rest of the 12 references asked staff and users of *TeleNex* to comment on their views, implying a reluctance to accept their authority. For example,

> Message 21/878
> I was told by some of *my colleagues* that the following sentence is grammatically acceptable — "The boy is playing a ball."
> *I always think* that a preposition "with" should be used after "playing" when it is not followed by any sports/musical instruments.
> If the sentence is acceptable, does it mean that another sentence like "The boy is playing a lantern" should also be accepted?

In the above message, the teacher is not so much challenging the authority of her colleagues, but rather she did not see their views as overriding her own views.

Own knowledge or judgement

Messages where the NNS teachers simply expressed their own opinions without citing other sources of authority made up the bulk of the messages. There were altogether 134 messages of this kind. However, this does not mean that in these messages, the teachers took themselves as the source of authority. A close examination of the discourse showed the following features.

Firstly, many NNS teachers prefaced their responses by disclaiming expertise, e.g., 'Although I don't confess to be an expert on usage …', 'I am not an expert in …, but …', 'I'm not sure if I am right', and the like; by hedging, such as 'As far as I know', 'To the best of my knowledge', 'I am not sure if all of the above are acceptable'; by agreeing with other teachers, e.g., 'I agree with so and so'; or by using tentative statements such as 'I usually/tend to use …'.

Secondly, they tended to end their responses by explicitly disclaiming authority, e.g., 'If I'm wrong, please let me know', 'Please comment if I am wrong', 'Please clarify (me) if I have made a mistake(s)!', 'Am I right?', 'Hope my interpretation is correct and useful to you', and so on. Alternatively, they would invite other teachers to express their views, hence implying that they did not consider their own responses as definitive. Typical expressions are 'What do other teachers think?', 'Does anybody have any other ideas?', 'Do you agree?', 'There would be better suggestions from corner readers' (meaning users who are logging into the Language Corner), and so on.

Native-speaker English teachers' discourse

NS teachers sent twice as many responses as queries and this probably springs from their confidence, as native speakers, that their views are of value. For example,

> Message 22/146
> As a native speaker, I would here say/write ... I'm not quite sure why, but I think that in this context ...

We can see from the above message that the NS teacher responded to the query by highlighting the fact that he is a native speaker as a source of authority. However, as this message indicates, some of the NS teachers recognize that while knowing what is normal NS usage, they do not always know the grammatical explanation, hence the 43 queries they did send.

Of the 152 messages from NS teachers, 93 were found to express language attitudes either explicitly or implicitly. In these 93 messages, there were 113 references to certain sources of authority or to their own knowledge and judgement to support those views. Results of the further analysis of these 93 messages and the references made are given in Table 2.2.

Native-speaker usage

The most frequent source of authority that NS teachers gave (apart from their own knowledge or judgement) was native-speaker usage (18.6% vs. 4.3% by NNS teachers). NS teachers of English in Hong Kong clearly regard native-speaker use of a linguistic form as indicating acceptability. They quite often overtly identified themselves on the network as native speakers as if to stress that this is the source of their authority. For example,

> Message 23/015
> *This native speaker* has also heard, and used, *shopaholic* — also *chocoholic*. There is a *book with a title* something like *Chocoholic's Handbook* on sale *in the UK*. Well, if it's in a BOOK TITLE it must be OK!!!!!?

Although slightly tongue-in-cheek, the final sentence here indicates a view that publication in a NS country confers additional acceptability. NS teachers also showed a belief that non-use of a form by NSs indicates non-acceptability. The following is an example,

> Message 24/429
> No normal native speaker would EVER use a construction like this ...

Sometimes the appeal to NS usage was less explicit, with terms like 'we'd say' when the message clearly gives a Western name for the author (rather than the anonymity that some teachers choose), implying that the 'we' refers to native speakers of English. This example is referring to tenses when talking about a photograph:

> Message 25/134
> If looking at a photo, for example, we'd say "Which girl is you?" ... If asking about someone's childhood character, we'd say "What kind of a girl were you?"

Native-speaker corpus

References to the corpus of NS English further indicate the importance that NS teachers attach to NS usage as showing acceptability. While they did not have access to the corpus themselves, ten of the NS teacher messages (8.8%) asked if TELEC staff could search the corpus for them on a particular issue:

> Message 26/274
> I was wondering what the corpus says on beginning a sentence with AND. I was taught in Primary school preferably never to begin any sentence with AND. Does anyone have any opinions?

This is clearly a resource teachers have come to appreciate through the extensive use of the corpus by TELEC staff as a basis for their judgements about acceptability as well as for illustration. (Over a third of all TELEC staff responses referred to the corpus).

Grammar and usage books

The next most frequently cited authority after NS usage was grammar and usage books (13.3% by NS teachers, similar to NNS teachers at 13.0%). As with NNS teachers, NS teachers referred most frequently to books by British authors, e.g. *Collins Cobuild Grammar* and Swan's *Practical English Usage*. The references were usually positive, indicating acceptance of their authority:

> Message 27/825
> The correct form is . ... The examples are from Eastwood's *Oxford Guide to English Grammar*.

It is only when conflicting statements were made by authoritative NS publications that they turned to *TeleNex* for jurisdiction:

> Message 28/681
> Quirk and Greenbaum say that DO is an auxiliary verb ... I guess there's no disputing the experts ... is there? ... (in) the first example DO does not act as an auxiliary verb according to the *Collins Cobuild Grammar*, but then what about Quirk et al? Please help ...

Dictionaries

NS teachers referred to dictionaries less often than NNS teachers (6.2% vs. 17.0%). When they did, they were usually British dictionaries, such as the *Collins Cobuild Dictionary*, and the references were positive, accepting their explanations as authoritative.

Textbooks

When the publication is a local Hong Kong one, however, the picture changes. Two of the three references to textbooks (2.7%) were negative (the third was neutral). The following message referred to a query about a 'grammar' textbook produced in Hong Kong and designated for Form 1. The NS teacher clearly regards the book as a poor authority:

> Message 29/1115
> This is not helped by grammar books like the one you mention that give "There is much food in the refrigerator" as an example of correct English. This sentence is clearly unacceptable and therefore I would probably not use that particular grammar book with my students.

Own teachers

A smaller number of NS teachers referred to the way they were taught in school (6.2%). This was often in terms of trying to reconcile more recent terminology and definitions with those they grew up with:

> Message 30/447
> I am puzzled. I think the descriptive terminology of grammar has changed since I was at school. (Then,) a clause by definition contained ONE finite verb. I don't know how to define the grammar of "... with the main two being X and Y".

The discourse and attitudes of English language teachers in Hong Kong

Media

We have already seen the positive reference to a UK-published book title in Message 23 above, as showing acceptability. However, one message referred negatively to film subtitles that were produced in Hong Kong:

> Message 31/1268
> There is a need, I think, to be a little careful with film subtitles. "Nightcap" refers to an alcoholic drink just before you go to bed; it cannot be applied to food (see *Cobuild*). Also, we would not really use the term "night snack". ...

By contrast, this message gave a British dictionary a better authority. The use of 'we' also implies NS usage.

Hong Kong Examinations Authority

Two responses (1.8%) referred to the public exams authority in Hong Kong. One was positive:

> Message 32/658
> I think there are too many adverbials in this text. I worry that giving this text to my students may encourage them to overuse these sorts of words. This, of course, is being discouraged in the various examination subject reports.

The other, while reluctant to accept the exam authority's view, showed a pragmatic recognition that the examining authority is a powerful determiner of students' futures:

> Message 33/223
> Generally it seems to me that usage of *Yours faithfully/sincerely* is becoming far more flexible than the rules that I learned at school allowed. However, I believe the HK examining board penalises usages such as ... Therefore, since exams are a matter of life and death in HK, it may be better to be strict with your students and stick to the ancient rules.

Own knowledge or judgement

NS teachers cited their own knowledge or judgement more often (38.9%) than any more formal authorities. There is a cline in the assertiveness of their responses as a source of authority. There were messages where they were very sure of their own judgement. For example, the following message was in response to a query about a NS writing angrily on an Internet bread forum about a new batch of wheat: 'It will NOT hardly rise for ANYTHING':

> Message 34/538
> It's just WRONG! I know grammar is descriptive and not prescription and all that but the expression "It will NOT hardly rise for ANYTHING" is just NOT ENGLISH! Somewhere the line has to be drawn. I really can't hardly tolerate this. You are right to question it: remember that not all native speakers of a language actually know how to use it, especially when they're furious with their wheat!

In the above message, the teacher, being a NS, pointed out that not all NSs know how to use the language. It is interesting, and perhaps significant, that no such statements were made by NNS teachers in the data.

NS teachers also resorted more to their own intuition about appropriateness of usage, for example:

> Message 35/1046
> My *gut feeling* is that this is wrong, but I can't find a rule about when to use "etc". Does anybody know the rule?

Messages in which NS teachers invoked certain grammatical rules to make a judgement about correctness were rare:

> Message 36/604
> Both sentences are *correct*. "The other children" must refer to a particular group, e.g. ... "Other children" is more general, e.g. ... . The *rule* which applies is about definite and indefinite articles.

However, there were also messages where they were tentative about their own judgement and they invited other teachers to comment in the same way that the NNS teachers did. Message 35 above is an example. Nonetheless, compared to NNS teachers, there were far fewer instances in which they were not sure of themselves as a source of authority.

Discussion

From the above analysis of the discourse of NNS and NS teachers, we can see that there are similarities and differences in their language attitudes. Both groups of teachers deferred to the authority of the printed media, mainly dictionaries, grammar books and usage books. In a way, this is hardly surprising because codification is an important means of establishing the status of a linguistic form or usage. What is interesting is the different attitudes of both groups of teachers towards local textbooks on the one hand, and, on the other hand, grammar and usage books and dictionaries published in Kachru's Inner Circle countries, mainly Britain. They were more critical and wary about the former, which were also written by native speakers of English. This may have to do with the poor quality of some of the textbooks published in Hong Kong, which has been a matter of concern for a long time. However, it may also have to do with the fact that teachers have more confidence in publications overseas, hence suggesting that even when they refer to exonormative models, they make a distinction between local and international sources of authority. Compared to codified sources, NNS teachers' attitudes towards oral statements made by native speakers, especially their own native-speaker colleagues, were less homogeneous. Instead, they perceived *TeleNex* as a source of authority because, as mentioned above, the staff members were all English language specialists or teacher educators, most of whom were native speakers of English. This is also congruent with the finding that they regarded their own former teachers as more authoritative than their own colleagues. This may well have something to do with the fact that deference to one's own teacher is very much ingrained in the Chinese culture. Finally, the most striking difference is perhaps the perceptions of these groups of teachers of themselves as a source of authority. The queries and responses from NS teachers show a very strong tendency to base their views on their own knowledge or experience as NS users of the language. Their interest in the corpus of NS English further illustrates their faith that NS usage confers acceptability. By contrast, NNS teachers lack confidence in their own authority over the language as English teachers. This was manifested firstly in their having to cite codified sources and other sources as supporting evidence before putting forward their own views, and secondly, in their having to preface their own personal opinions with hedges and qualifications, and to solicit views from fellow teachers as a signal that they did not consider their own words as final.

Concluding remarks

The data that we analysed in this study are in no way representative of the entire NNS teacher population in Hong Kong. However, because this network is open to all English teachers in Hong Kong and registration is voluntary, it can be reasonably assumed that those who logged onto the network are those who are interested in discussing language issues. The analysis shows that even for these teachers, the model that they adopted and accepted was exonormative. There was not a single reference which discussed deviations from the model with a more favourable attitude. Even when such deviations were codified in local textbooks, and other media such as newspapers, they were questioned by teachers. The exonormative attitudes of Hong Kong's English teachers, in common with those of the government and the business community, still show a preference for Standard English in formal communication. Given rapid globalization and the immense impact of the Internet on the language of communication amongst nations, it would be interesting to see whether there will be a change in societal attitudes towards the local variety of English in Hong Kong and towards varieties of English in general.

Notes

1. Hong Kong Immigration Department figures at the end of December 1999 showed that about 2% of the population is Filipino (136,100) and that there are another 359,100 'foreign residents' in Hong Kong. The figures do not show ethnicity, and many of these foreign residents would be ethnically Chinese. However, the top nine nationalities after the Philippines are Indonesian, USA, Canadian, Thai, Indian, UK, Australian, Japanese, and Nepali. If even a third of these foreign residents were non-Chinese, that would account for another 2% of the population — the same proportion that was often reported as being non-Chinese before the relatively recent increase in numbers from the Philippines. It is on this basis that we estimate the population of Hong Kong to be about 96% Chinese.
2. Hong Kong Telecom was renamed Cable and Wireless HKT in 1999. In Autumn 2000, the company was acquired by Pacific Century Cyberworks (PCCW).
3. We would like to thank the teachers on *TeleNex* for allowing us to cite the messages that they sent in as examples in this chapter. We would also like to thank Sonia Cheung, our research assistant for her help in organizing and analysing the data, and Mabel Sieh, the Project Manager of TELEC for administrative help.
4. All names in the message cited are pseudonyms.
5. Messages cited from the network are verbatim. No attempt has been made to edit them. Teachers gave us permission to cite their messages anonymously and every effort has been made to conceal their identities.
6. NET stands for Native-speaker English Teacher. In order to improve English language teaching in schools, the Hong Kong government introduced in 1998 a new scheme of bringing in native-speaker English teachers into secondary schools. Each school can apply for up to two NETs. So far, the government has brought in over 300 NETs.
7. *SCMP* stands for *South China Morning Post*, one of two English newspapers in Hong Kong.
8. RTHK stands for 'Radio Television Hong Kong', a local broadcasting station which produces radio and television programmes.

References

Axler, Maria, Yang, Anson, and Stevens, Trudy (1998) Current language attitudes of Hong Kong Chinese adolescents and young adults. In *Language in Hong Kong at Century's End*. Edited by Martha C. Pennington. Hong Kong: Hong Kong University Press, pp. 329–38.
Bacon-Shone, John and Bolton, Kingsley (1998) Charting multilingualism: Language censuses and language surveys in Hong Kong. In *Language in Hong Kong at Century's*

End. Edited by Martha C. Pennington. Hong Kong: Hong Kong University Press, pp. 43–90.

Bamgboṣe, Ayọ (1998) Torn between the norms: Innovations in world Englishes. *World Englishes*, **17**(1), 1–14.

Crismore, Avon, Ngeow, Karen Yeok-hwa and Soo, Keng-soon (1996) Attitudes towards English in Malaysia. *World Englishes* **15**(3), 319–35.

Giles, Howard (1998) Language attitudes and language cognitions: Future prospects for Hong Kong. In *Language in Hong Kong at Century's End*. Edited by Martha C. Pennington. Hong Kong: Hong Kong University Press, pp. 425–36.

Hirvela, Alan and Law, Eva (1991) A survey of local English teachers' attitudes toward English and ELT. *Institute of Language in Education Journal*, **8**, 25–38.

Kachru, Braj B. (1985) Standards, codification and sociolinguistic realism: The English language in the outer circle. In *English in the World: Teaching and Learning the Language and Literatures*. Edited by Randolph Quirk and Henry G. Widdowson. Cambridge: Cambridge University Press, pp. 11–30.

Lowenberg, Peter H. (1990) Standards and norms for world Englishes: Issues and attitudes. *Studies in the Linguistic Sciences*, **30**(2), 123–37.

Luke, Kang-kwong and Richards, Jack C. (1982) English in Hong Kong: Functions and status. *English World-wide*, **3**(1), 47–64.

Pennington, Martha C. and Yue, Francis (1994) English and Chinese in Hong Kong: Pre-1997 language attitudes. *World Englishes* **13**(1), 1–20.

Pierson, Herbert D., Fu, Gail S. and Lee, Sik-yum (1980) An analysis of the relationship between language attitudes and English attainment of secondary school students in Hong Kong. *Language Learning*, **30**, 289–316.

So, Daniel W.C. (1998) One country, two cultures and three languages: Sociolinguistic conditions and language education in Hong Kong. In *Teaching Language and Culture: Building Hong Kong on Education*. Edited by Barry Asker. Hong Kong: Addison Wesley Longman, pp. 152–75.

3

Cantonese-English code-switching research in Hong Kong: A survey of recent research

David C. S. Li

Introduction

Research on Cantonese-English code-switching in Hong Kong may be dated back to the late 1970s.[1] Most of the earlier studies tended to focus on speech data (e.g., Gibbons, 1979, 1983, 1987), but beginning with Bauer (1988), attention was gradually shifted to include written data as well (e.g., Yau, 1993; Li, 1996, 1998, 1999a; Lee, 1999). With the exception of Yau's (1997) study investigating the code-switching of bilingual legislative councillors and colonial government officials in the proceedings of Legislative Council debates, research has shown that code-switching in Hong Kong tends to be intrasentential – hence the preference for the term 'code-mixing' in many studies – and that switching involving linguistic units above the clause level is rare. Indeed, many researchers have pointed out that Chinese Hongkongers are subject to strong social norms disapproving the use of English for intraethnic communication (e.g., Fu, 1987; Li, 1996, 1998, 1999b; Luke, 1984/1998). The exact nature and extent of such disapproval against the exclusive use of English among fellow Chinese Hongkongers, especially beyond the education sector, remain largely unexplored (but see, e.g., Hyland, 1997), although intuitively it would seem reasonable to interpret this as being due to a perceived violation, or even betrayal, of the Cantonese speaker's ethnolinguistic identity.

As noted by Li (1996), owing to terminological problems in the field, practically no studies on code-switching and/or code-mixing could be spared the trouble of defining unambiguously how these two terms are used. My own preference on this issue has been indicated elsewhere, and may be cited here for the sake of convenience:

> Cantonese interspersed with English elements, especially single words, is generally referred to as mixed code, and the sociolinguistic phenomenon itself, code-mixing or (intra-sentential) code-switching. To avoid negative

connotations associated with the term 'code-mixing', in this study the more general term 'code-switching' will be used to cover switching at both the inter- and intra-sentential levels (cf. Clyne, 1991). There is, however, no other satisfactory term which can replace the substantive 'mixed code', and the adjective 'code-mixed', which is why they will be used to refer to intra-sentential code-switching typical of Hong Kong bilinguals' informal language use, both in speech and in print. (Li, 1999a: 7)

Code-switching research in Hong Kong

By far the most informative single volume devoted to various language-related issues in Hong Kong is Pennington (1998a), which is a collection of data-driven articles divided into specialized topical areas, supplemented by summary discussion papers by well-known experts in the field. The volume also contains a very informative introduction by the editor herself (Pennington, 1998b). In this introductory piece, Pennington examines code-switching in Hong Kong from a number of partly overlapping theoretical perspectives, including diglossia, genre analysis, act of identity, syntactic interaction, semantic extension, language symbolism, psychology of duality, and cognitive advantage. Not all of these 'current perspectives' are considered entirely felicitous. Thus, for example, to the extent that Hongkong-style mixed code may be interpreted as a linguistic compromise, a 'middle way' to avoid the extremes of 'pure' English or 'pure' Cantonese, mixed code presents a challenge to the theory of diglossia (p. 5). Pennington (1998b) also examines mixed code from a number of 'new perspectives', according to which there is room to analyse mixed code, respectively, as linguistic innovation, chaotic language behaviour, linguistic entrepreneurship for expressing a host of things foreign, and a sign of the bilingual expressing, and alternating between, metaphorical experiences. In sum, Pennington points the way by offering a very broad range of directions in which research on code-switching in Hong Kong is worth pursuing. In the rest of this chapter, I will outline and review other key contributions to research on code-switching in Hong Kong,[2] before presenting four contextually well-defined motivations of invoking English words in otherwise Chinese texts, as shown in the Hong Kong Chinese press. Lexical borrowings – words of foreign origin which have been assimilated to the phonology of the host language – are beyond the scope of this chapter.

The first major attempt to study code-switching in Hong Kong was made by John Gibbons (1979, 1983). He investigated 'U-gay-wa' ('university talk'), which was a genre of mixed code commonly used and heard among students at Hong Kong University. The findings from these earlier studies were later synthesized in a single volume (Gibbons, 1987), where the original designation 'U-gay-wa' gave way to a more general term 'MIX', in part out of recognition that intrasentential code-switching was not limited to university students, but was a Hong Kong-wide language phenomenon, especially among educated Hong Kong Chinese.

Gibbons (1987) used three complementary approaches – an ethnographic approach, a 'secular linguistic' or 'Labovian microsociolinguistic' approach, and a social-psychological matched guise approach – to analyse 'MIX' and to examine the correlation between the subjects' code choice and a range of situation-specific factors such as age, sex, setting and topic of conversation. The application of each of these approaches yielded interesting corroborative findings, confirming *inter alia* that (1) Cantonese was perceived as a marker of group and ethnic solidarity, (2) there was strong sanction against using English for intraethnic communication, (3) 'MIX' was preferred in informal settings, and (4) 'MIX' exhibits certain structural features which set it apart from its parent languages, Cantonese and English. The most significant claim from the theoretical point of view was that 'MIX' was undergoing koineization, which, Gibbons believed, was comparable to a similar process of levelling and simplification which culminated in koine Greek (Siegel, 1985), post-Norman-conquest English (Hymes, 1971) and Israeli Hebrew (Blanc, 1968). On the basis of this observation, Gibbons concluded that 'MIX' could be regarded as an 'incipient koine'. The koineization hypothesis, however, has been scrutinized and shown to be inaccurate (Li, 1999a). The thrust of Li's argument is that unlike prototypical koines reported in the literature (Siegel, 1985, 1993), mixed code in Hong Kong is not used between speakers of the contributing languages, Cantonese and English. In other words, to most non-Chinese English-speaking Hongkongers who do not understand 'pure' Cantonese, mixed code is just as inscrutable to them (except perhaps young ethnic Indians and Pakistanis brought up in Hong Kong, see Pannu, 1998; Patri and Pennington, 1998). Gibbons' research method has inspired two replication studies, one with students at City Polytechnic of Hong Kong (Pennington et al., 1992), the other with Indian adolescents in Hong Kong (Pannu, 1994). In both replications, the subjects reported that Cantonese was most often their preferred language when interacting with peers in informal settings on 'light' topics, such as their favourite singers and where to go for lunch.

The linguistic constraints approach to analysing code-switching data (Poplack, 1980; Sankoff and Poplack, 1981) has also inspired a number of studies investigating the extent to which Hongkong-style mixed code may be accounted for by the Free Morpheme Constraint and Equivalence Constraint (Leung, 1988; Chan, 1993, 1998). No syntactic constraints are supported by Hong Kong data, however. Instead, Chan (1998) found that Myers-Scotton's (1992) Matrix Language Frame model seems to provide a more adequate analytical framework, though not without residual problems: in a few rare cases, it remains indeterminate whether the phrase structure of the matrix language is Cantonese or English.

Based on examples of code-switching in the Hong Kong Chinese press, Li (1996, 1998) shows that English elements are commonly found in informal sections of Chinese newspapers, especially around six discourse topics: computer, business, food, fashion, showbiz and lifestyle. Since the style of informal writing in the Hong Kong Chinese press is close to the norms of speaking (cf. 'low' Cantonese, Luke, 1984/1998), Li (1996) argues that a massive amount of data from representative newspapers in both the quality and popular press over an extended period of time is no less instructive than speech data obtained from specific participants in particular contexts. In terms of motivations of code choice, Li argues that, given the strong social sanction disapproving the use of English (i.e., English entirely) for intraethnic communication, the Chinese Hongkongers' common practice of 'sprinkling' individual English words onto their Cantonese may be more satisfactorily accounted for by the absence of translation equivalents (i.e., lexical gap) or, where dictionary equivalents exist, by semantic discrepancy between the English expression and the Chinese/Cantonese translation, hence the two main linguistic factors 'availability' and 'specificity', especially at the formative stage of code-switching. In other words, in those cases the use of Chinese/Cantonese equivalents tends to bring about unwanted semantic loss or gain. This helps explain why sometimes even purists cannot help preventing English elements from cropping up in their speech or writing (Li, 1998).

Li (1999a) presents two types of evidence – lexicosyntactic transference of English words and specific functions assigned to individual letters of the English alphabet – to show that linguistic convergence has taken place in Hong Kong mixed code. Lexicosyntactic transference (Clyne, 1991) occurs typically when a VO structure of a transitive English verb supplants the intransitive OV structure of the corresponding Chinese/Cantonese verb. At the sublexical level, Li (1996, 1999a) shows that individual letters of the English alphabet are commonly used in the Hong Kong Chinese press to signal indefinite reference, or to serve the function of quasi-euphemism of 'bad language' in Cantonese. Particularly versatile are the letters B, D, N, Q and V, which are all charged with specific meanings. To give an example, for many Chinese Hongkongers, especially members of the younger generations, the letter Q (pronounced as kiu1 in Cantonese) stands for the adjective 'cute'; for advertisers it symbolizes the 'Quality' label; for horse-racing fans Q means 'quinella'; and finally for readers of pornographic literature, on the basis of its written form Q has taken on meanings associated with 'sexual intercourse' (Bauer, 1988). In addition, conventionalized strings of English letters, which are either recognizable English words or acronyms, may be invoked by columnists of Chinese newspapers to structure discourse topics in otherwise pure Chinese texts, thus making the English elements serve a well-defined rhetorical purpose at the discourse level. As for the actual layout, Li (1996, 1999a, 2000) notes that an English letter appearing in the Chinese press is often treated on a par with logographic Chinese characters, leading thereby to an intriguing question whether the English alphabet should be regarded as an integral part of the Chinese language.

More recently, Micky Lee (1999, 2000) adopts an interpretative approach to study 'fashion discourse' in Hong Kong Chinese printed media texts with a view to better understanding how texts in fashion discourse are produced and consumed. Data was constituted by three magazines collected over a period of one year. Using critical discourse analysis and the Hallidayan model of 'context of situation' as main analytical frameworks, supplemented by focus-group interviews with magazine producers and readers, Lee found a great deal of intertextuality and interdiscursivity in fashion discourse. This led her to conclude that media texts are never completely original; on the contrary, much of the day-to-day production of fashion discourse consists of appropriating other people's discourse – from the choice of language to printing style and fonts; from graphics to the nitty gritty details of fashion trends – to meet one's immediate writing needs. One of Lee's most interesting findings is that, seen from the point of view of members of fashion discourse, the terms code-switching and code-mixing, which are of primary interest to sociolinguists, have little reality for them in the text production process. Interviews with members of fashion discourse have shown that members have hardly any concern for allegiance to a particular language when producing or consuming texts in fashion discourse, let alone being conscious of what language they are using at a given moment and crossing language boundaries at the next. French words are sometimes 'mixed' into fashion discourse, largely for their iconic value, that is, for conveying a sense of Frenchness, plus all the meaning potential that French as a prestige language connotes, as in the case of an eye-catching title of a code-mixed feature called '白白度過 L'été blanc' (baak6 baak6 dou6 gwo3 *L'été blanc*, 'whiling away a white summer').[3] To account for these practices, Lee (1999) proposes the term 'voice-quoting', which in her view captures the exact motivation of language use among members of fashion discourse, in that language choice is largely driven by what is perceived as 'right'. This is not unlike Scollon et al.'s (1998) findings obtained from Chinese university students doing a hypothetical letter-writing task describing their feelings to their friends overseas just before the Handover in 1997. The findings show that some English expressions used in the 'discourse of transition' as found in print and electronic media (e.g., 'bright future') were appropriated when writing the letter. In addition, Lee's meticulous analysis clearly demonstrates a dialectic relationship between the individual member's appropriation from fashion discourse as one of the 'normal' practices for signalling legitimate membership, and the dynamic forces at work shaping, or even dictating, what constitutes the 'right' thing to say as well as in what language and form that 'right' thing should take.

Code-switching motivations: Expedient vs. orientational

Of all the works on code-switching in Hong Kong, Luke (1984/1998) comes closest to being a coherent theoretical model. To account for social motivations of code choice, he postulates six 'alternate means of communication': 'high' Cantonese, 'low' Cantonese, expedient mixing (pragmatically motivated), orientational mixing (socially motivated), code-switching, and English. An individual's speech repertoire is believed to be a subset of these. The use of English and code-switching – the latter being defined as 'the use of alternate segments of clause and sentence length from the two languages' (p. 149) – are rare, owing to strong societal disapproval against using English (except English words below the clause level) for intraethnic communication. 'High' Cantonese is modelled on standard written Chinese and is used in formal settings such as news broadcast and public speeches. 'Low' Cantonese, on the other hand, is used in informal settings. Language mixing between Cantonese and English may be motivated by two different reasons: 'expedient', when the object, institution or idea of Western origin (e.g., *walkman*) has no known equivalent in 'low' Cantonese, whereas the use of the 'high' Cantonese equivalent, if it exists (e.g, 隨身聽, ceoi4 san1 ting3), would result in stylistic inappropriacy; 'orientational', when there exist equivalents in both 'high' Cantonese (e.g., 午飯, ng5 faan6) and 'low' Cantonese (e.g., 晏, ngaan3), and the choice of English (e.g., *lunch*) shows the speaker's identification with the better educated as well as a Western outlook. In Luke's (1998) own words:

> The difference between the two kinds of mixing is that while in expedient mixing a term in the mixing category is 'chosen' because it happens to be the only informal term in the formal-informal contrast, in orientational mixing, a term in the mixing category is shown out of a two-term contrast between the 'mixing term' and its corresponding 'low' Cantonese term. (Luke 1998: 155)

In sum, expedient mixing helps fill a lexical or stylistic gap in Cantonese, while orientational mixing allows for dynamic manipulation, or 'display', of the speaker's social identities and distance vis-à-vis the interlocutor(s). According to Luke (1984/1998), this model of code choice helps explain why inherently Chinese notions such as food items and names of festivals are almost never expressed in English. Further, just as 'high' Cantonese and 'low' Cantonese can be differentiated phonologically, grammatically and lexically, so mixed code has its own linguistic features, which are discussed under four sections: phonology, grammar, semantics, and discourse markers (cf. Gibbons, 1987), the latter (e.g., 'anyway', 'in case') being a salient feature of orientational mixing.

While Luke's model of code choice is intuitively appealing, its explanatory power is dependent on the validity of a premise taken largely for granted, namely, the notion of 'translation equivalent'. Thus for those instances of code-switching characterized as orientational, there exist semantically congruent 'high' and 'low' Cantonese equivalents of given English terms. Where 'low' Cantonese equivalents are not found, the English words that surface serve pragmatically to fill a stylistic gap, hence expedient mixing. Such a relationship of semantic congruence between words listed as translation equivalents, however, does not always obtain. Li (1996) points out that a culturally neutral activity such as 'shopping' has functional equivalents in 'high' Cantonese (購物, kau3 mat6), and 'low' Cantonese (買嘢, maai5 je5), but their literal meaning, 'buy things', commits the speaker/writer to buying things in a way that the English word 'shopping' does not. Likewise, Lee (1999) sees ideological differences in these 'referential synonyms' and offers an interesting gloss as follows: her shopping activities are often labelled by her mother as 'shopping', implying that in the eyes of her mother, she tends to indulge in 'unnecessary, somewhat money-wasting and hedonist consumption', whereas her mother's own 'shopping' activities tend to be referred to as mai5 je5, which are 'necessary and inevitable' (p. 38).

In many other cases, it remains unclear whether the Chinese dictionary equivalent actually expresses the same content as the term in English. One such example is *keep fit*, which is ubiquitous in what may be called 'sports club discourse' among health-conscious Chinese Hongkongers; it is generally rendered in bilingual dictionaries as 保持健康 (bou2 ci4 gin6 hong1, literally 'stay healthy'). There is something in their meanings, however, which makes them less than a perfect match. The Chinese disyllabic word *gin6 hong1* depicts a state of being free from illnesses, whereas the English word *fit* means 'healthy' plus 'strong in bodily condition'. This latter meaning component helps explain why to describe someone with a strong build and a sporty outlook, the code-mixed expression 好*fit* (hou2 fit, 'very fit') is more often heard than 好健康 (hou2 gin6 hong1, 'very healthy').

In extreme cases, there exist more than one translation across Chinese varieties for a given English term. One most revealing example is *Internet*, which has been given the translation 互聯網 (wu6 lyun4 mong5) in Hong Kong, but which has been rendered as 網際網路 (wǎng jì wǎng lù) in Taiwan, and 因特網 (yīn tè wǎng) in the Mainland (Lam, 2000). It is not difficult to imagine, therefore, that the word *Internet* may tend to surface in communications between Mandarin-speaking Chinese from both sides of the Taiwan Straits, especially if neither side is ready to accommodate to the other's communication style.

An additional complication is that, given an English expression occurring in mixed code, it is not clear which Cantonese equivalents have been displaced. Luke's (1984/1998) examples, which are mostly nouns or noun groups denoting concrete referents such as *tennis* (pp. 154ff), suggest that he operates with denotation. There are examples in public discourse, however, showing that in actual language use, Chinese Hongkongers are less concerned about equivalence in terms of denotation so much as functional, referential identity. One interesting example is the ubiquity of *Y2K* in the Hong Kong Chinese press (generally pronounced as waai1 tu1 kei1), including cartoons (see Appendices). As is well-known, *Y2K* is a linguistic artifact of the 'millennium bug' problem confronted by practically all computer users worldwide, a trendy shortcut way of saying 'computer digital problem in the year 2000'. Like many other acronyms, part of the appeal of *Y2K* lies in its brevity, which helps explain a large number of collocations in English ever since the problem was detected, of which *Y2K bug*, *Y2K problem*, *Y2K compliance*, *Y2K threat*, and *Y2K attack* are just a few examples. Strictly speaking, *Y2K* denotes 'year 2000', but as a result of these and other collocations, it has come to mean practically the same thing as the longer, more explicit expression mentioned above. This is probably why the press conference given by Hong Kong government officials reporting on the switch-over was given the following bilingual title:

電腦公元二千年數位問題
Y2K
Press Centre

where the Chinese title reads:

din6 nou5 gung1 jyun4 ji6 cin1 nin4 sou3 wai2 man6 tai4
computer AD 2000 digital problem

Further, from the point of view of the referent, *Y2K* is not the only designation; there exists a referential synonym in informal English: *millennium bug*, which has been translated into Cantonese as 千年蟲, cin1 nin4 cung4.

Within the model of code choice proposed by Luke (1984/1998), the ubiquity of *Y2K*, both in code-mixed speech and writing, raises some interesting questions. For example, what are its 'high' and 'low' Cantonese equivalents? That is, should they be based on its denotation ('year 2000') or pragmatic meaning in context as shown above? Further, if *cin1 nin4 cung4* ('millennium bug') is taken to be the equivalent in Cantonese (which is not unreasonable), should it be regarded as 'high' Cantonese or 'low' Cantonese, or both? The same query may apply to the status of *wu6 lyun4 mong5* (*Internet*) discussed above. Luke (1984/1998) has made no mention of cases where the 'high' vs. 'low' distinction in Cantonese may be neutralized, which has a direct bearing on the kind of motivation in question. Given the myriad ways and domains in which *cin1 nin4 cung4* and *wu6 lyun4 mong5* are used, both in speech and in writing, it would be difficult not to classify them under *both* the 'high' and 'low' categories. These are some of the problems that a model based on lexical equivalents across languages has to reconcile.

Above all, in the age of information superhighway and globalization where the Internet along with 'computer speak' is heavily and clearly dominated by English, it seems doubtful how much 'Westernness' one can attribute to oneself by using computer jargon such as *Y2K*. What seems to be happening is that, apart from the fact that it is much easier to key in *Y2K* compared with 千年蟲, the spread of *Y2K* across language boundaries is a clear case of intertextuality (cf. Scollon, 1998; Scollon et al., 1998), where segments of text are appropriated at will for various situation-specific communicative purposes, such as attracting attention and luring the reader to read on in an otherwise mundane news story. This seems to be the case with the quarter-page international news story 'Yeltsin's man who would be president', which opens with: 'The Y2K bug struck Russia. The heating and lights stayed on, but the president went out' (Weir, 2000).

Apart from the slippery notion of 'translation equivalent' (cf. Snell-Hornby, 1988), there are other cases where the meaning of the English word is expressed by a syntactically more complex structure in Cantonese, suggesting that in such cases, code-switching spares the speaker/writer considerable linguistic effort, hence the 'principle of economy' (see below).

The above discussion shows that much more is at stake than Luke's (1984/1998) dichotomy: code-switching either as a result of a pragmatic move to fill a lexical or stylistic gap in 'low' Cantonese (expedient mixing), or as a social act of displaying one's inclination towards, and identification with, a more Western disposition (orientational mixing). Instead, much of the overt code-switching behaviour as manifested in informal interactions among Chinese Hongkongers may be accounted for by two main complementary forces: a lack of semantic congruence between English lexis and its Chinese/Cantonese counterparts, and a desire to express more precisely what one wants to say, especially at the formative stage of code-switching. In extreme cases, the syntactic properties of the English lexical item (including multi-word units) such as transitivity pattern are carried over in mixed code, resulting in what Clyne (1991) calls 'lexicosyntactic transference'. In what follows, four specific motivations of code-switching will be discussed based on examples collected mainly from the Hong Kong Chinese press: euphemism, specificity, bilingual punning, and principle of economy.

Four motivations for code-switching in Hong Kong

Euphemism

One of the pragmatic motivations for using English words is euphemism. To illustrate, consider an example taken from 'showbiz discourse' (Li, 1996). A quarter-page entertainment news story in *Apple Daily* (99/08/01/C9)[4] features the Taiwanese actress 林心如 (Lin Xinru) who became very popular in the

Mainland, Hong Kong and Taiwan after a very successful TV series 還珠格格 (huán zhū gégé, 'My fair princess') was broadcast in 'Greater China'. Of interest to us is the attention seeker cutting across the eye-catching picture of this actress in jumbo-sized print that says:

(1) Woo! 透 Bra 格格!
    tou3 BRA gaak3 gaak3
    visible bra princess
    'Wow! (a) princess (whose) bra is visible!'

Reference was made to a see-through long dress worn by the actress, making her bra clearly visible from the outside. The word and referent 'bra' is no more Western than pants and jeans nowadays; it does have equivalents in both standard written Chinese (SWC) and Cantonese:

胸罩 (hung1 zaau3, SWC): literally 'chest cover'
奶罩 (naai5 zaau3, SWC): literally 'breast cover'
胸圍 (hung1 wai4, Cantonese): literally 'chest wrap'
乳罩 (jyu5 zaau3, Cantonese): literally 'breast cover'

Following Luke's (1994/1998) framework, by preferring *bra* to its Cantonese/Chinese equivalents the infotainment reporter and/or copy-editor might have wanted to appear 'Western'. This analysis does not seem convincing, however, given that *bra* was the only English word used in this Chinese news story (other than the English-like interjection *Woo!* in the attention seeker). If 'orientational mixing' had been the intended motivation of language choice, one would expect other English elements to appear in that news story. I think a more plausible explanation for the preference of the English word *bra* lies in the literal meanings of its Chinese/Cantonese equivalents: compared with the analytically expressed Chinese counterparts 'chest cover'/'breast cover' (SWC) or 'chest wrap'/'breast cover' (Cantonese), using the word *bra* allows the speaker/writer to allude to the same referent without making explicit mention of that potentially embarrassing female body part denoted by 胸 (hung1, 'chest'), 奶 (naai5, 'breast') or 乳 (jyu5, 'breast'). In other words, the choice of the word *bra* was most likely motivated by a desire for euphemism. A similar explanation underlies the general preference for words like *toilet* and *washroom* in the mixed code of Chinese Hongkongers, with variations in pronunciation depending on the individual's language repertoire, including monolingual Cantonese speakers.

Specificity

Sometimes an English expression is preferred because its meaning is more general or specific compared with its near-synonymous counterparts. One high-frequency example in both the informal speech and writing of Hong Kong Chinese is the word *fans* (of a certain idol), which invariably appears in plural form in the Chinese press and, depending on the individual, may be pronounced as [fæns], which is close to British English norms, or [fæn si], which is arguably a borrowing comparable to 巴士 (baa1 si2, 'bus'). For example:[5]

(2)* 黎明有好多 FANS
lai4 ming4 jau5 hou2 do1 FANS
Leon Lai have very many fans
'Leon Lai (the singer/film star) has many fans.'

This basic meaning of 'fans' is expressed by the morphosyllable 迷 (mai4), but unlike English, Cantonese requires the speaker/writer to make explicit the talent(s) in question by having it specified in a premodifier. Compare:

歌迷 (go1 mai4): 'song fan'
影迷 (jing2 mai4): 'film fan'
球迷 (kau4 mai4): 'ball fan', especially 'soccer fan'

Given that many entertainers today have multiple talents, it may be troublesome to specify the types of fan a person is. The use of 迷 (mai4) alone is not a conceivable option either, partly because of a general tendency in modern Chinese in favour of polysyllabic words. It is against this background that the word *fans* offers a convenient 'solution', in that its meaning is more general, in addition to being a monosyllabic, high-frequency word. This may have been the principal motivation at the formative stage of code-switching this word into Cantonese before it caught on in public discourse.

If *fans* is preferred for its more general meaning, there exist opposite cases where the English expression is preferred for its more specific meaning. Thus the English verb *book* figures frequently in mixed code in such contexts as booking a table in a restaurant, a tennis or badminton court, a ticket for a flight or a show. For example:

(3)* 唔該, 我想 BOOK 三點, 一號場
m4 goi1 ngo5 soeng2 BOOK saam1 dim2 jat1 hou6 coeng4
please, I want book 3 o'clock no. 1 court
'Please, I want to book court no. 1 at 3 o'clock.'

The nearest equivalent in Cantonese is 訂 (deng6) which, as a noun, means 'deposit' or 'down payment'. As a verb, deng6 typically means 'to order something made to measure' such as 訂造張床 (deng6 zou6 zoeng1 cong4, 'have a bed made'), where a deposit is required. Since deng6 tends to bring to mind 'paying a deposit', it is highly probable that the English verb 'to book', which figures frequently in mixed code, was motivated at the formative stage by a desire to communicate the meaning 'make a reservation for which no money or deposit is required' unambiguously. The same may be said of the spread of the English preposition *vs.* (typographical variants *Vs*, *VS*), used with or without full stop, in the Hong Kong Chinese press, as in the following examples from the Chinese newspaper *Hong Kong Economic Times* (cf. Li, 1996: 93ff):

(4) a. 愛情 vs. 婚姻 (*HKET*, 93/08/18/48)
ngoi3 cing4 VS. fan1 jan1
'love vs. marriage'

b. 感情 vs. 理智 (*HKET*, 93/12/07/C8)
gam2 cing4 VS. lei5 zi3
'emotion vs. rationality'

The SWC/Cantonese counterpart of *vs.* is 對 (deoi3). Unlike *vs.*, however, *deoi3* is semantically not as appropriate in those contexts where the items on both sides of the preposition are merely juxtaposed for contrast (as in 4a and 4b above), with no sense of competition such as in a tennis match: 珊翠絲對嘉芙 (saan1 ceoi3 si1 deoi3 gaa1 fu4, 'Sanchez vs. Graf'). In other words, the two prepositions *vs.* and *deoi3* are only near synonyms, with the latter being restricted only to those contexts where competition or confrontation is involved.

Bilingual punning

One of the most interesting and conspicuous motivations of mixing English into Chinese/Cantonese is the deliberate attempt to create double meaning. This strategy, which relies on similarity in pronunciation between the English and Cantonese elements for its success, may be called bilingual punning. One such example is as follows:

(5) 'High Tech 揩嘢, Low Tech 撈嘢' (*Apple Daily*, 99/03/03/B9)
HIGH TECH haai1 je5 LOW TECH lou1 je5
high tech bring trouble low tech profitable
'High Tech brings trouble, while Low Tech is profitable'

This bilingual pun (involving English and Cantonese constituents) was found in a few columns of Hong Kong Chinese newspapers and feature articles of popular magazines at a time when the HKSAR was suffering from an economic downturn. In one newspaper column containing this bilingual pun, the columnist commented on the prospects of high-tech industries in Hong Kong, and voiced his concern by echoing this popular saying which, according to him, was commonly heard among local manufacturers. In this saying which has the strong flavour of a dictum, local manufacturers resorted to language play to produce what in their view was wisdom grounded in experience. Of interest to us here is that in making their point, they exploited rhyming between two pairs of disyllabic lexical units, in each case one from English, the other from Cantonese – *high* and 揩 (haai1, 'get into trouble'), *low* and 撈 (lou1, 'reap profit').

Bilingual punning is also a common feature in Hong Kong advertisements. One recent, interesting example may be found in light boxes of many MTR (Mass Transit Railway) stations promoting the avant-garde, yuppy monthly called *City Magazine*, whose Chinese title is 號外 (hou6 ngoi6, 'newspaper extra'). This magazine, written largely in Cantonese code-mixed with plenty of English, claims to be attractive among other things for being innovative in its language use – a feature which is directly reflected in the ad itself. Mandarin or Putonghua usually has no place in this magazine, but the attention seeker in the middle of the ad is made up of four jumbo-sized signs in two languages: on the left are the two characters 號外 representing the Chinese title, on the right are the English words 'how' and 'why'. The configuration is as follows:

號外   HOW ?
        WHY ?

Readers literate in both languages but who do not speak Mandarin may not be able to see the link; for those who do, however, the juxtaposition makes perfect sense, for the two characters are pronounced in Mandarin as hào wài, which are almost homophonous with English 'how' and 'why'. At the bottom, in small print, is a short response (in Cantonese) to the two eye-catching questions: 'Answer: buy a copy and read it on the first of each month'.

But in terms of frequency, probably no other English word comes close to the word *fun*,[6] which is commonly mixed into written Chinese for the explicit purpose of bilingual punning (Li, 1996). Being completely homophonous with the Cantonese morpho-syllable 分 (fan1; depending on collocation and context, 分 may mean 'point', 'score', 'mark'; 'to divide'; or 'to share'); or 紛 (fan1, 'many and various', 'profuse', 'numerous'), it often figures in soft news sections such as infotainment news, columns and ads in the Hong Kong Chinese press. Thus a standing column in *Apple Daily* bears the title:

(6) 著數有得 FUN
    zeok6 sou3 jau5 dak1 fan1
    offer exist have obtain fun/sharing
    'fun offer to share (with readers)'

This column usually gives a brief description of a new film or CD, plus a coupon which is good for some free gift such as a poster or film ticket. In the column title, *FUN* is embedded in a Cantonese clause featuring a bilingual pun and double meaning: '**fun** offer to **share** (with readers)'.

A few more examples containing the word *fun* will show that this word is really ubiquitous. They are all newspaper adverts collected from one of the most popular Chinese newspapers, *Apple Daily*, which appeared at different times over the last two and a half years since the Handover in mid-1997.

In one whole-page ad, Suzuki offers very special concessions and gifts at the venue of the car exhibition. The mid-page slogan reads:

(7) FUN FUN 鐘發放回歸的喜悅   (*Apple Daily*, 97/07/04/A22)
fan1 fan1 zung1 faat3 fong3 wui4 gwai1 dik1 hei2 jyut6
fun/every minute discharge Handover LP[7] joy
'discharging every minute, with fun, the joy of the Handover'

Since the word *fun* is completely homophonous with 分 (fan1, 'minute'), the bilingual expression FUN FUN 鐘 can also be read as meaning 分分鐘 (fan1 fan1 zung1, 'every minute'), hence the double meaning 'every minute with fun', which is further reinforced in the main text of the ad:

(8) 分分鐘有優惠, FUN FUN 鐘有禮送
fan1 fan1 zung1 jau5 jau1 wai6, FUN FUN zung1 jau5 lai5 sung3
every minute have special offer, fun/every minute have gift distribute
'there is special offer every minute, (and) there are gifts to be distributed every minute with fun'.

Another whole-page ad was jointly put up by Esso, Feoso and Tiger-Mart, offering coupons and special gifts to promote their gas station services in summer. To impress potential clients of the variety of attractive special gifts and offers, the slogan alludes to the Chinese expression 繽紛 (ban1 fan1, 'many and varied'), with the second morphosyllable of this disyllabic word being represented by the homophonous English word FUN, resulting in the double meaning 'many and varied, and fun':

(9) 老虎繽 FUN 夏日巡禮   (*Apple Daily*, 97/07/03/A5)
lou5 fu2 ban1 fan1 haa6 jat1 ceon4 lai5
Tiger many-and-varied/fun summer time carnival
'the Tiger-Mart many-and-varied/fun summer time carnival'

Next, Apple Charity Trust together with two other sponsors advertises a charity comics fair bearing the title:

(10) 夏日動畫 FUN FUN SHOW '99   (*Apple Daily*, 99/08/08)
haa6 jat6 dung6 waa2 fan1 fan1 show gau2 gau2
summer comics fun fun show '99
'1999 Summer Comics FUN FUN SHOW'

In this code-mixed title the choice of 'FUN FUN SHOW' was probably motivated by a number of intended associations:

1. the surface meaning of the English word *fun*;
2. the reduplication of FUN which is suggestive of the Cantonese meaning 'every' in a way similar to FUN FUN 鐘 (fan1 fan1 zung1, 'every minute') discussed above;
3. the meaning 'varied' based on similarity in pronunciation between FUN FUN and 繽紛 (ban1 fan1, 'many and varied') or its high-frequency variant in printed media: 繽 FUN.

In sum, the skilful blending of linguistic resources from Cantonese and English results in a title which conveys a semantically rich message in a most compact manner: 'The 1999 summer comics FUN FUN SHOW is fun every minute and is full of variety'.

Finally, TVB Pearl advertises a party to attract and enhance publicity of a new James Bond movie on TV. The party is given the name:

(11) 星光閃閃有得 FUN   (*Apple Daily*, 99/08/22/C10)
sing1 gwong1 sim2 sim2 jau5 dak1 fan1
star light shiny shiny have obtain fun/sharing
'starry, shiny light for fun and sharing'

The pun – 'fun' and 'share' – is justified by the fact that *Apple Daily* offers the reader a coupon for getting free tickets to join this party.

As shown in the above examples, the use of the word *fun* in Hong Kong Chinese media discourse is very common indeed. This point seems to have been recognized by the government which, until recently at least, exhibited a totally disapproving attitude towards the use of mixed code, especially in the education sector (Li, 1999b). A sign of change, however, was found in a Chinese brochure on curricular reforms proposed by the Curriculum Development Council of the Education Department, soliciting opinions and feedback from the general public. To stimulate students' motivation to learn and speak English, one of the proposed reform measures is to supplement the existing timetable system with a more flexible teaching and learning schedule, such as devoting one whole day (e.g., per month) to fun English activities. Of interest here is the name of such a day, which is expressed in mixed code as follows:

(12) 英文多 FUN 日   (Education Department, no date, 12)
jing1 man4 do1 FUN jat6
English much fun/mark day
'A day having great fun/high mark with English'

The additional gloss 'high mark' is justified by the near homophony between 'FUN' and 'fan1', here meaning 'score' or 'mark'. If this example is indicative of the beginning of a reversal from an uncompromisingly intransigent, hostile stance towards mixed code on the part of the government, it is a most welcome sign indeed. As pointed out by Li (1999b), banning mixed code from the education domain in the hope that some unwanted but salient patterns of language use in the students' everyday life could be kept at the doors of school premises, is simply unrealistic and counter-productive relative to the goal of effective second language learning. What I find encouraging in the recent round of educational reform initiatives undertaken by the HKSAR government, of which the Chinese brochure cited is an artifact, is the use of individual English words, whose meanings are well understood by students, to frame well-intentioned and communicatively effective messages targeting student audiences.

Principle of economy

In addition to any combination of the above motivations, an English expression may also be preferred because it is shorter and thus requires less linguistic effort compared with its Chinese/Cantonese equivalent. This is arguably the case with the high-frequency colloquial adjective *in*, which is commonly found in informal newspaper sections and in speech to mean 'fashionable', 'trendy', and the like. The nearest synonyms in Cantonese are 流行 (lau4 hang4) and 緊貼潮流 (gan2 tip3 ciu4 lau4, 'closely follow fashion/trend'), which are longer (two and four syllables) compared with the monosyllabic English word.

Another interesting example is *check in*, which is also ubiquitous in the mixed code of Chinese Hongkongers, especially in the discourse of seasoned travellers and many others who are engaged in the hospitality industry, for whom time is money. Consider the following example:

(13)* 你 check in 左未呀？
nei5 CHECK IN zo2 mei6 aa3
you check in ASP not yet FP
'Have you checked in already?'

This question could be heard in two kinds of context: getting a hotel room, or registering for a flight before take-off. In either case, the questioner is spared considerable linguistic effort (six syllables in place of ten) as compared with the 'pure' Cantonese version below:

(14) Hotel context: 你辦理左入住手續未呀？
nei5 baan6 lei5 zo2 jap6 zyu6 sau2 zuk6 mei6 aa3
you go through ASP in-stay procedure not yet FP
'Have you checked in (to your room) already?'

(15) Airport context:　你辦理左登機手續未呀？
nei5 baan6 lei5 zo2 dang1 gei1 sau2 zuk6 mei6 aa3
you go through ASP board plane procedure not yet
FP
'Have you checked in (for your flight) already?'

Similarly, English verbs with causative meanings such as *undo*, *unstar*, *update* and *upgrade*, which figure frequently in mixed code, may also be accounted for by the 'principle of economy' (Li, 1999a: 15ff).

The above examples show that, when the main purpose of communication is to convey one's meanings efficiently and unambiguously, Chinese Hongkongers who are bilingual/biliterate in Cantonese/Chinese and English to different extents would have no hesitation calling on all linguistic resources at their disposal to express more precisely what they want to say.

Conclusion

This chapter has reviewed the major works in code-switching research in Hong Kong, with Luke's (1984/1998) model of code choice and motivations of code-switching being discussed at greater length. The dichotomy 'expedient mixing' and 'orientational mixing' is intuitively appealing but probably overly simplistic because lexical and stylistic equivalents across languages may be difficult to establish owing to the slippery notion of 'translation equivalent'. Given the prevailing societal disapproval against Chinese Hongkongers using English exclusively for intraethnic communication, the more linguistically oriented motivations discussed above seem to offer more plausible explanations why English words and phrases, typically below the clause level, are used by Hong Kong Chinese to fulfill various communicative purposes in informal settings, resulting in overt code-switching behaviours. This, in turn, may be seen as manifestations of bilingualism and biculturalism as a result of sustained contact between English and Cantonese for well over a century in this former British colony.

Notes

1. I would like to thank Kingsley Bolton, Micky Lee, and an anonymous reviewer for their constructive comments on an earlier draft. I alone am responsible for any inadequacies that remain.
2. For more details, see Gibbons (1987), Lee (1999), Li (1996, 1999a), Luke (1984/1998), Pennington (1994, 1998a), and Poon (1997, in Chinese). Not included in this review owing to limitations of space is code-switching research in the bilingual classroom: see Li (1999b), Lin (1990, 1996, 1997), Johnson (1983, 1994) and Johnson and Lee (1987).

3. Cantonese expressions will be transliterated using the Jyutping system promoted by the Linguistic Society of Hong Kong (Fan et al., 1997). The number at the end of the segmental denotes the tone level: 1 = high level; 2 = high rising; 3 = mid level; 4 = low failing; 5 = low rising; 6 = low level.
4. The date and page reference of a newspaper clipping are indicated within brackets; for example, (99/08/03/C10) would mean 'dated 3 August 1999, p. C10'. In one or two cases the page number is missing due to oversight in the data collection process.
5. The examples (2), (3) and (13), which have their source in speech (as opposed to print) data, are marked by an asterisk.
6. Recent data involving ads of, and soft news about, mobile phones shows that the English word *phone*, which is nearly homophonous with Cantonese 風 (fung1, 'wind'), is fast catching up.
7. Key to abbreviations: ASP, 'aspectual marker'; FP, 'final particle', LP, 'linking particle'.

References

Bauer, Robert S. (1988) Written Cantonese of Hong Kong. *Cahiers de Linguistique Asie Orientale*, **17**(2), 245–93.

Blanc, Haim (1968) The Israeli Koine as an emergent national standard. In *Language Problems in Developing Nations*. Edited by Joshua Fishman et al. New York: Wiley, pp. 237–51.

Chan, Brian Hok-shing (1993) *In Search of the Constraints and Processes of Code-mixing in Hong Kong Cantonese-English Bilingualism*. Research Report no. 33. Department of English, City University of Hong Kong.

Chan, Brian Hok-Shing (1998) How does Cantonese-English code-mixing work? In *Language in Hong Kong at Century's End*. Edited by Martha C. Pennington. Hong Kong: Hong Kong University Press, pp. 191–216.

Clyne, Michael (1991) *Community Languages: The Australian Experience*. Cambridge: Cambridge University Press.

Education Department (no date) A comprehensive review of Hong Kong school curricula: Proposed reforms (in Chinese). Curriculum Development Council. See also http:\\www.cdc.org.hk

Fan, Gwok, Lee, Thomas, Lun, Caesar, Luke, Kang-kwong, Tung, Peter and Cheung, Kwan-hin (1997) 粵語拼音字表 (*Yueyu pinyin zibiao*, 'Cantonese Romanization and character list'). Hong Kong: Linguistic Society of Hong Kong.

Fu, Gail S. (1987) The Hong Kong bilingual. In *Language Education in Hong Kong*. Edited by R. Lord and Helen N. L. Cheng. Hong Kong: The Chinese University Press, pp. 27–50.

Gibbons, John (1979) Code-mixing and koineizing in the speech of students at the University of Hong Kong. *Anthropological Linguistics*, **21**(3), 113–23.

Gibbons, John (1983) Attitudes towards languages and code-mixing in Hong Kong. *Journal of Multilingual and Multicultural Development*, **4**(2/3), 129–47.

Gibbons, John (1987) *Code-mixing and Code Choice: A Hong Kong Case Study*. Clevedon: Multilingual Matters.

Hyland, Ken (1997) Language attitudes at the Handover: Communication and identity

in 1997 Hong Kong. *English World-wide*, **18**(2), 191–210.
Hymes, Dell (ed.) (1971) Introduction [to Part III]. In *Pidginization and Creolization of Languages*. Edited by D. Hymes. Cambridge: Cambridge University Press, pp. 65–90.
Johnson, Robert Keith (1983) Bilingual switching strategies: A study of the modes of teacher-talk in bilingual secondary classrooms in Hong Kong. *Language Learning and Communication*, **2**(3), 267–85.
Johnson, Robert Keith (1994) Language policy and planning in Hong Kong. *Annual Review of Applied Linguistics*, **14**, 177–99.
Johnson, Robert Keith and Lee, Paul L. M. (1987) Modes of instruction: Teaching strategies and student responses. In *Language Education in Hong Kong*. Edited by R. Lord and Helen N. L. Cheng. Hong Kong: The Chinese University Press, pp. 99–122.
Lam, Wing-kwan (2000) Interesting differences in the translation of *Internet* in three places (in Chinese). *Hong Kong Economic Times*, 12 January, p. A29.
Lee, Micky (1999) Code-switching in Hong Kong popular magazines: A critical discourse analysis of media texts. MPhil dissertation. Department of English, City University of Hong Kong.
Lee, Micky (2000) Code-switching in media texts: Its implications on society and culture in post-colonial Hong Kong. In *Language and Education in Post-colonial Hong Kong*. Edited by David C. S. Li, Angel Lin and Wai-King Tsang. Hong Kong: Linguistic Society of Hong Kong.
Leung, Yin-bing (1988) Constraints on intrasentential code-mixing in Cantonese and English. *Hong Kong Papers in Linguistics and Language Teaching: Special Issue*. The University of Hong Kong, pp. 23–40.
Li, David C. S. (1996) *Issues in Bilingualism and Biculturalism: A Hong Kong Case Study*. New York: Peter Lang.
Li, David C. S. (1997) Borrowed identity: Signaling involvement with a Western name. *Journal of Pragmatics*, **28**, 489–513.
Li, David C. S. (1998) The plight of the purist. In *Language in Hong Kong at Century's End*. Edited by Martha C. Pennington. Hong Kong: Hong Kong University Press, pp. 161–90.
Li, David C. S. (1999a) Linguistic convergence: Impact of English on Hong Kong Cantonese. *Asian Englishes*, **2**(1), 5–36.
Li, David C. S. (1999b) The functions and status of English in Hong Kong: A post-1997 update. *English World-wide*, **20**(1): 67–110.
Li, David C. S. (2000) Phonetic borrowing: Key to the vitality of written Cantonese in Hong Kong. *Written Language & Literacy*, 3(2), 199–233.
Lin, Angel M. Y. (1990) *Teaching in Two Tongues: Language Alternation in Foreign Language Classrooms*. Research Report no. 3. Department of English, City Polytechnic of Hong Kong.
Lin, Angel M. Y. (1996) Bilingualism or linguistic segregation? Symbolic domination, resistance and code switching in Hong Kong schools. *Linguistics and Education*, **8**, 49–84.
Lin, Angel M. Y. (1997) Hong Kong children's rights to a culturally compatible English education. *Hong Kong Journal of Applied Linguistics*, **2**(2), 23–48.
Luke, Kang-kwong (1998 [1984]) Why two languages might be better than one: Motivations of language mixing in Hong Kong. In *Language in Hong Kong at Century's End*. Edited by Martha C. Pennington. Hong Kong: Hong Kong University

Press, pp. 145–59. First published in 1984 as: Expedient and orientational language mixing in Hong Kong. *York Papers in Linguistics*, **11**: 191–201.

Myers-Scotton, Carol (1992) Constructing the frame in intrasentential codeswitching. *Multilingua*, **11**, 101–27.

Pannu, Jasbir (1994) Code-mixing in a trilingual speech community: Indian adolescents in Hong Kong. Unpublished MA dissertation. City University of Hong Kong, Hong Kong.

Pannu, Jasbir (1998) Language choice and identity: The world of the Hong Kong Indian adolescent. In *Language in Hong Kong at Century's End*. Edited by Martha C. Pennington. Hong Kong: Hong Kong University Press, pp. 219–42.

Patri, Mrudula and Pennington, Martha C. (1998) Acculturation to an ethnic minority: The language attitudes of Indian adolescents in a Hong Kong international school. In *Language in Hong Kong at Century's End*. Edited by Martha C. Pennington. Hong Kong: Hong Kong University Press, pp. 339–62.

Pennington, Martha C. (1994) *Forces Shaping a Dual Code Society: An Interpretive Review of the Literature on Language Use and Language Attitudes in Hong Kong*. Research Report no. 35. Department of English, City University of Hong Kong.

Pennington, Martha C. (1998a) *Language in Hong Kong at Century's End*. Hong Kong: Hong Kong University Press.

Pennington, Martha C. (1998b) Introduction: Perspectives on language in Hong Kong at century's end. In *Language in Hong Kong at Century's End*. Edited by Martha C. Pennington. Hong Kong: Hong Kong University Press, pp. 3–40.

Pennington, Martha C., Balla, John, Detaramani, Champa, Poon, Anita, and Tam, Frances (1992) *Language Use and Language Choice among Hong Kong Tertiary Students: A Preliminary Analysis*. Research Report no. 18. Department of English, City Polytechnic of Hong Kong.

Poon, Wai Yi (1997) An integrated study of Cantonese-English code-mixing in Hong Kong (in Chinese). Paper presented at the Annual Research Forum, Linguistic Society of Hong Kong, The University of Hong Kong, 6–7 December.

Poplack, Shana (1980) Sometimes I'll start a sentence in Spanish *y terminó en espagñol*: Towards a typology of code-switching. *Linguistics*, **18**, 581–618.

Sankoff, David and Poplack, Shana (1981) A formal grammar of code-switching. *Papers in Linguistics*, **14**, 3–46.

Scollon, Ron (1998) *Mediated Discourse as Social Interaction*. London: Longman.

Scollon, Ron, Wai-king Tsang, Li, David, Yung, Vicki and Jones, Rodney (1998) Voice, appropriation, and discourse representation in a student writing task. *Linguistics and Education*, **9**(3), 227–50.

Siegel, Jeff (1985) Koines and koineization. *Language in Society*, **14**, 357–78.

Siegel, Jeff (1993) Introduction: Controversies in the study of koines and koineization. *International Journal of the Sociology of Language*, **99**, 5–8.

Snell-Hornby, Mary (1988) *Translation Studies: An Integrated Approach*. Amsterdam: John Benjamins Publishing Company.

Weir, Fred (2000) Yeltsin's man who would be president. *South China Morning Post*, 2 January, p. 7.

Yau, Man Siu (1993) Functions of two codes in Hong Kong Chinese. *World Englishes*, **12**(1), 25–33.

Yau, Man Siu (1997) Code switching and language choice in the Hong Kong legislative council. *Journal of Multilingual and Multicultural Development*, **18**, 40–53.

Cantonese-English code-switching research in Hong Kong   99

Appendix 1

The expression *Y2K* is used in a 'Chinese' cartoon entitled 美麗新世界 (mei5 lai6 san1 sai3 gaai3, 'beautiful new world'). (*Apple Daily*, 00/01/02/E8)

Appendix 2

The expression *Y2K bug* is used in a cartoon in the English newspaper *South China Morning Post*. (*SCMP*, 00/01/02/16)

4

The English-language media in Hong Kong

Chan Yuen-ying

Introduction

The English-language news media in Hong Kong have always been minority media in circulation and audience. Normal market mechanisms do not explain why this minority of readers could wield such disproportionate influence until the mid-1980s, when Hong Kong began the transition to Chinese rule. This skewed influence is largely due to the fact that English was the only official language of Hong Kong until 1974. English was the language of the courts and government offices, and therefore the most important means for upward mobility. As Hong Kong old-timers would recall, the *South China Morning Post*, Hong Kong's leading English newspaper, was once considered a status symbol. The *Post* was the paper to be gripped while riding the bus or to be seen on one's doorstep in the morning. English conferred status and authority in a colonial setting. When every top manager in major companies read the *Post*, aspiring employees also had to follow it to track the minds of their superiors. As the official paper for placement of government recruitment advertisements, the *Post* also carried the largest number of classifieds on Saturdays.

Founded in 1903 by an Australia-born Chinese and a British journalist with funding from mostly non-Chinese business people, the *Post* was launched with the manifest goal of supporting the reform movement in China, where revolutionaries sought to overthrow the imperial Qing dynasty (Hutcheon, 1983: 11). While a detailed independent history of the *Post* still has to be written, numerous anecdotal accounts underscore the newspaper's elite status. For nearly the entire twentieth century, the *Post* represented the interests of the British government and the local Establishment. On his routine visits to Government House, the *Post* editor received official disclosures aimed at shaping public opinion. Similarly, the editor of the business section was given briefings at the Hongkong and Shanghai Bank, one of the newspaper's major shareholders. The bank's chairman was a member of the Governor's inner cabinet, the Executive Council. Bernard Fong, a writer at the *Post* from 1986 to 1992, vividly describes how, at the height of the newspaper's influence, *Post* editors dined with government officials and then returned to their offices to write editorials based on what they had heard around the dinner table. 'The *Post* sometimes appears to be the Tatler, a local glossy society magazine, writ large and an exclusive in-house newsletter of the Government', Fong wrote (1992: 12). At the time, the *Post* also was perceived to represent the interests of the rich and powerful. 'Assiduously wooed by powerful groups, companies and persons, [the editor] is privy to the very thoughts of the elite denied even to the most senior reporters' (1993).

These anecdotal reports are supported by an analysis of editorials in the *Post* and five other papers for the years 1956, 1961 and 1966 (Mitchell, 1996: 678). According to the study, the *Post* devoted more editorials to the United Kingdom than to Hong Kong and was the least critical of the colonial government among local newspapers. The *Post* 'has almost no criticism of government policies and programmes. Furthermore, this paper has been consistently non-critical over the years. It was more critical of Government in 1935–36'. Studying the editorial content of six newspapers at five-year intervals, Mitchell found that in the earlier years, 20 percent of *Post* editorials concerning government were critical, whereas only 14 percent of the comparable 1966 editorials voiced criticism. 'The paper appears to be anything but a member of the nonexistent loyal opposition to Her Majesty's Government,' Mitchell concluded.

In contrast, the study found that the other English-language newspaper, the *Tiger Standard*, later renamed *The Hong Kong Standard*, took a more critical stance towards the government. It devoted more space to local issues and gave less to news from the UK. Old-timers also recall that the *Standard* was more likely to cover both sides of a story. At times, colonial officials characterized it as 'leftist'. It was poorly managed, however, and was never able to attract much advertising from establishment companies (Henry Parwani, media consultant and ex-staffer at the *Standard*, personal communication, 2000).

In 1986, when the *Post* was acquired by Australian media tycoon Rupert Murdoch for a reported HK$2 billion, it was jointly owned by the Hongkong and Shanghai Bank (48.76%), Hutchison Whampoa (25%) and Dow Jones (18.93%). In 1992, it was sold again, this time to Malaysian business tycoon Robert Kuok. Through the years, it has remained one of the most profitable newspapers in the world even though its circulation is only about 100,000. Its only Hong Kong-based competitor, the *Hong Kong Standard*, has always remained a distant second. In the fiscal year ending 30 June 1999, the *Post* raked in nearly US$1 million in weekly profit. For the year, it netted US$50 million. Readership for a third English-language paper, the *China Daily*, owned by the Chinese government, is insignificant, judging by stacks of the paper collected at outlets such as the Seven-Eleven convenience stores.

Despite its strong financial performance, the *Post* has never succeeded in becoming a voice of Hong Kong or of Asia, speaking authoritatively to the world about the concerns of the local population. Nor, in my opinion, has it produced definitive reports or analysis of major issues on a regular basis. Situated at the crossroads of China and the larger world with a staff of bilingual writers, the *Post* is uniquely positioned to produce coverage that could compete with leading newspapers around the world. But it does not. In 1999, its performance on such stories as the NATO bombing of the Chinese Embassy in Belgrade or allegations of Chinese espionage in the United States has been less than stellar. Its story on these issues followed the lead of Western-based news agencies that reflects largely the views from Washington DC. Even after the Cox Report, a US Senate report that accuses China of stealing nuclear weapon secrets from weapon laboratories, had been roundly discredited by weapon experts and scientists, *Post* editorials continue to support the partisan positions of conservative legislators in the United States, mocking China for stealing secrets from the US.

> The problem is that the *SCMP* has for many years had all the resources necessary to become a great paper but has never shown any desire to be one. It has long been regarded as a cash cow for whoever happens to own it (HSBC, Murdoch, Kuok). The paper reinvests as little as possible in the editorial side. Kuok is an uncomfortable newspaper owner but was obviously regarded by Beijing as 'a safe pair of hands'. As for the *Standard*, it has never really summoned the will or energy to challenge the *Post*. Its many re-launches have been half-hearted and light on cash. (Jon Marsh, former managing editor of the *SCMP*, personal communication, February 2000)

In this editorial vacuum, the Chinese-language media have become Hong Kong's dominant media, setting the agenda and framing debates on major issues. The trend began in 1982, when China and the United Kingdom started negotiating Hong Kong's return to Chinese rule. Two years later came the Sino-British Declaration, which set a timetable for restoring Chinese sovereignty in 1997. Until the early 1980s, the Chinese-language papers were dominated by crime news and reports about events in mainland China. They paid scant attention to local political news. The Hong Kong population was largely apolitical, except in 1966 and 1967, when a ferry fare increase and communist activism led to street riots. The apolitical status quo was shaken in the early 1980s, when local activists demanded democratic reform and a voice in the Sino-British negotiations. Hong Kong's Chinese-language newspapers began to report intensely on the talks between London and Beijing.

Competition among the Chinese-language newspapers has since escalated as newspapers try to outshine each other with dazzling colour graphics, lurid tales and 'insider' reports.

> Little by little, line by line, the latest word on what moves Hong Kong is increasingly being found in the pages of local Chinese-language dailies. They

104   Chan Yuen-ying

have a natural edge in pulse-of-the-community reporting ... more significantly, the serious Chinese press is now breaking stories on policy changes – once the preserve of the top English daily, the South China Morning Post.
(Law Siu-lan, 1999: 40)

The circulation of English-language newspapers pales in comparison to the Chinese-language press. Hong Kong has 32 Chinese-language newspapers, 19 of which cover mainly local and overseas general news. Three focus on finance, while the others cover entertainment news, especially television and cinema news. The top-selling paper, *Oriental Daily News*, claims 31 percent of total readership of all papers. Capturing 29 percent, the *Apple Daily* is a formidable challenger. The *South China Morning Post* trails in seventh place with 5 percent, according to AC Nielsen's Media Index. Circulation figures released by newspapers show the *Post* in 8th place with only 4 percent of total readership.

Table 4.1: Daily circulation figures for newspapers in Hong Kong (December 2000)

Newspaper	Circulation
Oriental Daily News	639,400
Apple Daily	367,000
The Sun	344,337
Sing Pao Newspaper	170,000
Hong Kong Commercial Daily	150,000
Ming Pao Daily News	120,000
Hong Kong Daily News	120,000
South China Morning Post	107,129
Sing Dao Daily	105,000
Hong Kong Economic Times	*65,397
Hong Kong Economics Journal	63,120
Tin Tin Daily News	50,000
Hong Kong Standard	44,000
Total	2,345,383

(Audited figures provided by the newspapers, *for six-month period ending July, 1999)

When Jonathan Fenby, former editor of the *South China Morning Post*, stepped down at the end of his five-year contract in 1999 and suggested that his departure signalled 'part of a shift in the political wind in Hong Kong', Steve Vines, a former editor at the *Post*, quickly put it in perspective in a public rejoinder. 'Having been an editor of an English-language newspaper in Hong Kong, I can say that we come from the minority sector of the local media. Obviously newspapers written in English are more accessible to the international community, but the heartland of the Hong Kong media is and will remain in the Chinese medium' (Vines, 1999).

With the advent of the Internet and the arrival of broadband access in early 2000, the role of the *Post* as a news source is likely to further diminish. Increasingly, English readers in Asia are turning to international media and the Internet for information (Tsui, 2000). Distribution figures available for the region in February 1999 show that the highest circulating publications are international titles. Comparable rankings for circulation in Hong Kong are not available.

Of the top-selling English-language publications in the East and Southeast Asia, *Asia Inc* is the only one owned by an Asian entrepreneur, Timothy Ong of Brunei, who bought the magazine in early 2000. Until recently, two Hong Kong-based regional weeklies were owned by US-based media conglomerates – *Asiaweek* by Time-Warner and the *Far Eastern Economic Review* by Dow Jones but in November 2001, *Asiaweek* was suddenly closed by the owners, and is now no more.

Survey figures also show that the region's affluent readers regularly purchase international magazines. AC Nielsen Media International's 1999 Asian Target Markets Survey shows that affluent Asian readership of *Newsweek* increased from 276,000 in 1997 to 315,000. Affluent Asian readership of *The Economist* increased from 93,000 in 1997 to 94,000 and of *Time* from 306,000 in 1997 to 334,000 over the same period.

Table 4.2: Circulation figures for English-language periodicals in the Asia-Pacific market (February 1999)

Periodical	Circulation
Reader's Digest	1.9 million
Cosmopolitan	1.1 million
Computerworld/InfoWorld	486,565
National Geographic	479,679
PC World	423,710
Time	327,086
Newsweek Asia	240,000
Asiaweek	128,125
Far Eastern Economic Review	92,506
The Economist	79,500
Fortune	66,127
Asia Inc	61,675
The Asian Wall Street Journal	59,309
International Herald Tribune	45,818
USA Today International	17,500
Financial Times	13,912

(Source: Advertising Age International Supplement, 8 February 1999)

Radio and television

Hong Kong's English-language broadcast media plays an even more marginal role locally and internationally. Only two of seven channels offered by Radio Television Hong Kong, a publicly funded station, are broadcast in English. The two English channels offer a general format of news discussion and entertainment and a 24-hour relay of the BBC World Service. A third channel provides a mix of English and Chinese bilingual music and arts news. In the case of radio, two broadcasters provide limited English-language programming on AM and FM channels, which are otherwise dominated by music.

In commercial television during the 1990s, as the popularity of Chinese-language programming exploded and international broadcasters achieved higher local penetration, locally owned English programming declined. Until 1991, Hong Kong had only two television stations – ATV (Asia Television Limited) and TVB (Television Broadcasts Limited) – each broadcasting one channel in Cantonese and one in English. The top 10 programmes of the TVB Chinese channel command at least 75 percent of audience share, with 1.5 million viewers, according to the latest AC Nielsen survey. The two English channels are not rated, but a 1998 survey shows that 4.6 percent of 503 randomly selected households surveyed watched TVB Pearl, an English channel, while only 0.8 percent watched ATV World, the other English channel (Guo et al., 1998).

The two commercial stations are each licensed to broadcast one Cantonese and one English-language channel until 2000. During 1998, they broadcast about 600 hours of programming each week. Serialized dramas, entertainment magazines, game contests and variety specials are the most popular programmes. TVB, owner of the largest Chinese TV library in the world, is also the world's most prolific producer of Chinese-language television content.

In contrast, the audience for the two English channels, TVB Pearl and ATV World, have been limited. Under government regulations, the stations must provide these channels, but can broadcast up to 20 percent of their airtime in languages other than English and Cantonese. The government has been under pressure to lift the rule but has decided to keep the English channels intact. Original programming is limited at the channels, which have steadily increased their imported programmes. TVB's Pearl carries popular US programmes such as *NYPD Blue*, *The X-Files*, *ER*, *Friends*, *Mad About You*, *Spin City* and *When Good Pets Go Bad*. Rival ATV World airs a slate of CBS programming including *60 Minutes* and *60 Minutes II*, *The Late Show with David Letterman* and *The Wheel of Fortune*. Each broadcasts a half-hour daily national news programme produced by US networks (CBS, ABC).

Cable television is also dominated by Chinese-language and US and UK produced programmes. Hong Kong Cable Television Limited (HKCTV), launched in 1993, carries BBC World Service, CNNI, ESPN and Jet TV from

Japan. Its other services include a 24-hour Cantonese news service, and channels devoted to sports, movies, music, children's programmes, finance and horse-racing. Cable has about 450,000 subscribers, a penetration rate of only 26 percent.

Hong Kong is also the home market for Satellite Television Asian Region Ltd (STAR TV), which transmits more than 60 programming services in 8 languages on 28 channels. STAR TV, which started in 1991, claims to reach 360 million people across Asia, India and the Middle East. About 545,000 households in Hong Kong can receive regional satellite channels. The most popular are the four free-to-air channels. Star TV claims 750,000 viewing homes in Hong Kong and 44,978,766 in mainland China.

Galaxy Satellite Broadcasting Limited, another Hong Kong-based satellite TV broadcaster and a subsidiary of TVB, was started in August 1998. It offers an entertainment channel and a music channel, both broadcast in Putonghua (Mandarin) and serves countries outside Hong Kong. Video-on-demand Programme Service, the world's first commercial-scale programme of its kind, was launched in March 1998. Services include movies, entertainment shows, music videos, educational programmes and horse-racing information. Home shopping and home banking services are provided through the same network.

The international media

The Chinese language media have become more important for Hong Kong residents, yet people outside Hong Kong's Chinese-speaking community have few options but to see Hong Kong through the lenses of the international media. The limitation and parochialism of the indigenous media reinforce the outside world's dependency on Western sources for news and for analysis on Hong Kong affairs. In spite of its status as a world-class business centre, Hong Kong has to rely on the international media, especially TV, to present itself to the world. Often these mediated images are distorted and narrowly framed, reinforcing established stereotypes. In an age when people get most of their images of distant people, places and events from television, such distorted reports could have an even greater impact if delivered through television. 'Increasingly, the public gets its image of other places from television; the further the "event" from our own direct experience, the more we depend on media images for the totality of our knowledge' (Morley and Robins, 1995: 133).

Two recent examples – the 1997 Handover and the press-freedom issue – show how the international media employ narrowly framed master narratives for their Hong Kong reports.

The Handover

The 1997 Handover was a mega media event, with 8,000 journalists converging in Hong Kong. Many were 'parachute reporters', who had not spent time in Hong Kong previously, but flew in for a short period for the job. As journalists beamed live images of the Handover ceremony around the world, all eyes were directed to Hong Kong. As one study observed, however, missing from the international coverage of the Handover was 'any real attention to Hong Kong as a distinct space and identity' (Wilkins and Siegenthaler, 1997: 509):

> U.S. media analysis of Hong Kong generally reinforces, rather than questions, the dominant groups in power. Most media coverage focuses on the political tensions between the British and the [People's Republic of China] governments. Not surprisingly, in this framework U.S. journalists frame the PRC as the 'other' and openly admire the British ability to leave the territory with 'dignity'. When coverage does stray from this elite political focus, it glamorizes the economic prosperity of Hong Kong, questioning whether a change in political power will affect economic gains, a concern most relevant to the business elite.

Much of the coverage by the international media played on the theme of impending doom and danger of a communist takeover. Yet Hong Kong people were not merely helpless prawns to be devoured by authoritarian China; rather they are people with multiple identities who share cultural, economic and social ties with other Chinese on the Mainland and around the world. Most may oppose the communist system, but culturally they also strongly identify with China. Many also have vested economic interests in China.

'The Death of Hong Kong' proclaimed the cover of *Fortune* magazine (Kraar and McGowan, 1995). Other Western reports predicted the demise of freedom and democracy in Hong Kong. But few noted that Hong Kong was hardly a democratic place under British rule. For more than a century, the Governor appointed all members of the Legislative Council. Elections were introduced only in 1985, a year after China and the UK reached agreement on returning Hong Kong to Chinese sovereignty. In 1985, half of the legislature was elected. The elected proportion gradually expanded, and the council became a fully elected body in 1995, two years before the Handover.

Following rules laid down in the Basic Law, a 400-member Selection Committee nominated Tung Chee-hwa, a shipping tycoon with close ties to China's top leaders, as the first Chief Executive of the Hong Kong Special Administrative Region. While the international media characterized Tung as a candidate hand-picked by Beijing, they failed to note that before 1997 Hong Kong's Governor was appointed by the British government. The Governor held extensive executive and emergency powers, including the right to veto any legislation. The introduction of a Selection Committee for nominating the

Chief Executive under the Basic Law, while hardly a showcase for democracy, is more democratic than the procedures under the old colonial system. The Basic Law also imposes more checks and balances on the power of the Chief Executive and central government (Chen, 1989: 116–9).

Instead of placing the Handover in a historical context, the international media framed the occasion as a free and democratic Hong Kong being absorbed into an autocratic China. Mike Chinoy, CNN correspondent who has covered China for two decades, conceded that the images projected on TV are often poor reflections of reality. 'Both television and print coverage focused very heavily on China's determination to send in the troops with all the jitters that raised. There were thousands of soldiers, ramrod stiff, coming across the border. That was classic case of the image and the underlying reality not being the same' (Mike Chinoy, quoted in Knight and Nakano, 1999: 68).

Often, the international media tailor their reports for their audience. Knight and Nakano gave the example of *Newsweek*, which produced separate stories on the Handover for its Asian and American readers. The Asian edition featured a golden, upbeat cover that was titled, 'Hong Kong, The City of Survivors: What does the future hold?' Inside, stories profiled the resilience of Hong Kong people and the role of Hong Kong as a business and finance centre. In the US edition, the cover story 'China Takes Over: Can Hong Kong Survive?' focused on the threat posed by China. The words 'take over' were rarely seen or heard in Hong Kong; the public used 'Handover'. *Newsweek's* graphics also went from festive to provocative. The US edition featured a close-up of a woman blindfolded with a Chinese red flag (Knight and Nakano, 1999: 64–6).

The BBC World Service also projected China as a threat to Hong Kong. One report opened with a scene of Hong Kong from Victoria Peak, a panorama of the turf being abandoned by departing colonial administration. 'As the city stirred into life, they were preparing to welcome their new masters', droned the narrator, as though Hong Kong was heading into bondage. Here the reporter behaved as the typical outsider journalist seeing the object of his work as the 'other', to be selectively explained to his distant audience. There was no attempt to present the total situation of the people under his gaze. Instead, he hunted for what suited the taste of the reference group from where he came. It is a sample of the 'rhetoric of empire' that Spurr describes:

> The Western journalist's essential position does not change even beyond the confines of a Western preserve in Asia. The eye remains mobile and selective, constantly filtering the visible for the sign, for those gestures and objects that, when transformed into the verbal or photographic image, can alone have meaning for a Western audience by entering a familiar web of signification. The journalist is literally on the lookout for scenes that carry an already established interest for a Western audience, thus investing perception itself with the mediating power of cultural difference. (Spurr, 1993: 21)

Press freedom

The issue of press freedom in Hong Kong is another example of the narrow framing of the international media in its coverage of Hong Kong affairs. In numerous stories on the future of press freedom on Hong Kong, the international media focused on the threat to press freedom from Beijing and reported rise of self-censorship on the part of journalists. The reports evoked a Hong Kong press that has always enjoyed a blissful state of freedom, about to be put in chains at the stroke of midnight on 1 July 1997. The reports were reinforced by studies that polled journalists' perceptions that self-censorship was on the rise (Lee and Chu, 1998).

Once again, however, most reports on the Hong Kong press suffer from a 'romantic liberal ideology rooted in a deep nostalgic sentiment that Hong Kong has been enjoying press freedom' (Cheung, 1999: 2). Historically, Hong Kong had one of the most draconian media laws under British rule, though only rare crises provoked enforcement (Klein, 1997; Robertson, 1996). For example, under the Defamation Ordinance, malicious publication of a defamatory libel was a criminal offence punishable by two years' imprisonment. Under a 'General Clauses Ordinance', law enforcement officers could apply for a 'production order' at an open court to obtain journalistic materials from a reporter or a media organization (Cheung, 1999: 44–5).

The colonial government was not reluctant to use its power. In 1952, it charged three Chinese communist-backed newspapers for publishing seditious materials. The publisher and editor of one of the papers were found guilty and fined while publication of the newspaper was banned for six months. In 1967, three other pro-communist newspapers were charged and convicted of sedition and false reporting. The three newspapers were suspended for six months and their executives jailed (Klein, 1997; Lau, 1997). These convictions were clearly based on political grounds. In contrast, the 1999/2000 case against the *Apple Daily* newspaper for the alleged media bribery of police personnel is a criminal prosecution involving the corruption of government employees.

In Hong Kong, a statute to punish the publication of 'false news' was repealed only in 1988. Critics have observed that 'the freedom of press in Hong Kong is better understood as allowing the press great latitude to comment on Chinese politics, but not on the legitimacy of British rule' (Lau 1997: 159).

There is no question that self-censorship exists among Hong Kong journalists. All journalists practise self-censorship, unless he or she is financially independent. All media institutions impose control over their editorial products. Publishers and editors 'censor' stories for political and business reasons. Many stay away from hot topics that raise legitimate issues. Hong Kong journalists are no exception in this regard. Under more favourable legal protections, US TV networks recently censored stories on big tobacco companies. Rather than selectively targeting the Hong Kong press, researchers of press self-censorship would contribute to the scholarship on press freedom by using a comparative approach to examine how the practice operates under different legal and press systems.

At whatever level it exists in Hong Kong, self-censorship is not a new phenomena introduced with the Handover, and factual evidence does not convincingly prove that there has been a worsening of the problem in recent years. A fact-based comparative study would help to shed more light on this controversy. William Woo, former editor of the *St. Louis Post Dispatch*, who conducted a study of the Hong Kong media in 1998, criticized journalists for following a 'master narrative' when they write about press freedom in Hong Kong. Writing a year after the Handover, Woo found that the handful of examples of press self-censorship cited in mass media could not be verified and concluded that while there were reasons to be vigilant about the future of a free press, not much has changed since July 1999 (Woo and Shirk, 1998).

The future

As the new millennium dawns, government deregulation, technological convergence and globalization are remaking the media landscape the world over. Global media, which had a tough time cracking into the Asian market only five years ago (Vines, 1996: 131), is playing a much more dominant role in Hong Kong and Asia, forming alliances with local partners and carving up turf. They are also positioning themselves for the China market.

In early 2000, the Hong Kong government took aggressive steps to deregulate the telecommunication market, including cellular phones, fixed-line operators, Internet providers and the cable TV market. The new 'open sky' policy ended a six-year monopoly of the local cable television, unleashing a rush to the pay-TV market. By the end of the year, as many as 100 pay-TV channels could be available to viewers in Hong Kong. The digital revolution has also ushered in the convergence of the Internet, print, television, blurring the lines between traditional and new media.

Amidst the merger and acquisition frenzy, some trends of the new media order are emerging:

- The global media are developing pan-Asia English services but in East Asia, they will focus on Chinese-language services directed at the Greater China market. The influence of Hong Kong's English media will further diminish unless they reach out to forge regional alliances.
- The global media will continue to build alliances with local partners and to create more local content in Chinese. Lack of content will be the main obstacle to expansion.
- The Internet explosion has expanded the reach of the English language

and revived the region's belief in the primacy of the language, increasingly seen as a requirement for global literacy in the online world.

These trends are underscored by rapid expansion of international media organizations in the region. News Corporation, one of the top media conglomerates in the world, has been developing its Pan Asian offering through STAR TV. While most of its news programmes are 'feeds' from US-based networks, it has introduced a weekly hour-long TV news magazine named '*FocusAsia*' that feature stories about East, South and Southeast Asia. In Hong Kong, Phoenix, a Chinese-language cable television of the STAR TV group, has formed a partnership with a major telecommunications company in Hong Kong to provide 50 general entertainment, news and home shopping channels, video-on-demand and high-speed Internet access. On the Internet, News Corp has launched a Chinese-language Website called *ChinaByte* in a joint venture with the Chinese Communist Party.

Time Warner, which was taken over by AOL in the biggest media merger in the past decade, has launched *AsiaNow* (http://www.cnn.com/asianow), a multimedia Website that combines *Time*, *Asiaweek* and *CNN.com*, providing regional financial, weather, sports, entertainment and travel news as well as Web-exclusive news analysis. Meanwhile, CNN, a subsidiary of Time Warner, is offering Websites in languages other than English, including Spanish, Portuguese, Italian, Swedish, Norwegian, and Danish.

As the international media expand, they will increasingly win over viewers from local TV programmes, including the English-language TVB Pearl and ATV World. According to a 1999 Pan Asian Cross Media Survey, top picks among affluent Asian viewers are CNN International, Discovery Channel, Home Box Office and MTB Networks Asia. CNN International was the most popular cable and satellite channel among business decision makers and affluent viewers in Asia (Madden, 1999).

To expand its influence and reach, the Hong Kong English media will have to form alliances with other English media organizations in the region. Already, Asian newspapers are building alliances to boost their presence in the world scene. Nine English papers including *The Korea Herald*, *The Nation* of Thailand, and the *Philippine Daily Inquirer* have joined the Asia News Network (ANN), the first news-exchange cooperation programme among leading dailies in Asia. Network members share stories for use in each other's publications. Other members of the network include *The Jakarta Post* of Indonesia, *Vietnam News* from Vietnam, *Sin Chew Jit Poh* and *The Star* newspaper of Malaysia, *The Straits Times* of Singapore, and *The Statesman* from India. Plans are underway to set up a joint Internet website – carrying articles by ANN members – to convey reports and comments with an Asian perspective. The two Hong Kong-based newspapers are conspicuously absent, although *China Daily* has now joined the alliance.

While optimists believe that the global media will invigorate, not absorb, the local media, a rising chorus of critics have warned against the threats of globalization. 'Questions of cultural imperialism and even national sovereignty are raised with the privatization of Asian media that many countries are undertaking. These concerns are increased exponentially when there are no local players able to provide the competition ... Asians might end up in a position of being controlled by the same media conglomerates that control the US – and by individuals who do not even reside in their countries' (Zuraidah, 1999).

In response to the unprecedented expansion of global media, Asia and Hong Kong-based critics have called for a greater voice for Asians in the media (Stewart, 1999) and the training of indigenous writers and 'content producers' (Janviroj, 2000). 'Certainly, it could be argued that there are more Asian faces on CNN today than there were five years ago, but fewer Asians are serving as news producers. It is more difficult to name a single Asian journalists or syndicated columnist with international recognition and journalistic credibility...' (Shimatsu, 1999).

In Hong Kong and the rest of the region, the global economy has also revived the call for the revival of English and training in English. The paradox for Hong Kong is that while English represents Hong Kong's colonial past, it is also its global present. Hong Kong must develop and train its own journalists who can write in English on and for the global stage. Alastair Pennycook, who teaches English in Australia, argues the liberals who fought for the use of indigenous language have missed the point that indigenous people must master English so that they can 'confront the discourses that adhere to English'.

> We need alternative representations, alternative stories, alternative possibilities ... we need to work in and against English to find cultural alternatives to the cultural constructs of colonialism; we desperately need something different. But unless we can work alongside each other both to dislodge the discourses of colonialism from English and to generate counter-discourses through English, colonialism will continue to repeat itself ... (Pennycook 1998: 217)

Conclusion

This chapter is not a defence of the status quo in Hong Kong, nor of the Hong Kong Special Administrative Region (SAR) government. Rather, it seeks to deconstruct the master narrative propagated by the international media and the leading English media in Hong Kong, typical colonial discourses that often portray Hong Kong before and after the 1997 Handover in black and white terms. On 9 April 2000, the *South China Morning Post* splashed on its front page a banner headline, 'Clinton seeks progress on SAR's democracy', referring to the US president's meeting with Tung Chee-hwa, Hong Kong's Chief Executive, in the White House. The problem is that the headline was not supported in the text that followed: some editor's imagination had turned Clinton into a champion for democracy in Hong Kong. Such adulation of the US president as the champion of democracy in Hong Kong also prompts the question: where was the United States during the long years of colonial rule in Hong Kong? Where was the outcry for democracy then?

Granted, that the Chinese government does not allow a free press on its soil. It puts dissidents in jail and cracks down on free expression. It has also killed unarmed student demonstrators in the 1989 Tiananmen crackdown. It is true that Beijing's oppressive behaviour pose threats to Hong Kong's freewheeling ways. But the fact remains that by reclaiming the sovereignty of Hong Kong, the autocratic Chinese government has ironically unleashed the democratic aspirations of the Hong Kong people and ushered in a greater degree of protection for human rights and the press. As late as 1988. a United Nations Human Rights Committee meeting in Geneva found that the colonial British government had committed a litany of offences under the International Covenant on Civil and Political Rights (ICCPR), including the ban on 'teaching of matters of a political nature' in public schools, or the extraordinary power of the police to indiscriminately 'stop and search' citizens in the streets (Jayawickrama, 1989: 155–7). By 1985, even the far-flung Falkland Islands had received a constitutional instrument protecting their basic rights. Hong Kong was deprived of such protection until 1990 when China, in face of demands by the Hong Kong people, enacted a 'mini-constitution', the Basic Law for Hong Kong in preparation for its return to Chinese sovereignty.

To the Chinese government, Hong Kong has never been a colony: it was only once under British rule. Such an ahistorical stance completes the circle of pervasive denial of colonialism on the part of the governing and the governed. As the bearer of authenticated information, the news media would serve itself well by confronting Hong Kong's colonial past and beginning a genuine effort to develop post-colonial discourses, thus rendering the possibility of true representation of Hong Kong to the world.

References

Balakrishnam, N. (1993) A Proposal to Improve the Quality of the *South China Morning Post*. Unpublished manuscript.
Chen, Albert H. Y. (1989) From colony to special administrative region: Hong Kong's constitutional journey. In *The Future of the Law in Hong Kong*. Edited by Raymond Wacks. Hong Kong: Oxford University Press.
Cheung, Anne S. Y. (1999) The search for freedom of the press in Hong Kong: From misindentification to reassertion, unpublished MJS manuscript, Stanford University.
Fong, Bernard (1992) *Postscript: Inside the South China Morning Post*. Burnaby: Grapevine Press.

Guo Zhongshi et al. (1998) The Public, the Media and the 1998 Hong Kong Legislative Council Election: A Survey Report. Hong Kong: Department of Journalism, School of Communication, Hong Kong Baptist University.
Hutcheon, Robin (1983) *SCMP: The First Eighty Years*. Hong Kong: South China Morning Post.
Janviroj, Pana (2000) Thai media will need to be more responsive. *The Nation*, (Thailand) 19 January.
Jayawickrama, Nihal (1989) Protecting civil liberties. In *The Future of The Law in Hong Kong*. Edited by Raymond Wacks. Hong Kong: Oxford University Press.
Klein, Richard (1997) The empire strikes back: Britain's use of the law to suppress political dissent in Hong Kong. *Boston University International Law Journal*.
Knight, Alan and Nakano, Yoshiko (1999) *Reporting Hong Kong, Foreign Media and the Handover*. London: St. Martin's Press.
Kraar, Louis and McGowan, Joe (1995) The Death of Hong Kong. *Fortune*, **131**(12), 118–8.
Lau, C. K. (1997) *Hong Kong's Colonial Legacy*. Hong Kong: The Chinese University of Hong Kong.
Law, Siu-lan (1999) Chinese-language papers are gaining fresh clout in post-handover Hong Kong. *Asiaweek*, 8 January, 40–4.
Lee, Paul S. N. and Chu, Leonard (1998) Inherent dependence on power: The Hong Kong press in political transition. *Media, Culture & Society* **20**(1), 59–77.
Madden, Normandy (1999) Media powers in Asia take offerings to net. *Advertising Age International Supplement*. 1 December.
Mitchell, Robert Edward (1996) How Hong Kong newspapers have responded to 15 years of rapid social change. *Asia Survey*, **9**(7), 669–81.
Morley, David and Robins, Devin (1995) *Spaces of Identity, Global Media, Electronic Landscapes and Cultural Boundaries*. London: Routledge.
Pennycook, Alastair (1998) *English and the Discourses of Colonialism*. London: Routledge.
Robertson, Geoffrey (1996) The long arm of British law. *Media Studies Journal*, Fall, **10**(4), 83–7.
Shimatsu, Yoichi Clarke (1999) Can Asian Journalists think? *Newsletter*. Hong Kong: Centre of Asian Studies, The University of Hong Kong. September, **15**, 2–3.
Spurr, David (1993) *The Rhetoric of Empire: Colonial Discourse in Journalism, Travel Writing and Imperial Administration*. Durham: Duke University Press.
Stewart, Sarah (1999) Is Asia's voice being heard? *The Correspondent*. Hong Kong: The Foreign Correspondents' Club. August. 12–13.
Tsui Sio-ming (2000) Decline of the English-language media in Hong Kong (Chinese language) *Hong Kong Economic Journal*. 13 January, p. 15.
Vines, Stephen (1999) The Chinese press is real battlefield. *The Correspondent*. Hong Kong: The Foreign Correspondents' Club. September.
Vines, Stephen (1996) A very hard market. *Media Studies Journal*. Spring/Summer, 131–138.
Wilkins, Karin G., Siegenthaler, Peter D. (1997) Media and identity in Hong Kong. *Peace Review*, **9**(4), 509–14.
Woo, F. William and Shirk, Martha (1998) Hong Kong Handover: Impact on the press. A report to the International Center for Journalists. Unpublished manuscript.
Zuraidah, Ibrahim (2000) Asian Media Must Respond Aggressively or Else ... *The Straits Times*, 16 January. 35.

Part II
Language Form

5

Towards a phonology of Hong Kong English

Tony T. N. Hung

Introduction[1]

In the present chapter, I shall not concern myself with the question of whether there exists a 'variety' of English called Hong Kong English (HKE). Being a variety or dialect of English (or of any other language) involves not only phonological features but a set of lexical, syntactic and discoursal features, as well as a certain degree of indiginization, as exemplified by such well-studied 'new varieties' of English (NVEs) as Singaporean, Indian and Lankan English. I do not know enough about these other aspects of HKE to be able to make any claims about its status as a NVE. But such claims are, fortunately, not crucial to an investigation of its phonological system. I do not think there is any dispute about the existence of an identifiable HKE accent, which is just as easily recognizable as Indian, Singaporean or Australian English. The fact that native Hong Kongers speak with an identifiable accent means that they share a common underlying phonological system – regardless of whether HKE is characterized as an 'interlanguage' or a 'new variety' of English.

There has been much less published research on the phonology of HKE than on the phonologies of such NVEs as Singaporean and Indian English. Previous publications on the HKE accent were typically prescriptive, and dealt with 'common errors' in HKE pronunciation. I have nothing against teachers of English doing their jobs, but for the purposes of understanding and describing the phonological features of HKE, the prescriptive approach is not very helpful, and runs the risk of distorting or obscuring the true nature of the system (cf. Mohanan, 1992). For example, upon noticing that many HK learners pronounce the word *net* as [let], or *let* as [net], teachers often say that they 'confuse' [l] and [n]. To say that learners confuse two categories (either in phonology or syntax) is not very illuminating. Do they have two mental representations, or one? In syntax, learners who produce sentences like 'He very tall' are often said to 'confuse' adjectives with verbs. Now if they really did that, they would be inflecting the adjective *tall* with verb morphology and producing forms like *talling and *talled and so on, which they never do. But if we take the learners' grammatical system on its own terms, we will probably come to the very different conclusion that their sentence structure is based not on the notion 'subject-predicate' but on 'topic-comment'. To return to the [l]~[n] example, taking the learner's phonological system on its own terms, we may (among other possibilities) conclude that [l] and [n] are in free variation in the syllable onset in HKE, but are contrastive in other environments (see analysis below).

One of the earliest published papers on HKE which touched on its phonology was Luke and Richards (1982). The paper was mainly about the functions and status of English in HK, which the authors characterized as an 'auxiliary language' (i.e. 'a non-native language which is reserved for certain restricted functions in society and for use by a restricted section of that society'), but in the Appendix there was a brief outline of some characteristic phonological features of HKE, such as the substitution of /n/ for initial /l/, or /w/ for /v/. These observations were basically impressionistic, and many of them were over-simplifications (such as the two mentioned above), but then it was not intended to be a detailed description of HKE phonology. Pennington (1995) likewise made only incidental references to HKE phonology.

Bolton and Kwok (2000) was the first paper to attempt a broad description of the segmental and suprasegmental features of HKE phonology. It was based on an actual corpus of spoken HKE data, from which the authors made a number of important generalizations about the vowel and consonant systems of HKE. A particularly valuable feature of this paper was the use of instrumental analysis of intonation patterns. What it lacked was in-depth phonological analysis. For example, the observation was made that 'final consonants are sometimes deleted', without an analysis of the phonological conditions that tend to trigger such deletion – given that not all final consonants are equally likely to be deleted, and that the same final consonant is not equally likely to be deleted in all phonological environments.

Peng and Setter (2000) is an in-depth investigation of one particular phenomenon in HKE phonology, i.e. the simplification of consonant clusters. It was based on data from two informants reading from a substantial word list that incorporated all possible consonant clusters in English. Though the sample size was obviously too small for any valid generalizations to be made about HKE, the authors are successful in showing that there are systematic phonological rules applying in an interlanguage-speaker's phonological system, and that these rules (such as the deletion of alveolar stops in consonant clusters in specific morpho-phonemic contexts) may be unique to HKE. It was the only paper on HKE that posed any theoretical implications for interlanguage phonological systems in general, in the spirit of such earlier work as Eckman (1981).

This chapter is the first in a projected series of papers on the phonology of HKE. Describing the phonology or sound system of a language (or variety of language) involves a number of components, namely:
1. An inventory of **phonemes**, or sound segments which contrast with each other;
2. Systematic variations in the **phonetic** realizations of these phonemes, i.e. **alternation**;
3. The **distribution** of individual segments in relation to other segments.

In addition, there are higher-level or suprasegmental phenomena such as stress, rhythm and intonation. In this chapter, I shall confine myself only to the segmental phonology of HKE, in fact to the first two components listed above. As far as possible, I shall make use of instrumental data to provide objective support for my analysis, something which few previous investigators have done.

The data

The object of my study is the English spoken by educated young people who were born and raised in Hong Kong. For this purpose, I made recordings of 15 subjects from the first-year undergraduates of the Hong Kong Baptist University, of whom 8 were females and 7 males, and 6 were from the Arts and 9 from the Science Faculty. In three separate recording sessions, they read aloud from three different word lists, totalling 281 words in all. Each list was read twice by each speaker. The words were intended to capture all the vowel and consonant contrasts that potentially existed in English, in various phonological environments. As far as possible, common everyday words were chosen to minimize the effect of unfamiliarity. The words were jumbled up to ensure that similar-sounding pairs such as *heat* and *hit* or *seal* and *zeal* did not occur in juxtaposition, to minimize any preconceived notions that they were supposed to contrast. The data were transcribed by ear, as well as analysed acoustically by the Computerized Speech Lab (Model 4300B) software where necessary to confirm my subjective perceptions or reveal acoustic properties which were hard to hear.

For these recordings I chose to use word lists in preference to whole sentences because I was looking for phonemic contrasts and wanted to minimize the effect of other variables such as differences in sentence structure, word and sentence stress, intonation, stumbling over words in a sentence, and so on. And I preferred this to spontaneous speech for the obvious reason that it would be extremely cumbersome, if not impossible, to discover all the phonemic contrasts and allophonic variations in a speaker's phonological system from this sort of random data. In later stages of my research, I shall be resorting to sentences and texts to check my earlier conclusions, as well as to provide data on suprasegmental phonology.

Before I discuss my analysis of the data, I would like to point out what is well known, i.e. that there is a certain amount of variability in HKE data. There is of course variability in all speech data, including those from native varieties of English, but the degree of variability in HKE data is perhaps higher. In my analysis, I shall provide frequency counts only when I think they are essential, for I do not want to get unduly bogged down by statistics. My main interest is in the phonological phenomena themselves, not in their relative frequency of occurrence. As long as a particular phonological property is not idiosyncratic but shared by a number of HKE speakers, I have tried to incorporate it in my description. The internalized phonological system of an individual speaker of HKE is, like any interlanguage system, dynamic and evolving rather than static. We can conceptualize it as occupying some point in a continuum with an 'idealized' HKE phonology at one end and standard British or American English phonology (whichever happens to serve as that speaker's model) at the other. HKE speakers may differ among themselves with respect to which end of the continuum they are closer to, and how many features of the idealized HKE phonology they exhibit.

Vowels

Monophthongs

Previous researchers (e.g. Bolton and Kwok, 1990) have concluded, by subjective hearing alone, that HKE has a simpler vowel system than British RP (and other Old Varieties of English, or OVEs), and that certain vowel contrasts that exist in the latter are neutralized.

In the present research, I have relied on instrumental measurements as well as subjective hearing to capture the qualitative differences between vowels.[2] My spectrographic analyses of the vowels produced by the 15 subjects show that certain vowels which are distinctive in most OVEs, such as the vowels in words like *heat/heed* and *hit/hid*, are virtually indistinguishable in HKE, both perceptually and acoustically. As an illustration, Figure 5.1 shows the spectrograms for one subject's pronunciation of the words *heat* and *hit*, which show no significant differences in the formant frequencies of the two vowels.

Though there is a slight difference in vowel duration (0.131 vs. 0.108 second), that difference alone is not sufficient for the two words to be distinguished by ear, an impression confirmed by perception tests (see Figure 5.6). The formant frequencies and durations, and the formant chart, of the vowels in the key words as pronounced by this particular subject (Speaker 2) are given in Figures 5.2 and 5.3 respectively.

Towards a phonology of Hong Kong English 123

There is a remarkable degree of homogeneity among the subjects with respect to vowel contrasts. The average formant frequency readings for F1 and F2 for the 15 subjects for all the vowels in the key words, and the average formant chart, are given in Figures 5.4 and 5.5 respectively.

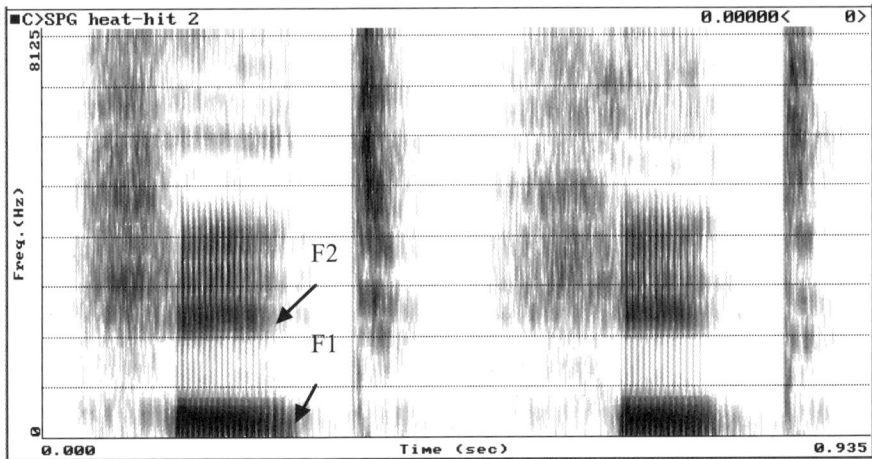

Figure 5.1 Spectrograms for *heat* and *hit* as spoken by one HKE speaker

Item	F1	F2	Duration (ms)
heed	292	2352	177
hid	285	2410	126
head	668	1863	179
had	652	1877	132
hud	695	1235	152
hard	818	1182	174
herd	524	1389	169
hawed	568	866	181
hod	460	875	176
whod	289	813	220
hood	296	935	163

Item	F1	F2	Duration (ms)
heat	351	2401	131
hit	320	2426	108
bet	629	1872	161
bat	609	1885	190
hut	813	1323	97
heart	879	1171	183
hurt	531	1414	161
caught	548	881	183
cot	557	872	141
hoot	319	950	116
hook	333	919	176

Figure 5.2 Formant frequency chart for speaker 2

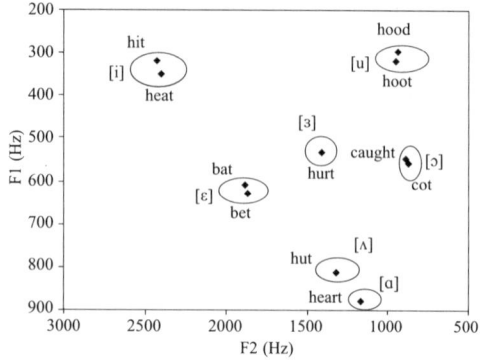

Figure 5.3 Formant chart for speaker 2

Item	F1	F2	Duration (ms)
heed	346 (72)	2572 (338)	188 (58)
hid	368 (77)	2601 (284)	138 (40)
head	668 (125)	1961 (200)	160 (23)
had	701 (105)	1941 (160)	144 (31)
hud	747 (144)	1457 (136)	99 (11)
hard	808 (132)	1289 (122)	156 (35)
herd	539 (70)	1521 (105)	173 (41)
hawed	577 (113)	944 (161)	173 (44)
hod	604 (138)	995 (140)	148 (23)
whod	372 (62)	796 (115)	224 (42)
hood	402 (82)	926 (168)	147 (28)

Item	F1	F2	Duration (ms)
heat	350 (72)	2604 (332)	134 (25)
hit	372 (75)	2557 (372)	117 (19)
bet	741 (152)	1919 (176)	169 (37)
bat	689 (114)	1959 (178)	179 (36)
hut	774 (135)	1504 (125)	91 (23)
heart	874 (175)	1334 (133)	159 (27)
hurt	569 (82)	1522 (128)	164 (29)
caught	640 (134)	1008 (161)	154 (23)
cot	609 (94)	1016 (115)	142 (26)
hoot	404 (79)	992 (126)	121 (20)
hook	485 (130)	973 (146)	109 (32)

Figure 5.4 Average formant frequencies for 15 subjects (*standard deviations are given in brackets*)

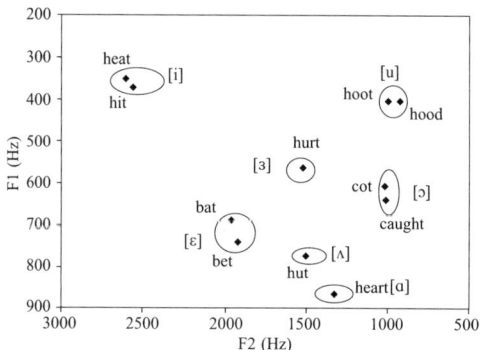

Figure 5.5 Average formant chat for 15 subjects

Towards a phonology of Hong Kong English   125

From the above data, we may conclude that HKE speakers in general operate with as few as 7 simple vowel contrasts (not counting the neutral vowel [ə]), in comparison with 11 for British RP speakers. In particular, the vowels in each pair of words given below are virtually identical for most HKE speakers, and must therefore be treated as tokens of the same vowel phoneme, rather than two distinctive phonemes as in RP and most other OVEs:

Words	HKE vowel	RP vowels
heed - hid, heat - hit	/i/	/iː/ - /ɪ/
head - had, bet - bat	/ɛ/	/e/ - /æ/
hoot - hood	/u/	/uː/ - /ʊ/
hawed - hod, caught - cot	/ɔ/	/ɔː/ - /ɒ/

One important systematic feature of the HKE vowel system is the lack of the tense/non-tense or long/short distinction, which more than anything else accounts for the smaller number of vowel contrasts in HKE.

Perception tests

To provide further support for the production data and acoustic analyses, a perception test was carried out with another group of 15 HKE subjects, who were different from the group who did the recordings. A number of key words, as pronounced by the first group of subjects, were played to the second group, and in each case they were asked to circle the word which they thought they heard, from a pair of choices (e.g. *heat/hit*). At a separate session, a different tape with the same words as pronounced by a native speaker of British RP, who distinguished all the vowels in the key words, was again played to the same group of subjects, who again circled the words which they thought they heard. The results of the test are given in Figure 5.6, which shows the percentages of correct identifications of each word as pronounced in the two different ways.

Item	HKE Speaker	Native RP Speaker	Item	HKE Speaker	Native RP Speaker
heat	60%	53%	hit	60%	67%
bet	40%	47%	bat	67%	60%
hoot	87%	73%	hood	93%	33%
cot	67%	80%	caught	73%	87%
heart	93%	87%	hut	87%	67%
hurt	100%	100%			

Figure 5.6 Perception tests results

Since it involves an 'either/or' choice, a totally random attempt to identify the words is expected to score an average of 50% on the recognition of each word. On that basis, it can be claimed that the pairs of vowels in *heat* and *hit*, and in *bet* and *bat*, cannot be distinguished by HKE subjects in general, even when they are pronounced distinctively by a native RP speaker. In the case of the vowels in *cot* and *caught*, they are close to being indistinguishable when pronounced by a HKE speaker; when pronounced distinctively by an RP speaker, they can be distinguished by the majority of the subjects. On the other hand, the vowels in *heart*, *hut* and *hurt* are distinguished more successfully by the subjects (close to or at 100%) when pronounced by a HKE speaker. The case of *hoot* and *hood* is the most interesting. The subjects were highly successful in distinguishing the two when pronounced by a HKE speaker, who exploded the [t] in *hoot* much more clearly than the (devoiced) [d] in *hood*. The RP speaker, on the other hand, did not explode either clearly, but distinguished the two vowels as [uː] (for *hoot*) and [ʊ] (for *hood*) respectively, but this was apparently not perceived by the subjects.

While the conclusions which can be drawn from these preliminary perception tests are at best tentative, there is evidence for claiming at least that the vowels in *heat* and *hit*, and *bet* and *bat*, are not perceived as different by HKE speakers in general, while those in *heart*, *hut* and *hurt* are.

Vowel system of HKE

On the basis of production data supported by acoustic evidence, the inventory of monophthongs in Figure 5.7 is postulated for HKE. One possible explanation for such a simplified (by OVE standards) vowel system is the influence of the HKE speakers' mother tongue, Cantonese, which has a much simpler vowel system than OVE's, as given in Figure 5.8. By comparison, the vowel system of British RP (which serves as a pedagogic model for English learners in Hong Kong) is much more complex (see Figure 5.9). Notice how much more 'cluttered' the vowel spaces in RP are in comparison with Cantonese, or indeed most other languages spoken in this region. It is not surprising that, in common with varieties of English spoken in Singapore, Malaysia, China and Japan (cf. Hung, 1995, 1997), HKE should have a much simpler vowel chart that utilizes vowel space in a more maximally contrastive manner. But one vowel feature that sets HKE apart from the other varieties mentioned above is the distinctiveness of [ʌ] and [ɑ]. The most probable explanation is again the influence of Cantonese, which (unlike the aforementioned learners' L1s) does have this particular contrast – as in [sʌm] 'heart' vs. [sɑm] 'three'.

Towards a phonology of Hong Kong English   127

Vowel	Examples
[i]	*heat, hit*
[ɛ]	*bet, bat*
[u]	*hoot, hood*
[ɔ]	*cot, caught*
[ɑ]	*heart*
[ʌ]	*hut*
[ɜ]	*hurt*

Figure 5.7   Inventory of HKE vowels

	Front	Central	Back
High	i, y		u
Mid	ɛ, ø		ɔ
Low		ʌ	ɑ

Figure 5.8   Cantonese Vowel Chart

	Front	Central	Back
High	i: ɪ		u: ʊ
Mid	e	ɜ: ə	o ɔ:
Low	æ	ʌ	ɒ ɑ:

Figure 5.9   RP vowel chart

Diphthongs

On the whole, the 15 subjects produced 8 diphthong contrasts. The acoustic properties of these diphthongs are given in Figures 5.10 and 5.11, which show the transitions in vowel quality which make them true diphthongs rather than monophthongs. In this respect, HKE differs from many NVEs, such as Singaporean or Indian English, which have a simpler inventory of true diphthongs.

128 Tony T. N. Hung

Item	First Element		Second Element		Whole
	F1	F2	F1	F2	Duration (ms)
hide	853 (188)	1435 (175)	446 (76)	2205 (268)	250 (53)
height	880 (190)	1577 (104)	375 (83)	2433 (361)	195 (38)
toyed	581 (82)	1013 (118)	407 (58)	2089 (307)	261 (63)
hoist	592 (97)	997 (123)	375 (77)	1994 (434)	224 (45)
loud	853 (193)	1436 (175)	491 (79)	1019 (123)	292 (48)
house	754 (126)	1272 (143)	404 (43)	912 (90)	215 (43)
bode	510 (154)	1010 (115)	352 (59)	741 (101)	275 (61)
coat	562 (105)	1068 (144)	384 (40)	787 (138)	229 (62)
paid	577 (81)	2192 (212)	357 (73)	2567 (228)	256 (46)
hate	538 (109)	2389 (164)	346 (44)	2737 (237)	228 (48)
here	348 (68)	2535 (322)	534 (73)	1792 (177)	292 (56)
hair	536 (54)	2247 (238)	639 (91)	1703 (145)	278 (44)
poor	427 (63)	915 (102)	500 (62)	1318 (78)	272 (33)

Figure 5.10 Formant frequencies for HKE diphthongs (*standard deviation is indicated in brackets*)

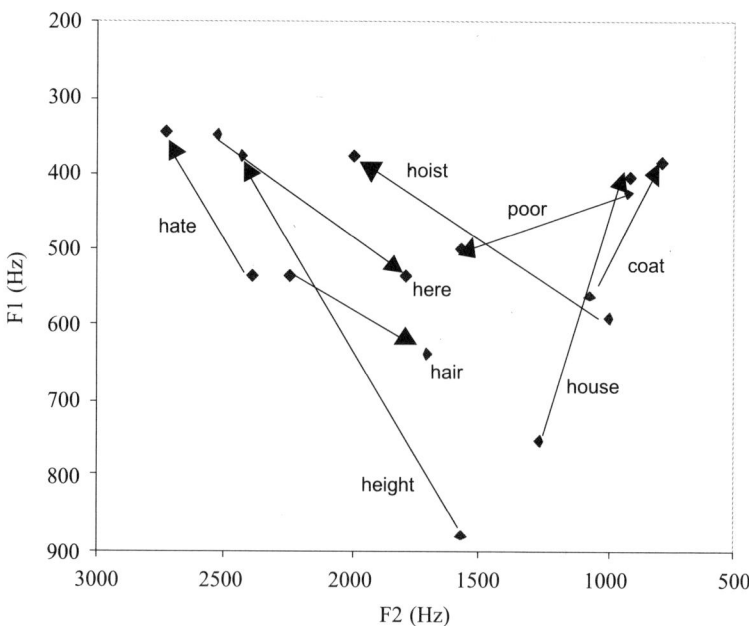

Figure 5.11 Formant chart for HKE diphthongs

Towards a phonology of Hong Kong English   129

The most interesting (and puzzling) feature of HKE diphthongs is the status of [ʌɪ] vs. [aɪ], in the following examples:

tries   [tʃwaɪs]   *twice*   [tʃwʌɪs]

Are these two diphthongs contrastive, or are they predictable allophones of the same phoneme? At first sight, the words *tries* and *twice* seem to suggest that they may be contrastive, and in a totally innovative way for English. Whereas these words are contrasted in OVEs by the voicing of the {s} suffix as well as by the [tr] vs. [tw] contrast, these contrasts do not exist in HKE, which appears to utilize a contrast in the diphthong instead, one which does not exist at the phonemic level in OVEs. This contrast is apparently influenced by Cantonese, where [ʌɪ] and [aɪ] are distinctive (as in [mʌɪ] 'rice' and [maɪ] 'buy').

To solve this puzzle, it is crucial to compare the broader distribution of [aɪ] and [ʌɪ] in HKE. My limited data include the following instances:

[aɪ]: *lie, lies, lice, try, tries, eye, eyes, wise, rise, rice, ice, size, tide, side, ride*
[ʌɪ]: *tight, site, rite, light, mice, twice*

One can draw a number of observations, but few conclusions, from the above data. In open syllables, only [aɪ] can be found. The contrast between *tide, side, ride* (all with [aɪ]) and *tight, site, rite* (all with [ʌɪ]) suggests that the voicing of the following consonant has something to do with the distribution of these two diphthongs. A similar phenomenon can be found in Canadian English, where the diphthong /aɪ/ is systematically 'raised' to [ʌɪ] when followed by a voiceless consonant, as in *right* [ɹʌɪt] and *rice* [ɹʌɪs]. However, the rest of the HKE data are not consistent with such a hypothesis, as both diphthongs can be found in similar phonological environments, as in *mice* [mʌɪs] and *rice* [ɹaɪs], where they are followed by the same voiceless consonant [s].

Further and more extensive research is needed to settle this intriguing question. Until then, I would postulate an inventory of eight (rather than nine) diphthongs for HKE, as given in Figure 5.12.

[eɪ]	hate	[ɔɪ]	toyed
[aɪ]	height	[ɪə]	here
[aʊ]	house	[ɛə]	hair
[oʊ]	coat	[ʊə]	poor

Figure 5.12   Inventory of HKE diphthongs

Consonants

Stops

My analysis of the data shows that there are six distinctive stops and two distinctive affricates in HKE, namely: /p/ *pea*, /b/ *bee*, /t/ *tie*, /d/ *die*, /k/ *cot*, /g/ *got*, /tʃ/ *cheap*, /dʒ/ *jeep*. Phonetically, the 'voiced' stops and affricate in HKE are not truly voiced, and are distinguished in the syllable onset from the 'voiceless' stops and affricate by the aspiration and greater delay in voice onset time of the latter. (Much the same is true of stops and affricates in OVEs). Since voice onset time is a matter of degree, and since the two sets of stops and affricates are just as phonologically distinctive in HKE as in OVEs, I shall continue to adopt the conventional 'voiced' vs. 'voiceless' labels for them in this chapter.

Voiced and voiceless stops and affricates in HKE maintain their contrasts in word-initial and intervocalic positions (as in *betting* and *bedding*) mainly through aspiration. In word-final position, stops are distinguished mainly by the non-release of ' voiced' stops vs. the aspirated release of voiceless stops, without any appreciable lengthening of the vowel before voiced stops.

Fricatives

The most significant feature of fricatives in HKE is that, for the great majority of speakers, there is no evidence of a voiced/voiceless contrast. For these speakers, all fricatives are voiceless, which means that instead of eight fricatives (/f/, /v/, /θ/, /ð/, /s/, /z/, /ʃ/, /ʒ/), there are only four in their consonant system. In this respect, HKE differs from Singapore and Malaysian English, where the voicing contrast exists for fricatives (though not for all four places of articulation), and from Mainland Chinese and Japanese English, where the contrasts are realized differently – e.g. in the form of a voiced alveolar affricate [dz] for /z/.

There is evidence for only one alveolar fricative, /s/, in HKE. In my data, there are no tokens of the voiced alveolar fricative [z] in any position – initial, medial or final – as shown in the examples below.

seal	[sil]	zeal	[sil]
race	[ɹeɪs]	raze	[ɹeɪs]
racing	[ɹeɪsɪŋ]	razing	[ɹeɪsɪŋ]

There are thus no grounds for postulating an underlyingly voiced alveolar fricative /z/ in the phonemic system of HKE. It would be reasonable to assume that the underlying representations for words like *zeal*, *raze*, and *razing* in HKE are /sil/, /reɪs/ and /reɪsɪŋ/ respectively.

Likewise, there is no evidence for an underlyingly voiced palato-alveolar fricative /ʒ/, as all tokens of a palato-alveolar fricative are voiceless ([ʃ]), as in:

pressure [pɹɛʃə]   *pleasure* [plɛʃə]

Contrary to popular perception, at least half of my HKE subjects did produce an interdental fricative [θ], as in:

thin [θin]   *clothing* [kloʊθɪŋ]

For these speakers, we can postulate a voiceless interdental fricative /θ/ in their consonant system. The other subjects produced [f] instead of [θ] in all environments. For those speakers, /θ/ is apparently not part of their system, and the above words would have the underlying representations /fin/ and /kloʊfɪŋ/ respectively.

For virtually all HKE speakers, however, there is no evidence of a voiced interdental fricative /ð/. Words such as the following are pronounced in HKE with a [d] in word-initial or intervocalic positions:

this [dis]   *brother* [bɹʌdə]   *clothe* [kloʊθ]

The phonetic realization of the consonant as a stop [d] in intervocalic position, as in *brother*, is particularly conclusive. If the consonant were underlyingly a fricative (/ð/), it would surely emerge as such in this of all positions, which has a tendency to 'weaken' consonants (cf. the lenition of /d/ to [ð] in Spanish in words like *nada*), and not the reverse. It is thus reasonable to claim that the voiced interdental fricative /ð/ is not part of the consonant system of most speakers of HKE, and that the underlying representations of *this* and *brother* for these speakers are /dis/ and /bɹʌdə/ respectively.

The most interesting 'fricative' in HKE from the phonological point of view is the one represented as /v/ in OVEs. Assuming that there is some such fricative in HKE in the first place, we have to account for data such as the following (stress is indicated with a vertical stroke ' preceding the stressed syllable):

vine   [waɪn]   *leave*   [lif]
advice [ɛd'waɪs]   *even*   ['ifən]
event [i'wɛnt]   *leaving* ['lifɪŋ]
revoke [ɹi'wʊk]   *rover*   ['ɹoʊfə]

The [w]-like quality of the medial consonant of *revoke* is shown in Figure 5.13 by the following spectrographic analyses of the words *revoke* and *awoke* as spoken by the same speaker, where the medial consonants are an identical [w]. The medial consonant in *revoke* can be contrasted with the medial consonant in *rover*, which is a voiceless fricative [f], as shown in Figure 5.14.

132 Tony T. N. Hung

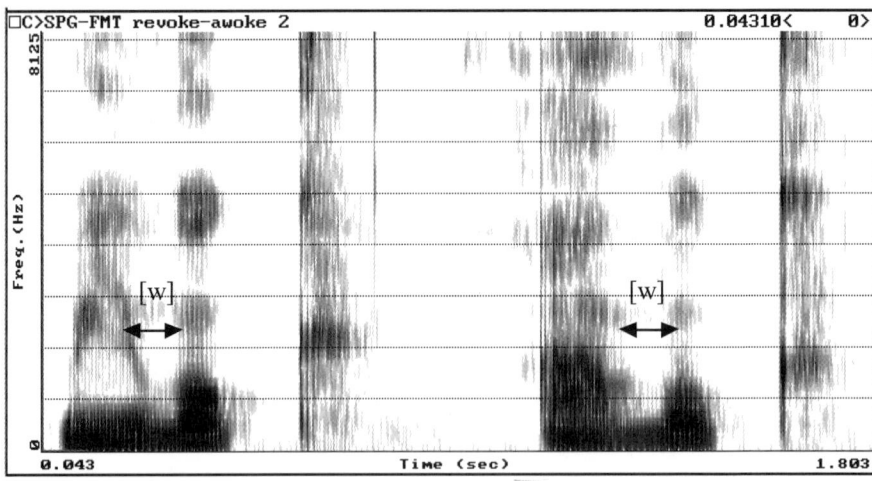

Figure 5.13 Spectrograms for *revoke* and *awoke*

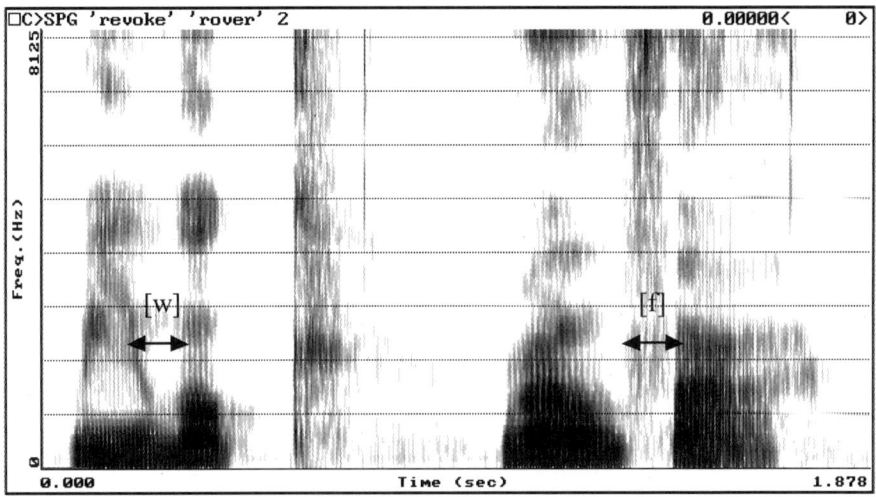

Figure 5.14 Spectrograms for *revoke* and *rover*

At first sight, there seems to be a regularity to the above data, which can be captured with the following hypothesis:

Hypothesis I: There is a phoneme /v/ in HKE, which is phonetically realized as [w] at the beginning of a stressed syllable, and as [f] at the beginning of an unstressed syllable.

While the above evidence would seem to support Hypothesis I, there is something amiss about an underlying /v/ which never surfaces as [v] in any environment. Edge (1991), for example, postulates a voiced labio-dental fricative /v/ in her Cantonese subjects' interlanguage which does not show up as [v] but only as a 'devoiced' [v̥] even in intervocalic positions. This is a dubious proposition, as one would surely expect an underlyingly voiced consonant to surface as a voiced consonant intervocalically, of all positions.

This leads us to consider an alternative hypothesis:

Hypothesis II: There is no phoneme /v/ in HKE.

Under this hypothesis, the underlying representations of the above words are much closer to their phonetic realizations and are as follows:

vine	/waɪn/	*leave*	/lif/
advice	/ɛd'waɪs/	*even*	/'ifən/
event	/i'wɛnt/	*leaving*	/'lifɪŋ/
revoke	/ri'wʊk/	*rover*	/'roʊfə/

The type of evidence that would help us decide between the two hypotheses would be words such as the following, where the 'v' consonant (whatever it is underlyingly) occurs alternately between a stressed and unstressed syllable within the same morpheme, as in '*advertise ~ ad'vertisement, 'province ~ pro'vincial,* and '*televise ~ tele'vision.* (NB: The stress pattern of *television* is based on HKE rather than RP.) The results from my subjects were as follows:

advertise	['ɛdwɜtaɪs]	*advertisement*	[ɛd'wɜtismənt]
province	['pɹoʊwins]	*provincial*	[pɹoʊ'winʃəl]
televise	['tɛliwaɪs]	*television*	[tɛli'wiʃən]

If Hypothesis I were correct, the subjects would have pronounced *advertise* as ['ɛdfɜtaɪs], and so on, but they did not. Hypothesis II is much more consistent with the facts. Under this hypothesis, the underlying representations of *advertise, province* and *televise* would be /'ɛdwɜtaɪs/, /'pɹoʊwins/ and /'tɛliwaɪs/ respectively. My conclusion is that there is no evidence for a voiced labio-dental fricative /v/ in HKE, but only for /w/ and /f/.

Other consonants

There are three nasal consonants, /m/, /n/ and /ŋ/, in HKE. Except for /n/ (see /l/ below), they are much like their counterparts in OVEs. So are the approximants /w/, /j/ and /h/ in HKE. The remaining consonants, /l/ and /r/, have certain interesting and perhaps unique phonological properties.

/l/:

In the syllable coda, /l/ is realized in HKE as a velar glide [w], not dissimilar to the 'dark' [l] in OVEs. This is illustrated in Figure 5.15, the spectrogram of one subject's pronunciation of *feel*, where a [w]-like glide clearly follows the [i].

The realization of /l/ as [w], however, takes place only when it is preceded by a [-back] vowel. The following data show that, when preceded by a [+back] vowel, /l/ is deleted in the coda:

feel	[fiw]	*feeling*	[filɪŋ]
dull	[dʌw]		
call	[kɔ]	*calling*	[kɔlɪŋ]
cool	[ku]	*cooling*	[kulɪŋ]

In *call* and *cool*, the presence of an underlying /l/ in the coda – and hence its deletion – is motivated by the fact that the same speakers pronounce *calling* and *cooling* with an [l], as [kɔlɪŋ] and [kulɪŋ] respectively rather than *[kɔɪŋ] and *[kuɪŋ]. The /l/ is not deleted because it is no longer in the coda but the onset of the next syllable.

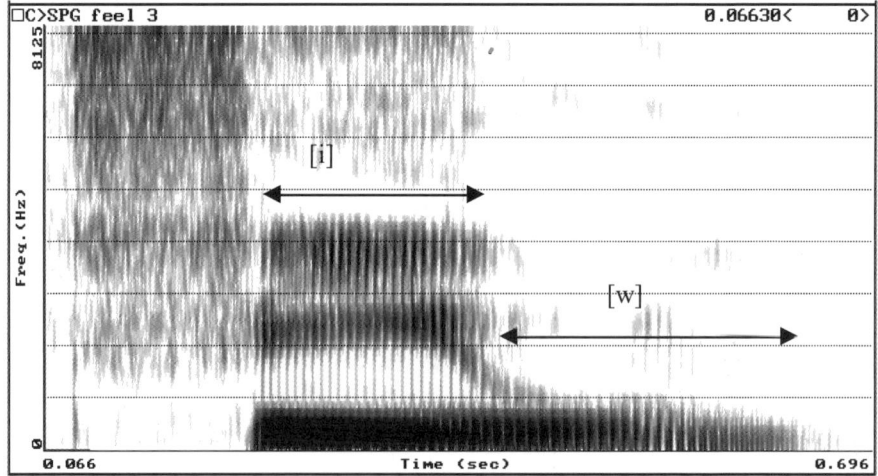

Figure 5.15 Spectrogram for *feel*

The most intriguing phonological property associated with [l] in HKE is its apparent interchangeability with [n] in the syllable onset. In the syllable coda, the two consonants are contrastive, as in *pill* [piw] vs. *pin* [pin], and therefore they have to be postulated as separate phonemes in HKE. We cannot dispense with the phoneme /l/ in the coda and postulate that the underlying representations of *feel* and *call* are /fiw/ or /kɔw/ either, because *feeling* and *calling* are realised as [filɪŋ] and [kɔlɪŋ] respectively (rather than *[fiwɪŋ] or *[kɔwɪŋ]).

The crucial position is the syllable onset, where [l] and [n] are often interchanged by HKE speakers. The question is whether the interchange happens with equal frequency both ways, and whether it is subject to any phonological conditions.

The following data elicited from my subjects show the frequency (in %) with which initial 'l' is pronounced as [n], and initial 'n' as [l], in the following 29 words, each pronounced twice by 15 subjects (a total of 30 tokens for each word).

pronounced with initial [n]		pronounced with initial [l]	
line	37%	night	33%
lame	27%	no	23%
longing	17%	naked	20%
lead	17%	number	20%
loose	17%	need	13%
loud	17%	not	10%
lower	17%	net	10%
lot	13%	now	10%
lake	13%	noose	7%
leafing	10%	nine	7%
long	10%	name	3%
low	10%		
leaf	7%		
let	7%		
leaving	7%		
light	7%		
leave	3%		
lumber	3%		

(Words with initial 'l' or 'n' showing no alternative pronunciations: 0%)

It is hard to discover any phonological patterns behind these distributions. The only thing approaching a pattern is the fact that *line* and *lame*, the two words in the 'l' list which are most frequently pronounced with initial [n], are mirrored in the 'n' list by *nine* and *name*, which are the two words least frequently pronounced with initial [l]. This suggests that the presence of a nasal in the same syllable increases the likelihood of an initial 'l' being pronounced as a nasal, just as it decreases the likelihood of an initial 'n' being pronounced as a non-nasal – some sort of 'nasal harmony' or 'nasal spreading' so to speak.[3] Apart from that, it is hard to draw any other conclusions from the above data.

Is it a case then of some HKE speakers having an underlying

representation with an /l/ for a word like *line* (i.e. /laɪn/), and others having an underlying representation with an /n/ for the same word (i.e. /naɪn/)? The crucial data turned out to be instances where the same speaker alternated between [l] and [n] within the same word in two separate readings. This happened with significant frequency, in the following cases:

>Speaker 8: 12 (*let, leaf, longing, lot, lake, lead, leafing, leaving, loose, not, light, night*)
>Speaker 14: 6 (*lot, light, long, loose, naked, need*)
>Speaker 1: 3 (*loose, loud, number*)
>Speaker 3: 2 (*line, longing*)
>Speaker 7: 1 (*number*)

The fact that the very same speaker pronouncing the same word may alternate between [l] and [n], together with the lack of any clear phonological pattern in their alternation, suggests that [l] and [n] are probably in free variation in HKE in the onset of a syllable.

/r/:

In syllable-initial position, /r/ is realized by the majority of my subjects as an alveolar approximant [ɹ], which is distinct from [w] or [l]:

>*rice* [ɹaɪs]
>*wise* [waɪs]
>*lice* [laɪs]

It is therefore legitimate to postulate /r/ as a separate phoneme from /w/ and /l/ for these speakers of HKE. For a minority of speakers, /r/ is realized as [w] in all contexts (including syllable-initial position), and for such speakers, /r/ is probably absent from their inventory of consonants.

When preceded by another consonant, however, the distinction between /r/ and /w/ is typically neutralized, both being realized as [w]. This happened with the majority of my subjects, including some who kept /r/ and /w/ distinct in syllable-initial position.

>*tries* [tʃwaɪs]   *twice* [tʃwʌɪs]
>*trim* [tʃwim]   *twin* [tʃwin]
>*crib* [kwib]   *quit* [kwit]

The spectrograms for *tries* and *twice* in Figure 5.16 show how similar the /tr/ and /tw/ clusters are, both being phonetically realized as [tʃw].

It needs to be pointed out that the phonetic realizations of /r/, /w/ and /l/ in consonant clusters are a relatively variable phenomenon (even for something as variable as HKE phonology), and more extensive investigations remain to be done. Any conclusions drawn at this stage are at best tentative.

Towards a phonology of Hong Kong English 137

The following is a summary of the phonemic contrasts that exist among the consonants in HKE, with examples:

/p/	pea	/tʃ/	cheap	/f/	fee, even	/l/	lice, pill
/b/	bee	/dʒ/	jeep	/s/	seal, zeal	/n/	nice, pin
/t/	tie			/θ/	thin, clothing	/m/	mice
/d/	die, this			/ʃ/	she, pleasure	/ŋ/	sing
/k/	cot					/r/	rice
/g/	got					/w/	wise, van
						/j/	yes
						/h/	hit

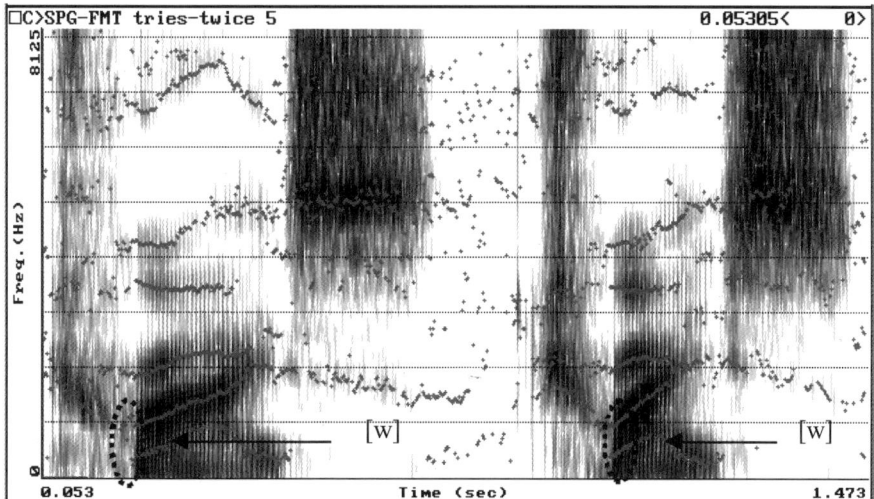

Figure 5.16 Spectrograms for *tries* and *twice*

Distribution

My research at this stage has not covered the distribution of individual segments, and syllable-structure constraints, in HKE in any systematic way. But this promises to be a fruitful area of investigation. Here, it is worth mentioning two interesting – and apparently well-motivated – distributional phenomena in HKE.

The cluster [kw], involving a velar stop followed by a labio-velar glide, does not occur before rounded vowels in HKE, but only before non-rounded vowels, as illustrated by the following:

quote	[koʊt] [kwotə]	*quit*	[kwit]
quarter	[kɔtə]	*quite*	[kwʌɪt]
	[kwɔrtə]		

The above distribution has an interesting counterpart in modern Cantonese (the speakers' L1), where, among the younger generation of speakers at least, the cluster [kw] has been simplified to [k] before rounded vowels, but maintained before non-rounded vowels, as in:

[kwɔŋ] → [kɔŋ] 'broad' vs. [kwʌi] ' 'expensive'
[kwɔk] → [kɔk] 'nation' vs. [kwai] ' 'strange'

There seems to be a constraint in HKE against syllable rimes consisting of the sequence diphthong + stop (oral or nasal), as evidenced by data such as the following:

awoke [əwʊk]   *rain* [ɹɪŋ]
line [laɪ]   *drain* [dʒwɪŋ]
loud [laʊ]   *train* [tʃwɪŋ]

The 'repair strategy' against violations of the constraint takes the form of either reducing the diphthong to a monophthong, or deleting the final stop.

The above observations (brief as they are) indicate that there is much of interest to be discovered about the distribution of segments in HKE, and some of it is likely to prove unique among accents of English.

Conclusion

At this stage of the present research, the following conclusions can be drawn:
1. There exists a ' phonology' of HKE, with systematic features of its own.
2. The phonemic inventory of HKE is considerably simpler than that of OVEs, both in its vowel and consonant systems.
3. Though HKE shows the influence of Cantonese, its phonological system cannot be reduced entirely to the phonology of either Cantonese or English, but needs to be investigated on its own terms.

The charts in Figures 5.17 and 5.18 capture, in brief, the phonemic system of HKE, based on the current stage of my research.

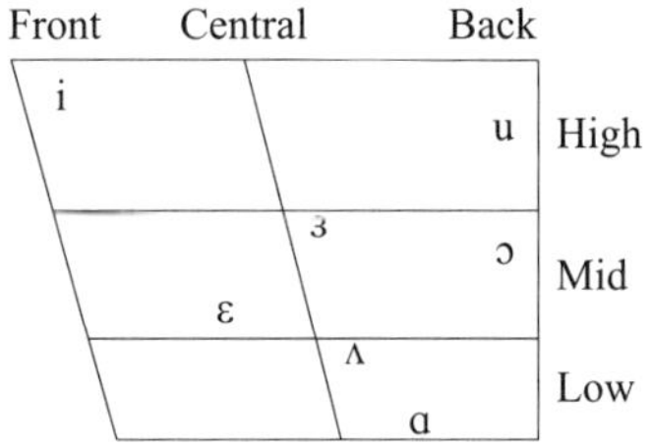

Figure 5.17 HKE vowel chart

Towards a phonology of Hong Kong English   139

	Bilabial	Labio-Dental	Inter-Dental	Alveolar	Palato-Alveolar	Palatal	Velar	Labio-Velar	Glottal
Stop	p b			t d			k g		
Affricate					tʃ dʒ				
Fricative		f	θ	s	ʃ				
Lateral Approximant				l					
Approximant				r		j		w	h
Nasal	m			n			ŋ		

Figure 5.18 HKE consonant chart

Notes

1. This chapter is based on research carried out by the author under an ERG-grant funded by the University Grants Commission (UGC) of Hong Kong. I would like to thank my research assistant, Vicky Man, for her extremely capable and resourceful support in all stages of my research, and Jean D' Souza, K.P. Mohanan, Peng Long, Lau Chunfat, and the anonymous reviewer for their valuable and insightful comments on the first draft of this chapter.

2. Just a brief word of explanation for those not familiar with acoustic phonetics. Because of the complex shape of the oral cavity in the production of each vowel, resulting from various tongue and lip positions, the air resonates at different frequencies all at once, which show up as dark bands of concentrated energy at various frequencies on a spectrogram. The lowest of these is called the First Formant or F1, the Second F2, etc. What is relevant for present purposes is that there is an inverse correlation between F1 and vowel height, namely: the higher the F1, the lower the vowel, and vice versa. There is also a correlation between F2 and vowel frontness or backness, namely, the higher the F2, the more front the vowel is, and vice versa.

   When F1 is plotted on the vertical axis of a graph, against F2 on the horizontal axis, with zero at the top right hand corner, the configuration of the vowels resembles what is found in traditional vowel charts, which are arranged according to vowel height and backness. (See for example Ladefoged, 1993: 197.)

3. Note that *lumber/number* is an apparent exception, in its greater than expected tendency for 'n' to be realized as [l] but not vice versa, perhaps because the word *number* has been borrowed into Cantonese as [lʌmba].

References

Bolton, Kingsley and Kwok, Helen (1990) The dynamics of the Hong Kong accent: Social identity and sociolinguistic description. *Journal of Asian Pacific Communication*, **1**(1), 147–72.

Eckman, Fred R. (1981) On the naturalness of interlanguage phonological rules. *Language Learning*, **31**, 195–216.
Edge, Beverly A. (1991) The production of word-final voiced obstruents in English by L1 speakers of Japanese and Cantonese. *Studies in Second Language Acquisition*, **13**, 377–93.
Hung, Tony T. N. (1995) Some aspects of the segmental phonology of Singapore English. In *The English Language in Singapore: Implications for Teaching*. Edited by S. C. Teng and M. L. Ho. Singapore Association for Applied Linguistics, pp. 29–41.
Hung, Tony T. N. (1997) The phonemic system of some Asian varieties of English. Paper presented at the Fourth International Conference on World Englishes, Singapore, 19–21 December.
Ladefoged, Peter (1993) *A Course in Phonetics*. Orlando: Harcourt Brace & Company.
Luke, Kang-kwong and Richards, Jack C. (1982) English in Hong Kong: Functions and status. *English World-wide*, **3**, 47–63.
Mohanan, K.P. (1992) Describing the phonology of non-native varieties of a language. *World Englishes*, **11**, 111–28.
Peng, Long and Setter, Jane (2000) The emergence of systematicity in the English pronunciation of two Cantonese-speaking adults. *English World-wide*, **21**(1), 81–108.
Pennington, Martha C. (1995) Language diversity in bilingualism: Preliminary speculations on varieties of Hong Kong English. *Language in Education Journal*, **1**, 1–19. Hong Kong Institute of Education.

6

Relative clauses in Hong Kong English

Nikolas Gisborne

Introduction

Kachru (1985) in an editorial statement in *World Englishes* discusses a range of factors that are relevant to the identification of world Englishes, and to identifying them as a research domain.[1] He identifies various functional and formal elements in the discussion of varieties of English. This chapter is primarily concerned with the formal properties of Hong Kong English, in particular the syntax of relative clauses. Trudgill and Hannah (1994) identify a range of formal elements at the levels of syntax and phonology which are relevant as criteria for establishing the identity of a distinct variety of English and this chapter is an essay within that tradition. Bolton and Kwok (1990) and Hung (see Chapter 5) focus on elements of the sound-system of Hong Kong English. Bolton (see Chapter 1) identifies a number of other elements in the sociolinguistics of Hong Kong English which are relevant to the identification of Hong Kong English as an independent variety. There are, however, very few materials on the syntax of Hong Kong English – those that exist are reviewed in the work that follows. None of the work on the syntax of Hong Kong English is concerned with it as a variety.

Below, I discuss work by Newbrook (1998), which is concerned with relative clauses as a variable in international varieties of English. Newbrook discusses Hong Kong English data among data drawn from native-speaker varieties of English as well as Singaporean English, whereas Yip and Matthews (1991) are concerned with Hong Kong English as an 'interlanguage' system. They discuss a number of syntactic phenomena which are shown to be typical of Chinese second-language learners of English.

From the syntactic point of view, whether Hong Kong English constitutes an independent variety or not involves a consideration of the following factors:

- whether it includes syntactic patterns or constructions that are not present in either standard English (British or American);[2]

- whether such patterns are systematic and regular;
- whether such patterns are independent of the patterns that emerge in learner English of Cantonese home speakers acquiring L2 English in Guangdong province (and elsewhere in Cantonese-speaking China).

Patterns of the kind described in the last criterion are something I only have anecdotal evidence for (Stephen Matthews, personal communication), which suggests that the constructions under discussion which are found in Hong Kong English are not found in the English of L2 speakers in China, whose English more closely matches the normative native-speaker variety.[3] There is evidence that Hong Kong English has syntactic constructions that are not found in native-speaker varieties of English and which are often found in contact languages.

The discussion that follows assumes that several of the phenomena of relative clause formation in Hong Kong English can be explained with reference to the Cantonese influence on Hong Kong English, as well as observing certain patterns that are generally found in contact varieties. While I acknowledge the force of Mohanan's (1992) argument that varieties of English need and deserve to be described in terms of their own systematic regularities, it becomes clear that without a full database and the concomitant opportunity to write a full grammar of Hong Kong English, the description of Hong Kong English requires some reference to both native-speaker varieties and Cantonese. The task of describing the syntax of Hong Kong English requires the opportunity of quantitative work which will be provided by the research tool of the Hong Kong database for the International Corpus of English (ICE-HK).[4]

One crucial area which will require close attention is the matter of register variation. Matthews and Yip (2000) establish that contemporary Hong Kong Cantonese has a stratified grammar, each stratum of which has its own internal structure; and the strata may not be mixed in a single utterance. While this is possibly rare in a non-contact language, it is the norm for contact languages, as work on post-creole continua such as that reported in Sebba (1997: 203–34) shows. Given that Hong Kong English shows some of the features of a contact variety, and that a grammar stratified by register is the norm within the daily linguistic experience of Hong Kong people, I would expect that Hong Kong English too would show internal grammatical variation, stratified by style – and perhaps by class, especially if it is an independent variety of English.

The constructions that I am concerned with are relative clauses and morphosyntactic mismatches such as those in the passive (with active participle) *I am boring*. I take these in turn. I also make one or two observations on this issue of what this kind of variation data means for theories of grammar. Much of what follows is a report on the work of other scholars, but I present data from the ICE-HK, and there has been no earlier work which has brought together all of the phenomena of relative clauses in this way.

Relative clauses

Relative clauses are a widely studied sociolinguistic variable because there are a number of elements which can vary in their behaviour. I present a typology from native-speaker varieties below. In (1–3), we can see a range of relative clause types, which can be classified by relative marker. The relative marker is italicized in these examples.

(1) I know the man *who* Jane married.
(2) I know the man *that* Jane married.
(3) I know the man *0* Jane married.

In examples in (1–3), the relative clause is introduced by WHO, THAT or 'zero', with the WH-relative clause as the most formal, and the 'zero' relative clause as the least formal. There is another dimension by which relative clauses can be classified presented in (4–7).

(4) I know the house *which* belonged to her.
(5) I know the house *which* she liked.
(6) I know the house *which* she lived in.
(7) I know the house *which* she liked the style of.

In (4), *which* is the subject of *belonged* – this is a subject relative; in (5), *which* is the object of *liked* – this is an object relative; in (6), *which* is the complement of *in* – this is an oblique relative; and in (7), *which* is the complement of *of* – Yip and Matthews (1991) call this a genitive relative. Further grammatical issues concern the word class of relative pronouns which can replace nouns, pronouns, determiners, and adverbial elements (preposition phrases and adverbs).

The two dimensions, formality and the grammatical function that the relative marker plays in the relative clause, interact. Therefore, both WH-relatives and THAT-relatives can perform all of the grammatical functions in the relative clause; and 'zero'-relatives can be object, oblique and genitive relatives, but they cannot be subject relatives except in existential contexts like (8):[5]

(8) There's the man *0* killed the dog.

In example (8), the subject of *killed* is 'zero'. There is a further grammatical dimension – the distinction between restrictive and non-restrictive relative clauses. This dimension also interacts with the choice of relative marker so that, for example, in standard British English a THAT-relative may not be non-restrictive.[6]

Both of these two dimensions of relative clauses are relevant in the study of variation. For example, Romaine (1982) discusses the formality variation in choice of relative marker. Newbrook's (1998) investigation of the features of variation in relative clauses in new varieties of English focuses on the dimension of grammatical variation. In what follows, I present the major features of variation in relative clauses in Hong Kong English. The discussion in part follows Newbrook's presentation, with additional data drawn from other sources.

'Zero'-subject relatives

In Hong Kong English, Newbrook identifies 'zero' subject relatives of the kind in example (9).[7]

(9) This is the student did it.[N, 8]

He claims (1998: 47) that this is 'virtually categorical' with 100% occurrence and that Hong Kong students are surprised to learn that it is non-standard or unacceptable in formal writing.[9] Newbrook asserts that 'zero'-subject relatives of this kind are less frequent in Singaporean English than they are in Hong Kong English, but he claims (p. 47) '[f]irst language interference would generate similar patters in the two cities and the much greater proficiency in English of most Singaporeans does not by itself seem to account for the disparity.' Other scholars also find 'zero'-subject relatives in Hong Kong English. Webster et al. (1987) give the examples in (10) and (11), which they in turn take from Chan (1970).

(10) Hong Kong is a small island has a large population.
(11) There was a fire broke out.[10]

The issue of 'zero' subject relatives in this discussion raises three questions:

- What is their frequency in native varieties of English?
- Are there similar features in Singapore English and how does Singapore English vary from Hong Kong English?
- Are there commonalities in the grammar of all of these examples which might suggest that the Hong Kong English variant simply displays an overgeneralization of a common pattern?

The first issue is discussed in various works by Newbrook (1998). He has established that examples like (9) are to be found in native-speaker varieties in both Australia and England. Therefore, this construction is not necessarily a contact phenomenon: it is also a native-speaker variant. Given that it does exist in native-speaker varieties, it possibly has the status of a marker or variable in the Labovian sense in Hong Kong English, rather than constituting a grammatical feature which is indicative of a particular (dialect or regional) variety. Whether patterns like (10) constitute further generalizations of the example in (9), or whether they constitute a particular contact phenomenon of Hong Kong English, is something which follows from a consideration of the second and third points above.

To tackle the second issue we can draw a comparison with Singapore English. Alsagoff and Ho (1998; 129, ex. 3b) identify a structure in Singapore English given in (12).

(12) That boy **pinch my mother one** very naughty.

In this example, there is no relative marker found at the beginning of the relative clause, and the relative marker discussed by Alsagoff and Ho is not a WH-word or THAT. However, they found good evidence to treat *one* in the example in (12) as a relative pronoun (pp. 133–6), which occurs clause-finally like relative markers in Cantonese, Hokkien, and Mandarin. Where the example in (12) differs from the Chinese examples is in the relative ordering of the relative clause and the nominal head. In Chinese, as in the examples in (13)–(15) (taken from Alsagoff and Ho (1998: 129; exx. 5–7)), although the relative pronoun is clause final the relative head then follows the relative clause in turn. I have marked off the relative clause in bold, and the head nominal is underlined.

(13) **Nie wode mama de** neige nanhaizi hen huadin[11]
pinch my mother RP that child very naughty
'That boy who pinched my mother is very naughty'

(14) **Ngiap wa-e lauba e** hi-le tabo gina jin pai[12]
pinch my mother RP that boy child very naughty
'That boy who pinched my mother is very naughty'

(15) **Mit ngo mama ge** go-go namzai ho kuai[13]
pinch my mother RP that boy very naughty
'That boy who pinched my mother is very naughty'

In each of the cases in (13)–(15), we can see that the relative clause precedes the modified noun phrase, and that the relative pronoun and the head noun are adjacent. What happens in the Singaporean examples is that the general pattern of the Chinese relative clause, with the relative marker clause final, is preserved, whereas the relative ordering of modified head and relative clause keeps to the usual English pattern. Alsagoff and Ho argue that ONE is pronominal in Singapore English, and that it functions like DE in Mandarin, in those contexts where DE is pronominal, but that it does not pattern after DE in those contexts where DE is not pronominal. The conclusion is important because it shows a particular kind of substrate influence, which is conditioned by a regulating effect of the superstrate grammar.

The Singapore English variety, then, shows a juxtaposition between the head nominal and the verb in the relative clause, which is a pattern very similar to 'zero' subject relatives. But it isn't a 'zero' subject relative because there is a relative marker in this example – *one*. Where Singapore English differs from Hong Kong English is in the grammaticalization of a particular relative pronoun, whose position internally in the relative clause is patterned on substrate models. (Alsagoff and Ho give a Malay substrate example which has the same structure as the native-variety English examples; this clearly does not particularly affect this feature of relative clauses in Singapore English.) Such an account assumes that Singapore English has creole-like features. In fact, Alsagoff and Ho's paper would support an analysis of Singapore English as creole-like because you see a substratal grammatical pattern (clause-final relative marker) instantiated by a superstrate lexical item (which has been grammatically reanalysed).

The third issue concerned the structure of the examples in (9) and (10). We can note that the example in (9) is similar in structure to the existential example in (8): instead of an existential THERE, the example is introduced by a deictic – *this* – which in turn allows the head noun to be definite rather than indefinite. Both constructions share the fact that the 'zero'-subject relative is modifying a predicative noun. With the exception of the classification of the word that introduces the construction, and the definiteness of the head noun phrase, this example has the same structure as example (8): the relative clause is dependent on a head noun which is the complement in the higher clause.

The Hong Kong English example in (10) arguably has a similar structure because of the equative BE structure *Hong Kong is a small island*. It could be argued that both existential THERE and the word *this* in (9) serve a kind of topicalizing function which helps to disambiguate a structure which is otherwise likely to cause processing difficulties. When the head noun is the complement of BE, irrespective of whether the subject of BE is existential, deictic or a fully referential noun phrase, the processing difficulty that Newbrook (1998: 47) identifies as a reason for dispreferring these examples no longer obtains. However, if such an argument holds, it should be possible to see 'zero' subject relatives whose head nominal is an object in the higher clause, and I have found no such examples in Hong Kong English.[14]

Reduced relatives with a relative marker

Another pattern Newbrook (1998: 47) identifies as occurring in Hong Kong English, and as largely confined to Hong Kong English, is shown in (16).

(16) This is the student **who admitted last year**.[N, 15]

Newbrook (1998: 48) claims that this is a reduced relative construction, which has a redundant subject relative pronoun added. If it were a standard reduced relative construction it would be like the example in (17).

(17) This is <u>the student</u> **admitted last year**.[N]

In reduced relative clauses, participles may serve as an adjunct of the verb, and there is no need for either the relative pronoun or for the verb BE. They pattern like postpositive adjectives like *keen* in (18).

(18) <u>A student</u> **keen on linguistics** came to my office.

As in the examples in (16) and (17), I have underlined the head nominal and put the modifying phrase in bold typeface. One reason why reduced relatives pattern like this is that participles have the same distributions as adjectives in English – among other things they can occur attributively as in *the setting sun*. For that reason I generally prefer the term participial relative for reduced relatives. The term 'reduced relative clause' is often used because they can usually be reconstructed so that they are in a clear variation with regular relative clauses. If (16) were a full tensed relative, you would expect *this is the student who was admitted last year*.

Examples like these can be construed in two different ways. One is that they are really evidence for the nature of the morphosyntactic feature system of Hong Kong English. Newbrook claims that such examples come about because of the ease of confusing tensed forms and participle forms in English and, as we shall see below, there are several areas where the morphosyntax of Hong Kong English shows fewer distinctions than native-speaker varieties. We shall also see that there are several suppletions in Hong Kong English which may be responsible for situations like this. The alternative possibility is that the use of relative markers in reduced relative clauses in Hong Kong English follows from a general lack of postpositive modification in Hong Kong English.

The lack of postpositive modification is found in Cantonese. Matthews and Yip (1994: 158) state that attributive adjectives 'always precede the noun' in Cantonese. It is also the case that adjectives very rarely follow nouns in the English noun phrase, so what we could be seeing here is a convergence of typological features in both Cantonese and English where both languages have a preference for Adj + N patterns, and so the unusual N + Adj or N + participle pattern is disallowed, resulting in relative clause marking even in participial relatives. This is just a speculation, however. It is necessary to determine what patterns of postpositive modification are permitted in Hong Kong English, and it is also necessary to establish the nature of its morphosyntactic system before clear explanations for this pattern can be ventured. Both tasks require the completion of the Hong Kong corpus of English.

Where with abstract head nouns

Newbrook (1998) identifies the use of where with abstract head nominals as a particular feature of Hong Kong English. The example in (19) presents a case of a relative with WHERE.

    (19) This is a basis where we can go on.[N]

Newbrook identifies (19) as typical of Hong Kong, with a standard variant being *this is a basis from which we can go on*. Newbrook also finds WHERE for *in which* as in (20). Newbrook does not attempt to provide an explanation for this distribution. We can see, however, that what has happened is that the sense of WHERE has been extended. Typically, WHERE is a locative prepositional phrase but what has happened in this example is that WHERE has replaced a directional prepositional phrase. It is common enough in language change for locative expressions to acquire directional senses by regular processes that give rise to polysemy.[16] The syntax is the same as in any other instance of where substituting for a preposition + WH-word structure, but the meaning is different. Newbrook presents two further examples, given here in (20) and (21).

    (20) This is a theory where transformations are used.[N]
    (21) This is a theory in which transformations are used.[N]

According to Newbrook, (21) is preferred in standard varieties, although (20) is typical of Hong Kong English. I confess that of the two variants I have no preference for (21). Neither of these examples involves a directional sense of *where* even though they both involve relative clauses modifying abstract nouns. Newbrook does acknowledge that this variant is found in mainstream varieties.

WH-words and prepositions

Newbrook identifies as typical of Hong Kong English examples like those in (22) and (23). In native-speaker varieties, these examples would include a preposition either stranded at the end of the clause or moved with WHICH to the beginning of the clause.

    (22) That was the accident which/that she was hurt.[N]
    (23) There are some words which/that there are no equivalents.[N]

In the example in (22), a more typical statement might be *that she was hurt in*. For the example in (23), either *for which there are no equivalents* or *which/that there are no equivalents for* would be more typically expected. Yip and Matthews (1991) also identify examples of this kind. The grammar of preposition stranding and pied-piping is particularly complicated in English. Pied-piping as in (24) involves the WH-features of the WH-word percolating up to the whole of the preposition phrase so that the whole phrase can have the distribution of the WH-word.[17]

(24) I bought the book in which I found the answer.

In (24), *in which* has the clause-initial distribution of a WH-word, although the preposition *in* would typically occur after the object NP if the subordinate clause were a main clause as in *I found the answer in the book*. The grammar of English differs substantially from the grammar of Cantonese in this respect. There are two ways of marking relative clauses, neither of which involves the 'movement' of a relative marker from a particular grammatical position within the relative clause (Killingley, 1993; Matthews and Yip, 1994; Matthews and Yip, 2000). They are given in (25) and (26) (both examples from Matthews and Yip, in press). The first kind of relative clause is the classifier relative. The second kind, (26), is a relative with GE (see also (15) above).

(25) **Keoi coeng** go sau go.
s/he sing that CL song
'the song she sings'

(26) **Keoi coeng ge** go.
S/he sing PRT song
'the song she sings'

I have given the relative clause in bold; the head noun is underlined. I am unsure about the status of *go* in (25), so I have not marked it for inclusion as part of either the head noun or the relative clause.[18] What is crucial for the discussion about prepositions is that although in the classifier relative the classifier and noun have to be assumed to be in a grammatical relationship within the subordinate clause as well as the main clause (perhaps mediated in (25) by *go*); and in the GE relative, GE functions in the subordinate clause much as THAT does in English, when there is a relationship in the relative clause mediated by a preposition, Cantonese has a resumptive pronoun strategy. That is – assuming a movement metaphor for structures like *the place in which she left her chequebook* – not only can prepositions not move in Cantonese but also the preposition's complement position must be filled by a resumptive pronoun as in (27) (example from Matthews and Yip, 1994).

(27) **ngoh sung fa bei keuihdeih ge** behngyahn
I send flower to them that patients
'the patients I sent flowers to'

Again, the head noun is underlined and the relative clause is given in bold. In (27), *keuideih* is the resumptive pronoun. Matthews and Yip (1994: 110) note that resumptive pronouns are also possible in object relatives. In addition to the examples in (19) and (20) in which prepositions are 'omitted', there are further examples of the omission of prepositions in Hong Kong English in (28)–(30), and an example of the double marking of a preposition in (31).

(28) There are also cases that boys are naughty and they pretend to be good.[Y]
(29) It is really a controversial issue that no one can find a definite answer.[Y]
(30) They think that language is another aspect that inferiority and inequality are shown.[M]
(31) Language activity is the basis on which social cohesion is to be consolidated on.[Y]

This phenomenon is related to the next phenomenon discussed, resumptive pronouns. Matthews and Yip provide an account of these phenomena which I discuss in the next section.

Resumptive pronouns

Yip and Matthews find examples of resumptive pronouns in Hong Kong English, as in (32)–(34) (1991: 117). Newbrook does not mention examples of this kind. Yip and Matthews are less concerned with establishing the particular features of Hong Kong English than they are with identifying elements which appear to be 'universal features of interlanguage' (p. 117).

(32) 'Go in for' is a phrasal verb **which the meaning of it** is very different from the literal meaning.[Y]
(33) There are thousands of crimes **of which** think and sex are two **of them**.[Y,19]
(34) They wanted to build a tower **which its top** can reach the heaven.[Y]

Yip and Matthews state that the only clear cases of resumptive pronouns in relative clauses they found involved genitive relatives of the kind found in (32–34). However, Stephen Matthews has also collected the following examples of resumptive pronouns in Hong Kong English.

(35) Spoken languages are produced by those vocal organs **that some of them cannot be seen**.[M]
(36) 'Whitewash', 'springclean', 'sunbathe', etc. are all compound verbs **which its part is not totally relevant to the meaning**.[M]
(37) Sign language is the combination of some compounds in a spatial dimension **which it occurs simultaneously** while spoken language is the linear sequence of sounds.[M]

(38) When we see a new chair at home **that we never see it before**, we can still form the concept of chair.[M]

The example in (35) is a further case of a resumptive pronoun used in a genitive example (we could recast this as *some of which cannot be seen* or *which some of cannot be seen*). But the example in (37) is a clear case of a resumptive pronoun as subject. To the extent that Cantonese does not allow subject resumptive pronouns, this example argues against a straightforward transfer account.

We have seen in the previous section that Cantonese uses resumptive pronouns always when there is a case of 'extraction' from a prepositional phrase and often in the case of object relatives. Yip and Matthews (1991) note that Hong Kong speakers of English often avoid relative clauses, which is a typical learner strategy in acquiring a language but also they note both preposition avoidance – the phenomenon we noted above – and resumptive pronouns are 'universal features of interlanguage' (p. 117) which can even be found when native speakers of English try to acquire other languages. Yip and Matthews adopt Keenan and Comrie's (1977) Noun Phrase (NP) Accessibility Hierarchy. The NP Hierarchy claims that subjects are more 'accessible' to relative formation than direct objects, which are more accessible than indirect objects, which in turn are more accessible than obliques. Matthews and Yip hypothesize that resumptive pronouns help in the grammatical processing of relative clauses, especially those which involve grammatical functions lower down the hierarchy. They provide a plausible account of the resumptive pronoun strategy found in Hong Kong English, but it does not explain the phenomena in the section above where prepositions in pied-piping and stranding environments are omitted.

Blurring of the restrictive/non-restrictive contrast

The final variant that Newbrook finds typical of Hong Kong English is given in (39).

(39) Hong Kong that is now a colony will soon change its status.[N]

n this example, the distinction between restrictive and non-restrictive relative is made unclear. Although proper nouns are not amenable to restrictive modification, this example has a relative marker that is typically only used in restrictive relatives; furthermore this example does not come with the phonological features which mark off non-restrictive relatives. Newbrook says that there is extensive use of non-restrictive THAT in Hong Kong English, but he also asserts that 'Hong Kong English is simply not as systematic, more generally, as more "nativized" varieties' (1998: 53).

I am not too exercised by this. It seems to me that in naturally occurring discourse the restrictive/non-restrictive contrast is apt to be blurred, even by native speakers. What is more, Cantonese scarcely makes a distinction between restrictive and non-restrictive relative clauses (Matthews and Yip, 1994: 110). I would expect that with variable judgements about native-speaker English, and no model of the restrictive/non-restrictive contrast in Cantonese, there simply is no restrictive/non-restrictive contrast in Hong Kong English.

Indeterminate or ambiguous structures

Webster et al. (1987) identify certain structures which are ambiguous between the categories above. For example, one of their citations is to cases like (40).

(40) I saw a big car only carried one person.

This is ambiguous between two possibilities: either this is a 'zero'-subject relative, of the kind described above, or it is a reduced relative clause, and *carried* is an active participle, with aberrant morphological marking of the active participle. This second possibility will be discussed further below. The example in (41), also from Webster et al., is a possible calque on Cantonese.

(41) The **unknown named** man (= 'the man whose name was unknown').

In this example, the relative clause precedes its head, and there is no relative marker. Furthermore, it shows a morphosyntactic confusion: *named* can hardly be assigned word class or morphosyntactic features on the basis of its form. But (40) could just as well not involve a relative clause.

Discussion of relative clauses in Hong Kong English

The main features of Hong Kong relative clauses that we have seen are:

1. 'Zero'-subject relatives
2. Participial relatives with a relative marker
3. Where-relatives with a directional sense as well as a locative sense
4. The omission of prepositions
5. Resumptive pronouns
6. The absence of the restrictive/non-restrictive contrast

Of these, (2) and (3) appear to be unique to Hong Kong English; (4) and (5) also occur in learner-varieties of other languages and are common second-language acquisition phenomena; and (1) and (6) appear to be extensions of phenomena which are found in other varieties of English, including native-speaker varieties.

I think that it is unsurprising that learner-variety, or interlanguage, phenomena should be found in Hong Kong English. English is not typically an acquired language in Hong Kong, it is a learnt one, and according to the 1996 census 88.7% of the population speak Cantonese as a usual language.[20] Only 3.1% of the population speak English as a usual language, and this must include a substantial 'expatriate' population (although expatriates do not make up all of the 184, 308 speakers of English in Hong Kong). As far as establishing the status of Hong Kong English as a variety, it would be interesting to establish whether the interlanguage phenomena that Yip and Matthews (1991) identify in Hong Kong English are also found in other Asian Englishes, such as Singapore or Malaysian English.

It is surprising for variables in native varieties to appear as variables in Hong Kong English. However, it is interesting that these phenomena are more widespread in Hong Kong English than in native varieties, which is probably due to Cantonese influence. I would hypothesize that with respect to 'zero' subject relatives and the restrictive/non-restrictive contrast Hong Kong English has established its own norms. But this hypothesis requires empirical research.

This leaves phenomena (2) and (3). Semantic change, the phenomenon found in (2), is rapid, common, and often found in cases where there is the possibility of polysemous inference. It is possible, just from the general principles of semantic change (McMahon, 1994: 174–99) to explain why WHERE should develop a directional sense (recall that I found the use of WHERE to modify abstract nouns unremarkable). This leaves, then, as a property unique to Hong Kong English which requires more investigation, the use of participial relatives with relative markers. This discussion requires a discussion of the morphosyntactic feature system of Hong Kong English, which leads us to the next section.

Morphosyntax

In varieties where there is an apparent morphosyntactic levelling, there is the possibility that it is due to phonological processes, rather than strictly morphosyntactic processes, as there is in new varieties and interlanguage varieties a tendency to reduce word-final elements. In Hong Kong English, this tendency becomes even more marked, as Cantonese does not permit syllable clusters of the kinds that are found in native varieties of English. However, there is evidence of both a reduction in the morphosyntactic distinctions made in Hong Kong English and of suppletion in those categories where there are morphosyntactic distinctions being made.

In a comparative discussion of Faroese and Norwegian, Trudgill (1983: 104) observes that 'we would expect high-contact, innovative varieties of language to have undergone more "non-natural" changes'. He notes that Faroese preserves more morphosyntactic feature categories than Norwegian does, and hypothesizes that this is due to the fact that the Faroes have been relatively free of language contact situations, whereas Norway has been far more open to contact. We should expect to see levelling in the morphosyntactic feature system of Hong Kong English.

Native varieties of English make the distinctions in the morphosyntax of the English verb shown in Table 6.1. One clear fact that emerges from Table 6.1 is that native varieties of English have a large number of suppletive forms. If we take a regular verb like KISS, we can see that it only has four forms: *kiss, kisses, kissed* and *kissing*. These four forms correspond to seven different morphosyntactic contrasts, and only one of them – *kissing* – displays one-to-one correspondence with a feature-value. However, the *ing* form of verbs is also used in the English gerund, so it too displays a certain degree of ambiguity even if that ambiguity is not strictly in the morphosyntactic feature system of English. In Table 6.1, features 1–3 are finite and features 4–7 are non-finite.

Table 6.1 The morphosyntactic feature system of native varieties of English[21]

Feature name	Form	Use	Example
1. **Imperative**	+ 'zero'	independent	Drive carefully!
2. **Past**	+ ED	either	I walked/drove
3. **Present**	+ 'zero' or +S	either	I walk/drive
			She walks/drives
4. **Infinitive**	+ 'zero'	dependent	She will walk
5. **Active participle**	+ ING	dependent	He was walking
6. **Perfect participle**	+ ED or +EN	dependent	He has walked/ driven
7. **Passive participle**	+ ED or +EN	dependent	He was driven

What we see in Hong Kong English is a reduction of the range of morphosyntactic features which are differentiated between, and a number of suppletions, which accounts for the typical student utterance *I am very boring in lectures*. In examples like this, students do not mean that they are boring, but that they are bored, no doubt as a result of the quality of the lecture. In this case, we can assume that speakers of Hong Kong English are maintaining the active/passive feature distinction, but that they have a suppletive form. This, in turn, is probably carried over from Cantonese. The Cantonese adjective *muhn* has both active and passive meanings, so one form is associated with two meanings, and two sets of morphosyntactic features.[22]

In the spoken part of the Hong Kong corpus of English, I have found forms like those in (42) and (43).[23]

(42) She like to go there.[1]
(43) Have you try.[1]

In example (42), the verb does not show third person feature marking. In (43), what is absent is a perfect form – instead of using the perfect participle as the complement of HAVE, this speaker is using the base form of the verb. Note that in Table 6.1, the base form of the verb is the most widely used form; whether we conclude from this that this speaker does not have perfect participle features or that they do not have participial marking is, however, another investigation which requires substantial empirical research over the completed corpus.

We could conclude tentatively, that it is an issue of morphosyntactic marking because of examples like (44).

(44) I think it's very difficult to described.[1]

In (44), a passive or perfect participle is used as the complement of infinitival TO. From this, it would appear to be more likely that speakers of Hong Kong English maintain the morphosyntactic features contrasts of Table 6.1, but are uncertain about the exponence of those features in morphosyntactic marking.

This conclusion is born out by Yip and Matthews's investigation into the passivization of unaccusative verbs like APPEAR. They found that Hong Kong speakers of English produce utterances like (45).

(45) The bus was appeared around the corner.

In (45), an intransitive verb is found in a passive structure. These verbs belong in a class of verbs whose subjects are analysed as being in a grammatical sense also their objects. The English pattern is typologically unusual in that most of the world's languages deal with these structures as passivized reflexives. However, it is clear that speakers of Hong Kong English have a passivization strategy, even if the morphosyntactic marking is irregular.

There is evidence of irregularity in passivization strategies in Hong Kong English in examples like (46)–(49).

(46) Then she had to **promote** to Accountant One[1]
(47) I've **been tried** hard to do that[1]
(48) You didn't expect the timetable would be that **pack**[1]
(49) If you want to go there **backpacked**[1]

These examples do not all show the same set of phenomena. In (46), an example which in native-speaker varieties would involve either passive BE or passive GET and a passive participle is a simple infinitive. This looks like a base form of the verb used as a variety of a passive construction. In (47), a passive construction follows perfective HAVE. This could indicate a generalization of the distribution of perfect and participles to passive environments, because they are syncretic. Example (48) is like (46): you would expect *packed* here, instead of which you find the base form of the verb. The final example uses either a perfect or a passive participle as an adjunct in a context where a native-speaker variety would use a present participle. There do not appear to be any regularities that emerge from this. There is a general levelling of the morphosyntactic feature system in Hong Kong English, but it shows a great degree of individual variation.

It is also the case that there is levelling of morphosyntactic features in finite verb forms, as is shown in (50)–(52).

(50) In my first year Cats come to Hong Kong[l]
(51) He is born in Hong Kong and then just go to Hong Kong[l]
(52) China want to took ... wants to take over[l]

In (50), *come* is a base-form of the verb, used to refer to a past time situation. In (51), we have the form of BE *is* for a past time event, and then the base form of go. And in (52) we have a revision of *want to took* to *wants to take*. This kind of correction is sometimes taken as a performance error, with the correction reflecting the competence of the speaker, but we could actually construe it differently as indicative of register variation in Hong Kong English. This requires more quantitative evaluation, but there is anecdotal evidence that students' email correspondence in Hong Kong English shows substantial register variation. It would be plausible to suggest that marking of morphosyntactic features would be more evident in higher registers, whereas levelling of morphosyntactic features would be more marked in lower registers.

Where does this leave relative clauses of the kind identified in example (16) above? I fear that it leaves them as a research problem. It is clear that the morphosyntactic feature system of Hong Kong English needs further investigation, but it also needs to be established whether it is a variety with register variation or not, and what the interplay between morphosyntactic features and the relative clause system might be. We are not yet placed to establish whether Newbrook is right in saying that this is an unusual kind of participial relative clause, or whether, in fact, it corresponds to a phenomenon of the morphosyntactic feature system of Hong Kong English.

Conclusions

In this chapter I have discussed a number of phenomena in the relative clause system of Hong Kong English and I have brought them together to provide the most comprehensive description of the relative clause in Hong Kong English to date. This discussion has identified a number of areas where Hong Kong English needs further exploration and clarification in research which will exploit the research tool of the ICE-HK. However, it is possible to make analyses of what is unique to Hong Kong English, and what it shares with other varieties. There are features of the Hong Kong English relative clause system which are apparently unique to the system of Hong Kong English; this merits further investigation. One important conclusion is that a full description of the relative clause system of Hong Kong English awaits a comprehensive discussion of the morphosyntactic feature system of Hong Kong English.

Notes

1. I would like to thank Kingsley Bolton and Steve Matthews for discussion and for their generous sharing of data. I would also like to thank an anonymous referee for useful comments and additional data. I have adopted the following conventions: examples taken from Newbrook (1998) are marked with a superscript N; examples taken from Yip and Matthews (1991) are marked with a superscript Y; examples from Steve Matthews's personal files are marked with a superscript M; and examples from the International Corpus of English–Hong Kong files are marked with a superscript I. The sources of the other examples are given in the text. If no sources are given, I have collected the examples myself.
2. Another issue concerns the transfer of grammatical patterns from Cantonese – the issue is specifically whether there are features of the syntax of Hong Kong English which are not explicable in terms of 'superstrate' (English) or 'substrate' (Cantonese) influence.
3. However, Yip and Matthews (1991) argue that Hong Kong English displays the same kinds of interlanguage phenomena as the varieties of English spoken by other Chinese L1 speakers.
4. The main objective of the ICE project worldwide is to enable comparative studies of the English language on an international scale, both with regard to the use of English in societies where it is the first language of the majority of the population, as in the USA, UK, and Australia, and with reference to its use in societies such as India, Singapore, and Hong Kong, where it is used as an 'additional' language. The research on the ICE project referred to throughout this chapter is funded by a grant from the Research Grants Council of the Hong Kong Special Administrative Region, China (Project No. HKU 7174/OOH).
5. Quirk et al. (1985) provide an account of the syntax and semantics of relative clauses in standard English.
6. Although this is the usual claim, I am a speaker of standard British English and I find that I occasionally use non-restrictive THAT-relatives.
7. Newbrook does not identify the provenance of his examples in this paper. However Newbrook (1988) relies on examples collected in Hong Kong, mostly from students.
8. Newbrook marks this example as ungrammatical with the notation '*', but as it is clearly grammatical in Hong Kong English, as well as other varieties that Newbrook describes, I leave it unmarked for (un)grammaticality.
9. I wonder at Newbrook's assertion that such examples are 'virtually categorical'. To reach 100% occurrence of such examples you would have to find no examples

of *this is the student that/who did it*. However, it is interesting to observe that zero-subject relatives are standard, and occur frequently, in Hong Kong English.
10. Steve Matthews has pointed out to me that (11) may not be in the same category as (10). Example (11) is an existential construction easily transferred from any variety of Chinese. See Yip (1995), Chapter 7. It may, therefore, not be a relative clause, lending support for Mohanan's (1992) observation that comparison of non-native varieties with native varieties can give rise to inaccurate analysis of the non-native variety.
11. Mandarin. As is well-known, there are several systems of romanization for Chinese. In this chapter, I have used the romanization of Chinese examples of the sources of those examples. This means that the romanization is slightly irregular. An anonymous referee observes that a better gloss of *nanhaizi* would be *boy*. The gloss given here is that of Alsagoff and Ho (1998).
12. Hokkien.
13. Cantonese.
14. I am thinking of a (fictitious) example like *he kicked the dog 0 bit him* where the underlined material is a zero-subject relative clause whose head is *the dog* which is the object in the main clause.
15. If this example is characteristic of Hong Kong English, it is hard to see how the omission of the subject relative pronoun in examples like (9) above can be 'categorical'. Steve Matthews has suggested that (16) may be a hypercorrection. That is, if (9) is typical, examples like (16) arise because of a sense that relative pronouns tend to be omitted in Hong Kong English. However, such a suggestion begs the question of why this is a target site for hypercorrection.
16. For a discussion of the relationships between different kinds of spatial sense see Lakoff (1987: 416–61); for a discussion of the relationship between polysemy and semantic change see Sweetser (1990).
17. Steve Matthews (personal communication) observes that a transfer/substrate account of examples like (22-3) can be established, as there are Chinese equivalents.
18. However, Steve Matthews (personal communication) suggests that it is in constituency with the classifier and the head noun.
19. In this example, *think* is not a misprint. The example comes from an undergraduate paper discussing Orwell's *1984*. The example means that both independent thought and sex are crimes in the novel's fictional world.
20. However, there is an increasing percentage of the local population being educated in international schools in Hong Kong. The 1996 census gives 38.1% of the population claiming to speak English as a second language. Bacon-Shone and Bolton (1998: 83–7) examine the spread of English in Hong Kong against a demographic account of Hong Kong society. They note that in 1995, 18% of the population were enrolled in higher education (by comparison with a figure of approximately 2% in 1980) and that proportionally more children are being educated at the secondary level, with the result that more and more children are learning English, and more and more people are speaking English. Their analysis shows how an increasing percentage of the population of Hong Kong claims to have knowledge of English.
21. Table 6.1 is adapted from Hudson (1990: 178), and the discussion in Hudson (pp. 172–8).

22. I am grateful to an anonymous referee for this fact.
23. As an anonymous referee observes, the analysis of past participles, and the morphosyntax of Hong Kong English more generally, is problematic because of the nature of the Hong Kong accent which typically deletes syllable-final stops and simplifies consonant clusters.

References

Alsagoff, Lubna and Ho Chee Lick (1998) The relative clause in colloquial Singapore English. *World Englishes*, **17**, 127–38.

Bacon-Shone, John and Bolton, Kingsley (1998) Charting multilingualism: Language censuses and language surveys in Hong Kong. In *Language in Hong Kong at Century's End*. Edited by Martha C. Pennington. Hong Kong: Hong Kong University Press, pp. 43–90.

Bolton, Kingsley and Kwok, Helen (1990) The dynamics of the Hong Kong accent: Social identity and sociolinguistic description. *Journal of Asian Pacific Communication*, **1**, 147–72.

Chan, E. P. (1970) Common Errors in Written English made by Chinese-speaking learners. *English Bulletin*, Education Department, Hong Kong, 1960–1970.

Hong Kong Government (1996) *1996 Population By-census*. Hong Kong: Census and Statistics Department.

Hudson, Richard (1990) *English Word Grammar*. Oxford: Blackwell.

Kachru, Braj B. (1985) Editorial. *World Englishes*, **4**, 209–12.

Keenan, Edward L. and Comrie, Bernard (1977) Noun phrase accessibility and universal grammar. *Linguistic Inquiry*, **1**, 63–99.

Killingley, Siew-yue (1993) *Cantonese*. Meunchen: Lincom Europa.

Lakoff, George (1987) *Women, Fire and Dangerous Things*. Chicago: Chicago University Press.

McMahon, April (1994) *Understanding Language Change*. Cambridge: Cambridge University Press.

Matthews, Stephen and Yip, Virginia (1994) *Cantonese: A Comprehensive Grammar*. London: Routledge.

Matthews, Stephen and Yip, Virginia (2000) Aspects of contemporary Cantonese grammar: The structure and stratification of relative clauses. In *Sinitic Grammar: Synchronic and Diachronic Perspectives*. Edited by Hilary Chappell. Oxford: Oxford University Press.

Mohanan, K. P. (1992) Describing the phonology of non-native varieties of a language. *World Englishes*, **11**, 111–28.

Newbrook, Mark (1988) Relative clauses, relative pronouns and Hong Kong English. *University of Hong Kong Papers on Linguistics and Language Teaching*, **11**, 25–41.

Newbrook, Mark (1998) Which way? That was? Variation and ongoing changes in the English relative clause. *World Englishes*, **17** (1), 43–59.

Quirk, Randolph, Greenbaum, Sidney, Leech, Geoffrey and Svartvik, Jan (1985) *A Comprehensive Grammar of the English Language*. London: Longman.

Romaine, Suzanne (1982) *Socio-historical Linguistics*. Cambridge: Cambridge University Press.

Sebba, Mark (1997) *Contact Languages: Pidgins and Creoles*. Basingstoke: Macmillan.

Sweetser, Eve V. (1990) *From Etymlogy to Pragmatics.* Cambridge: Cambridge University Press.
Trudgill, Peter (1983) *On Dialect.* Oxford: Blackwell.
Trudgill, Peter and Hannah, Jean (1994) *International English: A Guide to Varieties of Standard English.* London: Edward Arnold.
Webster, Michael, Ward, Alan and Craig, Kenneth (1987) Language errors due to first language interference (Cantonese) produced by Hong Kong students of English. *Institute of Language in Education Journal,* **3**, 63–81.
Yip, Virginia (1995) *Interlanguage and Learnability: From Chinese to English.* Amsterdam: Benjamins.
Yip, Virginia and Matthews, Stephen (1991) Relative complexity: Beyond avoidance. *Chinese University of Hong Kong Papers in Linguistics,* **3**, 112–24.

7

Hong Kong words: Variation and context

Phil Benson

Introduction

Much of the discussion on Hong Kong English over the last 20 years has revolved around the question of whether such a variety of English actually exists. The paradigm for this discussion was established by Luke and Richards (1982: 55): 'There is no such thing then as "Hong Kong English". There is neither the societal need nor opportunity for the development of a stable Cantonese variety of spoken English'. Many local scholars would continue to agree with this statement, while others have suggested that a distinctive variety of the kind described by Luke and Richards may be in the process of emerging. In a paper published in the same year, Platt (1982: 409), for example, argued that: 'At present there is probably less justification for speaking of a Hong Kong English than of a Singapore English as a variety in its own right. Nevertheless, certain typical characteristics appear to be emerging'. Similarly, Bolton & Kwok (1990: 163) suggested that:

> Whether or not one can speak of 'Hong Kong English' as a recognisable 'localised variety' of English remains a matter for further research and investigation. If one can establish that (in addition to identifiable local accent) there are clusters of shared lexical and grammatical items which contribute to a distinctive body of shared linguistic features then this may well legitimise recognition of Hong Kong English as a localised variety.

The aim of this chapter, however, is not to attempt to resolve the question of whether Hong Kong English can legitimately be described as a variety of English, but rather to question some of the premises on which the discussion is based in relation to distinctively localized items of vocabulary.

One of the most basic premises in the discussion is that, if Hong Kong English is indeed a variety of English, it should be recognizable as one that belongs to the Hong Kong English-speaking community as a whole. The specific problem that sociolinguists have identified with the idea of Hong Kong

English is, therefore, the fact that the English-speaking community is sharply divided into a small, largely expatriate, group of native English speakers and a much larger group of Chinese nonnative speakers who share Cantonese as their first choice medium of communication. Although this characterization is something of an oversimplification (see Bolton, Chapter 1), it remains broadly true that Cantonese speakers tend not to use English unless non-Cantonese speakers form part of their audience or the channel of communication demands it (for example, e-mail or ICQ).

The conclusion that a stable Hong Kong variety of English lacks sociolinguistic reality, however, dramatically fails to account for the data that has been presented in several studies of localized vocabulary (Chan and Kwok, 1985; Taylor, 1989; Davies and Roberts, 1990; Benson, 1993, 1994a, 1994b; Carless, 1995). Indeed, it is relatively easy to find descriptive evidence of localized vocabulary in any local English-language newspaper. In the following extract from a front-page news item in the *South China Morning Post* (21 June 1993), for example, we find no less than 8 items within 77 words of text that are arguably distinctive to Hong Kong in their form or meaning (my italics):

> CHINESE law enforcement agencies say they have declared war against *triads*, but *local legislators* last night received the news with scepticism. Some *legislators* said they were confused by China's stance at an unprecedented seminar between Hongkong and *mainland* police, because Public Security Minister Tao Siju had earlier noted that some *triad members* could be '*patriotic*' ... It was the first *anti-triad* seminar between the forces, although local and mainland police have had close co-operation on general *cross-border* crimes.

The words italicized in this extract are, in fact, only 8 examples of several hundred similar words that might well be included in a dictionary of Hong Kong English or an English dictionary covering Hong Kong. Their distinctiveness, however, lies not so much in the fact that they are characteristic of the speech of the majority of English speakers in Hong Kong, as in the fact that the reader must call upon knowledge of the Hong Kong context in order to fully understand their meaning and use. Indeed, it appears that the notion of 'regional context' may be more helpful than the notion of 'regional variety' in identifying and describing such words.

Regional context and regional variety

In descriptions of the vocabulary of regional varieties of English, several selection criteria are typically applied. In general, the word or sense of the word must have some degree of currency and stability. It should either originate in the region concerned or be formally, semantically or collocationally distinctive from usage elsewhere in the world. Although these criteria are often loosely applied, they tend to be basic to the compilation of regional English dictionaries and to the use of regional labels in general English dictionaries (Benson, 2001). In consequence, the lexical items deemed to 'belong to' a regional variety are often identified through a comparison with 'standard international English', which often turns out in practice to correspond to standard British or American English. These items may also be taken as defining, from the point of view of vocabulary, the distinctiveness of the usage of the speech community to which the regional variety belongs.

The chief problem with this approach is that it tends to identify the lexical component of regional varieties of English reductively and fails to describe localized words in terms that are specific to the variety itself. As Delbridge (1983: 34) has argued, the ideal description of a regional variety of English is a 'description of that variety by and for itself, so that all the pronunciations, all the spellings, all the definitions of sense for all the words are taken from the usage of the national community'. In the case of Hong Kong English, an additional problem arises that the items identified through the application of these criteria are not necessarily used by, or even known to, the majority of English speakers in the territory. In his entry on Hong Kong English in *The Oxford Companion to the English Language*, for example, McArthur (1992) lists three items: *nullah, dim sum* and *short week*. *Nullah* is a colonial name for a stream or gully and is not well known to Cantonese speakers. *Dim sum* refers to a kind of meal consisting of snacks ordered and served one by one, for which Cantonese speakers tend to use the word *yam cha*. *Short week* refers to a working week in which Saturday morning is a day off, and is widely known only among office workers. These words clearly *are* used in Hong Kong, but they do not fit well with the description of Hong Kong English as the language of the Hong Kong English-speaking community as a whole. They do, on the other hand, fit well with the idea of a Hong Kong word as one whose distinctiveness lies in its semantic and pragmatic relationships to the regional sociocultural context to which it refers.

An approach to the identification and description of localized words in terms of regional context differs in two respects from approaches that emphasize relationships to words that do not belong to the variety in question. First, a word is considered to be localized in so far its meaning or usage is related to some aspect of the local linguistic or sociocultural context in which it is used. Second, the description of the word will consist in the description of its relationship to this sociocultural or linguistic context. In the remainder of this chapter, I will attempt to illustrate this approach with reference to four possible types of relationship involving underlying definitions, taxonomies, semantic opposition and lexical productivity.

Underlying definitions

A relatively small number of words can be characterized as local to Hong Kong because their use and interpretation is dependent upon an underlying definition pointing to the local context. For several months of the year Hong Kong is subject to strong winds and typhoons, which have varying immediate social, as well as physical, consequences according to their degree of severity. These social consequences are mediated through a warning system based on the various *typhoon signals* using the categories designated by the Hong Kong Observatory as illustrated in Table 7.1.

Table 7.1 Hong Kong typhoon signals

Signal		Display		Meaning of the signal
		Symbol	Lights	
Stand by	1	T	White White White	A tropical cyclone is centred within 800 kilometres of Hong Kong and may later affect Hong Kong.
Strong wind	3	⊥	Green White Green	Strong wind is expected or is blowing in Victoria Harbour with a sustained speed or 41–62 kilometres per hour (kmh). Gusts may exceed 110 kmh.
Gale or storm	8 NW	▲	White Green Green	Gale or storm-force wind is expected or is blowing in Victoria Harbour with a sustained wind speed of 63–117 kmh from the quarter indicated. Gusts may exceed 180 kmh.
Gale or storm	8 SW	▼	Green White White	
Gale or storm	8 NE	▲▲	Green Green White	
Gale or storm	8 SE	▼▼	White White Green	
Increasing gale or storm	9	▼▲	Green Green Green	Gale or storm force wind is increasing or expected to increase significantly in strength.
Hurricane	10	✚	Red Green Red	Hurricane-force wind is expected or blowing with sustained speed reaching upwards from 118 kmh. Gusts may exceed 220 kmh.

The system is specific to Hong Kong and not entirely transparent since several numbers are missing. However, although the underlying meanings of the signals are highly technical and not widely known, their practical consequences would be clear to most residents of Hong Kong. The phrase 'the number eight signal will be hoisted soon' would convey the unambiguous meaning that it is time to go home before public transport stops running. Hong Kong has several similar classification systems with associated vocabularies covering, for example, dangerous goods, fires and films. The film censorship system currently divides films into Categories I, IIa, IIb and III. In everyday usage, an X-rated movie in Britain, would be a Category III movie in Hong Kong, but the two are not simply semantic equivalents for the term *Category III movie* draws its meanings directly from the definitions contained within the local system. One of the consequences of this is the generation of lexical items that have no clear equivalents beyond Hong Kong, such as *Category III movie star* – an actor who has become a public figure mainly because of her appearances in Category III films.

Underlying definitions are sometimes made explicit in text. In the following extract from the *South China Morning Post* (17 May 1992), the word *sandwich class* is defined:

> THE chairman of the Housing Authority hinted yesterday that the solution to the problems of the middle income 'sandwich class' was to rent a flat rather than to buy one. The sandwich class, so-called because it describes people who fall between those groups which are either eligible for public housing or can afford to buy their own home, is the subject of a new working group.

The definition is informal, but is grounded in more precise official specifications of the upper and lower incomes of the 'sandwich class'. *Sandwich class* is also commonly used without any definition at all, so that the reader needs to supply the definition unaided. Again the term is productive in expressions such as *sandwich class loan* and *sandwich class flat*. It should be added that the idea of a 'sandwich class' only makes sense if the reader is also aware of the way in which sharply rising property prices in the early 1990s caused middle income families in Hong Kong to feel that they were financially worse off than families who have lower incomes but are entitled to subsidized public housing. In this case, interpretation of both the word and its underlying definition is pragmatically dependent upon knowledge of the local sociocultural context.

Taxonomies

Taxonomies arising within specific sociocultural domains are also a source of localized words in Hong Kong. In an academic text published in Hong Kong

166 Phil Benson

by a sociologist at the University of Hong Kong, Vagg (1991: 58–9) offers the following description of the Hong Kong commercial sex industry:

> The current commercial sex scene is rather fragmented, but nevertheless caters to almost every need. There are *unlicensed massage parlours*, providing a more intimate service than the licensed variety. There are a few *'fishball stalls'* in which one sits in the dark, on a high backed bench seat and facing the high back of the seat in front, with one's hostess. More numerous are the *'villas'*, small hotels which let rooms by the hour ... Brothels as such are rare in Hong Kong, although *'one-woman brothels'* exist. They are small rooms – some are cubicles – each with a single girl both living and working in it. *'Private brothels'* do exist; they take only clients known to the prostitutes, or recommended by existing clientele. And finally – and much as in other large cities worldwide – one can find in telephone directories advertisements for escort and massage *'outcall services'* ... (Vagg, 1991: 58–9, my italics)

In this extract, there is a good deal of description and informal definition of the terms *unlicensed massage parlours, fishball stalls, villas, one-woman brothels, private brothels* and *outcall services*. The point to note, however, is that they collectively form a taxonomy of terms, each of which can be defined by reference to its differences from the others. In order to understand what a *villa* is, for example, we need to understand how it differs from a *fishball stall* or a *one-woman brothel*. Informal taxonomies of this kind are not uncommon in Hong Kong texts, and a later text from the *South China Morning Post* (7 July 1996) both repeats and adds terms:

> Hundreds of *villa apartments, one-woman brothels, karaoke bars* and *street walkers* – plus the number of people indulging in casual sex in nearby countries – create a dangerous environment for the spread of AIDS, they say ... Dr. Wong said interviews with police and health workers had revealed several tiers of commercial sex establishments in Hong Kong. There were 400 villa apartments, 250–300 karaoke bars or nightclubs, 80 *massage parlours* and an unknown number of private, *underground brothels* and *callout escort services*, Dr. Wong said.

We might note here that the word *karaoke bar* – now known internationally – gains a specific meaning in Hong Kong through its inclusion within the taxonomy of commercial sex establishments. Other sociocultural domains that are productive of localized words and senses in Hong Kong include crime (e.g. *cross-border crime, triad activities,* etc.) and migration (*expatriate, illegal immigrant, economic migrants*).

Semantic opposition

In the first extract from the *South China Morning Post* quoted in this chapter, the words *local* and *mainland* were noted as possible lexical items of Hong Kong English. One of the reasons for this is that in the phrase 'local and mainland police' the words *local* and *mainland* are semantically opposed. The local police are Hong Kong police and the mainland police are the police of the People's Republic of China. Although in isolation, neither word appears at first sight to be distinctive to Hong Kong, it is this semantic opposition that in part defines them in the Hong Kong context. The word *local* also regularly appears in texts in opposition to the words *expatriate* and *international*:

> Local and expatriate civil service unions have been holding confidential talks with the government for the past three weeks. (*Hongkong Standard*, 23 March 1994)

> Sponsored by legislator Mr Steven Poon Kwok-lim, members agreed that both the local and international phone networks should be opened for competition. (*South China Morning Post*, 4 June 1992)

In effect, the repetition of oppositions of this kind leads to a pattern in which the word *local* in the Hong Kong context becomes a synonym for the word *Hong Kong*. In certain linguistic contexts, these oppositions are implicit: 'Those local students who were apprehended in Beijing delivering Hong Kong's donations had to undergo harrowing interrogation before being deported' (Pomery, 1993: 33). The potential ambiguity in the reference of *local* in this extract (were the students local to Beijing or Hong Kong?) is removed by a knowledge of the linguistic context in which a 'local student' is, almost by definition, a Hong Kong student.

Semantic oppositions of this kind are quite common: for example, *pro-China* and *pro-Hong Kong*, *public housing* and *private housing* and, in the context of Vietnamese migration in the early 1990s, *economic migrants* and *refugees*. In each case, the meaning of one term is established by reference to the meaning of the other. *Public housing* is not *private housing* and vice versa. The significance of semantic oppositions of this kind can be illustrated by the word *mainland China*, which in Hong Kong is a widely used term for the People's Republic of China. The word is, strictly speaking, geographically inaccurate since the major part of the territory of Hong Kong, comprising Kowloon and the New Territories, is itself located on the mainland and separated from *mainland China* by a land border. However, the term has evidently reached Hong Kong from Taiwan (from the perspective of which it is geographically accurate). In the Hong Kong context, *mainland China* thus refers simply to the part of China that is not Hong Kong or Taiwan. Although the word is internationally known, its use in Hong Kong encodes a perspective that it is specific to the local sociocultural context.

Productivity

In an earlier paper (Benson, 1994a), I reported in detail on an investigation of the use of the word *local* in a one-million-word corpus of texts published in Hong Kong. It was observed that the frequency of the word and its derivatives was significantly higher in the Hong Kong corpus than in comparable corpora compiled in Britain and the USA. Moreover, when the senses of *local* in the Hong Kong corpus were compared with the senses listed in dictionaries of English, it was found that senses such as 'concerned with a small area' or 'belonging to the area in which you live or work' were effectively blocked by the dominant sense, 'concerning or belonging to Hong Kong'. A further observation concerned the productivity of Hong Kong usage in the words *localize* and *localization*. In Hong Kong texts, both words are typically used in contexts where they refer to the replacement of expatriate by Hong Kong workers or officials. In these contexts, *localize* might be broadly defined as 'to make something local' and *localization* as 'the process of making something local'. In most dictionaries of English, however, these senses do not appear. *Localize* is typically defined as 'to isolate or to identify the source of' (as in the phrase 'to localize a problem'). The word *localization* does not generally appear in dictionaries at all.

It should be noted that these senses of *localize* and *localization* are not specific to Hong Kong. Indeed, the use of *local* to refer to the country one is in, rather than an area within a country, is found in corpora of Indian and Australian English and is doubtless common to the Englishes of other former British colonies. The point to note, however, is that once a regional sense of a word is established, it is liable to become productive of new senses and derivatives defined in terms of that sense. Conversely, the production of derivatives is liable to point to something specific within the regional sense of the words from which they are derived. In Hong Kong, for example, *illegal immigrant* has produced the abbreviation *II* and in Malaysia *identity card* has produced the abbreviation *IC*. In each case, the meaning of the underlying word is apparently transparent internationally, yet the existence of the derivative suggests that there is more to the localized use of the word than meets the eye. Similarly, although a word may have spread internationally, it may be far more productive in its original regional context than it is elsewhere. The Hong Kong word *triad*, for example, is internationally known, but in Hong Kong it is also productive of words such as *anti-triad, triad activity, triad language* and *triad movie*, all of which have specific meanings in the Hong Kong context.

Conclusion

The aim of this chapter has been in part to suggest that, at least in regard to vocabulary, the problem of describing regional varieties of English is less a question of assigning linguistic features to the usage of particular speech communities and more a question of assigning them to particular sociocultural contexts of language use. In the inner and outer circles of world English, the use of English within the speech community and its use within the sociocultural context to which that speech community belongs tend to be coterminous. In the expanding circle of regions in which English is primarily used across, rather than within, regionally defined speech communities, however, the distinction is highly relevant to the description of regional varieties of English. Hong Kong, China, Taiwan, Thailand, Japan and other countries of the expanding circle each have their own distinctive vocabularies that cannot easily be accounted for in terms of conventional sociolinguistic paradigms for the description of world Englishes. The answer to the problem may well lie in greater attention to the relationship of words and their senses to the contexts in which they are used. In the Hong Kong context, it is clear that many localized words can be satisfactorily accounted for in terms of semantic and pragmatic relations that are internal to the contexts in which they are used. Such an approach may well also bring us closer to Delbridge's (1983: 34) ideal of the description of a regional variety of English 'by and for itself'.

References

Benson, Phil (1993) Localized vocabulary in Hong Kong English and Australian English. In *Studies in Lexis: Proceedings from a Seminar*. Edited by R. Pemberton and Elza S. C. Tsang. Hong Kong: Hong Kong University of Science and Technology, pp. 99–111.

Benson, Phil (1994a) Electronic text analysis and the lexis of Hong Kong English: What can it tell us that we don't already know? In *Entering Text*. Edited by L. Flowerdew and K. K. Tong. Hong Kong: Hong Kong University of Science and Technology, pp. 89–100.

Benson, Phil (1994b) The political vocabulary of Hong Kong English. *Hongkong Papers in Linguistics and Language Teaching*, **17**, 63–81.

Benson, Phil (2001) *Ethnocentrism and the English Dictionary*. London: Routledge.

Bolton, Kwok and Kwok, Helen (1990) The dynamics of the Hong Kong accent: Social identity and sociolinguistic description. *Journal of Asian Pacific Communication*, **1**(1), 147–72.

Carless, David R. (1995) Politicised expressions in the *South China Morning Post*. *English Today*, **11**(2), 18–22.

Chan, Mimi and Kwok, Helen (1985) *A Study of Lexical Borrowing from Chinese into English with Special Reference to Hong Kong*. Hong Kong: Centre of Asian Studies, The University of Hong Kong.

Davies, Stephen and Roberts, Elfed (1990) *A Political Dictionary for Hong Kong*. Hong Kong: Macmillan.

Delbridge, Arthur (1983) On national variants of the English dictionary. In *Lexicography:*

Principles and Practice. Edited by R. R. K. Hartmann. London: Academic Press, pp. 23–40.

Luke, K. K. & Richards, Jack C. (1982) English in Hong Kong: Functions and status. *English World-wide*, **3**, 147–64.

McArthur, Tom (1992) *The Oxford Companion to the English Language*. Oxford: Oxford University Press.

Platt, John T. (1982) English in Singapore, Malaysia and Hong Kong. In *English as a World Language*. Edited by R. W. Bailey and M. Görlach. Ann Arbor: University of Michigan Press.

Pomery, Chris (1993) *Hong Kong in Depth: An A-Z Guide*. Hong Kong: Guide Book Company.

Taylor, Andrew (1989) Hong Kong's English newspapers. *English Today*, **5**(4), 18–24.

Vagg, John (1991) Vice. In *Crime and Justice in Hong Kong*. Edited by H. Traver and J. Vagg. Hong Kong: Oxford University Press, pp. 57–69.

Part III
Dimensions of Creativity

8
Hong Kong writing and writing Hong Kong
Louise Ho

Introduction

'Writing, commitment of the word to space, enlarges the potentiality of language almost beyond measure, restructures thought …', writes the scholar-critic, Walter Ong (1982: 7). Being committed to space, language has its particular dynamics of time. Writing results from a studied, calculated, planned and controlled exercise of language which is then unravelled in the continuum of time by the reader. Written language is able to carry a burden of analytical thought, discursive argument, contemplation or even self-parody and ironic denial of its own statement; as Ong puts it, 'it restructures consciousness' (p. 78). Without writing, the mind would be tied to a reliance on memory and would not be freed for developing thought in its more original and abstract forms. All this is merely pausing to consider the obvious: the world has taken literacy for granted for a very long time.

Literary experience, however, is about awareness of distance between the reader and language; perception of the mechanics of literary language which gives language a life of its own; knowledge and awareness of the literary traditions against which any new literary creation is recognized and judged. Quite simply, the reading of literary language requires the process called education. How has Hong Kong society nurtured literary sensibilities? What are the features of the literary culture (if any) that are particular to Hong Kong? If one were to pursue this question far enough (beyond this chapter, certainly), one would be asking the question, what is Hong Kong?

While education amounts to self-education of the individual in the end, society from its multifarious angles and contexts must impact on individual consciousness. More immediately, Hong Kong society has nurtured sensibilities for stocks and shares and property prices rather than sensibilities in abstractions and aesthetics. But that development can be a source of strength: writers would then observe a highly unself-conscious, non-self-aware community, where people on the whole have no time to observe their own observations. Such unself-consciounsness can be a productive kind of rawness. The demise of the 'great' Victorian novel came about, perhaps, partly because English sensibilities became over-rarefied and over-articulated. We have no fear of that happening for Hong Kong in a very long time yet!

As Hong Kong is essentially a cosmopolitan city with a rock-hard Chinese core, one cannot talk about the generality of Hong Kong writing without a reference to Chinese writing, however cursory (writing in English is at best marginalized, when at all in existence). The very mention of Chinese writing in Hong Kong stirs many a hornet's nest. Is it a seamless continuation of the literary culture of mainland China or is it indigenous; and if so, in what way? While there are countless spoken languages in China, there is only *one* written language, and that is the language of literature, admittedly with regional variations that are culture-bound. Some poets in Hong Kong see themselves writing from the traditions of mainland China, while others want to start a radically new literary tradition by trying to write in dialect form. For Hong Kong that would be Cantonese. *Renditions: A Chinese-English Translation Magazine*, for example, aims at introducing Chinese literature and culture to the Western reader, and *Renditions* numbers 29–30, and 47–48 are special issues on Hong Kong writing and culture.

Hong Kong space is to be differentiated from Hong Kong place. The site is the socialized space of a place. Not many city-entities in the world would show a greater difference between site and place than that shown in Hong Kong. Insignificant in geographic size, it is significant on an international scale. Its site hovers above the place and is part of the globalized configuration. At the same time, the land holds a rich past, from pre-historic excavations to rural architecture going back to a thousand years. There are many Chinese and other languages spoken. Basically a Cantonese city, Hong Kong also caters to cosmopolitan tastes and cultures. The site of Hong Kong is both extensive and 'thick', although there is much country park and wilderness a stone's throw from its high urban densities. Such a geographic, cultural and political anomaly offers a new Pegasus waiting to be reined in and to be made to trot in iambics and other metres.

Writing in English

The novelist, Xu Xi (Sussy Chako), once noted that writing in English about Hong Kong is not problematic, although, arguably, writing in Swahili about Hong Kong may be. I do not know Swahili, but I can't see why writing in any language cannot be made to represent Hong Kong, provided it is done well. Literary language is an alienated language, anyway; it is foregrounded from ordinary discourse. What is essential is a literary awareness on the part of those who write and those who read; thus developing an overall literary sensibility within that society where writers and readers begin to cultivate and recognize a literary tradition. While mainland China and Taiwan have such traditions, the major critical assumption is that Hong Kong does not. On the part of the writer, this awareness is the basis of all writing in that however experimental or 'original' a piece of writing may be, it is, at least initially, to be read against the background of the literature of the language in which it is written. Homer was not the first Adam; at the time he sang, there was already plenty of literature around. At the same time, every poet is a new Adam naming and ordering the world she or he is writing about. Every poet gives to 'airy nothing a local habitation and a name'. Possibly the highest hurdle for the writer is to become 'original' *within* an existing literary tradition, 'To make it new', as Ezra Pound put it, with materials as old as the language used by countless writers before oneself. It is a new voice with ever-receding echoes.

While thinking of Hong Kong as mappable material, I couldn't help but be reminded of that map-maker of another new entity, Derek Walcott. Here is someone conscious of his task as marker of his land on the literary map of the world. Although his poetry has echoes of Western civilization all the way back to Homer (nothing more obvious than Omeros), as well as those of English and European literatures throughout the ages, his poetry is that of discovery and creation, of the Antilles, his home. In his speech upon receiving the Nobel Prize for Literature (1992), he says:

> There is a force of exultation, a celebration of luck, when a writer finds himself a witness to the early morning of a culture that is defining itself, branch by branch, leaf by leaf, in that self-defining dawn … Then the noun, the 'Antilles', ripples like brightening water, and the sounds of leaves, palm fronds, and birds are the sounds of a fresh dialect, the native tongue. The personal vocabulary, the individual melody whose metre is one's biography, joins in that sound, with any luck, and the body moves like a walking, a waking island … This is the benediction that is celebrated, a fresh language and a fresh people, and this is the frightening duty owed. (Walcott 1992)

The case of Hong Kong is not as pristine as that of 'a fresh language and a fresh people', we are both stretched and contorted by a 6,000-year-old civilization. As the writer makes a beginning he or she must feel the weight of the centuries bearing down, that is, if the writer is in any way sensitive to the Hong Kong site, and not having total recourse to externally imposed conceptualizations. But language is culture-bound and literarily bound. A writer using the English language to write about Hong Kong sensibilities is, in effect, translating them into English sensibilities: they become transformed as they surface through the writing. As a result, the 'duty owed' becomes more problematic as well as more exciting.

Nomenclature and locality in Hong Kong English

Hong Kong writing in English has not yet reached a critical mass whereby it can claim nomenclature and locality. For the moment, we look at what is available. The editor for this book suggested that I might discuss my own work. I shall comply by choosing a few pieces that speak quite directly of Hong Kong over a period of the recent past. The poems appear in the appendix to this chapter.

I shall briefly repeat what has been said of my work. Although it ranges over various subjects and styles, from emphasis on images to the leaner poetry of statement, it has been generally described as the poetry of wit and irony rather than that of romantic exuberance. The critic Michael Hollington, among others, has called me the unofficial Hong Kong laureate. The reason may be that I have written 'occasional' poems, for example, poems on the riots, on the 1989 Tiananmen episode, Hong Kong on the approach to the changeover in 1997, and so forth. It is not unusual for me to write on public themes and issues.

I see the poet primarily as a technician; in this, I share the sensibilities of the French nineteenth-century poet, Theophile Gautier, whose words on the poet's battle with language appear as an epigraph in my book, *Local Habitation* (1994): 'Lutte avec le carrare, / Avec le paros dur ...' An active poet is also competing with the living and dead; this aspect makes poetry allusive on the whole. I steal from and rewrite Shakespeare, Dryden, Eliot and others. Having attained a toehold on mainstream literature, I divert the course into local contexts, at times using Cantonese words or sounds within the poems. Unlike African and Carribean poets, we have no applicable patois or creole with which to work. One of my goals is to bring into existence a space where the English literary language expresses as well as is incorporated into the local ethos, thus becoming almost a *tertium quid*, but which remains at the same time definitely English. Ackbar Abbas says of my work:

> In [Ho's] poems ... , English literature is an initial point of departure that allows the poet to take her bearings on local life and politics, both of which are becoming increasingly elusive and hard to describe. English literature functions less as a form of poetic authority than as a convenient grid against which the metastasizing habitations of the local can be situated ... What is remarkable – her form of extremity – is that the cultural, political, and personal tensions of the city are so precisely focused by the tensions of her language. (1997: 125–6)

The unsung voices

I have mentioned that the Hong Kong literary scene in the English language is still at the stage of formation. I would like to show the work of yet unsung voices who have produced quality work. The two poems by Anita Cheung ('My Probe...', and 'How Many Times') speak for themselves in their mature technique and sophisticated irony.

My Probe ...

My probe
(not unlike that of a clairvoyant's)
dissolves
with that faint curl of the lips
Distant reminder
of that notoriously
ambiguous smile –
You perfected
the art of
equivocation

How Many Times

How many times we tried
to fix a time
to spend some quality time
only to find we're simply
ill-timed

'thought I've given (enough)
the best of my time
(knowing we are running short of time)
never imagined
such pains you have to take
to fit me in
to the precious odd slots
around your many priorities

Civilized as we are how could we stand
being a pain
in the name of sharing
How we hate to bother
as much as we hate to be bothered by
each other

Then why should anyone bother
to intrude
into anyone's
self-sufficient
self-complacent
solitude

Wong Ho-yin has entered two poems for a recent Hong Kong poetry competition. The topic given was 'Friendship'. He is aged 21: here are his two polished pieces ('The Three Gum Leaves', and 'The Kite'), showing a definite command of the English language and of the mechanisms of poetry.

The Three Gum Leaves

A sweet scent caresses my nose
When I eagerly open your letter:
Three gum leaves are carefully enclosed,
Pressed between a piece of folded paper.

These three leaves have travelled across
Time and space:
Will they find themselves at odds
With this alien and busy place?

You say koala bears like chewing
Gum leaves for their sweet fragrance:
I haven't eaten these three leaves,
But I can taste their sweetness.

The Kite

The Airport Express
Travels back along the time path:
The nearer it gets to its destination,
the closer comes the past.

Once the two of us played with kites.
You really wanted to be one.
High above the ground you fly
The line would always let you come

Home safe and sound. Now that you're
Leaving Hong Kong for real,
Keep this kite with you;
I will keep the reel.

In the below-sixteen section of the competition, here is an encouraging piece from Li Tsz-chiu, who shows enough of a sense of music in his piece to make it a poem, again the theme is that of friendship.

Friendship

Friendship, friendship,
We are friends playing together,
Friendship, Friendship,
We are the best of friends.

Friends, Friends,
We are playing together,
Friends, Friends,
How do we make friends?

More of these, and Hong Kong writing would make its proper nomenclature and would contribute substantially towards a Hong Kong identity, for then Hong Kong would have a voice of its own.

References

Abbas, Ackbar (1997) *Hong Kong: Culture and the Politics of Disappearance.* Hong Kong: Hong Kong University Press. (Originally published by the University of Minnesota Press.)
Ho, Louise (1994) *Local Habitation.* Hong Kong: Twilight Books Co./Department of Comparative Literature, The University of Hong Kong.
Ong, Walter (1982) *Orality and Literacy: The Technologizing of the Word.* London: Methuen.
Walcott, Derek (1992) The Antilles: Fragments of Epic Memory. The Nobel lecture. http://www.geocities.com/SoHo/Exhibit/6107/frameset.html.

Appendix

Four poems by Louise Ho

Hong Kong riots, 1967

As five this morning
The curfew lifted.
Receding, it revealed
Shapes that became people
Moving among yesterday's debris
Stones, more so than words,
Are meaningless,
Out of context.

Island

We are a floating island
Kept afloat by our own energy
We cross date lines
National lines
Class lines
Horizons far and near

We are a floating island
We have no site
Nowhere to land
No domicile

Come July this year
We may begin to hover in situ
May begin to settle
May begin to touch down
We shall be
A city with a country
An international city becoming national

End of era

End of era
Or change of chapter
Smaller than a speck on the map
A nerve centre in the world
Minuscule place
Global space
Several vortices
Suspended by their own velocity
Drive cogwheels that orbit like planets

Remembering 4th June, 1989

Yes, I remember Marvell, Dryden,
Yeats, men who had taken up the pen
While others the sword
That would have vanished
Were it not for the words
That shaped them and kept them.

The shadows of June the fourth
Are the shadows of a gesture,
They say, but how shall you and I
Name them, one by one?
There were so many,
Crushed, shot, taken, all overwhelmed,
Cut down without a finished thought or cry.

Presumably, that night, or was it dawn,
The moon shone pure,
As on the ground below
Flowed the blood of men, women and children.
The stunned world responded, and
Pointing an accusing finger, felt cheated.

But think, my friend, think: China never
Promised a tea party, or cakes
For the masses. It is we,
Who, riding on the crest of a long hope,
Became euphoric, and forgot
The rock bottom of a totalitarian state.

Then this compact commercial enclave,
First time, ever, rose up as one.
Before we went our separate ways again,
We thought as one,
We spoke as one,
We too have changed, if 'not utterly'
And something beautiful was born.

As we near the end of an era
We have at last
Become ourselves.
The catalyst
Was our neighbour's blood.

Whoever would not
For a carefree moment
Rejoice at a return
To the Motherland?
But, rather pick ears of corn
In a foreign field

Than plough the home ground
Under an oppressive yoke.

Ours is a unique genius,
Learning how to side-step all odds
Or to survive them.
We have lived
By understanding

Each in his own way
The tautness of the rope
Underfoot.

9
Defining Hong Kong poetry in English: An answer from linguistics

Agnes Lam

Introduction

In many former British colonies, English usually continues to prosper because of its instrumental functions in commerce and international communication. In Hong Kong, a former colony returned to China on 1 July 1997, English has also continued to play such a role. Given the international outlook of the city, that is to be expected. What is remarkable is that, apart from the use of English at work or as one of the languages in education, particularly at the tertiary level, there also appears to have been more public use of English as a medium of literary expression in the last few years. In this chapter, I shall focus on the development of poetry, often identified as the first literary genre to emerge with the enhanced use of English in a society. I shall first outline the salient indicators of the existence of Hong Kong poetry in English and then go on to define what it is. In the definition, I shall refer to some linguistic discussions on the nature of language and of poetry as well as to sociolinguistic concepts of the speech community (or a group of people communicating with each other) and how individual members in any specific community locate their own identity or identities. I shall end with an outline of a framework for tracking literary development.

A vibrant poetic community

In the last few years, the development of poetry in English in Hong Kong appears to have gathered momentum, as indicated by the publication of poetry, the scale of poetry readings, the interest in website discussion, and supportive press coverage.

Publication of poetry

Recent poetry collections include Louise Ho's *New Ends Old Beginnings* (1997), Agnes Lam's *Woman to Woman and Other Poems* (1997), Kavita Butalia's *An Amorphous Melody* (1998), Madeleine Slavick and Barbara Baker's *Round* (1998), Mani Rao's *The Last Beach* (1999) and Peter Stambler's *Coming Ashore Far from Home* (2000), all published by Asia 2000 (http://www.asia2000.com.hk) based in Hong Kong. Examples of anthologies are *Vs: 12 Hong Kong Poets* (1993) and Andrew Parkin's *From the Bluest Part of the Harbour: Poems from Hong Kong* (1995). Parkin's anthology includes the translated work of several poets writing in Chinese. Examples of other Chinese poems translated into English are Leung Ping-kwan's *City at the End of Time* (1992) and Laurence Wong's contribution in *Hong Kong Poems* (Parkin and Wong, 1997). Apart from books, three literary journals are of particular interest to English readers. *Renditions: A Chinese-English Translation Magazine* (http://www.cuhk.edu.hk/renditions) published by the Chinese University of Hong Kong has had a long history. A more recent journal is *Dimsum* launched by Chameleon Press on 11 May 1999. Based in Hong Kong, *Dimsum* (http://www.dimsum.com.hk) features English writing, mostly short stories, essays and, to a much lesser extent, poetry, from the Asia-Pacific region. Another journal launched around April 2000 by the Department of English at the University of Hong Kong is *Yuan Yang*.

Poetry readings

Various organizations have organized readings for both English and Chinese writers. Poets writing in English have been featured along with writers writing in Chinese in events such as 'Meeting Hong Kong Writers This Life' organized by the Hong Kong Arts Centre during the Handover period in 1997 and the 'Eye on books' Literary Festival organized by the British Council in 1998. While the Arts Centre seminars attracted primarily adult participants usually with an interest in writing, whole classes of secondary school students attended various readings in the British Council programme apparently in lieu of an English class at their schools, resulting in audiences of over a hundred. In January 2000, the Fringe Club also presented 'Citypoetry' as part of a 'City 2000 Festival', involving poets reading in the Soho area, just off the Central business district in Hong Kong. During the festival, poetry was displayed using various media in the windows of restaurants and shops.

Writers have also organized events themselves, especially in the last year or so. On 4 November 1998, Kavita Butalia organized a reading at a bar called *Steps* on Aberdeen Street, again just off the Central business zone. This soon became a monthly event announced over email by various poets such as Mani Rao, Alan Jefferies, Christopher Kelen and others. By May 1999, the regular crowd had reached 60. It became necessary to find a bigger venue. In October 1999, the readings moved to *Visage Free*, under the Mid-Levels escalator on Cochrane Street. By then, the announcement was emailed to a list of about three hundred people. At the end of 1999, Alan Jefferies, Christopher Kelen and Mani Rao put together a manuscript for an anthology consisting largely of poetry from some 26 writers who had presented their work at the *Steps/Visage* readings, and this has since been published (Outloud 2002).

Wed-based interaction

Besides face-to-face networking, writers and creative writing students can communicate further on website forums. Lawrence Gray hosts and active site at RLINK at http://www.lawrencegray.com/ and circulates an electronic newsletter entitled *The Wild East*. The site for the Hong Kong Writers' Circle can also be found at Gray's site. Stephen Richards, who teaches creative writing at the City University of Hong Kong, administers another on-line journal entitled *Expressions* (http://www.cityu.edu.hk/Is/research/xhk/). Primarily created for young Chinese students writing in English, it also welcomes contributions from other writer.

Press coverage

All the activity has received generally supportive coverage from the Hong Kong press. Articles introducing the local literary scene or reviewing locally published books including poetry collections have appeared periodically in the two daily English newspapers, *Hong Kong Standard* and *South China Morning Post*. There has also been coverage in various magazines ranging from in-house publications such as *Paroles* published by the Alliance Française to magazines for a wider audience such as *Asiaweek* or *B International*. See, for example, Clark (1997), Forestier (1997a, 1997b), Henry (1998), Hui (1998), Vee (1999) and Sun (1999). Radio interviews of writers are also aired occasionally.

Other conducive factors

Various explanations have been offered for this recent interest in poetry in English in Hong Kong. According to Vce (1999: 1) reporting on the readings at *Steps*, the demographic characteristics of the readers as well as the audience are relevant. The readers are 'mostly post-university Westerners, at the age when poetry and culture mean more than mortgages and investment plans'. The Chinese in the crowd have usually spent some time overseas. 'So the growth in the number of young-ish, arty, English-speaking intellectuals in Hong Kong could be one of the local reasons for the interest in poetry'. Vee also points to the international trend of poetry slams (or competitions for poetry performances) at bars, for example, in New York. Another reason could be that several of the poets know or, at least, know of each other through someone else in Hong Kong. There is therefore interest in maintaining social interaction, which enhances efficient communication when events are organized. The occupations of the poets are partly responsible for this. They tend to be working in the media, marketing, art or design, publishing, teaching and literary or language work. Electronic communication has also made it easier to disseminate information to a wider pool of people. Of course, there must be a core group who take sufficient interest to organize events. Publishers and editors like Mike Morrow and Alan Sargent of *Asia 2000* and Mohan Mirchandani and Nury Vittachi of *Dimsum* also contribute in no small measure to the networking between the press and the writers as well as among writers. The financial investment from publishers and grant support from the Hong Kong Arts Development Council (for example, for Slavick and Baker (1998), Rao (1999), Stambler (2000) and the special 1997 issue of *Renditions* by Hung and Pollard) also deserve mention (see Lam, 1999 for details on the development of poetry in Chinese and English in Hong Kong up to 1997).

The controversy

Amidst all the recent excitement in poetry, questions about literary quality and cultural identity have been asked. In July 1998, Hui reported on the 'identity crisis for English writers' in Hong Kong. A year later in August 1999, Vee (1999: 1) asked, 'Has anyone in Hong Kong really produced poetry, in the classic literary, timeless sense of the word, as opposed to doggerel or cute epigrams?' A few weeks later in September 1999, Lawrence Gray set up a website discussion with the title 'Are Hong Kong poets poets or Hong Kong poets?' They are all essentially questions about quality and identity. Subsumed under this controversy are at least three questions: (1) What counts as poetry? (2) What counts as good poetry? and (3) What counts as Hong Kong poetry?

What counts as poetry?

Modern poems are rather amorphous. Rhyme and rhythm are not always used. Some poets even talk of prose poems. Some poems tell stories. Others paint a character sketch, a picturesque scene or convey a mood. Still others are wishes, prayers or songs. The boundaries between poetry and other types of writing are unclear. In fact, the blurring of the distinction between poetic language and ordinary language is not just the concern of poets. In mainstream linguistics, there has also been a movement to reclaim the importance of figurative language in everyday language. More and more linguists now conceive of language as being inherently tied to thinking or the structuring of general experience. Some have referred to this position with the term *cognitive linguistics* but related theories have also been proposed under other names such as *cultural linguistics* (Palmer, 1996) or *cognitive poetics* (Tsur, 1992). Although these theories do not take into account exactly the same concerns, there is a common recognition that language, thought and experience are intricately related. Taken together, research such as Lakoff and Johnson (1980), Gibbs (1994) and Carter (1999) indicates that it is more helpful to think of 'a cline of literariness in language use' (Carter, 1999: 207) than to use an either-or opposition of literal versus non-literal language. If all language could be literary, then how do we characterize poetry? Apart from its appearance in lines, it is hard to identify a poem. Often, we shall have to take a poem as the poet offers it, at face value. A poem is a poem because the poet offers it as such. We may think it is a bad poem but it is still a poem. It is the same as when someone sends us a letter. We may think it is poorly written but it remains a letter.

What counts as good poetry?

How can we decide whether a poem is good? Some have offered indicators such as the poet winning a prize, good sales or positive reviews. All these indicate that the poet is reaching a certain readership but do not guarantee quality. Yet, although a poet's fame does not automatically mean quality, the strength of the communicative tie between a poet and readers is still a good key to quality because poetry, like all language, is a communicative act. The reader's understanding may not be entirely the same as what the poet intends to convey, but that could be so even in everyday communication. Apart from passing on information, good poetry normally has the effect of giving pleasure through heightening the empathic awareness of some experience in the reader. A final mark of good poetry is the appropriateness of the language used. These three characteristics of good poetry: communicativeness, empathic pleasure and linguistic appropriateness, need to be culturally articulated. Understatement may be valued in one culture while directness may be esteemed in another. Emotional expressiveness, humour and satire also vary from culture to culture. It takes therefore cultural openness to appreciate a poem from someone with a different background even if it is the same language that is used. It also takes discipline to write a poem in such a way so that at least the group of people it is intended for can have a good chance to understand it. Poets do not have the licence to be unnecessarily opaque though, like other writers, they can choose to write between the lines.

The fact that English is an international language makes it possible for writers writing in English to communicate with a very wide audience. But in the metaphorical use of English, there are cultural constraints in the sense that readers from some cultures may be able to identify more easily with a certain poet than readers from other cultures. Cultures, however, are not fixed entities to be contained in impervious boxes. Non-native poets writing in English in Hong Kong are likely to have at least two cultures at various degrees of convergence (or coming together). Because English is a global language, even poets with English as their native tongue have to take into account other cultures, both native and non-native, if they wish to reach readers from those cultures.

Since there is cultural variation, poets have to decide for themselves which readership they intend to reach. The more readers a poet manages to reach, the greater the communicative success. The more a poet is understood by readers from diverse backgrounds in different geographical locations and through various historical times, the more communicative success the poet has. Alternatively, instead of catering to readers from all cultures, the poet may wish to address only readers in a particular culture but a great number of them, say, every Chinese who can understand English. The choice of readership size does not determine how good a poet is *per se*, but relates to the degree of communicative success possible. A Hong Kong poet once remarked, 'As long as one person understands my poem, I am happy'. That is a valid position because as long as one reader understands a poem, the communicative exchange is complete. But I am tempted to ask, 'If a poem is worth understanding, isn't it better that it is understood by more people?'

What counts as Hong Kong poetry?

Some critics ask, 'Is there poetry in Hong Kong?' What they really mean is, 'Is there good poetry in Hong Kong? How international is Hong Kong poetry?' Hong Kong poetry can be defined as one or all of the following: (1) poetry written by Hong Kong poets; (2) poetry available in Hong Kong; and (3) poetry written about and for Hong Kong.

How do we define Hong Kong poets? For a start, perhaps we can refer to the conceptual basis of local varieties of English. Descriptions of local varieties tend to be based on the output from speakers native to that locality. Thus, Hong Kong English is often identified as that variety spoken by people of Hong Kong origin, not by foreigners residing in Hong Kong. If we take such a position in our definition of Hong Kong poetry, then there is only a very small corpus of Hong Kong poetry in English. Of the 26 writers who are included in the current manuscript of *Out Loud*, the proposed anthology for the Steps/Visage readers, only three have Chinese names: Louise Ho, Agnes Lam and Elbert S. P. Lee. Even if we include Juliette Chen (of Vietnamese and Taiwanese lineage and who came to Hong Kong when she was two years old but apparently now lives elsewhere), Yuen Che Hung (who writes mainly in Chinese but sometimes in English), and Liam Fitzpatrick (born in Hong Kong of Irish and Chinese parentage) from other anthologies, the corpus is still very small. If we include those poets writing in Chinese who have been translated into English (such as Leung Ping-kwan), the whole corpus of Hong Kong poetry available in English is larger.

In drawing up the list above, we seem to have taken Chinese ethnicity (or some indication of it) and/or whether poets spent a good number of their formative years in Hong Kong as defining characteristics of Hong Kong poets and thus of Hong Kong poetry. But what about poets who are already adults when they begin residing in Hong Kong? Is it not possible that they will come to know enough of the local culture to recount their experience of it? How long does a period of residence have to be to suffice as Hong Kongness for these visiting poets? For example, would Edmund Blunden count as a Hong Kong poet because he taught at the University of Hong Kong for a good number of years and published *A Hong Kong House: Poems 1951–1961*?

I do not know whether Edmund Blunden would have identified himself as both a British poet as well as a Hong Kong poet. I do know, however, that a good number of foreigners publishing in Hong Kong have presented their work with subtitles like *Hong Kong poems* or *Hong Kong writing* and certainly consider themselves to be part of the Hong Kong literary scene. Given the openness of visiting poets based in Hong Kong to be part of the Hong Kong poetic community, it would be unrepresentative to exclude their work from a discussion of Hong Kong poetry even if it may go against the conventional practice of linguistic discussions of local varieties and hence of local literatures in English.

Perhaps it is useful to take the broader perspective of Hong Kong as a cosmopolitan city with people from all over the world living here. Hong Kong poetry can therefore include all the poetry written in English either published or made available at poetry readings by anyone writing in English currently or once based in Hong Kong. The guiding principle is whether the poets have had sufficient experience of Hong Kong. Whether the poets writing in English are ethnic Chinese or not is irrelevant. We can take the stand that Hong Kong poetry means 'Poetry available in Hong Kong'. This is almost like saying Hong Kong French food is French food available in Hong Kong; whether it is cooked by French, Singaporean or Hong Kong Chinese cooks is irrelevant.

A final consideration is whether the poetry available in Hong Kong is written about Hong Kong or for Hong Kong. In other words, is there a Hong Kong flavour to the poetry? Not necessarily. Some poems in the corpus as defined above are about life in Hong Kong and some are not. This is regardless of whether the poet is of local origin. Poets not native to Hong Kong may write about Hong Kong life while those native to Hong Kong may not always write about Hong Kong. Compare, for example, these lines from Madeleine Marie Slavick's 'Passage' on an aspect of Hong Kong life (Slavick and Baker, 1998: 21):

> Red lights of family shrine,
> Red door gods,
> You know *a-ma* and *a-ba*'s sleep
> Inside their plastic-walled mattress.
> You know he'll rise at five to breathe good air,
> And she'll take exercises at six
> In the empty school playground.

with a few lines from Louise Ho's (1997: 52) 'Tree of life' on a more universal theme:

> All torn and twisted shredded and confused
> Meandering tree of life a weak pattern
> On a brick wall's worn whitish grey grouting
> Mere seepage along the way of least resistance
> And towards no end in particular

The above contrast is merely an illustration. Like many other non-Chinese poets writing in Hong Kong, Madeleine Slavick also writes on other less 'local' themes while Louise Ho has also written poems specifically about Hong Kong. Another approach to the issue is not to think of whether the poets write about Hong Kong but whether they write from the perspective of a Hong Kong person. In other words, is a poet speaking on behalf of Hong Kong people? Is there a distinct Hong Kong voice in the poetry? That question may only be answered by people who know Hong Kong culture in the first place. But what is Hong Kong culture? In the Hong Kong community, there can be several sub-groups with different sub-cultures, though they may overlap and, for certain aspects, share a common denominator. Each poet has to determine which of these sub-groups they want to speak for and speak to. There can be as many Hong Kong voices as there are sub-cultures, though on some issues, sub-groups may very well share the same perspective.

To summarize, Hong Kong poetry can have at least two definitions: one narrower and one broader. The first is that Hong Kong poetry is written by poets of Hong Kong origin as defined by place of birth and/or residence during their formative years. The broader definition includes poetry written by poets currently or once based in Hong Kong, as long as they have experienced Hong Kong. Whether the poetry is about Hong Kong does not seem crucial. Yet, it is likely that those poets who have had a long association with Hong Kong or at least with a certain sub-group in the community may be able to write more from the perspective of at least that sub-group. Hence, readers from that sub-group may find more resonance in their poetry. The more sub-groups a poet can speak for, the more likely will readers from different backgrounds identify with his or her poetry. The more universal the themes are, the more general the audience.

Speech communities and acts of identity

In the understanding of sub-groups or sub-cultures in a community, it is useful to refer to sociolinguistic concepts of the speech community and acts of identity by individual members of a community. Various definitions of the *speech community* have been given by Leonard Bloomfield (1933) through John Gumperz to Braj Kachru (1983) and others (see Hudson, 1996: 24–30 for a representative discussion). I would just define it as a community of individuals communicating with each other. A related concept is the *speech fellowship*. According to Firth (reprinted in Palmer, 1968: 208), 'it is useful to recognize a close *speech fellowship* and a wider *speech community* in what may be called the *language community*, comprising both written and spoken forms of the general language'.

Applying this distinction towards an understanding of the Hong Kong literary community, we can conceive of several overlapping small literary fellowships within it. For example, there is the fellowship of poets writing in Chinese, another of ethnic Chinese poets writing in English and a third group of other non-Chinese poets writing in English. These three may very well overlap and interact. They may also overlap with fellowships of writers writing in other genres such as novels, short stories, biographies and so on. Interaction between such fellowships is enhanced by translation or through bilingual individuals. Taken as a whole, the Hong Kong literary community can be conceived of as a fellowship overlapping with fellowships of other users of Chinese and English in other professions such as business, law, government, education and so forth in Hong Kong. In turn, the Hong Kong language community is itself a fellowship belonging to the wider speech community of Chinese users in the world as well as the international speech community of English users.

Because individuals, whether poets or readers, have different social networks (Milroy, 1987) and identify with the work of different poets, their perceptions of the poetic community in Hong Kong will differ. Le Page and Tabouret-Keller (1985: 4–5) go so far as to stress that 'groups or communities and the linguistic attributes of such groups have no existential locus other than in the minds of individuals, and that groups or communities inhere only in the way individuals behave towards each other'. The extent to which individual poets identify with other Hong Kong poets and the degree to which readers identify with the poetry produced by poets circumscribe the defining boundaries of the Hong Kong poetic community. While the outer limit of the Hong Kong poetic community can very well encircle all the poetry available from poets based in Hong Kong, within this community, each poet or each reader will have a possibly different concept of the Hong Kong poetic community and of Hong Kong poetry. The key is mutual identification between one poet and other poets and between a poet and his or her readers. Because poetry is a communicative act, a poet cannot be considered a Hong Kong poet unless the poet is accepted by Hong Kong readers. That brings us to the question of who the Hong Kong readers are. That also has two definitions: a narrower one based on readers who were born and/or grew up in Hong Kong and a broader one including visitors now or once resident in Hong Kong. That all seems very clear except that there are also readers of Hong Kong poetry in the international community who have never been based in Hong Kong. It is possible that these readers may identify a poet's work as that of a Hong Kong poet in that it is a voice *from* Hong Kong. Whether that voice is *of* Hong Kong may not be easily apparent or important to them.

Apart from all these fuzzy possibilities of mutual identification between poets and readers, it is also very likely that a poet will identify with more than one poetic community. An Asian American poet now based in Hong Kong is likely to continue to identify with the Asian American poetic community and maintain communicative ties with that community in terms of publication and personal interaction. At the same time, this Asian American poet may interact with the poets now based in Hong Kong as well. Likewise, a Hong Kong poet may read poems in other parts of the world and, on those occasions, will be part of the international poetic community. In spite of these multifarious interactions and acts of identity, for most poets, there is likely to be a dominant poetic community just as for each user of English, there is a dominant variety of English most frequently used.

How does our discussion of Hong Kong poetry affect traditional concepts of local varieties of English? If Hong Kong poetry in English suggests different entities to different people, granted that such individually defined entities are likely to overlap, does that mean that Hong Kong English will also mean different varieties to different people? Is Hong Kong English not one variety but a whole host of varieties? To start with, unlike some writers writing in Hong Kong who are open to adopting the label of Hong Kong writing for their work, foreigners in other professions are unlikely to claim they are using Hong Kong English just because they are based in Hong Kong. Yet, because of the interaction with so many varieties of English from outside of Hong Kong, users of English in Hong Kong, whether they are local Chinese or visiting foreigners, have to accommodate their use of English to allow for effective global communication. This constant accommodation is probably characteristic of the use of English in Hong Kong and other cosmopolitan cities. The users of English in Hong Kong can be mapped onto an entire continuum of users with low English competence as well as users of extremely high competence akin to that of speakers of standard varieties in countries where English is natively spoken. The users at the top end of the continuum are much fewer than those at the lower end, but their English is still a sample of Hong Kong English. Hong Kong is an international city peopled by individuals bilingual and bicultural in varying degrees, and we can expect to find a whole cline of Hong Kong English reflective of this variation.

A framework for the development of literary communities

Hong Kong poetry in English as affirmed in this chapter appears to be thriving in recent years according to a number of indicators and/or factors such as the emergence of poetry collections and anthologies, the developing culture of poetry readings in the community, animated discussion on the web, a favourable press environment, organizational leadership from a critical mass of poets, regular cohesive interaction among poets, investment in publication by publishers, and support from the Hong Kong Arts Development Council and other organizations.

To enhance its development, more of the above will of course help, but other support mechanisms are also desirable. Some recommendations might include writer-in-residence programmes at universities, the study of selected poems produced by Hong Kong poets at school or university, the encouragement of bi-directional translation between Chinese and English in publication and readings, more obvious display stands at bookstores for Hong Kong writing, more opportunities for poets to interact with other writers and artists, literary awards and competitions to attract young poets and writers, and a consistent policy to enhance English competence and use in the community. This list can be used to help track the development of literary communities in Hong Kong as well as other societies where English is used as an additional language in the community.

Conclusion

In this chapter, I have given an overview of how poetry in English has thrived in Hong Kong in recent years. Although questions of literary quality and cultural identity have been raised, in the light of recent linguistic theory, the existence of Hong Kong poetry has been affirmed. Poetry is viewed as a communicative act and hence good poetry depends on communicative success.

On the basis of this general definition of poetry, Hong Kong poetry is defined broadly as poetry available in Hong Kong. For individual poets and readers, however, their perception of what Hong Kong poetry is depends on whether and to what extent they identify with other members in the poetic community in Hong Kong. A poet is not a Hong Kong poet unless he or she chooses to identify himself or herself as such and readers accept him or her as such. This in turn is related to whether poets wish to have only Hong Kong readers as their audience and/or a wider readership. The challenge to poets writing in English is to be able to articulate their thoughts and cultures to readers from their native cultures while communicating some of their experiences to readers in other cultures as well. This is so whether they are native or non-native speakers of English. If literature is for the extension of human empathy, then writing in English poses immense possibilities for the very fact that it is a global language with speakers from myriad cultures.

References

Ambucher, Brent et al. (1993) *Vs: 12 Hong Kong Poets*. Hong Kong: Big Weather Press.
Bloomfield, Leonard (1933) *Language*. New York: Holt, Rinehart and Winston.
Blunden, Edmund (1962) *A Hong Kong House: Poems 1951–1961*. London: Collins.
Butalia, Kavita (1998) *An Amorphous Melody*. Hong Kong: Asia 2000.
Carter, Ron (1999) Common Language: Corpus, Creativity and Cognition. *Language and Literature*, **8**(3): 195–216.
Clark, Julie (1997) Poetic license. *B International*, October, 124–5.
Forestier, Katherine (1997a) A life and death journey. *South China Morning Post: The Review*, 14 June, p. 9.
Forestier, Katherine (1997b) Using verse to bridge the culture gap. *South China Morning Post: The Review*, 14 June, p. 9.
Gibbs, Raymond W. (1994) *The Poetics of Mind: Figurative Thought, Language, and Understanding*. Cambridge: Cambridge University Press.
Henry, Gerard (1998) Une litterature chinoise de langue anglaise. *Paroles*, July–August, pp. 7–9.
Ho, Louise (1997) *New Ends Old Beginnings*. Hong Kong: Asia 2000.
Hudson, Richard A. (1996) *Sociolinguistics* (2nd edn.). Cambridge: Cambridge University Press.
Hui, Polly (1998) Identity crisis for English writers. *Hong Kong Standard: Life*, 7 July, p. 1.
Hung, Eva, and Pollard, David E. (eds.) (1997) *Renditions Special Issue: Hong Kong Nineties*. Hong Kong: Chinese University of Hong Kong.
Kachru, Braj B. (ed.) (1983) *The Other Tongue: English Across Cultures*. Oxford: Pergamon Press. Reprinted 1997, Urbana, IL: University of Illinois Press.
Lakoff, George and Johnson, Mark (1980) *Metaphors We Live by*. Chicago and London: The University of Chicago Press.
Lam, Agnes (1997) *Woman to Woman and Other Poems*. Hong Kong: Asia 2000.
Lam, Agnes (1999) Poetry in Hong Kong: The 1990s. *World Literature Today*, **73**(1), 53–61.

Le Page, Robert B. and Tabouret-Keller, Andree (1985) *Acts of Identity: Creole-based Approaches to Language and Ethnicity.* Cambridge: Cambridge University Press.

Leung, Ping-kwan (1992) *Xingxiang Xianggang [City at the End of Time].* Translated by Gordon T. Osing. Hong Kong: Twilight Books in association with the Department of Comparative Literature, The University of Hong Kong.

Milroy, Lesley (1987) *Language and Social Networks* (2nd edn.). Oxford: Basil Blackwell.

Outloud (2002) *Outloud: An Anthology of Poetry from OutLoud Readings, Hong Kong.* Hong Kong: XtraLoud Press.

Palmer, Frank R. (ed.) (1968) *Selected Papers of J. R.. Firth: 1952–59.* London: Longman.

Palmer, Gary B. (1996) *Towards a Theory of Cultural Linguistics.* Austin: University of Texas Press.

Parkin, Andrew (ed.) (1995) *From the Bluest Part of the Harbour: Poems from Hong Kong.* Hong Kong: Oxford University Press.

Parkin, Andrew and Wong, Lawrence (1997) *Hong Kong Poems in English and Chinese.* Translated by Evangeline Almberg, Serena Jin, Wing-Yin Mok and Laurence Wong. Vancouver: Ronsdale Press.

Rao, Mani (1999) *The Last Beach.* Hong Kong: Asia 2000.

Slavick, Madelaine M. and Baker, Barbara (1998) *Round: Poems and Photographs of Asia.* Hong Kong: Asia 2000.

Stambler, Peter (2000) *Coming Ashore Far from Home: Selected Poems 1981–1998.* Hong Kong: Asia 2000.

Sun, Andrew (1999) Hungry for good writing. *Asiaweek,* **25**(46), 54, 56.

Tsur, Reuven (1992) *Towards a Theory of Cognitive Poetics.* Amsterdam: North-Holland.

Vee, Louis (1999) Taking a poetic licence. *Hong Kong Standard: Life,* 26 August, p. 1.

Vittachi, Nury (ed.) (1999) *Dimsum: The Journal of Good Reading,* **1** and **2**.

Vs: 12 Hong Kong Poets. (1993) Hong Kong: Big Weather Press.

Appendix

Two poems by Agnes Lam

Yellow flowers on a battlefield

You ask me what is happiness.
You ask me what is success.
I once was young like you.
Like you, I needed answers.

You tell me learning is difficult
in circumstances like yours.
Your teachers know that too.
I couldn't agree more.

There are not enough books,
not enough tapes or videos,
not enough teachers,
not enough anything.

How can I talk to you
about English on the Net
when there's only one computer
for each department?

Six days I have taught you.
Six days you have all come.
Always eager, always trying,
ever listening and asking.

You ask me for my poems.
You ask me for my photo.
You ask me for my signature.
My dear students, I am but a teacher.

Tomorrow I shall fly away
back to my office where I work
from eight to eight and I shall miss
your thirst for learning, your welcome.

I wish so much
you would be happy,
that you would find
meaning and success.

But all I can leave you
are but another's words –
zhan di huang hua fen wai xiang.
On a battlefield, yellow flowers are

sweeter than ever.

(16 June 1999, Yanan University)

I have walked on air

Last night
I had the dream again …

… a quadrangle,
on all four sides
walkways with high ceilings,
smooth stone columns.
A garden in the centre
filled with light.

I was sitting
on the cool tiled floor
in the shaded verandah
leaning against a column,
looking at the garden in the sun,
in a white nightgown,
a tinge of blue light,
thin cotton, loose and
long beyond my toes.

I heard footsteps coming
and started to walk away.
Lighter and lighter,
my feet a few inches
above the ground,
I did not climb the stairs.
I floated into the air.

So many times
in my dreams,
I have walked on air.

I move over houses,
mountains, water, fields,
between the clouds
into the stars

as my body sleeps.

(2 November 1997, Rodrigues Court)

10

Writing between Chinese and English

Leung Ping-kwan

Introduction

Growing up in Hong Kong, I have always written in Chinese. But there were exceptions. In the last years of my high-school studies, while I had already published poems in the literary supplements of the local newspapers, my Chinese was considered by my Chinese teacher, an old scholar graduated from Peking University, to be less than elegant. Each of my compositions was marked heavily by his red brush, and into my 'modern' style of experimental writing, the wisdom of old idioms was added. But I refused to incorporate them into my revisions, and therefore always ended up with a C – for all my works! At the same time, the English teacher was a kind-hearted young woman who encouraged us to read widely and lent us works by Virginia Woolf and George Orwell. We were also encouraged to write our diary in English, and I was not penalized for writing in the stream-of-consciousness style to sketch my daily thoughts. On the contrary, she offered very encouraging comments!

Though I was not good with English grammar, I found the freedom I did not find in the writing submitted for my Chinese teacher, and the pleasure in actually using language to reflect upon my daily experiences. Few of my readers know the secret that some of the first pages of my first book of essays were actually translated from early practices in English writing!

I started my writing career as a poet and a translator. While in the late 1960s and 1970s when Chinese Mainland still upheld Critical and Socialist Realism as the main doctrine for any kind of writing, I, in this city of Hong Kong at the edge of the mainland, wandered through the dubious magazine stalls in Central and Tsim Sha Tsui, discovered avant-garde and underground magazines from the outside world, and eventually discovered, through English translation, writers such as Kenzaburo Oe, Julio Cortarzar, Jan Kott, Jorge Luis Borges and Gabriel Garcia Marquez. Besides working as translator and then editor and arts editor in various newspapers, I also translated from English, for my own pleasure, the writers I liked. Translation was a practice and training in writing, it was also a means to oppose the dominant trend, a kind of manifesto to promote alternative visions.

Writing in English

I did not receive formal training in the study of English. In the society I grew up in, the use of English was associated with a particular privileged status, which I found myself quite removed from and immune to. English is valued as an asset in business, it is essential in the service professions, yet I am not interested in business English, and I am uncomfortable watching programmes on Hong Kong television teaching English only as 'service English'. I am more interested in the other possibilities of English, in how people from very different cultures have expressed themselves in modified forms of this language.

I began seriously considering writing in English in the 1990s, when my friend Gordon Osing collaborated with me in translating my poems from Chinese into English. The final product turned out to be the book *City at the End of Time*. In the process of moving from one language to another, we had a better understanding of each other's different culture, and looked for possible though difficult ways to carry over the subtleties and nuances. These exercises also helped me for the first time to use in daily conversation a language which I usually did not use. Using it had appeared artificial and snobbish in the past, but now I saw that it offered potential in communicating my own personal thoughts and my own process of creation.

The process of translation is a process of negotiation. Sometimes Gordon would frown and ask me to clarify, so that he could think of an equivalent way to express my words smoothly in English. But then perhaps it was my turn to protest, to say that it was much too smooth or too English than I really wanted it to be. I remember one example, of a poem written on the road leading to Le Shan, the Mountain of Happiness in Sichuan where the gigantic Buddha statue stood. After the first and second drafts of the translation, I was not satisfied, though the meaning seemed to have been conveyed clearly in another language. I did not understand what was wrong and kept looking back and forth at the two versions in two languages, until I realized, in order to make the sentence flow better, we had added in English the causal and explanatory expressions such as 'because', 'therefore', 'and then' etc., which were not there in the Chinese original. I understood that it was impossible to do away with the syntax or make the poem as flexible as the Chinese original, but we tried our best to cut away the explanatory syntax, allowing the scenes to flash and to reveal without conclusion these glimpses of China at the time of the mid-1980s when it was staggering forward towards some unknown goal.

On the Road to Le Shan

Everything indistinct in white fog,
where are we being driven?

We come upon suddenly a slow
oxcart and pass it immediately.

On the chilly, misted glass, with fingertips,
I sketch the picture of green fields passing –

a girl pumping along on her bicycle,
pulling, it seems, an old man's wooden cart.

Two headlights fly right at us
out of the wall of cloud.

The roadsigns are unreadable.
Where in the world are we?

Don't follow that lorry so close,
a flat-bed semi-wavering with sheet steel.

Suddenly we're surrounded by a market town
and booths: eels, dried meats, fresh vegetables.

In a window a mother sews and watches
little red-trousers fall, get up again.

Comes the grinding of overloaded trucks
catching up from behind.

Along the road, tree after tree,
one overturned lorry after another.

This is a modernized road,
no end to the bumping and jolting.

Everything indistinct in white fog,
in silence we ride on and on and on.

(Leung, 1992: 64–7)

Negotiation culture

To negotiate between cultures is not easy. The more 'Chinese' the poem is, the more difficult it is for one to translate it. This difficulty could easily influence people to translate only what can be easily transported into another culture. Also, on the style of translation, there is much advocacy for translators to 'naturalize', and harsh condemnation for those who 'barbarize' the English language. This latter criticism is often made when translators wish to maintain some of the special characteristics of Chinese syntax and expression. I actually have great sympathy for such translators, and I even think that, as in the case of immigrants in a new society, it is often not so easy to be 'naturalized'. If people retain traces of their original culture, does that mean they are trying to barbarize the host culture where they now find themselves?

I have wished in particular not to translate poems that would be easily accessible to the Western readers, but rather those that I do not intend for easy reading. One collection in Chinese, called *Museum Pieces* in English, contains some of my most difficult poems. When 'Cauldron' and two other poems from this collection were first translated by my friend John Minford, I was grateful that they had found a translator who, well-versed in both Chinese and English, helped to recreate what is subtly hidden in one language. Thanks to the hands of the translators, what was considered untranslatable has a chance to speak to new audiences.

I started my collaboration with Martha Cheung on the *Foodscape* project, an exhibition of my poems together with images from photographer Lee Ka-sing, which focused on food from different cities, and which meditates on issues of culture (Leung, 1997). Martha is a friend and colleague who is experienced in writing in both Chinese and English, and she therefore understands very well the excitement and confusion in moving in and out of two cultures.

Tea-coffee

Tea fragrant and strong, made from
Five different blends, in cotton bags or legendary
Stockings – tender, all-encompassing, gathering –
Brewed in hot water and poured into a teapot, its taste
Varying subtly with the time in water steeped.
Can that fine art be maintained? Pour the tea

Into a cup of coffee, will the aroma of one
Interfere with, wash out the other? Or will the other
Keep its flavour: foodstalls by the roadside
Streetwise and worldly from its daily stoves
Mixed with a dash of daily gossips and good sense,
Hard-working, a little sloppy ... An indescribable taste.

(Leung, 1997: 1)

Language boundaries

I understand that it is always easier for me to write in Chinese, and to rely on the talents of my translator friends to render them into another language. But from time to time there are poems that I have considered writing in English. 'Leaf of Passage', a poem I wrote in December 1998, was first intended as a response to a poem 'Astronaut' written by Canadian/Hong Kong poet Andrew

Parkin. I knew Andrew in Hong Kong, and met him again in Erfurt, Germany at a literary conference, where we read together, as a dialogue to one other, musing on different treatments of similar topics.

Andrew's poem 'Astronaut' is about the new emigrant fathers from Hong Kong who leave their wives and children in Vancouver in order to return to Hong Kong to earn a living. The term 'astronaut' has been borrowed in recent years to refer to this group of people commuting busily between two places, whom Parkin depicts as irresponsible and hedonistic:

> From *'Astronaut'*
>
> fly wife and parachute kids to passport-land,
> fly back, astronaut, coming in above love hotels
> of Kowloon Tong for a Kai Tak splash down.
> Rent a flat again in Happy Valley
> With a view of the races,
> Whatever the cost per square inch
> To my karaoke soul!
>
> (Parkin, 1997: 23–5)

I did not have a poem of similar topic at hand, but I told Andrew that I might one day write a different poem to answer his, since I had a different picture of this father in mind.

After my six months' residency in Berlin, on my way back to Hong Kong I stopped by Vancouver to make a visit. At the airport I saw the 'astronaut' fathers rushing back home for a reunion, carrying bulky presents, and being questioned critically by the immigration officers.

At the airport I also saw the monumental bronze sculpture, *The Spirit of Haida Gwaii* by the First Nation artist Bill Reid. I had first seen it at closer distance in Granville Island. The sculpture showed animal travellers from Haida Gwaii myths crowding in a jade-coloured canoe, trying to make their way to some place else. At the airport the sculpture was set against a background of travellers from different origins, wandering past pushing their heavy luggage carts.

The following poem came to me:

> *Leaf of passage*
>
> Is this a jade or a wooden canoe? Sailing through wails from both banks,
> Only to be stranded near customs officers, amidst immigrants waiting in line.
>
> Myths of Haida Gwaii at your elbow: Bear Father with young son sits at the bow
> Looking back at the past; Bear Mother rowing hard, gazes into the future of her children.

> The sharp-teeth beaver paddles away, the dogfish woman converses secretly
>   with the mysteries of the ocean.
> The Wolf, vying for position, tramples on whose back? The reluctant recruit
>   aids in silence, clinging on.
>
> Has our Chief with great vision disappeared from sight with his talking staff?
> Under our eyes only the amphibious frog crosses over the boundary between
>   two worlds.
>
> Not an astronaut bringing home legends of space odysseys. Not at all.
> Just a lonely father shuttling back with heavy twigs to build new nests.
>
> Worries add to one's age, diseases accumulate. Transit is never as smooth
> As sages on blades of weed. See those mottled stamps on a suspicious passport?
>
> Not so easy to roll a house into a backpack; lost forever are the familiar
> Land and language. Departing, you imagined yourself a snow goose flying
>   south,
>
> Crossing the frozen earth in search of a warmer port? What one foresees
> Are sneers from both soils: how can a leaf move that many woes?
>
> (December 1998)

The Bear father and mother, the beaver, the dogfish woman, the wolf, the reluctant recruit ... they are all Haida mythical figures, engaged in a mysterious journey, moving from one place to another. I can still see them vividly in my mind.

From my own experiences in Canada, and from what I learnt from friends in that same situation, I view so-called 'astronauts' not as privileged or 'hedonistic', as Parkin assumed them to be. Rather, they continue to face the problems that generations of Chinese immigrants in the past have faced. And in spite of their ability to move freely between two places, their anxiety of losing touch with both is doubled.

I started to write the poem in English first, but shifted halfway to Chinese and finished it, then I 'translated' it back to English. English first, then Chinese, then English. But the two languages must have tangled deeper in my mind. When I wrote in Chinese, the English lines started to emerge among the characters. When I wrote in English, I must have secretly brought some of the Chinese sentiments over to the passage. Only when I really worked on the poem in English did I discover the unconscious echoes to Li Po's lines 'Sailing through wails of monkeys from both banks, a light boat has passed thousands of mountains' in my first line; and Li Ching Chao's 'How can such a leaf of a boat move that many woes?' in my last line.

But then when I read through it again, I discovered that the original Chinese already carried with it images and sentiments that were not Chinese. The images from Chinese classical literature such as 'snow goose flying south' found themselves in the strange company of Haida mythical figures and sages who were supposed to cross the river on blades of weed were stopped by custom officers examining their suspicious passports. As the poem developed, it grew into the present form, which is a negotiation between a couplet and an eight-line Chinese regulated verse with parallel couplets.

References

Leung, Ping-kwan (1992) *City at the End of Time*. Hong Kong: Twilight Books Company.
Leung, Ping-kwan (1997) *Foodscape*. Hong Kong: The Original Photograph Club Limited.
Parkin, Andrew (1997) Astronaut. In *Hong Kong Poems*. Edited by A. Parkin and L. Wong. Vancouver: Ronsdale.

11

From Yinglish to sado-mastication

Nury Vittachi

How to spell?

A friend of mine made a phone call in Hong Kong. The conversation went as follows:

>'Hello. Can I speak to the managing director?'
>'Hello?'
>'Hello. May I speak to the managing director, please?'
>'How to spell?'
>'Is the MANAGING DIRECTOR available, please?'
>'What is your name?'
>'Hunter.'
>'Mr Hunter is not in.'
>
>[Click.]

There are several elements in this conversation that could attract comment from linguists. Clearly, the receptionist has a poor grasp of English. But by the end of the conversation, she appears to have a poor grasp of logic too, telling the caller that he is not in. Or perhaps the most amusing thing about the transcript is the transparency of the receptionist's desire to get rid of the caller as soon as possible.

Yet to the serious student of Hong Kong English, it may be the phrase in the middle – 'How to spell?' – that gets the biggest nod of recognition. Despite the ungrammatical construction, it is an extremely common phrase, and it seems to work. It is easy enough to understand, and it usually gets results. Why do people speak like this? Is it simply that Hong Kong people are poorly educated in English? Such phrases are usually dismissed as 'Chinglish'. Is this fair?

I suggest it is not. The word 'Chinglish' tends to be used to describe errors in English which educators want eradicated. 'Children could not master both languages and were speaking "Chinglish" ' said a report on Hong Kong education from Agence France Presse on 6 October 1997. We should 'minimize mixed-code teaching or the so-called Chinglish' said an article in the *Hong Kong Standard* on 14 March 1998. The common element of such references is that they are all pejorative. Chinglish is a bad thing. Chinglish is evil. Chinglish must be destroyed.

But the curious thing about the sentence 'How to spell?' is that it is accepted. Employers expect their receptionists to say it. Callers expect to be asked it. Reporters and other people who make a lot of phone calls are asked it on an hourly basis. And I have no doubt that there are office etiquette manuals used by secretarial schools in Hong Kong which actively instruct trainee office staff to use it. 'How to spell?' is well on its way to becoming an acceptable piece of Hong Kong English. There are other structures which also have unique Hong Kong usages. And some of them have gone even further along the road to legitimacy than 'How to spell?'. Some of them have reached full acceptability, which I suggest is when they are used in print, and professional editors and publishers consider them 'correct'.

Wong Wing-fai is chopped to death

My position as a senior editor in a Hong Kong English-language daily newspaper, and as editor of *Dimsum*, an English-language literary quarterly, provides useful observation posts from which to examine the different forms of English used in the territory.

It is hard for a fiction writer to be taken seriously unless he captures something of the speech patterns of the community about which he or she is writing. That challenge is particularly great for writers of English fiction in Hong Kong, where idiosyncratic English speech patterns often require a grasp of Cantonese to fully understand. There are two further challenges. Hong Kong English, up till now, has not been well documented. And fiction writers in the past have delivered few texts which could serve as precedents.

But what is Hong Kong English? And where do we find examples of it? Particularly useful in this respect is to watch novice newspaper sub-editors (editors whose job it is to polish 'raw' copy) being initiated into Hong Kong English. New sub-editors are often imported into Hong Kong from other 'native English' speaking places, such as Australia. They think they have been briefed to turn reporters' raw copy into standard English. Of course, academics know that there is no such thing as standard English. It is often a shock to the sub-editors that they have to turn the copy into Hong Kong English, a language they never knew existed.

Let us take one example. One of the first things they must learn is the correct Hong Kong uses of the word 'chopped'. The *South China Morning Post* reported on the 10 May 1998: '14K member Wong Wing-fai is chopped to death.' The same newspaper reported on 9 October 1998 that: 'Cheng was chopped by two assailants as he arrived for work at Commercial Radio on 19 August, leaving him bleeding heavily from six deep wounds.' In both cases, the individuals had been attacked with knives, and would almost certainly have been described in publications in other parts of the English-speaking world as 'stabbed' or 'slashed'. Yet using 'chopped' in this way is not considered grammatically erroneous in Hong Kong. It is considered the correct way of describing a knife-attack in Hong Kong. (It may, indeed, be more visually accurate too. Many triads are said to favour meat-cleavers over daggers, so the attacker might have actually used chopping motions.)

The imported sub-editor eventually learns that the apparently improper use of the word 'chopped' is perfectly proper here. The following week, he comes across a sentence like this: 'Feng said he needed his passport chopped.' So does it still mean 'stabbed' in this context? Or attacked with a meat-cleaver? No. He then has to be taught that 'chopped' also has another meaning in Hong Kong English. It means 'certified', usually by the use of a seal with which a document is stamped. The phrase comes from a time 100 years or more ago, when money-changers in Hong Kong used cleavers to cut distinctive chips into the edges of silver coins to show that they had been tested and declared genuine. If a coin had been 'chopped' (in other words, chipped, or marked) it was real – and so it is with documents in Hong Kong today; they must be chopped to be valid. A short essay like this cannot include a comprehensive list of terms, but here are three examples of common English words used in unique forms in Hong Kong.

First, *staff* – in most places, we would talk about one staff member or two or three members of staff. In Hong Kong, the word staff is a singular noun. One adds an 's' to make it plural. I am a staff, you are a staff, they are staffs. 'Mr Fan said: "Someone left lipstick prints on the male staffs' shirts to provoke misunderstanding from their wives"' (*South China Morning Post*, 6 April 1999). Second, *alphabet* – a letter of the alphabet is simply 'an alphabet'. A Cantonese speaker of English may tell you that there are 26 alphabets in the English language. 'He can memorise all the positions of the alphabets on the keyboard and types accordingly.' (*Hong Kong Standard*, 11 March 1999). Third, *elderly* – the word 'elderly' is seen as a noun rather than an adjective. It is made plural by the addition of an 's'. One becomes an elderly at the age of about 60. 'Elderlies began queuing as early as 8 am yesterday for the annual handout of four kilograms of rice and other gifts, which did not begin until 3.30 pm' (*Hong Kong Standard*, 25 August 1998).

Of course, I'm not suggesting that these publications are the final arbiters on questions of language, but I submit that they are a useful general guide to what people think is acceptable in English usage. In places where communication occurs in a truncated fashion, such as the classified advertising pages of newspapers, distinctive Hong Kong patterns can again be seen. Recruitment advertisers frequently ask for 'aggressive staffs', when they want hardworking, ambitious people. Some have even asked for 'aggressive waiting staffs' or an 'aggressive receptionist', creating the impression that the employers particularly favour surly staff. This may explain a good deal about the service – or lack of it – in Hong Kong restaurants.

Job ads very often ask for 'staffs' with 'good social connection'. This refers to skills in networking. At times, the terms used in such advertisements can be rather euphemistic. For example, a 'public relations girl' sometimes refers to a girl in a hostess bar, who has 'relations' with members of the public. Get that one mixed up, and you could find yourself in a very embarrassing situation.

Passenger: Please behave

Hong Kong English can also be found in the spoken language. Less common in print, but widely used in spoken English is the word 'marketing' for shopping. It means, simply, going out to buy things, particularly in reference to the food market. These days, the market may refer to an old-fashioned street market of fruit and vegetable stalls, or it may refer to a supermarket. Whatever, many a day starts with a domestic helper telling her employer: 'I go marketing now.'

Cantonese lacks definite articles, and singular terms often carry plural meanings. These two factors give rise to terms such as 'Beware of the man behind the door' on the front of toilet doors. Visitors to shops or rail stations will sometimes see signs telling them to 'Be careful of the pickpocket' or 'Mind the thief', as if the premises has its own pet villain. A park in Tuen Mun has a sign saying: 'Do not feed the living creature.' The number eight green-top minibus bears a sign saying: 'Passenger: Please behave.'

From Chinglish to Yinglish

Hong Kong English also interacts with Cantonese on a more intimate level, sometimes creating a hybrid language that only makes sense to people who know at least a little of both. There is a particular slang in Hong Kong known to Chinese speakers as Chung Ying Mun – literally Chinese-English-Language. This mixes English and Chinese to such an extent that it ends up indecipherable to people outside Hong Kong. It is spoken by taxi drivers, tailors, Indian business people and anyone positioned between the Cantonese-speaking and English-speaking communities.

This slang form of speech has been largely undocumented, and indeed the English press appears not to know of its existence. However, I brought it to the attention of English-only readers by dubbing it 'Yinglish' (Ying being the Cantonese for 'English') and presenting a series of lessons in a daily newspaper here. In the following example dialogue, mixed English and Cantonese vocabulary, phonetically rendered according to my own system of transcription, is presented on a mixed grammatical base. The inherent incongruities in such slang have been deliberately concentrated and exaggerated for humorous effect. In order to make this intelligible to beginning learners and people outside Hong Kong, I provide a literal translation of the Yinglish.

YINGLISH DIALOGUE: HOW TO NEGOTIATE RENT REDUCTIONS WITH YOUR LANDLORD

Landlord A: Yanwai ngoh hai yat goh soft-hearted pushover, ngoh wuih only put up leih-ge rent to seventy-cheen mun. O-mm-o-kay?
Tenant B: Mm-okay! Hai criminal! Seventy-cheen hai a baak per cent increase. Beengo lei think ngoh hai, Li Ka-shing or someone?
A: Mo need to get stroppy tung ngoh, pal. Hai inflation-aah.
B: Lapsap! Market rate hai down 40 per cent.
A: Tung pigs might fly. Forty per cent down hai what the Heung Gong Jingfu Census tung Statistics Department gong. Ngoh-ge own estimate hai market rental rate gone up gau-sup per cent.
B: Tung what do lei base lei-ge estimates on, pray tell ngoh?
A: Rent rises ngoh charge ngoh-ge tenants-aah.
B: Ngoh wuih haul leih-ge crooked ass to the Rent Tribunal.
A: Mo mun tai. Most judges hai ngoh-ge tenants too, sunshine.
B: Ngoh won't pay. Ngor wuih move to Mongkok tung become yat goh cage-yan.
A: Excellent. Ngoh yauh the concession on most cages. Lei require a ng foot suhp inch or a lokh foot saam inch? Gai-wire or metal bars? Leung-up or saam-up?

LITERAL TRANSLATION OF YINGLISH DIALOGUE

Landlord A: Because I am one piece of soft-hearted pushover, I will only put up your rent to seventy thousand dollars. O-not-o-kay?
Tenant B: Not-okay! Is criminal! Seventy thousand is a hundred per cent increase. Who you think I am, Li Ka-shing or someone?
A: No need to get stroppy with me, pal. Is inflation-aah.
B: Rubbish! Market rate is down 40 per cent.
A: And pigs might fly. Forty per cent down is what the Hong Kong Government Census and Statistics Department says. My own estimate is market rental rate gone up ninety per cent.
B: And what do you base your estimates on, pray tell me?
A: Rent rises I charge my tenants-aah.
B: I will haul your crooked ass to the Rent Tribunal.
A: No problem. Most judges are my tenants too, sunshine.

B: I won't pay. I will move to Mongkok and become one piece cage-person.

A: Excellent. I have the concession on most cages. You require a five foot ten inch or a six foot three inch? Chicken-wire or metal bars? Two-up or three-up?

Joint ventures

Other examples of intimacy between the two languages come in the form of joint constructions. 'Thank-you you' is often heard. This is a straight translation of the Cantonese 'Mmgoi lei' (Thanks, you). More complex is 'O-mm-okay-ah?' This comes from the verb-negative-verb construction of the typical Chinese language question. 'Sek-mm-sek-ah?' is literally 'eat [or] not eat, eh?' If the verb has two syllables, such as 'jung yi', which means 'like', the speaker uses only the first syllable before the negative 'mm'. Thus 'Jung mm jung yi-ah?' is literally 'Like [or] not like, eh?' In the same way, the word 'okay' is chopped into two pieces and has a negative 'mm' place in the middle. 'O-mm-okay ah?' (Is that okay, huh?)

Linguistic traps

There are some Cantonese words that appear, at first glance, to have direct English equivalents. It is only when such words are used in context that the difference becomes apparent. One is the word 'faan', meaning return. Let us go back to our office phone conversation. If you call a local Hong Kong Chinese office at nine o'clock in the morning, there is a good chance that the receptionist or secretary will say 'He's not back yet.' To the English ear, this means that the other party has been in the office, gone out and not returned. But has this really happened, so early in the morning?

The receptionist is saying that the other party has been in the office, gone out and not returned. But she is referring to his visit to the office the previous day, or week, or month. 'Keui mm faan sei-tze-lau' means literally 'He not return office.' Chinese receptionists always think of people 'returning' to the office rather than 'coming' to the office. This is simply a matter of convention. Even if you called a person's office early on the first day they were to start their new job, the receptionist would probably say: 'He has not come back.'

The same misunderstanding sounds even more curious to the English-speaking ear when a similar phone call is made to a person's private house. 'May I speak to your husband please?' 'He didn't return from the office.' Anyone not versed in Hong Kong English may be forgiven for thinking that the husband has absconded. The intention of the speaker was merely to say: 'He isn't home yet.'

Another word with what is apparently a direct translation is the word 'first', which is 'sin' in Cantonese. The two words do seem to have largely identical meanings, except 'sin' also carries the meaning 'now'. Your Hong Kong Chinese speaker will welcome you into his house and say: 'First, talk.' In English, we would expect 'And then we will ...' But nothing follows. In Chinese, the presence of the word 'first' does not mean that there is going to be a second item. The speaker is merely saying: 'Now let's have a chat.'

Take the baasee to the bohsee

Another area is the influence of the Chinese language on the actual sounds of Hong Kong English. English is famously full of difficult phonemes that speakers of other tongues find hard to grasp. This is certainly true with people with a Chinese mother tongue. Chinese, like many languages, doesn't have the stand-alone 's' sound that is so common in English. Some languages, such as the continental European languages, have a vowel in front of the 's'. So 'stereo' in Portuguese becomes 'estereo' and school in French becomes 'ecole'. Cantonese, in contrast, adds a vowel after the 's'. Thus we get 'baasee' for bus, and 'bohsee' for boss. This Cantonese habit has given rise to the mock Chinese spoken by Oriental villains in Western comic books. 'You wantee findee muchee goldee?'

The 'r' sound and the 'z' sound also don't exist as sounds without vowels. Thus children in many Hong Kong schools are taught that the letter 'r' is pronounced 'aarro' and the letter 'z' is pronounced 'ezed'. The letter 'r' is thus pronounced as if it was 'R. O.' and the letter 'z' sounds like 'E. Z.'. A girl called Roz making a phone call in Hong Kong would be likely to have daily conversations such as this:

> 'Who calling please?'
> 'Roz.'
> 'How to spell?'
> 'R. O. Z.'
> 'Aarro. Oh. Ezed.'
> 'No. There's only one "o". And there's no "e" at the end. Just "z".'
> 'Aah! Aarro. Oh. Ezed.'
> 'No! There's only one "o". It's R. O. Z.'
> 'Aarro. Oh. Ezed.'
> 'No!'
> Et cetera, et cetera.

Many English words with two tricky-to-say consonants together are simplified in the Cantonese mouth, so that only one vowel is used. 'John he say af-ter you eat san'wich, you contac' him, o-mm-okay-ah?'

Capturing speech in fiction

It is important for a writer and editor focusing on material set in East Asia to produce dialogue which is true to the speech patterns in the various countries in the region. This is tricky; unlike the playwright, the creator of dialogue has no vocal aids, such as an accent, to help him. The voice must be created purely on the page. A further challenge is the grim lack of precedents. It is hard to find texts in which writers have tried to create such speech patterns. Thus each writer has to be his or her own pioneer.

The best known novels about Hong Kong are the James Clavell ones, such as *Noble House*, written in the early 1980s. 'Joss! The round-eye barbarians are back,' his Hong Kong characters exclaim. While some mainlanders might still use 'barbarians' for Westerners, this type of dialogue certainly doesn't ring true as Hong Kong speech today. I have never heard the word 'Joss' used as an exclamation in Hong Kong. It does exist as a word – it comes from a local mispronunciation of the Portuguese word 'Deus' – but it is certainly not in common use.

In my novel, *Asian Values* (1996), the major characters all spoke English, but each spoke a different 'brand'. The Indian character would say, 'What you are going to do?'. The Singaporean would say, 'Can or not?'. Here's a short excerpt illustrating two Hong Kong Chinese and one Hong Kong Indian talking on the phone. Mr Dippy Sajbalani believes his daughter has been kidnapped by a pervert and he is on the phone, trying to hire a detective to get on their trail. 'Waai' is Cantonese for 'Hello'.

> 'Waai?'
> 'Hello? Is Mr J.A. Chan there?'
> 'Waai?'
> 'Is this the office of Mr J.A. Chan, private investigator?'
> 'He in a meeting.'
> 'Oh. Where? Where is it? Is the meeting in the office? Where is Mr Chan?'
> 'In toilet.'
> 'He's in a meeting in the toilet?'
> 'No. He tol' me to say he in a meeting if someone call him.'
> 'But he's actually in the toilet.'
> 'Yes.'
> 'Can you get him out of the toilet please? This is a very urgent call. This is Mr Sajbalani. Just tell him Mr Saj is wanting to talk to him. Very important. Much money.'
> Mr Chan, who was listening to this conversation from a small room a metre away from Ms Tik, his secretary-receptionist-partner-accountant-lover-office cleaner, flushed the toilet and kicked the door open.
> 'Ah. He come out of toilet now. He here, he here. Fei yando-yan.'
> Chan, a middle-aged man wearing a jacket and trousers which were almost but not quite the same shade of grey, threw his wet newspaper down on

his paper-covered desk and settled himself comfortably in his lopsided red leatherette chair before signalling to Ms Tik, who sat 40 centimetres away, to put the call through. He spoke indistinctly thanks to the Mild Seven cigarette in his mouth.

'Mr Saj. Ver' nice to call me. How you?'

'Fine, Mr Chan. Listen. I have no time for idle chitting and chatting. I need you to follow some people.'

'Yes sir, Mr Saj.'

'Two people. Man and woman. Man is Chinese man, thirty-something years old. Name is Davis Lee. Woman is gwaipor. Name is – what was that woman's name? What? Manley. Ms Manley. Don't know her first name. I want you to follow them. Take notes. Find out exactly what they are doing, where they are going, where they are sleeping, everything, all that. Follow them all day and night and give me regular reports every few hours.'

'Ohhhh, night-time work very expensive.'

'I'm paying you the same as last time, and I am hoping no arguments, please.'

'Where are the people?'

'What?'

'The people to follow. Where I go? Where they are staying?'

'I'm going to send you some help to put you on their trail. And, and …' Sajbalani paused. 'Look, there's a bonus if you catch them doing anything bad, you know, anything – well, sex and all that.'

'They are going to do sex?'

'Not just sex. Bad sex. Really bad sex. You know, perverted stuff. M and S. What do they call it? Sado-mastication. All that. That sort of thing. Can you also be taking photos?'

'My camera broken, Mr Saj. Also, big problem with photos last time, because targets, they see flash. They get suspicious. Hit me. Very bad. No, no, no.'

'Okay, okay, just be taking notes. Look, just phone this number – 9028 0801 – that's the mobile phone of my nephew Arvind, who is following Davis at this very precise moment. You see, Davis – the bad sex man – left my house about 20 minutes ago, with the gwaipor. He is hot on their tail. I …'

Sajbalani stopped speaking, but Chan felt there was something more coming. He was right. The old man continued in a whiney whisper: 'Listen, Mr Chan, this is all a very very delicate business, you know? Don't be speaking about it to all and sundry. And there's another thing … I am going to go and interview my daughter now, to see if this bad man has done anything bad to her, know what I mean? Sex things, you know. If he has, and still refuses to marry her … how would you feel about shooting him? Killing him dead, you know, with a gun?'

'Killing him dead?'

'Yes,' said Sajbalani, suddenly enthused with the drama of what he was asking. 'Yes, killing him absolutely stone dead.'

'No, no, I don't think I can do that, Mr Saj, not my cup of tea, not at all, not a service I offering, not possible. I am not experienced in this business. The answer definitely no. How much you pay?'

A Wanchai monologue

Another major area of social intercourse – the phrase is chosen advisedly – between English speakers and speakers of other Asian languages is Wanchai. This part of Hong Kong Island is one of the red-light districts in the territory. A particular joy for anyone interested in language is to spend time talking to the mama-sans in the girlie bars. They are usually middle-aged Cantonese women who have spent their lives talking to sailors from around the world.

Discussions with such women informed the creation of Maggie, a mama-san who appeared in the first draft of the 1997 play *Back to the Wall*, which I co-authored with Teresa Norton. Maggie is from the New Territories, a place where sexist laws have allowed her male relatives to steal her inheritance from her. She has heard that changes to the laws may be in the offing, and she hopes that the smartly dressed regular customer may be able to advise her on what to do. Following is Maggie's opening monologue. 'Maggie at the Puddy-tat Bar, basement of 35, Jaffe Road, Wanchai':

> Discount? Discount? What you think this is, supermarket or something? You think you in Buk Gai or Wai Hong or something? We no give discount on public holiday, you been here plenty enough time to know that, my frien'. But … I tell you something, my old frien'. You sit and talk to old Maggie-san, maybe I give you discoun'; after a while. I think about it. You see, today is very special day, and maybe you rich moneyman can give some advice to ol'; woman no money no children no nothing. We have drink. On house. I buy you a drink okay? Ah wai! Leung bui wai-si-gei. Fai-di-la.
>
> Me, I am the last mama-san who drink real whisky with customer. All other one, they dring tea. Tea! Call themselves mama-san and dring only tea. Remember you come here summer, many times, I not here? I go to my Heung Ha, you know what that mean? Ancestor village. Where father mother born. Ancestor village means Heung Ha. Anyway, I go to my Heung Ha, which is in Bayun County, Guangdong province, see my old doctor. Remember I stop smoking nine-ten month before? Instead of feeling better, I feel worse. Much worse. My doctor in Hong Kong no good. Don't understand.
>
> Doctor in Guangdong much better than doctor in Hong Kong. Better medicine, but also better service. You know why? He not only give you medicine. He give you advice, he read your, how you say it, star chart? Astro, astro-nomy? Astro-logy, yes yes. Doctor he tell me I will get some good fortune and some very bad fortune before year of rat finish. I ask him how I can, how you say, rejec' the bad fortune and welcome good fortune. He tell me – after I pay him money. He very expensive, more than $1,000 for one hour talking. Almost as expensive as one hour talking my girls here! But you already know this, ha ha. He tell me that I mus' focus on southwes' at all times, where my fortune is coming, and I mus' always remember to do bai-saan – you know what means bai-saan? – praying means bai-saan – [she mimes the action of holding chim sticks and bowing before an altar] before coming to work in this business. Otherwise this business will kill me. Kill me dead. That's what

he say. Very soon. This business will kill me dead.

I come back Hong Kong, I still feeling sick, so I go to gwailo doctor here. Very expensive. Insultan'. What? Yes, consultan';. He tell me I have ... upper, er, rester, er, restoration disease ... yes, that's right – upper respi-tory disease. Many my problem all cause by this upper respi-tory disease. And you know, he say if I have one more cigarette, I die. One more. Only one. I say, that's crazy. How come one cigarette? You know what he tell to me? He say: If you have one cigarette, you will stop being non-smoker and start being smoker again, and you will die soon. He tol' me to think like this. My body designed for sup baak maan cigarettes, that mean one million cigarettes, and I already had sup baak maan cigarettes. Any more cigarette, bye bye, all finish, all done. So I come back to work, wait for the other thing — the good fortune. You see my chair? Facing southwes'. I sit here all the time, many days, waiting for the good fortune. And you know what happen? I get good fortune. I get good fortune from evil imperialis' British government, even. I get letter from government, they say that because of new revise law, I entitle to land in Sheung Shui. You know, ancestor law. Yes, that right, inheri-tance of rural land for women or something. Before, if father die, have no boy childrens, only girl childrens, then boy cousins can come steal land.

You know, I should be very rich. Big old house in Sheung Shui with big – how you say, fa-yuen – garden? Courtyard? Big grass outside front, pavement back, very nice. Also field back. Big field. Now worth very much money. Ho dor cheen! But cousins, they steal from me, many many years ago, so I no money. I have to work here as mama-san, make little money, eat rice. So stinking British Hong Kong government they write to me five months before, they say they are changing laws I may get some money, compensation. They don't say how much, they don't say when. But my land, my house, very big. More than 40 million. If only ten per cent, still very much money. But you know, I am reading article about this in newpaper, very hard to understand, talking talking talking in Legco, but no money arrives. Why not they send the money firs', talking about it later?

Now is time for me to retire, you know. I wait so long for my good fortune to come. If my cousin not steal my property, then I could have had good life, nice house, many childrens. Me? Oh yes, I had children. I had three childrens. First one when I was 15 only, I give to Heung Yee Kuk. Somebody adopt her. Or maybe still there. I don't know. One more when I was 17, this time I have some money, I abort. Number three is boy. So I keep him, so he can look after me when I am old. He not interested. Take drugs. Go to Canada. Go to jail. Big problem. I forget him, he forget me. You do me favour, I do you favour. You scratch my back, I scratch your – better, I get one of my girls to scratch your – anything. Scratch anything you like. Special price. Ha ha. You read newpaper, you study this land inheri-tance law business, you tell me when I get my money or get some land for compenation.

Of course, I already have advisor. Ah-Beng. You know Ah-Beng. Young man, often hang around here. He is really my protector. Keep me safe. No he is not bodyguard. He is employed by, how you say, underworld elements. But if he look after me, collect small money, then everybody happy. You wan' more whisky, same-same? This time you pay, I cannot give away all the time.

Conclusion

Hong Kong English is a very real sub-category of English, created mainly by the collision between English and Cantonese tongues in Hong Kong. I think it is fair to say that until the emergence of the present volume, there have been few wide-ranging studies of how Hong Kong English works. Such a study is long overdue. No more should the round-eye barbarians storm the jade gates. Instead, we should try to capture a form of speech that breaks many grammatical rules, but succeeds in facilitating communication between people of two different worlds. The world of academia probably has a technical term to describe such a hybrid language. And if anyone wants to tell me what it is, I shall probably reply: 'How to spell?'

Nury Vittachi – selected publications

Vittachi, Nury (1991) *Reliable Sauce: The secret diaries of Lai See.* Hong Kong: Pacific Century Books.
Vittachi, Nury (1993) *Only in Hong Kong.* Hong Kong: Incom?rehens!ble Book.
Vittachi, Nury (1996) *Asian values.* Hong Kong: Chameleon.
Vittachi, Nury (1997) *Goodbye Hong Kong, Hello Xianggang.* Hong Kong: O'Donald Publications.
Vittachi, Nury and Whitehead, Kate (1997) *After Suzie: Sex in South China.* Hong Kong: Chameleon in association with Corporate Communications Ltd.

12

Writing the literature of non-denial
Xu Xi

Introduction

When Virginia Woolf penned *A Room of One's Own* in the 1920s, she gave voice to the issue of women's absence in the history of writing. In thinking about English language creative writing from Hong Kong today, it seems appropriate to recall her. A similar absence prevails in world Englishes, but I do not believe that seventy years from now, Hong Kong writers will fill this void with nearly as much enthusiasm as women writers have, thereby widening the scope of literature by their contribution. The reasons may be due to political and social dynamics, the force of history, even the publishing industry, as well as greater attention focused towards Chinese language writing in world literature, whether from Hong Kong, Taiwan or the Mainland. This attention can only increase as China enters the ranks of the first world. For the individual writer, the reasons are equally as myriad, not the least of which is the tenuous nature of Hong Kong's existence.

Having said this, the continued existence of any literature in English, alongside those voices who refuse to be silenced by the city's 'neo-colonial' position vis-à-vis China since the Handover, suggests an unwillingness to forget who we have been or who we thought we were. Those voices are disparate – the April 5 activists; protestors against the increasing lack of legal autonomy; liberal politicians who maintain focus on rights in our 'democracy'; the middle and upper classes who still favour English-language education for their offspring, thereby increasing the percentage of local students in so-called 'international' schools to the greater majority. At this time, the government engages in dialogue and action to remedy a perceived backslide in overall English language proficiency. In the meantime, its rival city Singapore actively promotes, as a government initiative, the development of 'creativity,' in which English language local literature plays its part.

I will consider this issue based on my own experience of the creative process to examine general problems and stumbling blocks peculiar to an

English-language Hong Kong writer, and discuss the creative solutions that evolved over the years into my most recently completed novel *The Unwalled City*, an excerpt of which appears in the appendix.

Ethnicity and culture

Writing contemporary fiction in English as a Hong Kong person serves up a creative conundrum. Am I, at some level, rejecting the Cantonese literary heritage of my native city? Does it not affect the creative process, enhancing or infecting it with 'foreign' influences inherent in contemporary English, further muddled by the weight of national and world literatures in the English language? Is my voice 'authentic' in any way, or is my writing merely a fringe literature, reflecting a minority perspective that simply cannot be considered the 'real Hong Kong'? Or worse, do I get relegated to *gwailo* 'foreign devil' Hong Kong literature, a voice for those who are 'belongers' only because of a residency status conferred alike to non-Chinese newcomers, long-term residents, as well as those who can claim actual birthright, all in the name of *laissez-faire* capitalism?

I am of partial Chinese ancestry, the lesser part being Indonesian. Pearl S. Buck cannot make this claim, but her Chinese literacy is far better than mine. Maxine Hong Kingston, on the other hand, can make a pure bloodline claim of ancestry, yet no one would mistake her for a Chinese writer, least of all the Hong Kong Chinese. I was born and raised in Hong Kong, and lived both a young and middle-aged adult life here in between sojourns and residencies in the West and elsewhere in Asia. The result is that my creative process is simultaneously constrained and heightened by ethnicity and culture.

I did not mean for it to be so. Like most novelists, I began writing to create characters and plots or describe places and moments, mostly because I needed to do so, because I had a story to tell, because I had a point of view that demanded release. Because I am a writer. Yet the more I drew upon the Hong Kong I know, the more I stumbled over the race and national origins of my characters, the languages they spoke, the food they ate, the lovers they chose and rejected, the families they hated and loved and ultimately, the lives they chose to live. A mania for balance permeated my work – for each 'foreign' character or scenario I wrote, an equal and opposite reaction urged me to create a 'local' one. Likewise, Hong Kong's society, culture and language, little known internationally except as a business centre or backdrop for *kung fu* movies, demanded space in my fictional universes; otherwise how could my 'authentic' characters be properly understood if not in context? The novelist's perspective became subsumed to all these perplexingly 'greater' issues. Autonomy? I was slave to the conundrum that is Hong Kong. The central creative problem became an inability to discriminate in favour of or against anything that could be characterized as 'real Hong Kong'.

Had I tumbled onto a peculiarly Hong Kong ethos, and if so, what does this mean for the gestalt of our literature? Notice that I say 'our,' as if by writing about and from this place, albeit in English, I can and do stake a claim to its literary heritage. By the standards of contemporary Cantonese literature from Hong Kong, this is a terrible conceit. Local Chinese language fiction excels in disclaimers – a single voice from a tiny colony or 'Special Administrative Region' would not dare utter much truth for its populace – since Chinese literature, like any other national literature, echoes its country's literary tradition, history and social condition. And a 'local' Hong Kong novelist is, by literary, political, geographic and even social definition, Chinese, despite whatever hyphenated suffix follows. So here I was, worrying about how 'real' my Hong Kong universe was, when the real Hong Kong writers (meaning Chinese-language ones), were scrambling for a place in the hierarchy of Chinese literature. After all, no matter where a Chinese writer comes from, her or his work must be translated into a 'foreign' language, such as English, if it is to be read in 'world literature'.

To write in English as a native from and about Hong Kong, I was forced to disavow any claims to being a Chinese novelist. Chinese became an adjective for ethnicity only and not for any characteristics of my writing. Yet I cannot deny the influence of the Monkey King's *Journey to the West* or *Dream of the Red Chamber* any more than I can deny *Jane Eyre* or *Huckleberry Finn*. My problem wasn't in drawing upon the wealth of the world's literature, but instead was in the failure to identify with and belong to a national literature.

Why should that be important? On one level, it is wholly insignificant. I create my own fictional universe, anchor its coordinates of time and space, define its people and the overriding moral perspective, and thus give birth to a novel. There's the problem. I am a novelist, and worse, a realistic novelist. I do not write science fiction or magic realism or fantasy. In giving voice to the interior life of my characters, I portray them against a social and cultural milieu. Perhaps if I had pursued short stories or poetry, I might feel differently. But novels and novelists tend to be defined, rightly or wrongly, by the reality of their national identity. So how else is verisimilitude created unless I select details from the 'real world' for my fictional universe? What is a plot if not grounded in a 'real' place and time? And isn't a character in part understood because of her particular history within her 'real' country?

Which brings me back to the Hong Kong I know. I grew up in a multiethnic, multilingual environment. My parents' friends and associates were Eurasian, Japanese, English, Portuguese, Indonesian-Chinese, Indonesian, Filipino, Singaporean, Malaysian, Welsh, Scottish and even the occasional American, all of whom visited our home. My schoolmates were mostly Hong Kong Chinese, but I also numbered among my friends several Portuguese,

Eurasians, Indians and the occasional English. At my local government-subsidized school Maryknoll, English was the medium for all subjects except Chinese and French. Maryknoll nuns were Americans, which meant our textbooks sometimes diverged from standard British colonial issue.

My early spelling was an indistinguishable mixture of British and American English, as was my grammar and colloquial sense of the language. Added to this were all the wonderful Chinese words we turned into English, like 'stuck wire' (crazy) or 'water dogs' (dumplings), thanks to the multiple homonyms of Cantonese and the delightful instability of tones.

Funny how like contemporary Hong Kong this is. Yet most 'real' Hong Kong people consider my history 'foreign'. My linguistic abilities in Cantonese and my familiarity with the city they know makes me suspiciously local. Also, I am not much of an Anglophile, an elite local type more common to an earlier generation who, by my time, had become slightly anachronistic. By choice, I have never held a Hong Kong British passport (taking instead the Indonesian one of my parents), never studied at a British university, never resided in any corner of the Commonwealth other than Hong Kong. My English language fluency leans towards North American, the preferred accent in the local business community today, of which I was a part for many years. Passport immigration to Canada as 1997 neared has given rise to a generation of young people who speak a vaguely North American English, or rather, a generic global English that is common all over Asia.

The Hong Kong I know permeates my novels. These are filled with ethnic Chinese and other people who have ties to China and Asia, but are 'Westernized' or more accurately, 'globalized', the way the city was and is in its colonial, neo-colonial, financial centre, multinational-business influenced, international trade dominated, Hong Kong-Chinese fashion. It is a cultural hodgepodge, with strong Chinese characteristics, and culturally at least, perpetually confused. Even ethnicity is becoming confused, as mixed-race children are accepted at all strata of society, no longer maligned as the *jaap jung* by-product of illicit relationships or prostitution even when they were not.

Such blatant racism was evident as recently as the 1970s. But a novelist must be true to history and society. This 'multi-culti' world that is Hong Kong is also denied by a Hong Kong that, at a benignly xenophobic level, fosters a 'Hong Kong Chinese' identity, and, at a more nationalistic level, insists on a 'real Chinese' identity. The more I wrote about it, the more I saw the conflict of that denial. What I want to consider is what writing in English did to the exploration of that conflict.

Language as stumbling block

The common reaction by most locals when I call myself a Hong Kong novelist, but one who writes in English, is a mixture of surprise and disbelief. Since returning to my other home city New York, I have begun to drop 'Hong Kong' as adjective, which spares me the reaction of 'Oh, are your books in Chinese?'.

For many years, I thought of myself as an 'Asian' writer. I liked the Englishes of Asia: the lilt in Singapore and Malaysia, the hesitation of Japan and Korea, the fluent musicality of India and the Philippines, the question mark in Thailand, the soft slur of Mainland China and Taiwan, and most of all, the slangy formality in Hong Kong. By trying to write a generic kind of anywhere English, I reasoned, I could properly convey this 'multi-culti' world that emanates from Hong Kong and the rest of Asia.

But while the English language may evolve and change, its traditions and origins cannot be denied. The language itself proved an enormous stumbling block. 'Generic literary English' is an oxymoron that refused to exist. For a while, I careened between both British and American English, resulting in schizophrenia as style. I felt forced to choose one or the other. British and American writers do not typically face this dilemma in developing their voice. They indulge in regional styles and dialects and pay tribute to different literary traditions – Lawrence instead of Forster or Twain rather than Hardy – the list is long on both sides of the Atlantic up till contemporary times. Even the slimmer canon of my gender offers sufficiently divergent paths – Eliot or Austen, Woolf vs. Mansfield, Parker as rebel daughter to Chopin. The English language itself is not the issue; a writer finds an appropriate shade suited to her or his work. So, thought I, could I. To do that, however, I had to find and own my shade of English, a language that cast long but uneven shadows in Hong Kong.

The literature syllabus was almost entirely English, T. S. Eliot being the only American writer we studied. The written language we were taught was indisputably British. But a language has to be heard for it to come alive. If I recall the spoken English of my school days, it was more British than American, albeit with a Hong Kong accent as most of my teachers were native Cantonese speakers. Outside the classroom, the majority of us spoke 'Chinglish'. The only 'real' English I consistently heard was television American, whether from a horse like Mr Ed, Mission Impossible spooks, or the wiseguy humour of Bugs Bunny and Jack Benny. American movies graced my ear with stage English, as Bette Davies and Audrey Hepburn enunciated. As for pop music, the Beatles enriched and confused my auditory linguistics, while the Doors turned Blake into a repetitive prayer. I was seventeen before I functioned entirely in English among native speakers at an American college in upstate New York.

Politics cast other shadows. In our colonial state, we 'locals' lived an existence divided from the British, attended different schools, went through a similar but separate public exam system that was not interchangeable and, if we were of a certain family background such as, say, the civil service, this existence might eventually converge with our colonial rulers at an English boarding school or university. This Anglophile British existence did not translate into a living English language for many locals, and certainly did not for me. How lucky the Indians were! Not only were they already post-colonial, they belonged to a large country where a sizeable population spoke fluent British English in that delicious Indian accent; even British writers peopled their novels with Indian characters who had 'speaking parts'. Likewise, in Singapore and Malaysia, English lived as a language after their people had fought for and won independence. Filipinos also were truly literate in a kind of American English that had succumbed to Tagalog's rich influence. As for the rest of Asia, English was insignificant enough among locals that literature in that language would be unlikely, and more germane, unnecessary.

The trouble with Hong Kong was the continued significance of our 'official' English language and our non-nation statehood. Not only was a Gandhi-like fight for independence improbable, a separation from China as our motherland was impossible. '1997', as the poet Louise Ho says, was a 'date to live by / a topic for conversation. / There's always something deadly / About deadlines, / They haunt before they occur.' In terms of language, however, English was pragmatic for work and dealing with foreigners, but shameful for a local who aped *gwailoes* by pretending to be one of them. Given this, the literary role models left were the foreigners – Mason, Clavell, Coates or Maugham – no language issues for any of them. The only significant exception was Han Suyin. How fortunate she was to be Eurasian, thereby staking an authentic half-claim to the language! But language isn't ethnicity, and can fare worse from forced divisions. Some of my early stories bear a strikingly similar theme: Eurasian child protagonists die prematurely or otherwise suffer at the hands of well-intentioned but misguided parents.

Writing as a young adult in Hong Kong of the 1970s was linguistically confusing; this was the decade when Cantonese finally achieved 'official language' status alongside English. In the meantime, society was undergoing a fundamental, albeit not historic, change. The Hong Kong I returned to post-college was a colony where a British governor and the *hongs* were undeniably in charge. 1997 gave us pause but did not obsess; until Britain and China agreed upon a political solution, we the people had little to contribute. The economy was expanding, but the inflationary growth of the 1980s had not yet begun. 1979 was a turning point of sorts when the US dumped Taiwan and recognized China in a political divorce and rebound.

More interesting was the decline of English culture and the broadening expression of modern local culture. The latter was Cantonese-dominated, distinct from the Mainland, and heavily influenced by international pop and elite culture but with Hong Kong Chinese characteristics. A ballet group was formed, led by and comprising Western-educated local Chinese. Western-style pop groups sang in Cantonese, whereas a decade earlier, local Chinese bands emulated the West and sang in English. Chinese-language advertising in all media began approaching a higher level of sophistication as copywriters and producers brought home skills from abroad, but adapted expression to local sensibilities. The Arts Centre was built, the annual Arts Festival was launched, followed a few years later by the Asian Arts Festival. If Hong Kong could claim a time of 'self-rule', I would date it from the late 1960s (especially after the '67 riots) till about 1994 or 1995, just before the reality of 1997 set in and eroded that confidence. The British were there and couldn't be entirely ignored of course, but during the 1970s, it almost felt as if Hong Kong people were in charge of their own destiny. My city offered wonderful material for fiction. But to create is to seek truth, and writing creatively in English made truth-telling difficult.

Consciously or unconsciously, I wrote my fiction into categories. There were the Chinese stories, where all the characters spoke Chinese only, and I was in effect 'translating' their thoughts and dialogue. Then, there was the 'unique English' category, meaning that I tried to write the English of local Hong Kong. That quickly became reductive because it felt stilted and limited to a pragmatic consciousness. In despair, I turned to Asia as the background, creating multinational characters who interacted in English, their only common language. Each 'lived' in an English natural to her or his background, although this demanded more explanation than is desirable in fiction. However, the narratives fell apart, since I still had to make a language choice for these. It didn't work to write British sometimes and American at others. My fiction was jammed between two national Englishes.

The truth about the creative process is that it is very much a process, embracing trial and error. I did not one day suddenly find the 'right' English for me. My 'native language' is English, but it is not a true 'mother tongue' since both my parents speak it as a second language. I did not grow up speaking either my father's Mandarin/Javanese or my mother's Javanese. Both parents speak English reasonably well, but lapse into Javanese when annoyed or excited. Likewise, neither can write 100% 'correct' English, although their overall fluency is much higher than that of the average Hong Kong Chinese. By contrast, their Cantonese ability is poor; my mother can barely read characters while my father was literate in Chinese and conversed fluently in Mandarin but badly in Cantonese. I became far more fluent in Cantonese than they, thanks to my Hong Kong upbringing.

One story from that period captured my unease. When the MTR first opened in 1978, Hong Kong people shunned it briefly. Once the undeniable fact of its speed and convenience hit home, it quickly became the preferred public transport. What most piqued my creative sensibilities, however, was the way its existence 'collapsed' my city, connecting disparate districts and social classes in this democratic conveyance. I wrote 'The Yellow Line' to express this. The protagonist is a young boy from Lok Fu who lives in public housing with an abusive mother. One stop away is Kowloon Tong, an upper middle-class area of houses with gardens. The station's exit is near an English school (the former St George's) where he sees golden haired children in what is, to him, a paradise of grass, trees and open space. Until the MTR existed, the boy has never seen such an environment. It was in writing this story that I felt dumbstruck. The boy's consciousness is in Cantonese, which I was trying to render in English. In the narrative, I found myself using very basic words, partly because this was the consciousness of a child, but also because it seemed the only kind of English that sounded right for Hong Kong. After the story was broadcast on the BBC and published in Short Story International, my late aunt, an English teacher in a local boys' school, used it in her class. She taught in Choi Hung, a district quite similar to Lok Fu of the story. What she told me was that it was difficult to find reading material that had any relevance to her students' lives. This story was later broadcast on RTHK and translated into Mandarin for BBC World Radio.

This piece was pivotal in my creative development vis-à-vis language. It made me see that my linguistic environment limited scope. Other fiction from that time with adult characters set in Hong Kong was less successful. The problem was that the English I 'heard' from these characters was second language fluency, and as such, limited in expression. Their Cantonese would be the utterances of adults, but writing in English did not mean I wanted to translate Cantonese. Another problem was that as the influence of British culture waned, British English did not resonate accurately in the voices of fictional local characters, unless it was a British person or British-educated local speaking English. This became true for narrative as well. If I was attempting to portray an environment that felt like 'self-rule' (even if it was self-deceiving), could I really use the language of the colonizing power? What I discovered was that I needed a different kind of English to speak across the actual language of my characters and for the Hong Kong world I rendered.

The path to discovery became an element of my work. The day I read *The Woman Warrior*, I heard the first, truly clear echoes of myself. At the time of its publication, the book was unavailable in Hong Kong, and could be obtained only in pirated editions in Taipei. Kingston was dismissed locally as fraudulent. It is ironic that her legacy is as a literary model for many Asian-American as well as Asian writers in English. Although there are few similarities in my fictional themes compared to those of Kingston, what resonated was that she transformed language in an exciting new way, freeing English language fiction from its Anglo/Euro-American bonds. Her novelistic consciousness was uttered in English but informed by Cantonese, and she wrote of contemporary lives weighted by histories, cultures and ethnicities that were not entirely theirs. While she is undeniably American, it was her linguistic lack of self-consciousness that was most engaging. Although *The Woman Warrior* was originally issued as 'autobiography' due to the publishing industry's lack of vision, it has since been recognized as literature that is significant in the development of the contemporary novel.

While Kingston's work has been and continues to be an important influence in my battle with language, other writers left their mark. Conrad, Nabokov, Naipaul, Narayan and Rushdie were probably the most useful. Walcott sums up the dilemma best in 'Codicil' – 'To change your language you must change your life.' Although Walcott's declaration refers to the language of journalism – a 'hack's hired prose' – by which he made a living, it speaks to this question of the ownership of language. It was my linguistic life that had to 'change'. My early experience at college in America made me realize how lacking the life for English language fiction was when I first returned to Hong Kong in the 1970s. I wrote and published stories, began my first novel, and did all the things writers do while filling the daily rice bowl. What I lacked at the time was an environment that cultivated writing or appreciated literature. It is only in retrospect that I understand how little sustenance Hong Kong offered in my attempts to 'own' the English I wrote.

In the early 1980s, I left business life and went to Massachusetts to do a MFA in fiction. I remained in the US until the early 1990s, returning to Hong Kong only to visit. As I reined in and developed English for creative work, my fiction saw publication in the US. It was during this period that I dealt with my other linguistic stumbling block: Chinese. I am relatively fluent in Cantonese and my accent is almost indistinguishable from Hong Kong native speakers, but this is not matched by my Chinese literacy. Although I studied the language as a child, I did not continue into secondary school, opting for French instead, which proved easier. I was an aberration in Hong Kong's education system. I studied English, my first language, as a second language; conversely, Cantonese was a second language, but the education system assumed native language ability. As a result of early exposure, I write traditional characters easily. But from secondary school onwards, I read hardly anything in Chinese except for the occasional glimpse at my father's newspapers.

During my graduate studies, I found the American perspective on writing fiction wanting with respect to my own process. The workshops I attended helped enormously with craft and technique, and I read a useful amount of contemporary American fiction that was instructive, especially minority literature. In the development of voice, the programme was less helpful. Although I became far more comfortable 'hearing' American English for narrative and even dialogue, I was missing the critical Chinese language element for my work. The wonderful thing about large American universities is that you can study almost anything. I took Mandarin, not because I had to fulfill any language requirements (already met with French), but because it was available. The challenge was having to convince programme administrators that this was crucial to my writing; an English-speaking, English-writing creative programme evaluated things differently. Despite almost losing my fellowship, I knew this was right for me.

The Chinese studies programme was run by Taiwan-educated academics, which meant I could revisit Chinese through traditional characters. Studying it as a second language meant I could entirely ignore Cantonese and absorb Mandarin. My primary goal was to read a newspaper and contemporary fiction. Later, I learnt simplified characters from Mainland teachers in New York. Yet I do not claim much literacy in Chinese; given the choice, I prefer to read Chinese literature in translation, confining my Chinese-language reading to practical business needs or in chasing up references for my novels. Not till years after such linguistic schizophrenia did a fictional voice begin to emerge with confidence. For approximately the last fifteen years, my fiction has conformed to American grammar and usage, except when I deliberately use a British expression, or assign dialogue to British-English speaking characters. In the last eight to nine years, I have allowed Chinese (both Cantonese and Putonghua – 'Mandarin' has become rather like British English for me) into my sentences in both their romanized and translated form as if they were English words. My English is enriched by Chinese, in particular by pinyin. This form of romanization sensitized me to the accurate rendering of speech to flavour my work. For Cantonese, I generally use the Yale-Chinese University dictionary which feels right. Unfortunately, there isn't a single Cantonese romanization system that has been established as well as pinyin, especially in literature.

Despite my multilingual upbringing, I do not learn languages easily. Perhaps if this weren't the case, language would have been less a problem in my creative development. Somehow, I don't think so. Language is a schizophrenic issue for Hong Kong. Since the Handover, local government initiatives are now focused on upgrading the quality of English language education. Ironically, ESL training on the Mainland produces an elite modern Chinese who functions better in English than many Hong Kong educated folks. As Hong Kong confronts its linguistic schizophrenia, today's young creative writers may write in English if they choose with a little more confidence. My path was fraught with missteps, but I am not sure if the next generation of writers will find their paths much easier. They now have to face a growing nationalism that may more vehemently deny 'Hong Kong literature' in any language but Chinese. The exception will continue to be the 'foreigners' regardless of ethnicity; whether or not they are native to Hong Kong or have merely passed through (e.g. Paul Theroux's *Kowloon Tong*) will be virtually irrelevant.

Like Walcott, I had to 'change my life'. Today, I live between Hong Kong and New York. The combination provides both inroads to 'multi-culti Asia' and ensures the stimuli of and exposure to contemporary fiction in English. While I have no illusions about America's hard-won diversity, at least its history and culture does embrace the concept of cultural and linguistic immigration. In 1999, the National Book Award was given to a Chinese novelist for the first time. Ha Jin (*Waiting*) immigrated as an adult from China but writes in English. Unsurprisingly, Nabokov is one of his significant influences. Beyond culture, ethnicity and language, however, is the outcome of creativity. I would now like to turn to the novel itself, using as example my most recently completed work, *The Unwalled City*, excerpted in the appendix.

Beyond the denial of self

When I first conceived of the book, I called it my 'woman's novel'. I imagined I was writing my own 'golden notebook' á la Lessing since the question of a 'room of (my) own' had long been solved. Being a little too young to have burnt my bra, but old enough to have witnessed the sexual revolution before AIDS, I came of age empowered to earn a good living at multinationals in Hong Kong and New York, but only with my gaze fixed firmly towards the 'glass ceiling'. This gave me sufficient credentials to belong to a new wave of feminism that was perpetually confused. Not, it seemed, unlike my Hong Kong resume.

Conception occurred while completing an earlier novel *Hong Kong Rose*. My protagonist, Rose Kho, was so Hong Kong that she had begun to irritate me. I was writing about personal courage and cowardice, and the novel's angst was tied up with the compromise of being a Hong Kong person in the 1970s. Rose is a sexually thwarted, complex character who wears her Eurasian husband's homosexual adultery and her own affair with an American Sinophile as some kind of badge of honour. There are reasons of Chinese family honour and family love to vindicate her, but she is ultimately a timid woman, whose truth is a distortion of raw, and perhaps more honest, feelings. What personal courage she exhibits did not inspire me the way feminist courage did, and there were days I longed for a more powerful voice to emerge from my work.

Creativity is, however, a mercurial mistress. By the time my heroine emerged fully formed, slightly less confused, but still true to character, I had made peace with her brand of courageous compromise. Up till this point, the Hong Kong of most of my fiction was the colonial city. In one major exception, a novel begun in the 1970s, I had created a close-to and post-1997 Hong Kong which becomes a place that divides one pair of lovers – the long-time foreigner prefers to leave while a local girl chooses to stay, knowing that this way, she can remain close to family since travel overseas is easily accomplished. The trouble with accurate forecasting is that people refuse to believe it, which is why I returned to the city as it had been and was for subsequent work. By the time I set out to complete *The Unwalled City*, the city had been handed over, and the big media moment had passed. It was a time to reflect on the lives and loves of ordinary Hong Kong people before and up till this historical moment of their existence. But who were these 'ordinary' people? As work progressed, I began to see the extraordinarily global-cum-'multi-culti' nature of my four main characters, who were therefore questionably 'real Hong Kong'. Two were Americans and culturally 'foreign' to Hong Kong in some way: Vince da Luca, because he had never lived in Asia, and Colleen Leyland-Tang, because she was a cultural Sinophile with fairly strong pro-China leanings. Both had previous and current connections to Hong Kong. The other two were local Hong Kong women – Andanna Lee (Lee You Fun), a twenty-something musician/singer who has done 'immigration prison' and college in Canada and sings jazz to please her boyfriend but really prefers pop; the other, Gail Szeto, a middle-aged, divorced Eurasian and single mother, is determinedly Hong Kong Chinese in identity despite her American work style and behaviour. These characters evolved out of the contemporary Hong Kong I knew. In the earliest drafts, the working title was *The Duration of Loneliness*. Vince da Luca, divorcing for the second time and alienated in his Hong Kong expatriation, was the centrepoint around whom the lives of all three women revolved. By the second or third draft, this model had become unworkable, because it wasn't really what I was writing about. I then renamed it *Lives and Loves in the Unwalled City*. This proved a more resilient anchor for the process of unearthing the novel within.

To develop the landscape of this 'unwalled city', I added various minor characters who were more clearly 'local' Hong Kong, even if they had had some life experience overseas. The most significant minor character, Albert Ho, a questionably asexual man, functioned as the pivot for three of the main characters, but in particular, the male protagonist. By the fourth or fifth draft, Albert had become 'my Hong Kong', as Vince notes in the last third of the novel. Albert, a wealthy and successful businessman who appears to be a playboy, invests in and promotes local artistic endeavours, although no one really knows why. While loneliness worried my subtext, the nature of Hong Kong's evolution during this pre-Handover period – what people did with their lives and the societal and even linguistic context of their days – dominated the main text. The growing importance of Putonghua over Cantonese affects Andanna the pop singer, as Colleen reminds her, which the former reluctantly acknowledges but considers highly inconvenient and just plain tiresome. Despite what might be considered the extraordinary circumstance of my characters' lives, I like to believe that the way they love is pretty universal. When I finished the novel and handed it off to my agent, he observed that the book was as much about the character of the city as it was about the 'lives and loves' of the characters. It was then we made the decision to rename the book *The Unwalled City*. This editorial change is the outcome to date of the creative process.

What intrigues me is my own desire to render the lives of 'ordinary' Hong

Kong people. As a novelist, I understand that the process of any book is filled with edits and more edits, so what occurred is not more or less unusual than my experience with other novels. Yet I also wish to render the unique landscape and characters I have chosen into a fictional context that resonates universally. What emerged were ordinary emotional lives with Hong Kong characteristics. I trust I have done my job and made my characters engaging enough to fulfill a novel's function. The shape of those lives and their connections, however, defined the city in a way I had not previously understood.

A 'wall' or 'to wall in' are words that have a meaning in English; an 'unwall' or 'to unwall' is non-existent in the language, although we can guess at its likely meaning and even reason for usage in the right context, as we can in 'twas brilling, and the slithy tove'. There is a wonderland feel to my city I want to capture. Perhaps the Handover rang of an odd unreality, because it set an unsteady rhythm to the movement of the novel. Also, the complexity of three women protagonist vis-à-vis a Chinese vs. Western acculturation threaded its way through the novel's evolution, although this was far from the main issue in each of their lives. The male protagonist is otherwise confused; as a twice-divorced (left both times by a wife) absent father, he must come to terms with the meaning of family in his mid-life. My decision to 'unwall' them, and hence Hong Kong, was a reaction to the exaggerated quality of life prior to the Handover. The influx of sudden 'residents' or 'observers' struck me as comical, and the din of voices pontificating on the 'historical significance' of the event drowned out the continuance of ordinary life. Hong Kong believed itself extraordinary because of that moment, and hyped up an emotional (or fearful) 'return' to the motherland alongside a sad (or happy) 'farewell' to the colonial master. It was a convenient moment for enterprise; Hong Kong desperately sought to profit from exaggeration.

By imagining that world as an 'unwalled' city, did I wish to imply an earlier walling in of my own creative voice, muffled because of its need for English? And by altering the language to fit the Hong Kong I know, was I attempting to re-define that world? I am a novelist and not an academic, and therefore prefer to limit my attempts at analysis. All I know is that this novel allowed me to write beyond whatever real or imagined denial I felt as a result of being the kind of Hong Kong person and writer I am.

Conclusion

Not having written an academic piece, this is a difficult essay from which to draw conclusions. By presenting personal experience, I cannot claim anything more than the validity of that experience. Since at this time there are few of us who write creatively in English, whether or not 'Hong Kong English' exists in contemporary literature remains a question for academics to explore in the years ahead. What I can tell you is this: Hong Kong readers (i.e. readers with a real, personal knowledge of Hong Kong through residence and work/life experience), both 'local' and 'foreign', find my work 'very Hong Kong', whatever that means. I only know my Hong Kong. It's the one I write about, and will continue to write about in fiction, in English. Someone else can decide what that English is.

Books and recent works by Xu Xi
(former bylines: Sussy Chako/Sussy Komala)

Novels/fiction collections

Xu Xi (1997) *Hong Kong Rose* (novel). Hong Kong: Asia 2000.
Xu Xi (2001) *History's Fiction* (story collection). Hong Kong: Chameleon Press.
Xu Xi (2001) *The Unwalled City* (novel). Hong Kong: Chameleon Press.
Xu Xi (2002) *Chinese Walls* (novel). Second edition (first published in 1994 by Asia 2000). Hong Kong: Chameleon Press.
Xu Xi (2002) *Daughters of Hui* (fiction collection). Second edition (first published in 1996 by Asia 2000). Hong Kong: Chameleon Press.
Ingham, Michael and Xu Xi (eds.) (forthcoming) *City Voices: An Anthology of Hong Kong Writing in English*. Hong Kong: Hong Kong University Press.

Stories

Chako, Sussy (1990) The fourth copy or dancing with skeletons and other romances. In *Home to Stay: Asian American Women's Fiction* (anthology). Edited by Sylvia Watanabe and Carol Bruchac. New York: Greenfield Review Press, pp. 154–65.
Chako, Sussy (1991) Rage. *The Little Magazine*, **17**, 113–20.
Chako, Sussy (1991–1992) Rubato. *Hawaii Review*, 16 (1), 61–6.
Chako, Sussy (1992a) Blackjack. *South China Morning Post*, November 28, 6.
Chako, Sussy (1992b) Dannemora. *Phoebe*, 4(2), 79–87.
Chako, Sussy (1992c) Philip and me. In *Lovers* (anthology). Edited by Amber Converdale Summrall. California: The Crossing Press, pp. 42–50.
Chako, Sussy (1992d) The raining tree. *Hawaii Pacific Review*, 7, 25–31.
Chako, Sussy (1993) My father's story. *Manoa*, 5(2), 1–8.
Xu Xi (1999) Insignificant moments in the history of Hong Kong. *Dimsum*, 1, 71–5.
Xu Xi (2001a) Light of the south. *Great River Review*, **33**, 10–19.
Xu Xi (2001b) Democracy. *Dimsum*, **5**, 113–26.
Xu Xi (2001c) Until the next century. In *The Best of Carve Magazine* (anthology). Edited by Melvin Sterne. California: Mild Horse Press, pp. 131–45.

Essays/OP-ED

*Chako, Sussy (1995) Wah kiu wanderers. *Asia Magazine*, 24–26 March.
*Chako, Sussy (1996) Burnt out ambitions. *Asia Magazine*, 2–4 February.

Xu Xi (1999a) Rocking the sampan. *Rice Paper,* **5**(1), 37.
Xu Xi (1999b) Light shines from the east. *Rice* Paper, **5**(3), 12–13.
Xu Xi (1999c) Fulfillment on a path less traveled. *The Asian Wall Street Journal,* 24 December, *Personal Journal.*
Xu Xi (2000a) Linguistic erotica: to disclose is to conceal. Lit, **3**, 63–5.
Xu Xi (2001a) Multiple meanings of being Chinese. *Rice Paper,* **6:3**, 16–17.
Xu Xi (2001b) Life as a colony rat. *The Correspondent,* Dec Jan issue.
Xu Xi (2001c) Solace in the map for 'lonely hearts'. In *The Map of Sex and Love* (screenplay) by Evans Chan. Hong Kong: Youth Literary Book Store.
Xu Xi (2002) Asian space. *Ten,* **7:1&2**, 8–9.

Appendix

The Unwalled City

The latest novel by Xu Xi is called The Unwalled City, *which was published in 2001 and is set in Hong Kong at the time of the Handover. In this excerpt, we meet two very different characters from the ensemble of Hong Kong people whose lives and loves are played out in the city in the months leading up to June 1997. These are Andanna Lee, a young Hong Kong fashion model-cum-singer, and Vince da Luca, a 45-year-old American photographer.*

In the reception area of JB&D, Andanna You Fun Lee paced, glancing impatiently at her watch. *Gwailo* photographers, always late. Why had she accepted this assignment anyway, killing her only free day? She despised modeling, and this whole ad agency scene. But the money was good, and playing hotel lobby piano gigs didn't pay the rent. Sometimes, she wished she'd stayed in Vancouver where everything was cheaper and no one complained about what she did since she was far enough away. It was just too boring there though. Despite all its transplanted Hong Kong life, it wasn't the real thing.

She glanced at the pictures adorning the walls. A section titled 'FMCGs' was empty. When she'd met Jake Wu, the agency's creative director a year ago, he had called her that and laughed. She hadn't dared ask him what it meant and pretended to know, laughing along with him even though she suspected an insult. Fast Moving Consumer Goods. Every agency's rice bowl and the work the creatives hated. Andanna knew that JB&D paid the most, had the best facilities, and handled the highest profile fashion accounts. Next to the empty wall was testament to their success: the 1994 agency of the year award for Asia. But that was last year, and this year, what she'd been hearing was that they'd lost two of their big FMCGs. Easy come easy go, just like her piano gigs. The modeling jobs, on the other hand, were there as long as she could play the part.

Someone called her name.

The photographer introduced himself, apologizing for his tardiness. They shook hands. He was a tired, middle-aged American, a bit thick around the waist. Didn't look like he'd shaved, although perhaps he simply had too much hair.

They headed towards the studio area, past rows of open cubicles lining the window. JB&D's office was at the east end of Hong Kong island, and their premises in Taikoo Shing framed a perfect view of the airport runway across the harbor. A green and white Cathay Pacific plane rose towards the clouds. Behind it, a purple and gold Thai International aircraft waited in line for takeoff. Sunday afternoon traffic jam.

'Did you just graduate from college?'

The photographer's voice interrupted her thoughts. She had been thinking about Albert Ho, whom she'd run into last Saturday night at Club 97. He hadn't called even though he said he would. Men.

'Ages ago, almost three years.'

'Oh, what did you study?'

He didn't want to talk, did he? She hated these foreign guys who tried to draw her out. Everyone knew that all they wanted was to fuck. 'Music.'

'That's cool.'

Mentally, her eyes rolled. But she remained polite, smiling. No point being rude. He couldn't help being old. Of course, Albert wasn't all that young either, but he not only liked her music, he was rich. Very rich. Perhaps she could get him to fund a music video or CD. After all, it wasn't as if she were interested in him for anything else.

At the art department, Jake was trying to sort out which outfit would be used for the shot. The assignment was for some Italian sounding designer brand which Andanna had never heard of. She picked up a very short, lime green dress with orange flowers that was absolutely hideous. The price tag read HK$4,500 or ¥52,000, half of almost a month's rent for the 300-foot flat she shared with her boyfriend. 'That's it, put that one on,' he yelled in Cantonese, gesturing towards the bathroom. She made a face and he snorted. 'Women,' she heard him say, 'always so critical.'

When she returned, the photographer was setting up. Jake was telling him about the house he was restoring in Beijing. 'One of those old places with a courtyard, you know the kind? I'm preserving all the historic detail but modernizing the plumbing and putting in central air. It's not far from Tiananmen, about a ten minute taxi ride. Very convenient. You come as my guest some weekend, okay?' He gazed meaningfully at the photographer, his fingers lightly brushing the hair on his arm.

It was ludicrous, Andanna thought, the way Jake ran after Western men. She knew that was the only reason this guy had the assignment, since he wasn't one of the regulars. Couldn't Jake tell this one was straight? Jake was one of the hot directors, but for all his talent, he could be a total dope.

The photographer continued setting up. It astonished her how much time was spent lighting and preparing to get one silly shot. And the rolls of film these photographers went through! Could the creatives who hired her really see any difference in all those rows of contact sheets? In the past year, she'd turned down a couple of local art photographers who had asked her to pose. After all, they couldn't pay much and it wasn't like she was a real model. Would they work as slowly as this guy, she wondered.

He framed her through his camera. 'Photogenic.'

'Really?'

'Sure. Andanna's a pretty name, by the way.'

'Thank you,' she replied automatically, thinking, no it wasn't, now that she knew better. All her friends had made up their English names too when they were thirteen. Living in Canada, she had come to realize how ridiculous that was. Thank god she'd at least not accidentally used a real English word like her best friend Clitoris Ho – pronounced 'Cly-toris' to rhyme with fly – who survived the embarrassment when they'd first got to Vancouver for grade twelve. She went by Clio now, but had thought the whole thing a big joke. Andanna would have died if it had happened to her.

'Did you go to school abroad?'

This guy didn't give up! Perhaps she should tell him she already had a boyfriend, although that probably wouldn't stop him. It didn't stop other *gwailoes*. 'Yeah, Canada.'

'No wonder you speak English well.'

'Thanks.' She smiled but knew he was just looking for an opening. When she was growing up, she hated studying English. The grammar was difficult, and no one spoke it anyway. Her father, who was in business, wanted her to master it because he believed it would be important for her future. He insisted she study abroad, saying her English would improve faster. She had wanted to go to the Academy of Performing Arts at home with her friends. If her mother hadn't begged her to go for the passport, and if Clio hadn't been going, she would have refused. Music was easier. Tones sang in her head and her fingers obeyed. Fortunately, Mother didn't give her a hard time about

English, but then, she didn't speak it all that well either. As long as she knew the language, Andanna couldn't understand why speaking mattered.

Back in Vancouver, it hadn't mattered, except in high school classes. She hung around with Clio all the time and spoke Cantonese. Clio liked speaking English and made Canadian friends. What was the point of making friends she'd never see again? She knew she was going home. Fortunately, music teachers didn't talk a lot, even in Vancouver. Once she was in college, she avoided classes where speaking up contributed to the grade. Yet since she'd been back – was it already three years? – she found herself holding conversations in English with foreigners at her hotel gigs. So maybe the old man had a point, even if he was ashamed of what she did. English helped her make money.

'Vincent...' Jake began. He had come around from his side of the art table and was standing right next to the photographer.

'It's Vince,' he corrected, lighting a cigarette. 'I'm ready, let's work.'

Jake turned towards Andanna and went all businesslike. 'Over there,' he barked, 'and make like Lolita.'

'Lo-who?'

'Kids today. Don't know anything.' Jake was huffing, hands on his waist, disgusted.

Vince ambled over to her and pulled up a tall stool. 'Here, sit-lean on this. Legs slightly apart, one foot on the rung of the stool. Tip your head down a little and pretend you don't want your boyfriend to kiss you.'

She tried to do what he asked, feeling like an idiot. It wasn't working. Jake was becoming increasingly impatient which irritated her. But she didn't know what he wanted. It had been much easier the last time she worked for him in that sanitary napkin ad. No brainers she could handle: all the brief demanded was that she look 'fresh as a morning sunrise'. At least Vince seemed reasonable, patiently suggesting different poses. After about thirty minutes of this, Jake finally blew up with 'oh, give me a break, what does he have to do, fuck you?' in Cantonese, so Vince wouldn't understand.

'I don't need this,' she said coldly, in English, and began to walk towards the bathroom. She didn't care if Jake gave her a lot of work or paid big bucks; it didn't give him the right to yell at her.

'Okay, time out,' Vince declared. 'You,' he pointed at Jake, 'out of here. I'll get this done myself.'

Jake resisted, face simmering, and then flounced off. Andanna glared at Vince. 'Now what?'

'Relax. Sit a minute.' He gestured at the vending machine. 'Want something?'

'Diet Coke.'

He handed her one. 'By the way, what was that he said?'

She tilted the popped can to her mouth. Hesitant, surprised at her own coyness, she translated Jake's remark. Vince laughed, but quickly turned it into a cough saying, 'how rude of him.' She felt suddenly better about being here, about doing this ridiculous assignment and smiled, genuinely happy for the first time in days.

He picked up his camera. 'So what d'you think of all this?' 'Borr-ring,' she said. He shot her. 'And the dress?' 'Want to rip it off.' 'Who'd buy it?' 'Girls trying to be foreign, trying to be fashionable.' He took more shots. 'So why're you doing this?' 'Need money.' Andanna realized he hadn't stopped shooting. Whatever he was doing, she hoped it was right because she didn't want to have to listen to Jake grumble.

They wrapped up an hour later. Vince barely looked at her as she departed, although he did wave a cursory good bye. For just a second, it bothered her. But she forgot this as soon she boarded the MTR beneath Taikoo Shing headed back home to Sheung Wan.

Part IV
Resources

13 Analysing Hong Kong English: Sample texts from the International Corpus of English

Kingsley Bolton and Gerald Nelson

Introduction: The International Corpus of English (ICE) worldwide and in Hong Kong

The International Corpus of English (ICE) project is an international research programme which involves the parallel collection of similar data in some 20 countries worldwide. The principal motivation for this database is to permit a comparative analysis of the English language used in various locations worldwide. The countries involved include, first, those where English is a dominant language in the society, i.e. an 'inner circle' Englishes, such as the varieties spoken and written in the United States, the United Kingdom, Canada, Australia, and New Zealand. Second, the project also surveys those societies where English is an official (or co-official) language, and/or is also a second language for a substantial proportion of the population. Such 'outer circle' Englishes include those of India, South Africa, East Africa, Nigeria, Zimbabwe, and parts of the West Indies. In the Asian region, corpora are currently being compiled in India, Malaysia, Singapore, the Philippines and Hong Kong. The main objective of the ICE project worldwide is thus to enable comparative studies of the English language on an international scale, both with regard to the use of English in societies where it is the first language of the majority of their population, as in the USA, UK, and Australia, and with reference to its use in societies such as India, Singapore, and Hong Kong, where it is used as an 'additional' language.

The chief objectives of the ICE project in Hong Kong may be summarized as follows:

(i) to promote systematic empirical research on the English language in Hong Kong;
(ii) to provide a computerized database of English in the HKSAR that is available to academics, researchers, graduate students, and educationalists;
(iii) to encourage collaboration between researchers in Hong Kong and other

Asian universities, and between Asian researchers and those working in this field in European and North American institutions.

At this stage of our research (early 2002), we are currently concerned to realize the objective set out in point (ii) above, i.e. completing a computerised database of English in Hong Kong.[2] In fact, we have already progressed quite some way towards this aim. Essentially, the data-collection phase of research aims at collecting 500 texts each comprising 2,000 words. These 500 text units essentially provide samples of a wide range of different 'text types', spoken and written, including such *spoken varieties* as direct conversations, class lessons, broadcast discussions, parliamentary debates, legal cross-examinations, business transactions, commentaries, legal presentations, broadcast news, and speeches (not broadcast); and such *written varieties* as student untimed essays, social letters, business letters, learned informational texts from the humanities, social sciences, natural sciences, and technology; press news reports, and creative writing. The 500 texts each with 2,000 words will eventually provide a total of 1,000,000 words of English spoken and written in Hong Kong. Approximately, some 80 % of the data has now been collected, and in recent months the Hong Kong team has been mainly engaged in checking this data, and carrying out the computerisation of texts, and tagging the corpus for grammatical parts of speech. As of March 2002, a total of 320 texts have been computerized, of which 233 have been grammatically tagged for parts of speech. We intend to complete a fully computerized version of the corpus by autumn 2003.

ICE text types

In comparison with some other contemporary corpora, those in ICE may be considered by some researchers to be relatively small, especially for lexical studies. At just one million words, they are certainly smaller than 'megacorpora' such as the British National Corpus (100 million words) and the Bank of English (500 million words). However, we would contend that the number of words is far from being the only criterion by which to judge the usefulness of a corpus. The number of individual samples is also highly relevant. Each ICE corpus consists of 500 'texts', though in reality the number of different samples is much greater than this, since many of the texts are composite. In the category of Social Letters, for instance, several individual letters must be combined to make up a single corpus 'text'. In the ICE-GB corpus, a total of 1,001 samples have been included; we expect that the Hong Kong corpus will sample an approximately equal number.

An even more important criterion is the number and range of text types that are sampled. In ICE, a total of 32 text types are included, covering a broad of the possible situational, social, and communicative task variation occurring in the language. The range of different text types to be collected was agreed when the project began in the early 1990s. The text types are shown in Table 14.1 below:

Table 14.1 International Corpus of English text types

SPOKEN (300)	WRITTEN (200)
DIALOGUE (180)	NON-PRINTED (50)
Private (100)	Non-professional writing (20)
Direct conversations (90)	Student untimed essays (10)
Distanced conversations (10)	Student examination essays (10)
Public (80)	Correspondence (30)
Class lessons (20)	Social letters (15)
Broadcast discussions (20)	Business letters (15)
Broadcast interviews (10)	
Parliamentary debates (10)	
Legal cross-examinations (10)	
Business transactions (10)	
MONOLOGUE (120)	PRINTED (150)
Unscripted (70)	Informational (learned) (40)
Spontaneous commentaries (20)	Humanities (10)
Unscripted speeches (30)	Social sciences (10)
Demonstrations (10)	Natural sciences (10)
Legal presentations (10)	Technology (10)
Scripted (50)	Informational (popular) (40)
Broadcast news (20)	Humanities (10)
Broadcast talks (20)	Social sciences (10)
Speeches (not broadcast) (10)	Natural sciences (10)
	Technology (10)
	Informational (reportage) (20)
	Press news reports (20)
	Instructional (20)
	Administrative/regulatory (10)
	Skills/hobbies (10)
	Persuasive (10)
	Press editorials (10)
	Creative (10)
	Novel and stories (10)

Typically, each ICE project team is aiming at producing at least two types of corpora: a (i) lexical corpus (marked-up for computer processing), and (ii) a tagged corpus (with the whole corpus, or subsets of the corpus, grammatically tagged for parts of speech). In the case of the HK-ICE corpus, the project may be seen as a three-stage project:

- **Computerization:** all samples will be transcribed on to computer;
- **Lexical corpus:** after computerization, the researchers will then finish the markup of the data, thus producing a lexical corpus, containing

approximately five hundred texts, each with 2,000 words, using the ICE standard markup system;
- **Tagged corpus:** after the completion of a lexical corpus, subsets of texts will be grammatically analysed and 'tagged' for parts of speech; this will be carried out semi-automatically across the Internet, using the Amalgam tagger at the University of Leeds;

Following the completion of the tagged corpus, the Hong Kong ICE corpus will be transferred to CD-Rom and this will be made available for academic research, internationally and in Hong Kong.

In this chapter, our intention is to illustrate, first, the range of texts (spoken and written) that will be included in the completed database, and, second, to provide examples of the markup used to prepare the lexical corpus. The first sample text (Text 1) presented in the next section below illustrates the phases of data processing through the three stages of *computerization* (basic transcription), *markup* (for the lexical corpus), and *tagging* (for parts of speech). The other texts included in the following section (Texts 2–9) are all presented in their lexical corpus markup form. An explanation of markup symbols is provided in the endnotes of this chapter. Details of the grammatical tagging scheme may be found at http://www.ucl.ac.uk/english-usage/ice-gb/grammar.htm

A sample HK-ICE text throughout three phases of processing

Text 1 is an extract from a speech entitled '1997: A New Era of Accountancy in Hong Kong'. The speaker is a certified public accountant, male, aged 36–40. The speech was presented in February 1992 during a business seminar organized by the Department of Accountancy, Hong Kong Polytechnic.

Text 1 – A business talk

Phase 1 – Monologue, unscripted speech – transcribed and computerized

Mrs Chow talked about state own enterprise and joint venture Uh in fact that's true They are basically two as far as I understand two two sets of uh uh systems using in China One set is for state own enterprise and the other one is for joint ventures Based on my observation the state own enterprises system basically is a fund accounting which is to to uh record the source and the application of funds And then at the end of the financial period they will report it through several financial statements such as uh uh what they call the Balance of Funds Statements And then they also have uh uh Income Statements but uh they are very much related to operations of the enterprise This kind of system is not allowed for examples in Hong Kong because in

Hong Kong uh s if I remember correctly should be set two We cannot do reserve accounting But there is a lot of reserve accountings in China I mean particularly in state own enterprises Uh I first read a set of financial statements about states own enterprise in China is about two years ago I spent probably half an hour to understand one accounting entry which was the purchase of fixed asset So I must say it's quite confusing to the Western accountant

Phase 2 – Monologue, unscripted speech (with lexical markup)

<#42:2:A> Mrs Chow talked about state own enterprise and joint venture <,>
<#43:2:A> Uh in fact it's true <,> <#44:2:A> They are basically two as far as I understand two two sets of uh <,> uh systems <,> using in China<#45:2:A> One set is for state own enterprises <,> and the other one is for joint ventures <,,>
<#46:2:A> Based on my observation <,> the state own enterprises system basically is a fund accounting which is to <,> to uh record the source and the application of funds <,>
<#47:2:A> And then at the end of the financial period they will report it through several financial statements such as uh <,> uh what they call <,> the Balance of Funds Statements <,> <#48:2:A> And then they also have uh uh Income Statements but uh they are very much related to operations of the enterprise <,,>
<#49:2:A> This kind of system is not allowed for examples in Hong Kong because in Hong Kong <,> uh <.> s </.> if I remember correctly should be set <?> two </?> <,>
<#50:2:A> We cannot do reserve accounting <,>
<#51:2:A> But there is a lot of reserve accountings in China I mean particularly in state own enterprises <,,> <#52:2:A> Uh <,> I first read a set of financial statements about state own enterprise in China is about two years ago <,>
#53:2:A> I spent probably half an hour to understand one accounting entry which was the purchase of fixed asset <,>
<#54:2:A> So I must say it's quite confusing to the Western accountant <,,>

Phase 3 – Spoken monologue, unscripted speech (with grammatical tagging)

<#42:2:A> Mrs <N(prop,sing):1/2> Chow <N(prop,sing):2/2> talked <V(intr,past)> about <PREP(phras)> state N(com,sing):1/3> own<N(com,sing):2/3> enterprise <N(com,sing):3/3) and <CONJUNC(coord)> joint <N(com,sing):1/2> venture <N (com, sing) :2/2> <#43:2:A> Uh <INTERJEC> in <ADV(ge):1/2> fact <ADV(ge):2/2> it <PRON(pers,sing)>'s <V(cop,pres,encl)> true<ADJ(ge)>
<#44:2:A> They <PRON(pers,plu)> are<V(cop,pres)> basically <ADV(partic)> two <NUM(card,sing)> as <CONJUNC (subord):1/3> far <CONJUNC(subord):2/3> as <CONJUNC(subord):3/3> I <PRON(pers,sing)> understand <V(montr, pres)> two <NUM(card,sing)> two <NUM(card,sing)> sets<N(com,plu)> of <PREP(ge)> uh <INTERJEC> uh <INTERJEC> systems<N(com,plu)> using <V(montr,ingp)> in <PREP(ge)> China <N(prop,sing)>

<#45:2:A> One <NUM(card,sing)> set <N(com,sing)> is <V(cop,pres)> for <PREP(ge)> state <N(com, plu):1/3)> own <N(com, plu):2/3)> enterprises <N(com, plu):3/3)> and <CONJUNC(coord)> the <ART(def)> other<NUM(ord)> one <PRON(one,sing)> is <V(cop,pres)> for <PREP(ge)> joint <N(com, plu):1/2)> ventures<N(com,plu):2/2)>
<#46:2:A> Based <V(montr, edp)> on <PREP(ge)> my <PRON(poss,sing)> observation <N(com,sing)> the<ART(def)> state <N(com,plu):1/3> own <N(com,plu):2/3> enterprises <N(com,plu):3/3> system<N(com,sing)> basically <ADV(ge)> is <V(cop,pres)> a <ART(indef)> fund <N(com,sing):1/2)> accounting <N(com,sing):2/2)> which <PRON(rel)> is <V(cop,pres)> to <PRTCL(to)> to<PRTCL(to)> uh <INTERJEC> record <V(montr, infin)> the <ART(def)> source <N(com,sing)> and <CONJUNC(coord)> the <ART(def)> application <N(com,sing)> of <PREP(ge)> funds <N(com,plu)>
<#47:2:A> And <CONNEC(ge)> then<CONNEC(ge)> at <PREP(ge)> the <ART(def)> end <N(com,sing)> of <PREP(ge)> the <ART(def)> financial <ADJ(ge)> period <N(com,sing)> they <PRON(pers,plu)> will <AUX(modal,pres)> report <V (montr,infin)> it <PRON(pers,sing)> through <PREP(ge)> several <PRON(quant,plu)> financial <ADJ(ge)> statements <N(com,plu)> such <CONNEC(appos):1/2> as <CONNEC(appos):2/2> uh <INTERJEC> uh <INTERJEC> what <PRON(nom)> they <PRON(pers,plu)> call <V(cxtr,pres)> the<ART(def)> Balance <N(prop,plu):1/4> of <N(prop,plu):2/4> Funds <N(prop,plu):3/4> Statements <N(prop,plu):4/4>
<#48:2:A> And <CONNEC(ge)> then <CONNEC(ge)> they <PRON(pers,plu)> also <ADV(add)> have <V(montr,pres)> uh <INTERJEC> uh <INTERJEC> Income<N(prop,plu):1/2> Statements <N(prop,plu):2/2> but <CONJUNC(coord)> uh <INTERJEC> they <PRON(pers,plu)> are <AUX(pass, pres)> very <ADV(inten):1/2> much <ADV(inten):2/2> related V(montr, edp)> to <PREP(ge)> operations <N(com,plu)> of <PREP(ge)> the <ART(def)> enterprise <N(com,sing)>
<#49:2:A> This <PRON(dem,sing)> kind <N(com,sing)> of <PREP(ge)> system <N(com,sing)> is <AUX(pass,pres)> not <ADV(ge)> allowed <V(montr,edp)> for <CONNEC(appos):1/2> examples <CONNEC(appos):2/2> in<PREP(ge)> Hong <N(prop,sing):1/2> Kong <N(prop,sing):2/2> because<CONJUNC(subord)> in <PREP(ge)> Hong <N(prop,sing):1/2> Kong <N(prop,sing):2/2> uh <INTERJEC> s <UNTAG> if <CONJUNC(subord)> I <PRON(pers,sing)> remember <V(intr,pres)> correctly <ADV(ge)> should <AUX (modal,past)> be <V(cop,infin)> set <N(com,sing)> two <NUM(card,sing)>
<#50:2:A> We <PRON(pers,plu)> cannot <AUX(modal,pres,neg)> do <V(montr,infin)> reserve <N(com,sing):1/2> accounting <N(com,sing):2/2>
<#51:2:A> But <CONNEC(ge)> there <EXTHERE> is <V(intr,pres)> a <PRON(quant,sing):1/2> lot <PRON(quant, sing):2/2> of <PREP(ge)> reserve <N(com,plu):1/2> accountings <N(com,plu):2/2> in <PREP(ge)> China <N(prop,sing)> I <FRM:1/2> mean <FRM:2/2> particularly<ADV(partic)> in<PREP(ge)> state<N(com,plu):1/3> own <N(com,plu):2/3> enterprises <N(com,plu):3/3>
<#52:2:A> Uh <INTERJEC> I<PRON(pers,sing)> first <ADV(ge)> read <V(montr,past)> a <ART(indef)> sets <N(com,plu)> of <PREP(ge)> financial

<ADJ(ge)> statements <N(com,plu)> about <PREP(ge)> state <N(com,sing):1/3> own <N(com,sing):2/3> enterprise <N(com,sing):3/3> in <PREP(ge)> China <N(prop,sing)> is <V(cop,pres)> about <ADV(inten)> two <NUM (card,sing)> years<N(com,plu)> ago<ADV(ge)>
<#53:2:A> I <PRON(pers,sing)> spent <V(montr,past)> probably <ADV(ge)> half <NUM(frac,sing)> an <ART(indef)> hour <N(com,sing)> to <PRTCL(to)> understand <V(montr,infin)> one <NUM(card,sing)> accounting <ADJ(ingp)> entry <N(com,sing)> which <PRON(rel)> was <V(cop,past)> the <ART(def)> purchase <N(com,sing)> of <PREP(ge)> fixed <ADJ(edp)> asset <N(com,sing)>
<#54:2:A> So <CONNEC(ge)> I <PRON(pers,sing)> must <AUX(modal,pres)> say <V(montr,infin)> it <PRON(pers,sing)>'s <V(cop,pres,encl)> quite <ADV(inten)> confusing <ADJ(ingp)> to <PREP(ge)> the <ART(def)> Western <ADJ(ge)> accountant <N(com,sing)>

Other sample ice texts with lexical corpus markup

Text 2 — *Popular writing*

The following extract is from a social science article published in *The Foundation*, No. 16, 1991, p. 1.

(Written, printed, informational/popular/social sciences)
<h> <#1:1> HEDGING AGAINST A BELLICOSE CHAMBER </h>
 <#2:1> The public will witness a new order in the Legislative Council after September's elections .
<#3:1> The legacy of colonialism , which has enabled the administration to exert unrestricted control over its legislative body , is becoming Hong Kong's history .
 <#4:1> The council will no longer be dominated by appointees , who have been for years toeing official lines .
<#5:1> Instead , the forthcoming elections will simply create a large majority of elected members in the Legco , To be returned in different constituencies , the elected members will overwhelm their counterparts .
<#6:1> Underpinned by massive ballots , the directly elected members may exploit their representativeness to the limit .
 <#7:1> A demagogue-ridden chamber is emerging . <#8:1> It is anticipated that the legislative councillors will be
uncompromising and deviating from government lines .
 <#9:1> It is well known that bridging the gap between the administration and the law-making body has been the job of unofficial members of the Executive and Legislative Councils . <#10:1> They are in turn supported by other appointed members in the Legco . <#11:1> But the institution of a democratically constituted chamber , though
subject to qualification , ruins that practice .

 <#12:1> In strictly legal sense , the Governor is empowered to dissolve the chamber of blatantly veto bills already approved by it , if he finds the situation beyond control .
<#13:1> This may p erhaps help reassert government authority .
<#14:1> This measure may also compel members to take to compromises in order to avoid another election .
<#15:1> Be that as it may , the question then lies in whether the administration could survive the subsequent constitutional crisis .
 <#16:1> Could the administration continue to gain enough support from legislators to pass its bills ?
 <#17:1> The Government's idea of reviewing again rules governing the proceeding of the Legislative Council , though having been keenly discussed over the past couple of months , could not be seen as a measure to rule out the possibility of a stalemate .

Text 3 – A business letter

The following business letter was written in 1994 by a Hong Kong teacher in a school for the deaf to a local museum.

(Written/ Non-printed/Correspondence/Business letters)

<I> <#81:5> 17th May , 1994 .
<#82:5> The Curator
<#83:5> Flagstaff House Museum of Tea Ware
<#84:5> Cotton Road
<#85:5> Hong Kong
<#86:5> Dear Sir , <h>
<#87:5> <ul> Visit of Observation </ul> </h>
 <#88:5> As learning of the deaf students depends a lot on experience , therefore , great emphasis has been put on activities especially visits of observation for them .
 <#89:5> I venture to request for your kind permission for a group of 38 students &obrack; Lower and Upper Secondary Year 3 &cbrack; accompanied by 7 teachers to visit your Museum and learn about its works on Tuesday , 28th June , 1994 from 10:00 a.m. to 11.00 a.m .
<#90:5> I should be grateful if you could kindly arrange a Guide for this visit as well .
 <#91:5> Thank you for your kind attention and hoping this will meet your kind approval .
<#92:5> Yours sincerely ,
<#93:5> <O> signature </O>
<#94:5> &obrack; Miss &cbrack; BOW Sui-may
<#95:5> Principal/Supervisor
<#96:5> BSM/tyy </I>

Text 4 – A social letter

The social letter below was written in 1994 by a female university student in Hong Kong, to a fellow student.

(Written/Non-printed/Correspondence/Social letters)

<I> <p> <#137:12> Why not send me a mail ?<#138:12> You care only Cheng Siu Chau , Pao Kung &ampersand; William <-> Shakespear </-> <+> Shakespeare </+> at the expense of your best , kindly and friendly schoolmates .
<#139:12> How did you spend your Christmas vacation , reading again or doing essays ?
<#140:12> Oh !
<#141:12> Pat , you are a really a dull and boring girl with “ usual ” interests &ampersand; hobbies such as listening to classic instead of the “ Four Kings ” , playing piano at the contrast of playing majong .
<#142:12> You are an extremely out of fashion girl . </p>
<p> <#143:12> I have saw Andy Lau concert organised by Chase Credit card .
<#144:12> It is extremely wonderful &ampersand; successful and full of guests such the Anita Mun , Sally Yip , plus the “ five tigers ” .
<#145:12> I guess you would enjoy it if you were there .
<#146:12> Remember to sent me a mail . </p> </I>

Text 5 – A broadcast talk

The following extract is from the popular radio programme *Letter to Hong Kong*, broadcast on RTHK on 13 November 1995. The speaker is a male member of the Legislative Council.

(Spoken/Monologue/Scripted/Broadcast talks)

<$A><#1:1:A> Last Saturday I went to a wedding banquet of my cousin
<#2:1:A> One of my distant relative Auntie Ming snatched me by my arm once when I arrive <,>
<#3:1:A> She was not in a particular good mood and she was complaining about Housing Authority's new policies on property <.> in </.> ownership
<#4:1:A> She <?> blamed </?> me for setting such a harsh rule to bring so much distress to her family
<#5:1:A> Auntie Ming live in a public housing estate with her husband and two sons
<#6:1:A> Auntie Ming is a housewife
<#7:1:A> Her husband <,> Uncle Sum is a taxi driver
<#8:1:A> He purchase a taxi some years ago by installment
<#9:1:A> He has just paid off <.> hit </.> his mortgage recently
<#10:1:A> Their two sons both <,> are in late twenties have been working for

five to seven years since they graduate from tertiary education
<#11:1:A> Their total household incomes per month just exceeds forty thousand dollars per month
<#12:1:A> And the taxi is counted as a fixed asset of a value over one point five million dollars
<#13:1:A> According to the new policy proposed on property ownership they are rich enough to pay full market rent
<#14:1:A> It is estimated that the revised rental payment will be <?> around </?> ten thousand dollars per month
<#15:1:A> The market rent will take up more than half of the Uncle Ming's <.> inc </.> income
<#16:1:A> My two cousins are nice young men who always manage their personal finance well
<#17:1:A> They have to as they are saving up for their marriage in the near future
<#18:1:A> Though each of them earn over ten thousand dollars per month we can imagine that they are not have too much money to spare <,>
<#19:1:A> Auntie Ming and Uncle Sum have been working hard and particularly thrifty of their life
<#20:1:A> The taxi they own crystallizes all their <.> s </.> <?> wealth </?> for the past forty years
<#21:1:A> This property they invested in the means to earn a living and not for our speculation <,>
<#22:1:A> I share Auntie Ming's resentment for the punitive measure on them <,>
<#23:1:A> She was taught to believe that diligence and thrift should be ventured to be rewarded
<#24:1:A> However she is disillusioned now as they are punished for not being lazy enough in order to live hand to mouth <,>
<#25:1:A> While Auntie Ming was ventilating her emotion the guest sitting next to me made a very sensible suggestion to her
<#26:1:A> He said <,> you have to let at least one of your sons get married as soon as possible and so to move out of the unit
<#27:1:A> Then you may transfer the ownership of the taxi to him <,> who is no longer on the tenancy
<#28:1:A> And subsequently you have no asset in hand at all under your roof
<#29:1:A> Even a casual onlooker can think of such a trick to elude the <unclear> one-word </unclear> of <.> porty </.> property ownership
<#30:1:A> I am quite sure that the asset declaration is doomed to failure <,>
<#31:1:A> Auntie Ming's neighbour Mrs Wong's case even worse
<#32:1:A> She ran a food stall and own a flat in Shum Shui Po twenty twenty years ago <,>
<#33:1:A> The area she live was affected by a Land <?> Resumption </?> exercise and the government re-settle her family in a public housing unit <,>
<#34:1:A> Her food stall's business grew under the toil of all the family members
<#35:1:A> At present it has been expanded into a decent restaurant <,>
<#36:1:A> They are obviously too rich to be subsidized by the tax payers'

Analysing Hong Kong English   251

money <,>
<#37:1:A> We said her case is even worse because our consciences will not stir if this well-off restaurant boss has to pay market rent
<#38:1:A> Unfortunately we have overlooked the fact that <,> the Wong's family move in the public housing estate upon the government's invitation without any means test in the first place <,>

Text 6 – Broadcast news

The following television news bulletin was broadcast on TVB Pearl on 15 July 1992. Speaker A is male, aged 26–30; speaker B is female, aged 41–45.

(Spoken/Monologue/Scripted/Broadcast news)

<$A> <#1:1:A> The government makes public one of Hong Kong's best kept secrets <,>
<#2:1:A> The pope undergoes surgery in a Rome hospital <,>
<#3:1:A> And Chinese dissidents appeared at the Democratic National Convention <,>
<$B> <#4:1:B> Good evening <,>
<#5:1:B> Thanks for joining us
<#6:1:B> The government has departed from tradition to disclose how much Hong Kong has in its exchange fund
<#7:1:B> And from now on the balance sheet of the fund will be published every year
<#8:1:B> Making public one of Hong Kong's best kept secrets is seen as a move to impress prospective lenders especially for the new airport
<#9:1:B> Hong Kong's exchange fund until now one of the best kept financial secrets in town is used to safeguard the territory's exchange rates stability <,>
<#10:1:B> At the end of nineteen ninety-one it stands at two hundred and thirty-six billion Hong Kong dollars
<#11:1:B> The bulk of which are foreign currency assets worth twenty-nine billion US dollars equivalent to about two hundred and twenty-five billion Hong Kong dollars <O> speech by Hamish Macleod Financial Secretary of HK </O>
<$B> <#12:1:B> It gives Hong Kong a per capita foreign currency holding of five thousand US dollars <,>
<#13:1:B> The exchange fund has accumulated earnings of almost ninety-nine billion Hong Kong dollars
<#14:1:B> This fund is separated from Hong Kong's fiscal reserves of seventy-six billion Hong Kong dollars which can be used for public spending
<#15:1:B> And there's also twenty-five billion Hong Kong dollars excluding interests in the land fund for the future's Special Administrative Region
<#16:1:B> Pledging to publish annual balance sheets of the exchange fund from now on <,> Hamish Macleod obviously saw it as a political move conducive to attracting lenders for projects such as the new airport <O>

speech by Hamish Macleod </O>
<$B> <#17:1:B> It also reflects the new Open Government Policy <O> speech by Hamish Macleod </O>
<$B> <#18:1:B> The fund has been kept a secret before <,> for good reason says Macleod
<#19:1:B> But circumstances have changed
<#20:1:B> Hong Kong's monetary framework has strengthened significantly in recent years so that the territory is less vulnerable to speculative pressures on the exchange rate <,>
<#21:1:B> Disclosure of foreign currency reserves is also established practice in other major market economies <,>
<#22:1:B> The new governor Chris Patten also hailed the move as a show of Hong Kong's financial strength

Text 7 – Legco debate

The following extract from a debate in the Hong Kong Legislative Council (Legco) was recorded on 22 October 1992. The speaker is a male Legislative Councillor, then in his early forties.

(Spoken/Dialogue/Unscripted speech/Parliamentary debates)

<$A> <#1:1:A> Mr Deputy President I refrain from telling fairy tales because I've done it quite enough
<#2:1:A> I have to do it every night when I try to put my daughters to bed <,>
<#3:1:A> I welcome the Governor speech <,> although there are areas I have doubts <,>
<#4:1:A> On the whole <,> it is cleverly crafted and packaged <,> <#5:1:A> That is why it has received such wide support even though the spending proposals are well within our fiscal guidelines <,>
<#6:1:A> I'm glad to hear that the government's approach to business will remain one of minimum interference and maximum support <,>
<#7:1:A> I'm glad to know <,> that we will provide more assistance to those in genuine need <,>
<#8:1:A> I also welcome the establishment of the Governor Business Council <,> which has gone a long way <,> to allay the business sector's fear over the fast pace of the outline democratic development in Hong Kong <,>
<#9:1:A> The experience and insight of the members of the Business Council should provide useful input to the government in formulating business policies <,>
<#10:1:A> Since many of my colleagues have already commented extensively on the Governor's policy proposals I will confine my comments to a few specific areas which I feel strongly <,>
<#11:1:A> The first area is competition <,>
<#12:1:A> I agree with the Governor that competition <,> is the key to our economic success <,>

<#13:1:A> It holds down costs <,> raises efficiencies <,> and benefits consumers <,>
<#14:1:A> We must therefore <,> allow as much competition as possible in each and every sector of our economy <,>
<#15:1:A> However <,> we also have to bear in mind that competition is only a means to an end
<#16:1:A> The end is whether consumers can benefit <,> and equally important whether the market would continue to deliver goods and services at a speed and with such quality that the society's demands can be fully met <,>
<#17:1:A> While competition is conducive to consumer protection <,> we must avoid equating competition to consumer protection <,>
<#18:1:A> If we look at the complaints made to the Consumer Council we will find that many of these complaints are not in areas where we lack competition <,>
<#19:1:A> Rather many of those complaints are on unethical business practices of individual businessmen who cannot face competition and therefore have to resort to unethical and indeed illegal means to generate revenue <,>
<#20:1:A> In addressing this issue the government must distinguish between unethical business practices of individual businessmen <,> such as some electrical appliances shops <,> and some second-hand car dealers <,> and genuine collusion on an industry-wide basis <,>
<#21:1:A> It must also bear in mind that competition does not lie in the number of suppliers <,>
<#22:1:A> If there is no surplus production capacity <,> there will be no competition <,> regardless of the number of suppliers because suppliers find no incentive to compete when demand outstrips supply <,>
<#23:1:A> I would like to lay down the criteria of how I see a good competition policy <,>
<#24:1:A> A good competition policy should encourage production <,>
<#25:1:A> It should encourage investors to <.> pro </.> to produce more <,> better goods and services
<#26:1:A> It should eliminate whatever non-market barriers to entry for newcomers <,>
<#27:1:A> A good competition policy should recognize the limit on the optimum number of firms imposed by the size of the market and do not sacrifice efficiency for competition <,>
<#28:1:A> A good competition policy should recognize the need for market stability <,>
<#29:1:A> In industries where stability is essential to the society <,> we have to accept arrangements of markets participants provided <,> that such arrangements are transparent <,> known to the public and produce benefits without penalizing consumers <,>
<#30:1:A> In other words <,> these arrangements are not used by firms for profit maximization <,>
<#31:1:A> Some colleagues have ask for more legislations and more watchdog bodies to protect consumers <,>

<#32:1:A> While I'll support any legislation which would give consumers more protection <,> I'm sceptical about legislations which would discord distort markets and resource allocations <,>
<#33:1:A> Indeed I think I oppose those legislations
<#34:1:A> We must allow market forces full play <,> if we want genuine and not artificial competition <,>
<#35:1:A> Already there are legislations giving customers the <?> full </?> redress against unscrupulous business practices
<#36:1:A> However consumers seldom resort to legal proceedings because of the troubles they have to go through in undertaking such an act <,>
<#37:1:A> I also disagree with the setting up of more committees or quangos as watchdogs <,>
<#38:1:A> The Consumer Council has done a great job and we should continue to support their work <,>

Text 8 – *Informal conversation*

The following extract from a conversation was recorded in Hong Kong in 1994. Speaker A and speaker B are female undergraduates, aged 21–25. Speaker Z is a non-Cantonese-speaking student.

(*Spoken/Dialogue/Private/Direct conversations*)

<$A> <#71:1:A> Uh the hotel is uh relatively cheap
<#72:1:A> Uhm it cost for <,> just about <,> uhm <,>
<#73:1:A> I I can't recall exactly the amount
<#74:1:A> About <,> three hundred dollar
<$Z> <X>
<#X75:1:Z> Hong Kong </X>
<$A> <#76:1:A> Hong Kong dollar per night
<#77:1:A> Double room
<#78:1:A> And <,> if <,> uh if you're sharing a room with uhm you can just book a double room and <,> you can <,> uh three persons can live there
<#79:1:A> They won't <,> charge you extra money <{1> <[1> <,> </[1>
<#80:1:A> And the manager of the hotel are Hong Kong people
<#81:1:A> <{2> <[2> You can speak </[2> in Cantonese
<#82:1:A> They are very nice
<#83:1:A> Uhm <,> they will teach you uh how to <,> how to get to the scenic spots
<#84:1:A> Uh they will make some <,> arrangement for your transportation if you want them if you ask them
<#85:1:A> They are really nice
<$B> <#86:1:B> <[1> Uhm </[1> </{1>
<#87:1:B> <[2> Oh really </[2> </{2> <&>$B laughs </&>
<#88:1:B> Uh uh
<$Z> <X>
<#X89:1:Z> Do you speak Mandarin </X>

<$B> <#90:1:B> No
<$Z> <X>
<#X91:1:Z> How is she going to get by <,> in Beijing <|> <[> without any Mandarin </[> </X>
<$B> <#92:1:B> <[> Is it a big </[> </{> problem if I don't speak Mandarin <#93:1:B> Uh because I just finished uhm beginner's course <&> $Z laughs </&> and I I don't think I can <,> tackle the real problem <&> $Z laughs </&>
<$A> <#94:1:A> Uh I think that's a real problem for you
<#95:1:A> I speak Mandarin
<#96:1:A> I've finished the advance course <,> but <,> I think the local <.> Bei </.> Beijing people speak <,> the the <,> the Mandarin they speak is a little bit different because uhm <,> the Putonghua we we speak <,> uhm <,> include just part of the Beijing dialect
<#97:1:A> But in Beijing most people especially the <,> uhm people who are less educated they speak Beijing dialect which is really difficult for us to understand
<#98:1:A> Even I myself I finished advance course I <,> can't hear what they say <,>
<#99:1:A> So if you don't <,> know Mandarin that will be a big problem
<#100:1:A> You have to write all the time
<$B> <#101:1:B> Oh <&> laughs </&>
<$Z> <X>
<#X102:1:Z> Uhm </X>
<$B> <#103:1:B> So I have to prepare a lot of <,> paper <&> laughs </&>
<$A> <#104:1:A> Yes <,>
<#105:1:A> I <|> <[> think </[> so
<$B> <#106:1:B> <[> Oh </[> </|>
<#107:1:B> How long is your trip
<$A> <#108:1:A> Uhm <,> twenty days
<$B> <#109:1:B> Twenty days
<$A> <#110:1:A> I <,> I went to Beijing then I <,> then I travelled by train to <,> uh <,> Shandong <|> <[> <,> </[>
<#111:1:A> Uhm up
<#112:1:A> Do you know the Shandong Peninsula
<$B> <#113:1:B> <[> Uhm </[> </|>
<#114:1:B> <|> <[> No </[>
<$Z> <X>
<#X115:1:Z> <[> No </[> </|> <&> laughs </&> </X>
<$A> <#116:1:A> Uh <,> well
<#117:1:A> I went to <,> Ji Nan <{1> <[1> <,> </[1> Qianghai <O> one word in Mandarin </O> <{2> <[2> <,> </[2> Qingdao <O> four words in Mandarin </O> <&> laughs </&>
<#118:1:A> Then I
<$B> <#119:1:B> <[1> Uh uh </[1> </{1> <[2> Uh uh </[2> </{2>
<$Z> <X>
<#X120:1:Z> Sorry <{1> <[1> <,> what was that </[1> </X>
<$B> <#121:1:B> <[1> <&> laughs </&> </[1>

<$A> <#122:1:A> <[1> Then I </[1> </{1> went back to Beijing
<#123:1:A> But it's very difficult to uhm <,> get a ticket
<#124:1:A> Uhm <,> get a train ticket <{1> <[1> <,> </[1> uh from <,> north down south <{2> <[2> <,> </[2>
<#125:1:A> And it's <,> uhm <,> a problem if you want to travel from Beijing to the south
<$B> <#126:1:B> <[1> Uh </[1> </{1>
<#127:1:B> <[2> Uhm </[2> </{2>
<#128:1:B> Is it <?> difficult </?> to uh buy a <,,> ticket
<$A> <#129:1:A> There's there's a special office for <,> foreign visitors in uh Beijing uhm train station <{1> <[1> <,> </[1>
<#130:1:A> You can get a <,> you can bet you can get better seats and at a lower at a higher price <&> $B and $Z laugh </&> at the at the <,> foreign visitors <?> <.> tic </.> </?> uh ticket office
<#131:1:A> Uhm <,> last uh when I <,> went there last year they use the uhm <,> exchange coupon <{2> <[2> <,> </[2> but <,> that's that's no longer use now
<#132:1:A> <{3> <[3> I don't know </[3> whether the <?> <.> pri </.> </?> but I assume the price will be <,> much higher than
<$B> <#133:1:B> <[> Uhm uhm </[> </{>
<#134:1:B> <[2> Uh uh </[2> </{2>
<$Z> <X>
<#X135:1:Z> <[3> Uhm uhm </[3> </{3> </X>
<$B> <#136:1:B> Because uh some of my friends told me that uhm it's a <,> big confusion to have uhm <,> seats in the train <,> is it
<$Z> <X>
<#X137:1:Z> Uhm uhm </X>
<$A> <#138:1:A> Uhm <,> you get no problem if you book your seat in Hong Kong <,> then <,> you travel from Hong Kong to uhm <,> Guangzhou
<#139:1:A> Uh then from Guangzhou to Beijing

ICE corpus data – potential research applications

The ICE-HK corpus will provide an invaluable resource for the study of the linguistic features of Hong Kong English at all the major levels of linguistic analysis, notably phonology (accent), lexis (vocabulary), and grammar.

Phonology (accent)

Previous research by Bolton and Kwok (1990) and Hung (2000) has provided an extensive description of segmental features of the Hong Kong English accent. Such features include the neutralization of long versus short vowel contrasts in words such as *bit* and *beat*, *pot* and *port*, *foot* and *food*; the absence of a contrast between /e/ and /æ/ in *beg* and *bag*; and the allocation of full value to what is in other varieties of English the unstressed schwa /ə/ vowel, so that *grammar* may be pronounced /græmɑ/, and *China* /tʃaɪnɑ/ (Bolton and Kwok 1990: 152). In the case of consonants, patterns of regularly occurring substitution include the replacement of /θ/ by /f/ as in /fiŋks/ for *thinks;* /ð/ by /d/, as in /deɪ/ for *they,* and /ð/ by /v/ in final position as in /wɪv/ for *with;* /v/ by /w/, e.g. /diwaɪ/ for *divide;* /ʃ/ by /s/, as in /iŋglis/ for *English;* /l/ by /r/ as in /kɔrek/ for *collect;* /l/ by /n/ and vice versa, as in /lit/ and /nɔŋ/ for *neat* and *long;* and the vocalization of final /l/ (or 'dark l') as in /wiu/ for *will,* etc. Patterns of non-release and deletion also regularly occur in the case of final stops (pp. 153–4). Bolton and Kwok argue that 'Hong Kong English speakers typically share a number of localised features of a Hong Kong accent' (p. 166), and that such features are not restricted to mid- or lower-range speakers, but cluster in varying proportions in the speech of locally-educated upper-range speakers as well. More recently, Hung has suggested that (i) 'there exists a "phonology" of HKE [Hong Kong English], with systematic features of its own; (ii) 'the phonemic inventory of HKE is considerably simpler than that of OVE's ["other varieties of English"], both in its vowel and consonant systems'; and that (iii) 'though HKE shows the influence of Cantonese, its phonological system cannot be reduced entirely to the phonology of either Cantonese or English, but needs to be investigated on its own terms' (2000: 354). Although this previous research points the way forward to a more detailed agenda for phonological research, there still remains much to be done. For example, very little work has been carried out on such suprasegmental features of the Hong Kong accent as stress placement, and intonation (see Bolton and Kwok 1990). In addition, there are still many basic questions concerning the modelling of phonological variation, and the role that social variables such as age, educational level, and residence overseas may play in influencing the speech patterns of individuals and groups. In this context, the HK-ICE corpus will offer an accessible and relevant database for work in this area. All of the 300 spoken texts in the corpus are being transferred from audio tapes into digitally-recorded sound (*.wav*) files, and will be included in this form in the final computerized version of the HK-ICE database, which will be released to students and researchers in 2003.

Lexis (vocabulary)

A number of studies of a distinct Hong Kong vocabulary have been published in recent years, including Chan and Kwok (1985), Taylor (1989), Benson (1993, 1994, 2000). In addition, over the past ten years, the Sydney-based *Macquarie Dictionary* team have compiled wordlists for Asian Englishes including Hong Kong English. Examples of Hong Kong words in one recent *Macquarie* publication include such items as *ABC* (American-born Chinese),

AO (a public servant in the most senior career grade of the Hong Kong Civil Service), *astronaut* (a breadwinner repeatedly commuting by air between his job in Hong Kong and his emigrant family in Australia or Canada, etc.), *bak choi* (a variety of Chinese green and white cabbage), *Canto star* (a singer of Cantonese pop songs), *chit* (a bill or receipt), *chop* (a personal or company seal or stamp), etc. (Maquarie 2000). As noted above, a 1 million-word corpus is generally considered to be small, and this is especially true in lexical studies. Nonetheless, careful analysis of such a database can still yield interesting results. Chow (2001), following Benson's (1994) study of the political vocabulary of Hong Kong English, investigated 'the localised English vocabulary of official and political usage' in the HKSAR through the description and analysis of HK-ICE data, specifically the subset of data from the corpus known as 'parliamentary debates' (see above). Through a comparison of Hong Kong corpus data with data from the British corpus (ICE-GB), Chow was able to establish that a significant number of vocabulary items displayed a 'unique' local reference (in comparison with parliamentary debates from ICE-GB) within Hong Kong. These included such words and expressions as *abode, administration, autonomy, boatpeople, continuity, convergence, Exco* (Executive Council), *Hong Kong Special Administrative Region, ICAC* (Independent Commission Against Corruption), *Legco* (Legislative Council), *legislature, localisation, PRC* (People's Republic of China), *run-up*, and *self-censorship*. Interestingly, a number of such items can be found in the sample texts above, including *the Executive and Legislative Councils* (Text 2), *Legco* (Text 2), and *Special Administrative Region* (Text 6). In addition, even in this small sample of texts, there are other examples of localized vocabulary, including *food stall* 'a small open air restaurant' (Text 5), and the *Four Kings* 'four Hong Kong popstar celebrities' (Text 4).

Grammar

A substantial body of earlier work on commonly-occurring errors in Hong Kong English has been published over the last two decades. This includes such research papers as Webster, Ward and Craig (1987), Webster, and Lam (1991), and Bunton (1994), which have broadly adopted a contrastive analysis approach to the description of features of learner English and 'interlanguage' in the writing of Hong Kong secondary students. Somewhat similar in approach are a number of book-length studies, including Bunton (1989), a local Longman guide to 'common English errors'; Boyle and Boyle (1991), another Longman guide to 'spoken English errors'; and Potter (1992), another Longman guide to 'common business English errors'. More recently, Milton's (2001) detailed corpus-based study of the 'written interlanguage' of Hong Kong Chinese students represents a significant step forward in research methodology and analysis in this field. In addition to analysing grammatical patterns of 'overuse' versus 'underuse' in the writing of Hong Kong students in comparison to that of 'native' students, Milton also provides a taxonomy of local learner errors. These include, in rank order of frequency of error in category, the *indefinite article*; *prepositions*; *personal and relative pronouns*; *genitive*; *definitive article*; verbs, auxiliaries, and *participles*; *nouns*; *word order*; *adjectives*; *adverbs*; *possessive pronouns*; *conjunctions*; *determiners*; and *punctuation* (Milton, 2001: 43).

The precise relationship between labels such as 'error', 'interlanguage' and 'feature' in the description of the grammatical patterning of English in such 'outer circle' or 'ESL' societies as India, Singapore, the Philippines, Hong Kong, is a contentious one. Kachru and Nelson (1996: 79–80) note that the concept of interlanguage 'accounts for the observable differences between varieties of English in the Outer as compared with the Inner Circle' and that '[t]he *inter*-prefix refers to the notion that the linguistic system that any given learner or community of learning or users has at any particular moment is quantitatively and conceptually somewhere between the first language and the target'. There are a number of weaknesses with this approach, however:

> The validity of an interlanguage concept of Outer Circle Englishes would hinge crucially on two elements: the desire of learners of English to emulate one or another Inner Circle English model, and the availability of such models in accessible materials, not only in the classroom but also in broader social and cultural interactions. Neither of these conditions can be shown to obtain in broad ways in the Outer Circle. To be sure, one could find individuals in, say, India who actively seek to speak British English, and in countries such as India, Nigeria, and Singapore one often meets such people. There is thus a confusion between the perception of use and the linguistic reality (Kachru and Nelson, 1996: 80).

Much could be said about this issue. In many previous studies of Hong Kong English, the terms contrastive analysis, error analysis, interlanguage, have tended to overlap, as have such labels as 'errors' and 'interlanguage constructions', with the use of such terms contributing to the notion of Hong Kong English as a sub-standard or deficient variety. Nevertheless, Milton's adoption of the term here is a reasoned one. The data he analyses are drawn explicitly from learner corpora at both secondary and university level, and he later argues that many of the differences he identifies between Hong Kong student English and the 'Standard English' norms of UK students may be attributable to 'institutional' influences, such as teaching practices and coursebook materials, that promote the 'conservative production strategies' of students (2001: 110).

The approach of the ICE researchers in 'outer circle' societies worldwide is to adopt a 'features-based' rather than an 'error analysis' or 'interlanguage' approach to the analysis of grammatical variation. There are at least three broad justifications for this approach. The ICE project internationally and in the HKSAR (see above) is not simply restricted to the analysis of 'learner English' in the educational domain. In fact, student texts collected in the domain of education account for only 40 of the total of 500, i.e. (spoken) *class lessons* (20), *student untimed essays* (10), and *student examination essays* (10). Otherwise, the text types sampled by the HK-ICE are drawn from a wide range of communicative domains, including the business world, the civil service, the law courts, the legislature, television, radio, the print media, as well as the domains of friendship and social life. Second, many of those providing texts for ICE-HK are relatively older members of Hong Kong's bilingual speech community, particularly those bilinguals who regularly feature as commentators or spokespeople in the HKSAR media. Typically, they have graduated from university some years ago, now occupy middle-ranking and senior positions in business, government or the law, and may thus be regarded as mature language users, whose speech and writing is not untypical of 'English-knowing bilinguals' in Hong Kong. Finally, and perhaps more generally, the ICE project is, first and foremost, descriptive in orientation, and it is important, we feel, to counter the attitude that somehow 'Hong Kong English', even at the grammatical level, is somehow to no more than a clustering of error-ridden utterances or sentences. As in other parts of the world where the ICE is in progress, the main strand of our approach at the grammatical level is to identify and chart patterns of the relative frequency and distribution of particular grammatical structures, and to strive for a more adequate and ultimately more useful description of Hong Kong English grammar. Part of this description will involve the identification of language 'errors', but such labels need a precise definitional and descriptive explanation to distinguish an 'error', however defined, from a frequently-occurring 'feature' of local usage.

The texts in the HK-ICE corpus will provide an unprecedented resource for the study of the grammar of Hong Kong English. Each word will be annotated for its part of speech (as illustrated in Text 1, Phase 3), which will allow linguists to retrieve and study a wide range of grammatical features. By comparing these features with other components of ICE, we expect to be able to determine with a high degree of accuracy which features are distinctive in Hong Kong English, and which features are shared as part of a 'common core' of international English. The extracts shown above in this chapter are provided for illustrative purposes only, but even in these we can observe grammatical features that call for further investigation, once the entire corpus has been compiled. More specifically, three categories of features are suggested by a reading of the above examples, i.e. noun phrase structure, phrasal verbs, and coordination.

Features of noun phrase structure visible in the data thus include:
(i) The use and non-use of determiners, as compared with British English:

giving customers *the* full redress (Text 7)
In strictly legal sense (Text 2)

(ii) Number contrast:

the *proceeding* of the Legislative Council (Text 2)
Some colleagues have ask for more *legislations* (Text 7)
Already there are *legislations* (Text 7)

(iii) Noun complements and postmodifiers

I share Auntie Ming's *resentment for the punitive measure* (Text 5)
the *criteria of how I see a good competition policy* (Text 7)

Text 7 also contains an unusual noun phrase structure, in which *whatever* appears to be used as a determiner, equivalent to *all*, in 'It should eliminate *whatever* non-market barriers to entry for newcomers'. It will be interesting to see whether this usage is more general in Hong Kong English, and whether other distinctive aspects of the determiner system can be revealed.

In the case of phrasal verbs, there are a number of interesting instances of usage. In the following example, the verb phrase contains an intrusive preposition *for*, by comparison with British and American English:

I venture to *request for* your kind permission (Text 3)

In the next example, the preposition *to* is selected, rather than *with*:

we must avoid *equating* competition *to* consumer protection (Text 7)

Our final example omits the preposition altogether, from what is usually a phrasal verb:

You care only Cheng Siu Chau (Text 4) [cf. You care only *about* ...]

With reference to coordination, even a cursory reading of the extracts here suggests that coordination in Hong Kong English may be a fruitful area of investigation. In canonical use, coordination involves similar structures (noun phrases coordinate with noun phrases, for example). There are several instances of what we might call 'dissimilar' or 'disparate' coordination in the extracts in this chapter. In the following example, the participial adjective *uncompromising* is coordinated with the progressive form verb *deviating*:

... the legislative councillors will be *uncompromising* and *deviating* from government lines (Text 2)

In the next example, *been* fulfils a dual grammatical role in the coordinated structure:

> Auntie Ming and Uncle Sum have been working hard and particularly thrifty ... (Text 5)

In the first conjoin (*have been working hard*) *been* is a progressive auxiliary. In the second conjoin (*have been ... particularly thrifty*) it is the main, copular verb.

The final example, involves a coordinated predicate:

> A good competition policy should recognize the limit on the optimum number of firms imposed by the size of the market and do not sacrifice efficiency for competition (Text 7).

Rather than 'disparate' coordination, this may simply be a lack of subject-verb agreement (cf. 'A good competition policy *does* not sacrifice ...'). On the other hand, it may indicate a more general pattern of modal verb use in Hong Kong English. Many more instances from the corpus would be needed before we could reach any conclusions.

The grammatical features discussed here are, of course, found in other varieties of English, and no conclusions about Hong Kong English should be drawn from such limited data. Only when the ICE-HK corpus has been completed will we be able to determine whether these are isolated instances – perhaps part of an individual speaker's idiolect, or simply performance errors – or whether they have a wider and more general distribution in Hong Kong English. At that point, too, we will also be able to investigate more rigorously the similarities between learner corpus data and the community-wide ICE data study, and, perhaps, the description of 'errors' versus 'features'. In addition, the ICE-HK promises to provide an important resource for the study of discourse and pragmatics (Leung 1995, Woo 1999).

Conclusion

In this chapter, we have discussed the background to the International Corpus of English project in Hong Kong (ICE-HK), and present a number of different texts taken from the Hong Kong corpus. These include a business talk, an example of popular writing, a business letter, a social letter, a broadcast talk, broadcast news, a Legislative Council (Legco) debate, and an informal conversation. We have also presented, for illustration, one of these texts at the three stages of transcription or 'processing', i.e., first, basic transcription and computerization; second, with lexical markup; and, third, with grammatical tagging. With the completion of the ICE-HK corpus in the near future, we would hope to move forward descriptions of Hong Kong English in order to provide a more comprehensive and accurate description of this variety, at the lexical and phonological levels, as well as that of grammar and discourse. The project has not only an immediate relevance to the study of Hong Kong English, but will also help illuminate theoretical issues relating to the study of linguistic variation in outer-circle English-using societies throughout Asia and elsewhere.

Notes

1. The research described in this chapter has been supported by a grant from the Research Grants Council of the Hong Kong Special Administrative Region, China (Project No. HKU 7174/00H).
2. The ICE-HK academic team now comprises Kingsley Bolton, Gerald Nelson, and Joseph Hung of the Chinese University of Hong Kong. Our thanks too to Philip Bolt, who led the ICE-HK corpus team from 1990–1997.

References

Benson, Phil (1993) Localized vocabulary in Hong Kong English and Australian English. In *Studies in Lexis: Working Papers from a Seminar*. Edited by Richard Pemberton and Elza S. C. Tsang. Hong Kong: Hong Kong University of Science and Technology, pp. 99–111.

Benson, Phil (1994) The political vocabulary of Hong Kong English. *Hongkong Papers in Linguistics and Language Teaching*, 17, 63–81.

Benson, Phil (2000) Hong Kong words: Variation and context. *World Englishes*, 19(3), 373–80.

Bolton, Kingsley and Kwok, Helen (1990) The dynamics of the Hong Kong accent: Social identity and sociolinguistic description. *Journal of Asian Pacific Communication* 1, 147–72.

Boyle, Joseph and Boyle, Linda (1991) *Common Spoken English Errors in Hong Kong*. Hong Kong: Longman.

Bunton, David (1989) *Common English Errors in Hong Kong*. Hong Kong: Longman.

Bunton, David (1994) *Common Social English Errors in Hong Kong*. Hong Kong: Longman.

Chan, Mimi, and Kwok, Helen (1985) *A Study of Lexical Borrowing from Chinese into English with Special Reference to Hong Kong*. Hong Kong: Centre of Asian Studies, The University of Hong Kong.

Chow, Pok Man Susanna (2001) The study of Hong Kong English vocabulary, with particular reference to the study of official and political discourse in the HKSAR. MA Dissertation, Department of English, The University of Hong Kong.

Hung, Tony T. N. (2000) Towards a phonology of Hong Kong English. *World Englishes*. 19(3): 337–56.

Kachru, Braj B. and Nelson, Cecil L. (1996) World Englishes. In *Sociolinguistics and Language Teaching*. Edited by Sandra Lee McKay and Nancy H. Hornberger. Cambridge: Cambridge University Press.

Leung, Mei Chun May (1995) The use of the discourse markers you know, well and so in Hong Kong English and British English. M. Phil. Dissertation. Hong Kong Polytechnic University.

Macquarie (2000) Entries for Grolier International Dictionary. In *Grolier International Dictionary*. Sydney: The Macquarie Library Pty Ltd.

Milton, John (2001) Elements of a written Interlanguage: A computational and corpus-based study of institutional influences on the acquisition of English by Hong Kong Chinese students. *Research Reports*. Volume Two. Edited by Gregory James. Hong Kong: Language Centre, The Hong Kong University of Science and Technology.

Potter, John (1992) *Common Business English Errors in Hong Kong*. Hong Kong: Longman.

Taylor, Andrew (1989) Hong Kong's English newspapers. *English Today*, **20**, 18–24.

Webster, Michael and Lam, William C. P. (1991) Further notes on the influence of Cantonese on the English of Hong Kong students. *ILE Journal*. Special issue no. 2, 35–42.

Webster, Michael, Ward, Alan and Craig, Kenneth (1987) Language errors due to first language interference (Cantonese) produced by Hong Kong students of English. *ILE Journal* (H.K.), 3, 63–81.

Woo, Ka Hei Michelle (1999) An analysis of gender and discourse with reference to data from the Hong Kong International Corpus of English. MA Dissertation, Department of English, The University of Hong Kong.

14 Cultural imagination and English in Hong Kong

Shirley Geok-lin Lim

Hong Kong students' creative writing

The domain of the imagination finds expression through all kinds of media: paint, stone and marble, music, movement, and so forth; and, with the invention of new technologies, through photography, film, digital art and more. We can agree that imagination and the arts it produces are not limited to language. Even should we restrict our analysis to imagination in the language arts, the relationship between imagination and language arguably has not yet been fully plumbed; and, despite the many political controversies around the debate, neither has the relationship between a people's identity and their language of use been clarified. Imagination is a mysterious force, an ability or power we know little about, and particularly, about how to teach, encourage, strengthen, or nurture it.

What is the language of the imagination, when it is not limited to language? When it expresses itself through language, are certain languages more empowering, appropriate, and affirming for the life of certain people's imaginations? Are individual imaginations intrinsically, organically, and originally constituted through one kind of language (the mother tongue) and inevitably weakened, falsified, or deadened, if reconstituted through another (foreign) language?

If we view language as an immensely plastic medium, more plastic than paint or film, for example, can we then argue that all languages may be accessed by the imagination? In short, can we argue that imagination generates the arts of language, even as we acknowledge that language works to generate acts of imagination? Taking this dialogical approach to the relations between language and imagination, linguists such as Braj Kachru have theorized that the English language today, often situated as a 'Western' language producing 'Western' literature, is itself susceptible to the world's imaginations which collectively are generating the language arts of World Englishes.

Attentive to Kachru's thesis, this introduction does not seek to reduce the

English language to an instrument, receptive and plastic to any user. For example, I do not quarrel with the near universal view that language is a particularly cultural specific and sensitive phenomenon — not simply a social tool but a constitutive force that reproduces culture and culture makers. This view has been deployed to support the resistance to using a language, seen as non-indigenous to a community, to express the community's identity and culture. Such use of a non-'mother-tongue', it has been argued, results in identity loss and community death, in the destruction of original cultures constituted through indigenous languages. Historical evidence of vanished communities lends support to such concerns.

If I were in the business of conserving original cultures and communities, I would probably be erecting barriers to the spread of English, the most global language in human history and viewed by many as the most predatory. But I am in the business of change and transformation, on the side of the future, including the future for economic survival of the disadvantaged in human society. I cannot see how protecting disadvantaged communities from learning English could ensure their survival, except perhaps as 'boutique' communities patronized through benefactor efforts and resources; communities dependent on the protection of world agencies. While we lament the ravages of globalization, which include coercive integration into global capitalism and increasing loss of cultural autonomy, these changes can be ameliorated and political agency asserted should transformation come under these communities' critical control. That is, change is inevitable, but whether or how much it leads to destruction or to transformation is not predetermined. Thus, I have few qualms about whole-heartedly encouraging the young Hong Kong writer to consider writing also in the English language.

After over 150 years of British colonial education, it is remarkable that only a minority of Hong Kong people are comfortable speaking or writing the English language. Reasons for this may include the heavy representation of Cantonese speakers in the population, the continuous flow of immigrant Chinese from the Mainland, and the linguistic chauvinism of local people. But one over-riding factor, to my mind, is the utilitarian approach to English language education that has historically characterized colonial education in Hong Kong.

Unlike the West Indies, India, Ghana, Singapore and Malaysia, just to offer a few examples, Hong Kong has not yet generated its own style of colloquial spoken English, or been moved to accept its recognizable accent (although see Hung, Chapter 5). In Hong Kong, two types of English appear to prevail: 'proper' English, whether the received pronunciation is BBC or CNN, and 'bad' English. The concept of a Hong Kong English has little purchase, unlike the wide acceptance of the status of versions of Indian English with its variations of syntax and lexical items, or 'Singlish' with its noted mixture of Malay and Hokkien phrases and syntactical markers. When Hong Kong people speak English, they are supposed to speak proper English. When Singaporeans speak English, they have recourse to recognizable, communally shared registers. This implies that English has become indigenized in Singapore but remains foreign in Hong Kong, where English usage continues to depend on external benchmarks in Britain and the United States for validation.

Teaching at the University of Hong Kong, I have been able to practise what I have perhaps intuitively believed: that language is above all a cultural medium. I have heard over many decades and in many nation-states (Malaysia, Singapore, the United States, the Philippines) concerns that learning English (and losing the mother tongue) leads to anomie, cultural imperialism, colonized inferiority, and other social ills. But in my own writing and teaching experience, I have attempted to disarticulate English from its colonial history. The threat of cultural death, to my mind, rises not from learning English, but from the absence or presence of agency over English use. If English is learnt as the compulsory language of a colonial master, then the speaker must always remain in the position of imitator and borrower. If English is seized, even looted, as one's possession, then it may be taken as an empowering medium that opens the world's markets and cultural emporium not only for the consumer but for the producer in English. Hence, my goal as a creative writing teacher, whether in the US or in Asia, has been to offer to my students English as weapon of choice, as domain for their imaginations, and as cultural wealth to enrich their resources of feeling, thought, and knowledge.

Of course, my students in Hong Kong had their own responses to my agenda, located responses more persuasive and eloquent than those I can sketch from my position as their teacher. Ellen Lai, a University of Hong Kong final-year student, noted about my course (during which time she produced a remarkable portfolio of fiction and poetry):

> I could not have been or 'pretended to be' a writer if I had not attended this class. Of course I dare not have the ambition to be a Shakespeare. Though our professor is very kind to encourage us, I don't even have the ambition to be a lifetime professional poet because I'm afraid ambition will kill a poet's instincts. Yet as a loser in the public examination game, I regain a sense of identity in creative writing and a silly moment of pride. Sometimes after I've created a nice poem, I walk on the street feeling as if I were different from the crowd, as if I had done something big. Having been spoon-fed for fifteen-odd years from kindergarten to secondary school, here I taste a brave new learning experience in a liberal environment, melted with an instinctive joy of creating and a real global space with classmates from all over the world. But I find myself facing a bunch of dilemmas between living and earning a living, art and market, Chinese and English.
>
> Living or earning a living? Being a writer, especially a poet, whether for a lifetime or a second, is a little proof that I, a visitor in the world like anyone else, have lived, thought, felt and yelled. I've been young at heart and true to myself. It's a proof I rarely find elsewhere. Who knows when the Creator

of our disappointing world (if there is one) will force me to stay with him or her up in the clouds without sending me a notice beforehand? Who knows if one day I'll lose the courage or feel too tired to live on? My life will be deleted by a click, quietly, as if it's just an email in the Internet Sea of billions of emails while more and more are gushing into it every second. Yet to be a writer is my greatest luxury in this materialistic society. It's spiritual orgasm with no monetary value. I can't put it in my resume lest employers will be scared away by such an impractical soul. It's one of my biggest (among the very few) achievements in my life, though. Some even suspect that poets are insane. I suspect it too when I can't stop the urge to write, like I can't stop the urge to pee, when I'm rushing towards a term essay's deadline or when I find myself hooked to poems in midnight.

Art or market? As a writer, my duty is to write and write and nothing else. But as a marketing editor, I have to be embarrassingly pragmatic when I negotiate with bookshops. Today Professor Lim told me that the University's *Bulletin* might wish to publish my poem, 'At the Main Building, The University of Hong Kong'. Of course I'm excited. But it's not that I'm particularly gifted compared to my classmates. It's a combination of luck and 'market'. By sheer coincidence I've written such a poem during the University's 90th Anniversary. My poem fits the scene perfectly.

English is a world language. This means potential readers are all over the world. But how many people are lucky enough to cross borders? I'm lured to write in Chinese as I feel myself attached to my mother tongue. Chinese writings, though far from optimistic, attract a bigger crowd here too. Chinese or English?

Professor Lim says English creative writing is sprouting in Hong Kong. I'm stunned. I always think that Literature, especially English Literature, is dead here, and our creative writing class is a ghost shadow, a lovely accident created by an optimistic and well-intended professor and writer. To me it's next to impossible to get any creative writing to sprout in such a society where people find it useless. It's more so for English creative writing when our English standard is dropping drastically; when (my secondary school English Literature teacher tells me that) the Education Department finds so few English Literature students that it would like this subject closed in public exams; when I feel we have rarely any audience except ourselves; when Hong Kong is no longer a colony of the English world. I'll have to ask my professor why.

To write, I search into myself, my fears, obsessions, lusts, and dilemmas. By writing, I clarify my subconscious, my deepest desires. I'm amazed at how little we humans know. I didn't even know myself before.

'[A]n instinctive joy of creating and a real global space with classmates from all over the world.' For Ellen, English-language creativity permits both, at the same time that her commentary cautions that, for the Hong Kong writer, the Chinese language offers a larger attachment and audience in the region. Still, her poem on the Main Building (see pp. 269–70), one of the oldest, loveliest structures extant in the SAR, demonstrates how her acts of imagination confirm the value of her life. Even when her imagination has to work with the unique features of the English language rather than with her mother tongue. Even when the writer herself doubts the status of English in post-colonial Hong Kong. Ellen's experience illuminates my faith that working in, claiming English as a language of cultural imagination, leads to internalized possession of the language that no other schooling, no examinations can achieve.

The poems and stories gathered here represent only a little part of the work produced in two short years (1999–2001) by a very small self-selected group of Hong Kong University students. The selection, offered without commentary, suggests some of the range of themes, stylistics, and concerns that preoccupied these writers. We can generalize from the larger collection published in two issues of *Yuan Yang*, edited by the students as an editorial collective, that Hong Kong English-language writing at this moment tends to be culture-specific and ethnic-identified even as the choice of English results in interesting hybrid formations referentially and stylistically. British and other Western references are framed in the same narrative as Chinese and other Asian images, allusions and references. Common social phenomena in Hong Kong, such as the presence of Filipino maids, fortune-tellers, and multi-generational family dinners, may strike the Western reader as exotic, but for these writers, they delineate everyday experiences that carry emotional weight and critique. If one asks where is Hong Kong writing in English, part of the answer must be in its potential as a future production, when young Hong Kong people are given the opportunity to write their own stories in the language that has been a part of Hong Kong history for over a century.

Poems and short stories from Hong Kong students[1]

At the Main Building, University of Hong Kong
(By Ellen Lai)

Here time freezes
in the colonial age.
Red bricks think, the clock
sighs, slowly, as a sage.
Wind breezes in each corner,
from dawn to sunset.
Sun shines on the ivory tower,
in the east of the west.
Here I stand behind a stone pillar,
pretend to be a thinker.
All four courtyards look the same:
benches, balconies,
ponds and palm trees.

Everyday I lose my way
in this maze, but find my way
among van Gogh's
shadows, Plato's
whispers, Shakespeare's
sneezes, and a dozen scholars who
muse with music, who
are bizarre and romantic.
Here I pretend to be a
poet, for a season or so.
The world loves internet not
intellect, says we are fossils.
So I am, proud to be one.
At night
cellos croon in Loke Yew Hall, once
fallen in the war. Diners
walk along corridors
with water, wine and waltz.
Next summer, when
the apple still
lingers on the tree,
I shall leave with
an honor,
enlightened as
an unripe learner.

Old Kai Tak
(By Keon Woong Lee)

Flicker of shutter blades on this big blackboard
Cuts into the murmur of the hall.
Young wives at the side stare at the slope
Watching for familiar faces to fall.

Children wound with curious energy
Held tightly yet eager to explore
This beige-brown home of flyers,
Whispering and crying at the chaos of it all.

Travelers in leisure suits and summer cloth
Carry spice and smells into the melting
Humidity of our air, adding fragrance
And heat to an endless harlequin parade.

Hours turn into minutes into days,
Waiting for the sound of wheels to fade.

When
(By Eliza Wong Fong-ting)

I hopscotch
My shadow flickers on the ground
Jumping into strange silhouettes
My childhood
Like hopscotch
Shifts from one abode to another
Drifts apart my hordes of buddies
I had to
Farewell
My home
Clotheslines
Passageways
Ladder Streets
Slip down
To greet the
Skycrapers

Fireworks
(By Christie Cheng)

I light a match.

Fireworks sparkle above the Bank of China.
Red beams fall into the Victoria Harbour.
At the Convention Exhibition Centre,
the British flag comes down.
Chris Patten[2] shakes hands with Tung Chee Wa.[3]
A square foot rises to eight thousand Hong Kong dollars.
Citizens cheer.

The fire burns my fingers and I remember:
A square foot shrinks to four thousand HK dollars.
And my iron bowl disappears.[4]

Food For Thought
(By Shalini Nanwani)

Dancing in water,
tail and fins flop.
Free at sea.
Until those nets
lurch at it.
But that's how we like it.
Fresh, fried, filleted, chopped,
salted, sautéed, served with chips.

The same story unfolds
in Noah's Ark:

chickens, lambs, pigs, cows.
Meat, sanitized, wrapped in plastic
blinds us.

Our stomachs a graveyard.

At The Round Table
(By Venus Tsang Chiu-ying)

My memory was tested.
Who were Father's third uncle and sixth aunt?
Before any dish was tasted,
I addressed all my seniors.

Their eyes dashed between Grandfather and the food.
Respect prevented the revolt of saliva.
After Grandfather had taken his first bite,
Their hands hurried for their chopsticks.

Chopsticks coming out of different mouths
Arrived at the same dishes.
The sauce was mixed
With our mouths' dew.

Mother picked my meat,
Tenderest of all.
She crushed it into tiny pieces
And fed them to my wide-stretched mouth.

When all the words were swollen,
Father knocked the crab claws on the table.
Removing their obstinate shells,
He revealed their flesh.

Rounding up the meal was the red bean soup.
Cleansing the grease,
It soothed our mouths
And immersed our tongues in the sweet.

Fried Chestnuts
(By Michelle Fok Ka-ling)

Next to the ditch and rubbish bin,
where flies and cockroaches linger,
I meet a man
who waits for customers
from midnight film shows.

With a rusted metal spade in his hands,
he grins and says,
'Twenty four dollars for a pound.'
He fries
the chestnuts in the wok.

Wounds
on his finger-tips expose
the soft flesh under his wrinkled skin.
You had hands coarser than his,
but I like the way you patted my face.

Cracks
on the reddish-brown shells
show the golden kernel.
You bought me fried chestnuts
and the yellow mist in your eyes thickened.

Your last days in the white prison,
no snack but glucose.
I won't buy fried chestnuts again,
as soaked with tears,
they are bitter.

Neighbour
(By Venus Tsang Chiu-ying)

Jumping and hopping on your floor,
You rock my ceiling,
And shake the smell of herbs away.

Pills in bottles crowd my balcony.
Petals dropped from your potted flowers
Blanket my bald head like hair.

A ballet dances on your piano.
Breaking through the solid air,
Your music makes my bamboo sticks sway.

The Maid
(By Venus Tsang Chiu-ying)

Under the same roof
Guarded by the left and right Men Shen:
Their stare shakes my legs
When I shut the door
To open the Bible in my soul.

Around the same table,
Among the pinching chopsticks,
My fork becomes a slingshot,
Rebounds when it shoots
At the Guangdong food.

On the upper deck,
The dragon boy crashes the plane above my head.
Seeing the same black hair,
The same brown eyes,
I hug my son in my dream.

A foam bath for the Benz,
A cha-cha with the broom,
A massage for the windows:
I collect credits
For a Sunday ticket to Statue Square.

But when can I collect enough credits
For a ticket back to the Philippines?

Turning point
(By Addy Ng)

|

We share our red wine
at the Christmas party.
We prepare our sandwiches
for the school picnic.
We go for the fireworks
during Chinese New Year.
We quit college
before final exams.
We join the gangsters
right after your birthday.
We share the needle
nearly every day.
I die with you
yesterday.
|
|
|

The Importance of Having an 'R'
(By Nicholas Y. B. Wong)

Dea   Shopkeepe ,
May I complain about the p inte   I bought
at you   shop
last week? Today when I am p inting
the manusc ipt of my new play
at home,
I discove   the ' ' key is not wo king
at all.

The efo e, I call the publishe
immediately
to cancel the new d ama
tea pa ty.
I tell him the   eason,
but he thinks I am making fun
of him.

He asks me which model
I've bought.
It's a mechanical bet ayal
I've caught.

I leave a note at home fo the ca etake ,
telling him he'd bette
not to touch the p inte
in the oom.
But he doesn't know how to ead,
so he asks fo a night out
fo the night school,
and he claims he will unde stand
my note by the end of next week.

I look fo anothe p inte in the basement,
but the e is none.
So I go out and feed myself
in a café with live band
called No Man's Land.
I am se ved by a dumb waite ,
I o de a c ab f om Alaska,
and she gives me a Baked Alaska,
which is also a kind of Alaska.

I go home with a slight ache
in my stomach,
the neighbou next to my flat
is having a bi thday pa ty.
Noisie than the live band
in No Man's Land,
I just want a piece of silence
fo one night,
so that I can sit down
at my desk and w ite.
But I emembe
I am dep ived of the lette .
I feel like missing a finge .
Gone is the fun of life afte I have lost it.
Finally
I hope you'd unde stand
the impo tance of having an ' '
to me.

You s faithfully
Ha old Pinte [5]

Fortune Teller
(By Stephanie Lui Po-man)

Wang Shi Fu told me that the Year of the Hare would not be good for me because I was born in the Year of the Tiger. Don't do any business or investments throughout the year so as to avoid incurring losses. Speculation will not yield any profit for me. Especially don't invest in the property market since my *bazi*[6] belongs to the gold out of the five elements. Investing in the stock market is only advantageous in June, September and October. Don't buy and sell stocks in the other months even though there are opportunities to reap profits because his words are always true. Don't change jobs. Stay in the original work position and the chance of promotion will come in winter. No matter how nasty my boss is, I will not quit my job. Besides, put a copper vase on my desk facing the south to increase my career luck. Remember, it must be made of copper, not any other material. Don't drive or ride in my car in August for I may have a fatal accident. I will try to avoid travelling in the car by going to work on foot and travelling to Kowloon by ferry. What should I do if I have to go to the New Territories? I should ask him about that. Don't travel abroad during Chinese New Year since I may be robbed on the trip. April is very crucial for me because I will meet a man who was born in the Year of the Dragon. He will become my husband and be the person who brings me luck and happiness. So if I meet a man who was born in the Year of the Dragon in April, whatever he looks like I will grasp the chance to date him. Don't wear any black clothes throughout the year because the water out of the five elements will bring bad luck. Black represents water, so I'd better use another color leather wallet instead of my black leather one. Don't wear the black-rimmed spectacles as well. However, red is good for me because my *bazi* needs more fire and red represents fire, so I should buy more red clothes and dye my hair red. Finally, don't lend money to friends because they will not pay me back and will run away. Oh, when Ka Wah asks me to pay for his lunch next time, I will definitely reject him. Don't be skeptical about the words of the Feng Shui Shi Fu because they are always right.

Back Street
(By Nicole Wong Chun-chi)

'Papa, where are we?'
'At the back street, at the end of the street we live in.'
'Why are we here?'
'Because I have to come here.'
'Why do you have to come here?'
'I come here to play.'
'Can I play here too?'

Papa raised his other hand. I struggled to tear my hand out from his. He was standing against the sun; his face was dark. I drew a deep breath to stop myself crying. I did not want to be slapped on the cheek.

'We're going up to a flat. I'll take you to have dessert later. And don't tell anyone that we have come here today. Do you hear me?'

I nodded. My head was heavy. I kept trying to tear my hand out from his and turn around – if I ran inside the crowd Papa could probably not catch me. It was just one street. It is the 'Women's Street' in Mong Kok. The whole street is a fair, where people are always thronging back and forth, grabbing and bargaining over the cheapest goods. Clocks, watches, accessories, bags, clothes – the panties with pink fur. Mama yelled at me when I asked her if she had got any.

It was no use running home. Grandpa and Mama were working. Grandma had gone out. I could not go to my neighbour. I had had a fight with XiXi the day before. Maybe I could get lost in the crowd. Then when Papa found me, he would be crying and would not beat me. But I did not want Mama to cry. The only time I got lost I went to a policeman. The moment I saw Mama again I grinned and thought she would praise me, but she just held me and cried.

'My life is hard enough!' Her tears rolled down to my forehead. Mine rolled down too but I wiped them away at once. Mama would cry harder if she knew I had been crying also.

So we came to this back street. Trash was spilling out from the black plastic bags. Soft drink cans, plastic bottles, paper boxes – red and orange, blue and green – the colors clashed with one another and the smell of rotten food. Next to the trash was a metal gate. The sun shone on the silver but not the rust. Above the gate were the thin black frames and old posters of movie stars on the windowpane. On the walls torn pasted advertisements blew lightly in the wind. They read: second-hand cars for sale. I must have made some of these details up. But I have come back from time to time to make sure it is the right back street, and it does not look much different from how I remember it to be.

Papa pushed the gate open. I could hardly see the stairs. So I clenched Papa's hand.

'Why are you pouting?' Papa's voice was soft again. 'Mind your step.'

I smiled. Then I stopped at once.

'Ahhhh the stairs are so long! It takes all my strength away. How can I have fun then!'

I had never seen Papa giggle like that. I was panting too but I did not want Papa to know. We might be climbing up the stairs panting in the dark forever. We would never get out from this building. It should be better than lying dead in the Woman Street. I would scare those hawkers to death. Papa and Mama always fell sound asleep before I did. Sitting between them, I could not help looking out of the windows.

But the stairs ended. There stood another metal gate, painted in green. The dark brown of the wooden door looked like dark red – like blood that had dried – in the very dim light. Father strode towards the door and pressed the doorbell which was covered with dirt and fingerprints.

'Honey, I'm coming!'

Papa drew his hand out from mine. 'Hey sweetie, hurry up!'

So the blood melted. A pair of fake eyelashes were flashing behind the gate. The eyeline and eyeshadow had melted into a thin dark circle. As she opened the gate, Papa started giggling again.

'Hey sweetie, how have you been? Busy?'

'Yes, so many customers today. Oh, why did you bring this little girl with you? Is this your daughter?'

'Yeah.' Papa dragged me into the flat and we sat on the sofa. 'Her mom has to work today and I have to look after her. So troublesome.'

'Why bother to have a family then?' The woman closed the door and leant against it.

She was wearing a purple, semi-transparent dress and brick red lipstick. 'You can always have fun here, right?'

'Of course! My wife can never do the things that you can.' Papa stood up, strode towards her and held her by the waist. As Papa leant forward to kiss her she gently pushed him away.

'Let's take a shower first.' She was smiling into Papa's eyes, then she glanced at me. 'Oh, no, let's deal with your daughter first.' Now she stared right at me. 'Little sweetheart, will you be a good girl? Just sit on the sofa, don't run around or touch anything. If you're bored, just watch the streets. Papa will take you home soon, ok? Oh, by the way, how old are you?'

'Four.' My voice was trembling. I often saw Papa with different women. Sometimes it was the same woman. Sometimes it was a new one. They all asked the same question, 'Has your Papa taken you to see another woman?' I always said 'No' as Papa told me to. And I did not want to upset them. Sometimes they told me how I looked and acted when I was a baby. I thought they liked me because of Papa. But this woman kept staring at me till I sat up on the sofa and looked out of the windows. Her voice was so thin that I wanted to cover my ears. I had never imagined seeing Papa with such a woman. I had to clench my fists to stop myself from shivering. I had to look at the sky; the cars moving on the road; the pedestrians walking on the zebra crossing – to forget the sound of the shower.

The door opened. I turned around and sat down on the sofa, my ankles on my knees, my hands on my ears. A door closed. I stopped shivering. So I put my hands down and scratched some plastic off the black sofa with my fingernails. There were lots of scratches on the white walls. Some longer ones were filled with dirt. In front of the sofa was a white plastic table. As I stood up I saw a bowl of soaked noodles and a pair of chopsticks. Next to the bowl lay a heap of magazines. Noise was coming out from the room in the dark corridor. It thundered in my ears but I had given up covering them. This woman had her whole body bound with ropes, and she was spreading her legs. Papa was growling and the woman screaming. I knew what they were doing, but I could not picture it in my head. Now a woman was squeezing her breasts. I stood there and read on. The noise stopped. I jumped up to the sofa at once and knelt there, looking out of the windows. The clouds were moving fast in the sky. I heard Papa's footsteps and begged myself to weep or at least look shocked.

'Hey, girl,' Papa was combing his hair with his fingers, 'we're going.'

I sat gazing at Papa although I knew I should stand up at once. Then came the woman, her semi-transparent dress swaying under the fan. She grinned. This grin was different from those of other women whom Papa went out with. But it did not matter. I was waiting for Papa to look at me again, but he was smiling and whispering something in the woman's ears. I had seen

Papa doing this to women for a good many times. Maybe a man always does this to a woman other than his wife.

'Now, girl,' Papa dragged me up from the sofa, 'we're going to have dessert. Don't mention this to anyone, not even Mama, ok?'

I nodded. I always told Mama that it was only Papa and I when we went out. I did not lie because Papa told me to. I did not want to share the bed with Papa alone.

The woman hugged Papa and pinched my cheek as she said 'Goodbye!'. The blood melted again. Papa pushed the green metal gate and closed it. I was glad he forgot to hold my hand as we walked down the stairs.

The Return
(By Sanaz Fotouhi)

She threw a rock instead of a flower on his descending coffin.

She threw a rock as the earth was swallowing him up, as the mourning others celebrated his Return with flowers. The rock landed on a soft petal. The game was over and she had won. 'Dust to dust, ashes to ashes. ...'

Her last memory of him was his playing with her cousins and uncles the night before she left. That evening the uncles had come back from one of their fox-hunting events. He had been the star, carrying over his shoulder a dead orange-red fox. Afterwards, everyone had sat in the garden practicing their aiming skills. They set out cans and other objects and threw stones at them. Everyone was better than she was. She remembered him the most clearly. Laughing every time she missed. He tried very hard that evening to teach her how to aim. Being impulsive, she aimed at him instead: missing him. Who could possibly miss him but her?

It had been 25 years since. She did not wish to see him again, wanting to put behind her his piss-yellow watery eyes, stinking alcoholic breath and hanging beer belly. She had wanted to slide the image out of her subconscious, to make believe it was only her childish imagination. To make herself almost believe it had never happened. But she still woke up in the middle of night sometimes, feeling helpless like when she was seven. Afraid he would walk into her room, drunk, half-naked in the summer heat, and touch her delicate soft child-skin with his rough coarse scaly hands. She could still smell the alcohol mixed with his stinking sweat and cologne against her skin. How odd children can be to think that this was normal uncle-love.

Today she had deliberately come to see him again: to celebrate his Return. She came to see how she had seen him in her dreams during those long summer nights when she was made to stay at her aunt's house: dead and cold in a coffin.

Now he was lying in front of her, cold and lifeless, just as she had wished to see him. His eyes were closed and his belly was hidden in a good suit such as he never gotten to wear in life. How serene and peaceful he looked now. Suddenly he opened his eyes and winked like so many times he had done so at the dinner table when her aunt asked what the problem was. She started to cry helplessly like she had back then in her dark room, knowing that he hunted her still. She left the church weeping. An elderly woman, one of the few people who had shown up, patted her on the shoulder. 'He sure was a good man. We all miss him, honey.'

But when she saw the coffin descending in the gray autumn afternoon, she knew he was gone. And she threw a rock. She knew he was no longer the hunter. As the coffin slowly descended, she prayed for him. 'I hope when you rot down there with the worms you feel them eating away at your brain like you ate away mine for so many years . ... And may God bless you, Uncle, as you deserve.' She threw a rock on his coffin as the earth was swallowing him up. 'Dust to dust, ashes to ashes ...'

Notes

1. Many of the poems and stories here have been previously published in *Yuan Yang: A Journal of Hong Kong and International Writing*, which is written and edited by students in the English Department of the University of Hong Kong. *When* (by Eliza Wong Fong-ting), *At the Roundtable* (by Venus Tsang Chiu-ying), *Fried Chestnuts* (Michelle Fok Ka-ling), *Neighbour* (Venus Tsang Chiu-ying), *The Maid* (Venus Tsang Chiu-ying), *Turning point* (Addy Ng), *Fortune Teller* (Stephanie Lui Po-man), and *Back Street* (Nichole Wong Chun-chi) were published in *Yuan Yang*, Volume 1, in 2000. *Old Kai Tak* (Keon Woong Lee), *Fireworks* (Christie Cheng), *The Importance of having an 'R'* (Nicholas Y. B. Wong), and *The Return* (Sanaz Fotouhi) were published in *Yuan Yang*, Volume 2, in 2001. Inquiries concerning the availability of *Yuan Yang* may be sent to Ms Samantha Chan, email: english@hkucc.hku.hk.
2. Chris Patten was the last British governor of Hong Kong, serving from 1992 to 1997.
3. Tung Chee Wa (or 'Tung Chee-hwa') is the first Chief Executive of the Hong Kong Special Administrative Region. Christie Cheng explains that *Fireworks* is 'a scene about the Handover to China'.
4. An 'iron rice-bowl' is an idiomatic reference to a job in the Hong Kong civil service, previously thought to be safe and secure. In recent years, the civil service has been restructured and most new recruits are no longer offered permanent jobs.
5. Nicholas Wong notes that 'the name Harold Pinter (a British dramatist) inspired me to write this poem. I wondered what would happen if one day Pinter discovered the letter "r" could not be printed on his printer.'
6. Stephanie Lui notes that '*bazi*' refers to the precise time and date of a person's birth according to the lunar calendar.

15 Researching Hong Kong English: Bibliographical sources

Kingsley Bolton

In 1982, Luke and Richards noted the lack of detailed linguistic research in Hong Kong, commenting that: '[l]ittle detailed data ... is available on language usage, language shift, language networks or language learning within Hong Kong society' (Luke and Richards, 1982: 58). Since that time, a great deal of work has been carried out on the sociolinguistics of Chinese and English in Hong Kong society.[1] There is now an active research culture in linguistics in the Hong Kong Special Administrative Region (HKSAR), and this is reflected in the substantial numbers of research publications published by Hong Kong scholars in international journals in the fields of linguistics, sociolinguistics, and applied linguistics.[2]

A good indication of the quantity of linguistic research carried out in the last twenty years is provided by Bruce's informative (1996) bibliography of research publications on 'Language in Hong Kong education and society', which groups publications on language in Hong Kong into a number of topic categories. This was published in a print version in 1996, but is also available on the Internet (see below). A tabulation of the numbers of articles by topic area published during the period 1980–96 (excluding earlier years) from Bruce's bibliography gives an indication of the major areas of interest in language research in these years. This information is set out in Table 15.1.

The last seven categories in Table 15.1 might broadly be regarded as dealing with topics chiefly related to issues of language learning and language teaching, i.e. 'applied linguistics', which account for 54 per cent of the total number of academic articles written in this field for the years 1980–96. One explanation of the high total for research of this kind is growth of 'ELT professionalism' in Hong Kong and the importance accorded to issues of pedagogy during this period. A second reason is perhaps that 'applied linguistics' as a discipline expanded greatly in the late 1980s and 1990s at university level, particularly in the years after 1989, when the number of tertiary institutions was increased from two to eight. By the mid-1990s, a local applied linguistics industry had developed with significant numbers of international language teaching 'experts' employed at Hong Kong colleges and universities, bringing with them their disciplinary and research orientations. A third factor is that at many such institutions, English linguistics has often been harnessed to programmes of academic writing, 'language enhancement', and English for specific purposes.

Table 15.1 Linguistic research 1980–96 by topic area

Topic area	Number of publications	Percentage
Language attitudes and policies in Hong Kong	118	16.2%
Bilingual and multilingual Hong Kong	56	7.7%
Language alternation: Code-switching and code-mixing	30	4.1%
Language standards	9	1.2%
'Hong Kong English': Errors, bilingualism and 'transfer'	39	5.4%
Chinese language(s) in Hong Kong and South China	83	11.4%
Language learning: Attitudes and motivation	33	4.5%
Language learning: Problems and approaches	75	10.3%
Language teaching: Problems and approaches	71	9.8%
Teacher development and curriculum renewal	104	14.3%
Language assessment and programme evaluation	25	3.4%
Language(s) for specific purposes in Hong Kong	36	5.0%
Tertiary education in Hong Kong	49	6.7%
Total	728	100.0%

Source: Figures extracted from Bruce (1996)

For language scholars in Hong Kong or overseas scholars interested in linguistics and language issues in Hong Kong, there is now a wealth of bibliographical materials available. Printed bibliographies with coverage of English in the HKSAR include Foo and Cox (1994), Bruce (1996), and Foo (1997). In addition, Bruce (1996), Bruce, Tam, and Tse (1998), Candlin and Keobke (2000), and Chinese University of Hong Kong (2000) are available electronically on the Internet. Given the abundance of available material, the bibliography set out below is by necessity highly selective, and is restricted in a number of ways. First, the bibliography is limited to the last two decades, and lists books, book chapters, and journal articles published after 1979. Second, it is broadly limited to those topic areas most relevant to the study of world Englishes, and is thus skewed towards work in the fields of the sociology of language, sociolinguistics, and areas of applied linguistics relating most closely to the study of localized varieties of English. This bibliography thus omits a great deal of published work on curriculum design, language teaching, and other 'educational linguistic' concerns.

A number of Bruce's categories are used to classify the selective bibliography, although there are also some differences. There is a separate section for languages in education with particular reference to the 'medium of instruction' issue, and another section lists work of relevance to the study of creative writing in Hong Kong. In all, the bibliography contains eleven sections: books and journal special issues; the sociology of language and language planning; languages in education – with particular reference to the 'medium of instruction issue'; bilingualism and multilingualism; code-switching and code-mixing; pragmatics and discourse analysis; error analysis and interlanguage studies; Hong Kong English as a 'new English'; Hong Kong creative writing; and bibliographies – printed and electronic. In the first category of books and journal special issues the most comprehensive guide to the sociolinguistics of English in Hong Kong previously published was Pennington (1998). Gibbons (1987) and Li (1996) focus on Cantonese-English code-switching and mixing, Lord and Cheng (1987) on language planning issues in the 1980s, and Wright and Holmes (1997) on macrosociolinguistic issues. Other books and dissertations of more specific interest are listed in the individual sections that follow.

Hong Kong English: A selective bibliography

Books and journal special issues

Bolton, Kingsley (ed.) (2002) Special issue on 'Hong Kong English: Autonomy and creativity'. *World Englishes*, **19**(3), 263–452.
Bolton, Kingsley (In Press) *Chinese Englishes: A Sociolinguistic History*. Cambridge: Cambridge University Press.
Gibbons, John (1987) *Code-mixing and Code Choice: A Hong Kong Case Study*. Clevedon: Multilingual Matters.
Li, David C. S. (1996) *Issues in Bilingualism and Biculturalism: A Hong Kong Case Study*. New York: Peter Lang.
Lord, Robert and Cheng, Helen N. L. (eds.) (1987) *Language Education in Hong Kong*. Hong Kong: The Chinese University Press.
Pennington, Martha C. (ed.) (1998) *Language in Hong Kong at Century's End*. Hong Kong: Hong Kong University Press.
Scollon, Ron and Flowerdew, John (eds.) (1998) Special issue on 'Language and discourse issues in Hong Kong's change of sovereignty'. *Journal of Pragmatics*, **28**, 417–553.
Wright, Susan and Holmes, Helen K. (eds.) (1997) *One Country, Two Systems, Three Languages: Changing Language Use in Hong Kong*. Clevedon, Philadelphia: Multilingual Matters.

The sociology of language and language planning

Bacon-Shone, John and Bolton, Kingsley (1998) Charting multilingualism: Language censuses and language surveys in Hong Kong. In *Language in Hong Kong at Century's End*. Edited by Martha C. Pennington. Hong Kong: Hong Kong University Press, pp. 43–90.

Boyle, Joseph (1997) Imperialism and the English language in Hong Kong. *Journal of Multilingual and Multicultural Development*, **18**(3), 169–81.

Boyle, Joseph (1998) What hope for a trilingual Hong Kong? *English Today*, **14**(4)56, 34–9.

Cheung, Yat-shing (1984) Conflicts in the uses of English and Chinese languages in Hong Kong. *Language Learning and Communication*, **3**(3), 273–87.

Cheung, Yat-shing (1985) Power, solidarity and luxury in Hong Kong: A sociolinguistic study. *Anthrophological Linguistics*, **27**(2), 190–203.

Evans, Stephen, Jones, Rodney, Rusmin, Ruru S. and Cheung, Oi Ling (1998) Three languages: One future. In *Language in Hong Kong at Century's End*. Edited by Martha C. Pennington. Hong Kong: Hong Kong University Press, pp. 391–415.

Hamlett, Tim (1997) English in Hongkong: The future. *English Today*, **13**(3), 10–11.

Hirvela, Alan (1991) Footing the English bill in Hong Kong: Language politics and linguistic schizophrenia. *Journal of Asian Pacific Communication*, **2**(1), 117–37.

Johnson, Robert K. (1994) Language policy and planning in Hong Kong. *Annual Review of Applied Linguistics*, **14**, 177–99.

Li, David C. S. (1999) The functions and status of English in Hong Kong: A post-1997 update. *English World-wide*, **20**, 67–110.

Lord, Robert (1987) Language policy and planning in Hong Kong: Past, present and (especially) future. In *Language Education in Hong Kong*. Edited by Robert Lord and Helen N. L. Cheng. Hong Kong: The Chinese University Press, pp. 3–24.

Lord, Robert and T'sou, Benjamin (1983) The language bomb. Four articles published by the *South China Morning Post* in June 1983.

Luke, Kang kwong and Richards, Jack (1982) English in Hong Kong: Functions and status. *English World-wide*, **3**(1), 47–64.

Pennington, Martha C. (1998) The folly of language planning: Or, a brief history of the English language in Hong Kong. *English Today*, **14**(2)54, 25–30.

Pierson, Herbert D. (1998) Societal accommodation to English and Putonghua in Cantonese-speaking Hong Kong. In *Language in Hong Kong at Century's End*. Edited by Martha C. Pennington. Hong Kong: Hong Kong University Press, pp. 91–111.

Pierson-Smith, Anne (1997) English for Promotional Purposes. *English Today*, **13**(3)51, 6–8.

T'sou, Benjamin (1994) Language planning issues raised by English in Hong Kong: Pre- and Post-1997. In *English and Language Planning: A Southeast Asian Contribution*. Edited by Thiru Kandiah and John Kwan-Terry. Singapore: Times Academic Press, pp. 197–217.

Tsui, Amy B. M. (1996) English in Asian bilingual education: From hatred to harmony: A response. *Journal of Multilingual and Multicultural Development*, **17**(2–4), 241–47.

Yau, Francis M. S. (1997) Code switching and language choice in the Hong Kong Legislative Council. *Journal of Multilingual and Multicultural Development*, **18**(1), 40–53.

Languages in education – with particular reference to the 'medium of instruction issue'

Adamson, Bob, Lai, Winnie Auyeung (1997) Language and the curriculum in Hong Kong: Dilemmas of triglossia. *Comparative Education,* **33**(2), 233–46.

Benson, Phil (1997) Language rights and the medium of instruction issue in Hong Kong. *Hong Kong Journal of Applied Linguistics,* **2**(2), 1–21.

Boyle, Joseph (1997) Native-speaker teachers of English in Hong Kong. *Language and Education,* **11**(3), 163–81.

Cheung, Anne (1997) Language Rights and the Hong Kong Courts. *Hong Kong Journal of Applied Linguistics,* **2**(2), 49–75.

Gibbons, John (1982) The issue of the medium of instruction in the lower forms of Hong Kong secondary schools. *Journal of Multilingual and Multicultural Development,* **3**(2), 117–28.

Johnson, Robert K. (1983) Language policy in education in Hong Kong. *Asian Journal of Public Administration,* **5**(2), 25–43.

Kwo, Ora W. Y. (1992) The teaching of Putonghua in Hong Kong Schools: Language education in a changing economic and political context. In *Education and Society in Hong Kong.* Edited by Gerard A. Postiglione. Hong Kong: Hong Kong University Press, pp. 203–13.

Lin, Angel M. Y. (1997) Hong Kong children's rights to a culturally compatible English Education. *Hong Kong Journal of Applied Linguistics.* **2**(2), 23–48.

Pennington, Martha C. (1999) Framing bilingual classroom discourse: Lessons from Hong Kong secondary school English classes. *International Journal of Bilingual Education and Bilingualism,* **2**(1), 53–73.

Poon, Anita Y. K. (1999) Chinese medium instruction policy and its impact on English learning in post-1997 Hong Kong. *International Journal of Bilingual Education and Bilingualism,* **2**(2), 131–46.

So, Daniel W. C. (1989) Implementing mother-tongue education amidst societal transition from diglossia to triglossia in Hong Kong. *Language and Education,* **3**(1), 29–44.

Tung, Peter C. S. (1990) Why changing the medium of instruction in Hong Kong could be difficult. *Journal of Multilingual and Multicultural Development,* **11**(6), 523–34.

Yau, M-S. (1989) The controversy over teaching medium in Hong Kong – an analysis of a language policy. *Journal of Multilingual and Multicultural Development,* **10**(4), 279–95.

Walters, Steve and Balla, John (1998) Medium of instruction: Policy and reality at one Hong Kong tertiary institution. In *Language in Hong Kong at Century's End.* Edited by Martha C. Pennington. Hong Kong: Hong Kong University Press, pp. 365–89.

Yu, V. and Atkinson, P. (1988) An investigation into the language difficulties experienced by Hong Kong secondary school students in English-medium schools: I - The Problems; II - some causal factors. *Journal of Multilingual and Multicultural Development,* **9**(3 and 4), 267–84; 307–22.

Bilingualism and multilingualism

Afendras, Evangelos A. (1998) The onset of bilingualism in Hong Kong: Language choice in the home domain. In *Language in Hong Kong at Century's End.* Edited by Martha C. Pennington. Hong Kong: Hong Kong University Press, pp. 113–41.

Bacon-Shone, John and Bolton, Kingsley (1998) Charting multilingualism: Language censuses and language surveys in Hong Kong. In *Language in Hong Kong at Century's End.* Edited by Martha C. Pennington. Hong Kong: Hong Kong University Press, pp. 43–90.

Chan, Mimi and Kwok, Helen (1986) The impact of English on Hong Kong Chinese. In *English in Contact with Other Languages: Studies in Honour of Broader Carstensen on the Occasion of his 60th Birthday.* Edited by Wolfgang Viereck and Wolf-Dietrich Bald. Budapest: Akademiai Kiado, pp. 407–31.

Fu, Gail Schaefer (1987) The Hong Kong bilingual. In *Language Education in Hong Kong.* Edited by Robert Lord and Helen N. L. Cheng. Hong Kong: The Chinese University Press, pp. 27–50.

Gibbons, John (1984) Interpreting the English proficiency profile in Hong Kong. *RELC Journal*, **15**, 64–74.

Harris, Roy (1989) The worst English in the world? *Supplement to the Gazette*, **36**(1). Hong Kong: The University of Hong Kong.

Johnson, Robert K., Shek, C. and Law, E. (1993) *Using English as the Medium of Instruction.* Hong Kong: Longman.

Lin, Angel M. Y. (1996) Bilingualism or linguistic segregation? Symbolic domination, resistance and code-switching in Hong Kong schools. *Linguistics and Education*, **8**, 49–84.

Pennington, Martha C. (1998) Colonialism's aftermath in Asia: A snapshot view of bilingualism in Hong Kong. *Hong Kong Journal of Applied Linguistics.* **3**(1), 1–16.

So, Daniel W. C. (1987) Searching for a bilingual exit. In *Language Education in Hong Kong.* Edited by Robert Lord and Helen N. L. Cheng. Hong Kong: The Chinese University Press, pp. 249–68.

Code-switching and code-mixing

Chan, Brian H. S. (1998) How does Cantonese-English code-mixing work? In *Language in Hong Kong at Century's End.* Edited by Martha C. Pennington. Hong Kong: Hong Kong University Press, pp. 191–216.

Gibbons, John (1987) *Code-mixing and Code Choice: A Hong Kong Case Study.* Clevedon: Multilingual Matters.

Johnson, Robert K. (1983) Bilingual switching strategies: A study of the modes of teacher-talk in bilingual secondary school classrooms in Hong Kong. *Language Learning and Communication.* 2,3, 267–85.

Johnson, Robert K. and Lee, Paul L. M. (1987) Modes of instruction: Teaching strategies and student responses. In *Language Education in Hong Kong.* Edited by Robert Lord and Helen N. L. Cheng. Hong Kong: The Chinese University Press, pp. 99–121.

Kamwangamalu, Nkonko and Lee, Cher Leng (1991) Chinese-English code-mixing: A case of matrix language assignment. *World Englishes*, **10**, 247–61.

Li, David C. S. (1996) *Issues in Bilingualism and Biculturalism: A Hong Kong Case Study.* New York: Peter Lang.
Li, David C. S. (1998) The plight of the purist. In *Language in Hong Kong at Century's End.* Edited by Martha C. Pennington. Hong Kong: Hong Kong University Press, pp. 161–90.
Lin, Angel M. Y. (1996) Bilingualism or linguistic segregation? Symbolic domination, resistance and code-switching in Hong Kong schools. *Linguistics and Education,* **8,** 49–84.
Pennington, Martha C. (1996) Cross-language effects in biliterarcy. *Language and Education,* **10**(4), 254–72.
Yau, M. S. (1993) Functions of two codes in Hong Kong Chinese. *World Englishes,* **12**(1), 25–33.

Language attitudes

Axler, Maria, Yang, Anson, and Stevens, Trudy (1998) Current language attitudes of Hong Kong Chinese adolescents and young adults. In *Language in Hong Kong at Century's End.* Edited by Martha C. Pennington. Hong Kong: Hong Kong University Press, pp. 329–38.
Bickley, Gillian (1990) Plus ça change, plus c'est la meme chose: Attitudes towards English language learning in Hong Kong. *World Englishes,* **9**(3), 289–300.
Boyle, Joseph (1997) The use of mixed-code in Hong Kong English language teaching. *System,* **25,** 83–9.
Boyle, Joseph (1998) Changing attitudes to English. *English Today,* **13**(3), 3–6.
Flowerdew, John, Li, David and Miller, Lindsay (1998) Attitudes towards English and Cantonese among Hong Kong Chinese University Lecturers. *TESOL Quarterly,* **32**(2), 201–31.
Gibbons, John (1983) Attitudes towards language and code-mixing in Hong Kong. *Journal of Multilingual and Multicultural Development,* **4**(2) and **4**(3), 129–47.
Lin, Angel M. Y. and Detaramani, Champa (1998) By carrot and by rod: Extrinsic motivation and English language attainment of Hong Kong teriary students. In *Language in Hong Kong at Century's End.* Edited by Martha C. Pennington. Hong Kong: Hong Kong University Press, pp. 285–301.
Pennington, Martha C. (1994) Forces shaping a dual code society: An interpretive review of the literature on language use and language attitudes in Hong Kong. *Research Report.* City Polytechnic of Hong Kong, Department of English. 25 September, iii–171.
Pennington, Martha C. and Yue, Francis (1994) English and Chinese in Hong Kong: Pre-1997 language attitudes. *World Englishes,* **13**(1), 1–20.
Pierson, Herbert D. (1987) Language attitudes and language proficiency: A review of selected research. In *Language Education in Hong Kong.* Edited by Robert Lord and Helen N. L. Cheng. Hong Kong: The Chinese University Press, pp. 51–82.
Pierson, Herbert D. (1992) Cantonese, English, or Putonghua: Unresolved communicative issue in Hong Kong's future. In *Education and Society in Hong Kong: Toward One Country and Two Systems.* Edited by Gerard A. Postiglione. Hong Kong: Hong Kong University Press, pp. 183–202.

Pierson, Herbert D. (1994) Ethnolinguistic vitality during a period of decolonisation without independence: Perceived vitality in Hong Kong. *International Journal of the Sociology of Language*, **10**, 43–61.

Pierson, Herbert D. and Fu, G.S. (1982) Report on the linguistic attitudes project in Hong Kong and its relevance for second language instruction. *Language Learning and Communication*, **1**(2), 289–316.

Richards, Stephen (1997) Learning English in Hong Kong: Making connections between motivation, language use, and strategy choice. In *Language in Hong Kong at Century's End*. Edited by Martha C. Pennington. Hong Kong: Hong Kong University Press, pp. 303–28.

Pragmatics and discourse analysis

Bhatia, Vijay K. (1997) Democratizing government decision-making: A study of public discourse in Hong Kong. *Journal of Pragmatics*, **28**(4), 515–32.

Bilbow, Grahame T. (1997) Cross-cultural impression management in the multicultural workplace: The special case of Hong Kong. *Journal of Pragmatics*, **28**(4), 461–87.

Flowerdew, John (1997) The discourse of colonial withdrawal: A case study in the creation of mythic discourse. *Discourse and Society*, **8**(4), 453–77.

Flowerdew, John (1997) Competing public discourses in transitional Hong Kong. *Journal of Pragmatics*, **28**(4), 533–53.

Flowerdew, John, and Scollon, Ron (1997) Public discourse in Hong Kong and the change of sovereignty. *Journal of Pragmatics*, **28**(4), 417–26.

Kong, Kenneth C. C. (1998) Politeness of service encounters in Hong Kong. *Pragmatics*, **8**(4), 555–75.

Li, David C. S. (1997) Borrowed identity: Signaling involvement with a western name. *Journal of Pragmatics*, **28**(4), 489–513.

Lin, Angel M. Y. (1997) Analyzing the 'language problem' discourses in Hong Kong: How official, academic, and media discourses construct and perpetuate dominant models of language, learning, and education. *Journal of Pragmatics*, **28**(4), 427–440.

Scollon, Ron (1997) Attribution and power in Hong Kong news discourse. *World Englishes*, **16**(3), 383–93.

Scollon, Ron (1997) Handbills, tissues, and condoms: A site of engagement for the construction of identity in public discourse. *Journal of Sociolinguistics*, **1**(1), 39–61.

Error analysis and interlanguage studies

Boyle, Joseph and Boyle, Linda (1991) *Common Spoken English Errors in Hong Kong*. Hong Kong: Longman.

Bunton, David (1989) *Common English Errors in Hong Kong*. Hong Kong: Longman.

Bunton, David (1994) *Common Social English Errors in Hong Kong*. Hong Kong: Longman.

Green, Christopher F. (1996) The origins and effects of topic-prominence in Chinese-English interlanguage. *IRAL*, **34**(2), 119–34.

Huang, T. S. (1974) A contrastive analysis of the syntactic errors in English made by Chinese students and its implications for the teaching of English syntax to Chinese.

PhD thesis, Southern Illinois University. Ann Arbor, Michigan: University Microfilms Int.

Hung, Joseph H. W. (1987) Interlanguage and temporal expression: The development and use of tense-aspect and some time adverbials in Cantonese learners. PhD thesis, University of Edinburgh.

Potter, John (1992) *Common Business English Errors in Hong Kong.* Hong Kong: Longman.

Webster, Michael, Ward, Alan and Craig, Kenneth (1987) Language errors due to first language interference (Cantonese) produced by Hong Kong students of English. *ILE Journal* (HK), **3**, 63–81.

Webster, Michael and Lam, William C. P. (1991) Further notes on the influence of Cantonese on the English of Hong Kong students. *ILE Journal*, special issue **2**, 35–42.

Wong, Sau-ling, Cynthia (1988) What we do and don't know about Chinese learners of English: A critical review of selected research. *RELC Journal*, **19**(1), 1–20.

Yip, Virginia (1995) *Interlanguage and Learnability.* Amsterdam/Philadelphia: John Benjamins.

Yip, Virginia and Matthews, Stephen (1995) I-Interlanguage and typology: The case of topic-prominence. In *The Current State of Interlanguage: Studies in Honor of William E. Rutherford.* Edited by Lynn Eubank, Larry Selinker and M. Sharwood-Smith. Amsterdam: John Benjamins, pp. 17–30.

Hong Kong English as a 'new English'

Benson, Phil (1993) Localised vocabulary in Hong Kong English and Australian English. In *Studies in Lexis: Proceedings from a Seminar.* Edited by Richard Pemberton and Elza Tsang. Hong Kong: Hong Kong University of Science and Technology, pp. 99–111.

Benson, Phil (1994) The political vocabulary of Hong Kong English. *Hong Kong Papers in Linguistics and Language Teaching*, **17**, 63–81.

Bolt, Philip and Bolton, Kingsley (1996) The international corpus of English in Hong Kong. In *Comparing English Worldwide.* Edited by Sidney Greenbaum. Oxford: Clarendon Press, pp. 197–214.

Bolton, Kingsley (2000) Language and hybridization: Pidgin tales from the China Coast. *Interventions*, **2**(1), 35–52.

Bolton, Kingsley and Kwok, Helen (1990) The dynamics of the Hong Kong accent: Social identity and sociolinguistic description. *Journal of Asian Pacific Communication*, **1**, 147–72.

Budge, Carol (1986) Variation in Hong Kong English. PhD dissertation, Monash University.

Cannon, Garland (1998) Chinese borrowings in English. *American Speech*, **63**, 3–33.

Carless, David R. (1995) Politicised expressions in the South China Morning Post. *English Today*, **42**(11)2, 18–22.

Chan, Mimi and Kwok, Helen (1985) *A Study of Lexical Borrowing from Chinese into English with Special Reference to Hong Kong.* Hong Kong: Centre of Asian Studies, The University of Hong Kong.

Harris, Roy (1989) The worst English in the world? *Supplement to the Gazette*, **36**(1). Hong Kong: The University of Hong Kong, pp. 60–73.

Joseph, John E. (1997) English in Hong Kong: Emergence and decline. In *One Country, Two systems, Three Languages: A Survey of Changing Language Use in Hong Kong.* Edited by Sue Wright and Helen Kelly-Holmes. Clevedon, Philadelphia: Multilingual Matters, pp. 60–73.

Peng, Long and Setter, Jane (2000) The emergence of systematicity in the English pronunciation of two Cantonese-speaking adults. *English World-wide,* **21**(1), 81–108.

Platt, John (1982) English in Singapore, Malaysia and Hong Kong. In *English as a World Language.* Edited by Richard W. Bailey and Manfred Görlach. Cambridge: Cambridge University Press, pp. 384–414.

Tay, Mary W. J. (1991) Southeast Asia and Hongkong. In *English Around the World: Sociolinguistic Perspectives.* Edited by Jenny Cheshire. Cambridge: Cambridge University Press, pp. 319–32.

Taylor, Andrew (1989) Hong Kong's English newspapers. *English Today,* **20**, 18–24.

Hong Kong creative writing

Abbas, Ackbar (1997) *Hong Kong: Culture and the Politics of Disappearance.* Hong Kong: Hong Kong University Press. (Originally published by the University of Minnesota Press.)

Chako, Sussy (Xu Xi) (1994) *Chinese Walls* (novel). Hong Kong: Asia 2000.

Chan, Mimi (1994). Hong Kong. In *Traveller's Literary Companion to South-east Asia.* Edited by Alastair Dingwall. Brighton: In Print Publishing, pp. 405–43.

Cheung, Martha P. (ed.) (1998) *Hong Kong Collage: Contemporary Stories and Writing.* Hong Kong: Oxford University Press.

Ho, Elaine Y. L. (1994) Women in exile: Gender and community in Hong Kong fiction. *The Journal of Commonwealth Literature,* **29**(1), 29–46.

Ho, Elaine, Y. L. (1999) 'People like us': The challenge of a minor literature. *Journal of Asian Pacific Communication,* **9**(1 and 2), 27–42.

Ho, Louise (1977) *Sheung Shui Pastoral.* Hong Kong: Hong Kong Arts Centre.

Ho, Louise (1994) *Local Habitation.* Hong Kong: Twilight Books Co./Department of Comparative Literature, The University of Hong Kong.

Ho, Louise (1997) *New Ends and Old Beginnings.* Hong Kong: Asia 2000.

Hung, Eva (ed.) (1988) *Renditions: A Chinese-English Translation Magazine.* Special issue: Hong Kong, 29, 30. Hong Kong: The Chinese University of Hong Kong.

Hung Eva (ed.) (1997) *Hong Kong Nineties.* Special issue, 47, 48. Hong Kong: The Chinese University of Hong Kong.

Ingham, Michael and Xu Xi (eds.) (forthcoming) *City Voices: An Anthology of Hong Kong Writing in English.* Hong Kong: Hong Kong University Press.

Lam, Agnes (1997) *Woman to Woman and Other Poems.* Hong Kong: Asia 2000.

Lam, Agnes (1999) Poetry in Hong Kong: The 1990s. *World Literature Today,* **73**(1), 53–61.

Leung, Ping-kwan (1992) *City at the End of Time.* Translated by Gordon T. Osing. Hong Kong: Twilight Books in association with the Department of Comparative Literature, The University of Hong Kong.

Leung, Ping-kwan (1997) *Foodscape.* Hong Kong: The Original Photograph Club Limited.

Parkin, Andrew and Wong, Laurence (1997) *Hong Kong Poems in English and Chinese.* Vancouver: Ronsdale Press.

Parkin, Andrew (ed.) (1995) *From the Bluest Part of the Harbour: Poems from Hong Kong.* Hong Kong: Oxford University Press.
Vittachi, Nury (1996) *Asian Values.* Hong Kong: Chameleon.
Vittachi, Nury (ed.) (1999) *Dimsum: The Journal of Good Reading,* 1–3. Hong Kong: Chameleon Press. [http://www.dimsum.com.hk]
Vs: 12 Hong Kong Poets (1993) Hong Kong: Big Weather Press.
Wong, David T. K. (1996) *Hong Kong Stories.* Hong Kong: CDN Publishing Ltd.
Xu Xi (1996) *Daughters of Hui* (fiction collection). Hong Kong: Asia 2000.
Xu Xi (1997) *Hong Kong Rose* (novel). Hong Kong: Asia 2000.
Xu Xi (2001) *The Unwalled City* (novel). Hong Kong: Chameleon Press.

Bibliographies – printed and electronic

Bruce, Nigel (1996) *Language in Hong Kong Education and Society: A Bibliography.* Hong Kong: The English Centre, The University of Hong Kong . Available online at http://ec.hku.hk/njbruce/LANGBIBF.htm
Bruce, Nigel, Tam, Lawrence and Tse, S. K. (1998) *Language in Hong Kong Education and Society (LIHKES): HKU Dissertations and Theses Since 1945.* Hong Kong: English Centre and The University of Hong Kong Library. This is an online database, at http://asterix.lib.hku.hk/lihkes/.
Candlin, Christopher N. and Keobke, Ken (2000) *Bamboo: A Digest of English Language Education and Applied Linguistics Research from Asia.* An online database at http://www.cityu.edu.hk/lib/bamboo/. Hong Kong: City University of Hong Kong.
Chinese University of Hong Kong (2000) *ELT Matters.* Research Institute for the Humanities, the Faculty of Arts, the Chinese University of Hong Kong. http://www.arts.cuhk.edu.hk/~cmc/eltmatters/index.html.
Foo, Rebecca (1997) *ELT in Hong Kong: A Bibliography.* Vol. 2. Hong Kong: Department of English, Hong Kong Polytechnic University.
Foo, Rebecca and Cox, Ah Fong (1994) *ELT in Hong Kong: A Bibliography.* Hong Kong: Department of English, Hong Kong Polytechnic University.
Standing Committee on Language Education and Research (SCOLAR) (1998) *Hong Kong Language Education Research Database.* An online database established by the Standing Committee on Language Education and Research of the Hong Kong Government at http://www.language.com.hk/.

Notes

1. I wish to thank Nigel Bruce of the English Centre at the University of Hong Kong for his generous advice concerning bibliographical research on language issues in Hong Kong.
2. I also wish to apologize to those whose research I have overlooked. Given the abundance of linguistic research now available in Hong Kong, omissions are perhaps inevitable in a selective guide such as this. I trust that whatever gaps exist may be filled by utilizing the other bibliographies listed above, including those accessible through the Internet.

Part V
Future Directions

16

Futures for Hong Kong English

Kingsley Bolton and Shirley Geok-lin Lim

This book contains a range of voices and perspectives on the issue of Hong Kong English, from linguists, educationalists, and creative writers.[1] Here, issues of 'autonomy' and 'creativity' overlap and at a number of levels. For linguists such as Benson, Gisborne, and Hung one major aspect of these issues is that of linguistic description, and the identification of distinctly local features of language at the levels of lexis, syntax, and phonology. These contributions are complemented by Li's chapter, which provides a description of the 'code-switching' which occurs in parallel to the localized use of English; and Tsui and Bunton's description of the normativity of English teachers' behaviour in Hong Kong schools. For Bolton, the issue of Hong Kong English is also linked to broader sociolinguistic questions and the role played by such factors as culture and identity. For writers such as Ho, Lam, Leung, Vittachi, and Xu Xi such questions are of importance to literary creativity in the community, and their contributions point to a growing creativity in poetry and fiction produced by Hong Kong writers.

The autonomy of Hong Kong English – attitudes and ideologies

The notion of 'autonomy' has a number of instantiations in linguistics. Within dialectology and sociolinguistics, the autonomy of a variety helps determine the strength of its claim to the status of 'language', as Romaine (1994: 15–16) explains:

> Some linguists have found the terms '*autonomous*' and '*heteronomous*' speech varieties useful as alternative labels to language and dialect. Thus, we can say, for instance, that the Dutch dialects are dependent on or heteronomous with respect to standard Dutch, German dialects to standard German, etc ... The term 'language' is employed for a variety that is autonomous, together with all those varieties that are heteronomous upon it.

Within the discourse of world Englishes, the term autonomy has a parallel application in relation to the strength and vitality of 'new' varieties of English throughout the world, as McArthur (1992) indicates in his entry for 'New Englishes' in the *Oxford Companion to the English Language:* 'A term in linguistics for a recently emerging and increasingly autonomous variety of English, especially in a non-Western setting such as India, Nigeria, or Singapore' (McArthur, 1992: 688–9).

An early debate on the autonomy of world Englishes began in applied linguistics in the 1960s, when Halliday, MacIntosh and Strevens (1964) noted that 'during the period of colonial rule it seemed totally obvious and immutable that the form of English used by professional people in England was the only conceivable model for use in education overseas' (p. 292), but they then noted that, by the 1960s, ' "to speak like an Englishman" is by no means the only or obvious target for the foreign learner' (p. 296). The publication of such views by Halliday et al. (1964) and others prompted Clifford Prator to publish a spirited yet, it seems, historically misplaced attack on what he called 'The British heresy in TESL' (Prator, 1968; for critiques of this paper see Kachru, 1976 and Romaine, 1997). Prator's central argument was that 'in a country where English is not spoken natively but is widely used as the medium of instruction, to set up the local variety of English as the ultimate model to be imitated by those learning the language' is 'unjustifiable intellectually and not conducive to the best possible results' (p. 459). That 'the doctrine of establishing local models for a TESL ... appears to be a natural outgrowth of the much deplored colonial mentality' is, he suggests, plainly seen in former British colonies such as India, Pakistan, Ceylon, Ghana, and Nigeria, and is linked to the prolonged use of English as a medium of instruction which moves people to start feeling 'possessive' about the language (p. 460).

Prator then queries the notion that in an ESL society English could emerge as one of the indigenous languages of that society. He identifies seven fallacies associated with the British heresy: (1) that second-language varieties of English can legitimately be equated with mother-tongue varieties; (2) that second-language varieties of English really exist as coherent, homogeneous linguistic systems, describable in the usual way as the speech of an identifiable social group; (3) that a few minor concessions in the type of English taught in schools would tend to or suffice to stabilize the language; (4) that one level of a language, its phonology, can be allowed to change without entailing corresponding changes at other levels; (5) that it would be a simple matter to establish a second-language variety of English as an effective instructional model once it had been clearly identified and described; (6) that students would long be content to study English in a situation in which, as a matter of policy, they were denied access to a mother-tongue model; and that (7) granting a second-language variety of English official status in a country's schools would lead to its widespread adoption as a mother tongue.

According to Prator these attitudes were definitely a *British* heresy, as the Americans were united with the French in asserting that the only possible model of pronunciation was a 'mother tongue' one, that: 'in the eyes of both the French and the Americans, ... if teachers in many different parts of the world aim at the same stable, well documented model, the general effect of their instruction will be convergent', and that, just as there was increasing homogenization in mother-tongue societies, the forces of 'greater mobility, new media of communication, urbanization, mass education' would also influence second-language varieties. Prator suggested that the reasons for the British view included (1) the elitist model of Received Pronunciation (in contrast to the more democratic General American); (2) the 'British' distrust of the foreigner who speaks English *too* well (unlike the French who were willing to assimilate their colonial subjects into French culture and language; (3) a British-promoted 'instrumental motivation' towards English (as opposed to an American and French 'integrative' motivation). Finally Prator concluded:

> The limitation of objectives implied in the doctrine of establishing local models for TESL seems to lead inevitably in practice to a deliberate lowering of instructional standards. ... The total British effort on behalf of the teaching of English as a second language is too intelligently planned, too well executed, too crucial to the successful development of the emerging countries to allow for an indefinite prolongation of this flirtation with a pernicious heresy. (1968: 474)

Romaine (1997) provides a point-by-point refutation of Prator's arguments, and then turns to a discussion of the ideologies embedded in Prator's paper, with reference to the notion of 'hegemony'. She quotes Gramsci (1985: 183–4) to the effect that:

> Every time the question of the language surfaces, in one way or another, it means that a series of other problems are coming to the fore: the formation and enlargement of the governing class, the need to establish more intimate and secure relationships between the governing groups and the national-popular mass, in other words to reorganize the cultural hegemony.

The issue here is concerned with who controls the language, and who has the right to decide questions of language planning and policies, and Romaine compares the Prator debate in the late 1960s to domestic debates in Britain in the late 1980s and early 1990s about the question of 'language standards', the discussions that accompanied the Kingman Report and Cox Report, and the development of a national curriculum. Whatever the outcome in Britain, developments in Asia have generally seen an eclipse of the viewpoints expressed by Prator, whose views were partly moulded by his experience as a visiting professor in the 1960s Philippines. Some thirty years later, in 1996, the Philippine poet Germino Abad was able to assert to the apparent delight of a conference audience and the Manila media that 'English is now ours, we have colonized it' (*Philippine Daily Inquirer*, 12 August 1996, p. 13). Similarly, in journals and the international literature generally, it seems clear that those voices in favour of a recognition and tolerance of diverse English(es) enjoy a position of rhetorical and numerical dominance. Only in Hong Kong, of all Asian 'outer-circle' English-using societies, do numbers of local linguists apparently cling so steadfastly to the the axiom that English is an 'exonormative' or 'externally-imposed' variety of language.

Bolton's (see chapter 1) partial explanation of the persistence of such views points to the power of 'ideologies of language' in the Hong Kong speech community, which he characterizes in terms of the 'monolingual myth' and 'invisibility myth'. A third ideology also relates to the question of 'instructional standards' that Prator refers to above. For at least thirty years, Hong Kong has had its own localized complaint tradition about 'falling standards' of both English and Chinese, an ideology we might gloss as the 'falling standards myth'. In the period of the formation of modern Hong Kong, such an ideology seems to have emerged among academics in the early 1970s, and then gathered steam in the 1980s with the description of Hong Kong students as 'cultural eunuchs' from T'sou (1983). In a subsequently much-quoted article, T'sou charged that the rapid expansion of the education system in the early 1980s was producing a maimed generation of local students:

> The end result of the educational system, based on complaints and opinion commonly expressed, is very often a product which can be generally described as a 'cultural eunuch' – someone who knows what things could or might be like in cultural terms but who is not able to take part. This product is brought about by the encrustation of a light veneer of Western culture, glimpsed through exposure to the English language in schools and the media, on to a less than wholesome body of Chinese values and culture. (T'sou, 1983)

The debate concerning 'low' or 'falling' standards of English has continued from the mid-1980s to the late 1990s and to the present, although it probably reached a peak in the late 1980s, when a *South China Morning Post* editorial declared that '[t]he decline in the standard of spoken and written English in recent decades is obvious and measurable, and efforts by the Government and the tertiary education institutions have been insufficient to stop the slide' (*South China Morning Post*, 1989: 18). This was a debate not confined to academics in the 1980s, but was rehearsed and expressed in the broadcast media and the local press. During the mid-1980s, editorials on language policy, feature articles, news reports and letters to the editor on this topic regularly appeared in the *South China Morning Post* and other newspapers. Many of the arguments turned on the choice of language for schools, English, Cantonese and Putonghua, but as Lin (1997) notes, a strong and recurrent strand of argument in discussions on English was economic, expressed through an identification of English with business, trade, and prosperity. One editorial in the *South China Morning Post* in November 1986 made the case for English thus:

> English is pre-eminently the language of international trade, which is, and for the foreseeable future will remain, Hongkong's *raison d'etre*. There are indications that the territory's role in world commerce, far from diminishing as 1997 approaches, will increase in importance. Southeast and East Asia is widely seen as the growth area of the future and we are ideally placed to take advantage of this. Hongkong, as a stable and sophisticated oasis, is the obvious choice of any overseas company wishing to participate in the boom years ahead. The widespread use of English is an obvious added attraction. (*South China Morning Post*, 1986a)

A second editorial appeared in the same newspaper some two months later expressing concern about the effects of the promotion of Cantonese might have on business and finance:

> It is honourable for the people of Hongkong to feel a sense of 'nationalism' as we move towards 1997 and the change of sovereignty which will again make the territory part of China. ... Cantonese is and should always be the mother tongue of Hongkong. There is no dispute in this. But it is a fact of life that Hongkong has grown to become a world leader in trade and finance on the back of and assisted by the English language. It cannot be disputed that the international language in trade and commerce and a plethora of other interactions is English, and so it should be in Hongkong. (*South China Morning Post*, 1987)

The reference to nationalism in the editorial also pointed to another strand in this debate, which was overtly political. In fact, some months earlier, the *Post* had published another editorial in response to a warning from a Chinese Education Ministry official, Mr Yang Xun, that the promotion of Cantonese as the teaching medium ran against the grain of mainland policy, and would be 'a step backward for Hongkong'. The *Post*'s response in those pre-Tianmanen days was to endorse such concerns:

> Mr Yang has made an important point. We would recommend a fresh look at the subject. Putonghua and English are the languages which Hongkong should be stressing. English has, because of its adaptability, subtlety and richness, plus historical accident, become the language of international contact. Hongkong's status as a centre of world trade must be maintained, and our children must learn English to prepare them for the role they will one day assume. Putonghua is the official language of the nation to which Hongkong will be irrevocably joined after 1997. Our children will also become citizens of China, and should speak the language of their compatriots as well as English. (*South China Morning Post*, 1986b)

The political was to take a number of other forms in the language debates of the era. One news report even suggested that many schoolchildren were beginning to lose the motivation to study English because there was 'a different political atmosphere with Hongkong coming under Chinese rule' (Lau, 1986). Ten years later, the politics of English took a new turn when significant numbers of the Chinese elite in business and the government started to 'drop' the use of English first names in favour of the Chinese given names. One prominent civil servant explained his decision to do this by explaining that 'I do not have a Christian name, because I am not and have never been a Christian', adding that 'I have always been an atheist and the name "Brian" is, in fact, a product of colonialism' (*South China Morning Post*, 1996).

By the early 1990s, a *Time* magazine article was suggesting that 'Many [secondary school] students are not very good at either Chinese or English', and that 'The decline in English standards is clearly visible at the University of Hong Kong' (16 September 1991). By 1996, according to a *Far Eastern Economic Review* special feature, the situation had deteriorated still further, and the University of Hong Kong was once again the whipping-boy (or perhaps girl):

> Founded in 1911 and still the colony's premier institution of higher learning, the university today has become a symbol of the decline in local English standards in Hong Kong. At a time when other parts of Asia are trying to boost their skills, on the surface, the battle for English on this campus appears to be a losing one. ... There are number of factors at work here. To begin with, at least since the 1970s, Hong Kong's English-speaking middle class has been steadily sending its children to overseas universities. A Hong Kong government decision, announced in 1989 in reaction to the loss of confidence following Tiananmen Square, exacerbates the effect of this trend: To democratize Hong Kong's system of higher education, the government expanded enrolment to 18% of the relevant age group from about 7%. Here at the University of Hong Kong, that has meant a jump to 12,965 students today from about 7,000 only 10 years ago. ... And because the university no longer reflects simply the cream of Hong Kong society, the general level of English has declined as the numbers have increased. (McGurn, 1996: 43)

McGurn's sociology may contain nuggets of truth, but the piece was also penned a year or so before the 1997 change in sovereignty, at a time when the international media were inclined to publish copy that fitted into a preset agenda for 'Handover coverage'.

Journalistic attitudes to falling standards in the past decade or so were often matched by those of local academics and educators. Yu and Atkinson (1988) express attitudes similar to those of T'sou (1983), when they suggest that 'Hong Kong students suffer from an inferiority complex and identity conflict which prevents them from learning English effectively and being fluent in Chinese'. Another academic, Yee (1989: 228–9) quotes a local banker (and Hong Kong University Council member), Mr David Li:

[We are] dissatisfied with the educational level of the people (we) are forced by necessity to employ – whether products of our secondary schools, colleges or universities. The main grievance is the poor level of English. But complaints extend to the breadth and depth of knowledge. The constituency's consensus seems to be that Hong Kong students have been schooled to memorise what will get them through examinations and, thus, lack analytical skills.

From an empirical perspective, very little hard research was conducted on the issue of 'falling' language standards during these years, and what was done was inconclusive at best. King (1987) reported on the results of the Hong Kong Examinations Authority's (HKEA) English language examination for the years 1984 and 1986. After revealing a substantial number of statistics relating to 15,000 students, his conclusion was that there was no 'convincing evidence to suggest the English standard of the best students coming through the Hongkong system has deteriorated in recent years'. However, King also went on to add that '[i]t is clear that the whole of the secondary system is being seriously affected by the presence of large numbers of students whose English language standards are quite inadequate to cope with an education in the medium of English', which suggested that the root cause of such perceptions was the rapid expansion of the educational system. Educational research on levels of reading literacy was carried out by Johnson and Cheung in the mid-1990s as part of the International Association for the Evaluation of Educational Achievement (IEA) World Literacy Project. The results of this registered good levels of attainment in Chinese-language reading proficiency, but relatively poor levels of proficiency in English literacy. The research report suggests that this result might be influenced by the quality of schools as much as the choice of language, as '[g]ood schools produce good results in both Chinese and English and poor schools are equally consistent in producing poor results' (Johnson and Cheung, 1995: 10).

In the long view, the notion that standards of language have 'fallen' is clearly risible if we pause to reflect that in 1931 only 18% of females could read and write Chinese (compared to 69% of men), and around only 6% of the Chinese population could speak English (Bacon-Shone and Bolton, 1998: 47, 51). More than anything else, the public debates on language standards in this period indicate that 'attitudes' took on an ideological edge that seemed to 'scapegoat' the very people intended to benefit from education in Hong Kong, i.e. the many thousands of schoolchildren and college students undergoing public education. This points to a local 'pathology' in the language debates of a particularly perverse nature (Harris, 1989: 41). Very often, it seemed, the anger and scorn of educators and community leaders was aimed at the children of the community, who were routinely 'scolded' for their linguistic shortcomings in the media. At times, the barrage of criticisms aimed at the supposedly linguistically-inept young seemed to verge on parentally-instituted child abuse, or might have done, had such community leaders and academics been educating their own children in local schools instead of overseas.

As has been shown in many other societies, ideologies about 'falling standards' are often related to other factors, including social class divisions. Romaine (1994) suggests that '[s]tandards of language use and standard languages are essentially arbitrary conventions which can be learned only by going to school', and that '[t]his is precisely why they are so effective in maintaining barriers between groups'. She also points out that such debates have existed in Britain since the fifteenth century, and have continued to the present, even at Oxford University (Romaine, 1994: 202). In the Hong Kong context, one plausible inference with reference to the much publicized 'language standards' debates of the 1980s and 1990s is that, in large part, they were a reaction to the rapid and unprecedented expansion of education, as well as the pace of political and social change in the society at large. These ideologies continued to be voiced until the 1997 Handover (Boyle, 1997: 163), and notions of a 'decline' in English persist to the present. However, if there was ever a 'golden age' of English in the colonial period, it was arguably during the 1950s and 1960s and was particularly associated with the years of Edmund Blunden as Professor of English at the University of Hong Kong from 1953 to 1964. Blunden's students were drawn from a very narrow section of the population and then went on to take up high positions in the business world and civil service. In the 1960s, such alumni could perhaps claim a 'superiority' through their command of English, an ability shared by only 9.7% of the population in 1961, according to the census report. By the 1980s, with the rapid spread of varying proficiencies in English through the newly expanded education system, the graduates of the 1960s and early 1970s could no longer argue that few other people had a command of this language. They could, however, argue that standards had fallen. Which they did, thus contributing to a peculiar variety of neo-colonial nostalgia.

The Blunden era seems to retain an iconic importance as a high watermark for the 'monoglossic' normativity of British English in Hong Kong, although in retrospect little of lasting creative literary merit seems to have survived from the golden age. In a *Festschrift* produced by his students for Blunden in 1961, contributions from members of the British political and literary establishment were supplemented by essays from former students, some of which attest to the love of the English countryside that he had communicated to them:

> Many visitors to England have told me about the fog, the soot, the rain of London's streets; from him I know that trees and grass and rivers and hills bask in warm sunshine in the English countryside. I know this year white flowers are found everywhere, and like Wordsworth's daffodils 'flutter and dance in the breeze'. (Chang, 1961: 63–4)

In an era of educational high colonialism, such contributions from the 1961 alumni illustrate a 'mimicry', 'indeterminacy' and '*ironic* compromise' which Bhabha identifies with the 'ambivalence' of colonial discourse (1994: 85–6). For 'high standards' read 'high colonialism'.

Forty years on, the young people who enter the English Department of the university today are drawn from the top 10 to 20 per cent of English achievers from the territory's secondary schools, and our best students are impressively bilingual and bicultural, in spite of the fact that they often come from homes in housing estates where little or no English is spoken. But they also arrive at university burdened by years of 'scolding' and propaganda concerning the deteriorating language standards of themselves and their classmates. One area in particular where a 'paradigm shift' of the Kachru model is badly needed in Hong Kong is in this convoluted tangle of language attitudes. Notions of linguistic proficiency and linguistic potential may need to be revised to accommodate both the 'sociolinguistic realities' of Hong Kong, and the call for sensitive and imaginative agendas for language education. What those agendas might involve is outside the scope of this present discussion, but one would hope for a revitalized attitude to the teaching of English that is fully prepared to accept and utilize the power of creativity and intellectual inspiration that the study of the language can provide. Within this context, one would also hope that a discourse of 'Hong Kong English' as a new cultural space will allow for the increased ownership of the language by users such as our students, as well as a measure of joy and spontaneity in the creative potential that English and Englishes allow.

Creativity in Hong Kong English

What is or should be the difference between the categories of 'creative writing' and 'literature'? 'Creative writing' implies the active labour of imagination within specific forms and genres of written communication; a set of provisional dynamics, in which cultural, social, historical, and individual forces are evolving subjects in process, subjects still open to revision and re-formation. 'Literature', as befitting its nominal status, suggests, on the contrary, an already shaped text or body of texts; a contributory reproduction in the horizon of literary traditions and expectations that help frame the larger discursive universe of a social culture.

This distinction may lead a critic of Hong Kong society to conclude that while English language creative writing is possible in Hong Kong, an English language Hong Kong literature may be an impossible project. Abbas argues in his study of Hong Kong culture that it is marked by the 'paradox' of disappearance: 'A central issue that Hong Kong culture poses is the question of subjectivity in a space of disappearance. ... The problem is usually posed more misleadingly as a question of "Hong Kong identity" or "postcolonial identity" ' (Abbas, 1997: 10). In brief, because Hong Kong subjectivity is constructed 'in the very process of negotiating the mutations and permutations of colonialism, nationalism, and capitalism', Hong Kong culture is 'coaxed into being by the disappearance of old cultural bearing and orientations ... it is a subjectivity that develops precisely out of a space of disappearance' (p. 11). If we accept Abbas's thesis, then Hong Kong 'literature' must remain a figment of substance. A canon, a stable body of privileged cultural texts embedded in a matrix of traditional significations and signatures, cannot be established when stability of meanings and namings is impossible, in a culture of extreme provisionality, speed, contingency, transformation, and loss.

But creative writing is possible, because writers entering or coming from this social space of disappearance will provisionally offer representations of the space of the moment. Such creative writing, to expand on Abbas's argument, may partake of three options, the local, the marginal, and the cosmopolitan.

Indeed, critics have examined works loosely and casually named Hong Kong writing through lenses that appear to match these categories. In Chan's essay, for example, published in 1988, categorizes novels 'about Hong Kong', written by Anglo-American expatriates such as James Clavell, Anthony G. Hooper, Robert Elegant, and Christopher New, as 'Hong Kong Fiction Written in English'. In including the novel, *Running Dog*, written by a Hong Kong Chinese woman, Lee Ding Fai, in its analysis, Chan's essay elides any boundary markers of authorial origin, cultural specificity, and location. Interestingly, the essay does differentiate these markers in readers, identified as 'Hong Kong Chinese', who, apparently by virtue of their ethnicity, are 'enraged' by the insulting or simplistic characterizations of Hong Kong often found in these cosmopolitan fictions (1988: 273).

In contrast, Chow's 1992 essay analyses the lyrics of a Chinese songwriter originally from Taiwan, Luo Dayou, that illustrate a more 'local' cultural production. According to Chow, Hong Kong is a unique post-colonial society in its 'in-betweenness. . . an awareness of impure origins [marking] the untenability of nativism and postmodernism' (p. 157). Chow quotes Leung Ping-kwan, the Hong Kong poet, in her construction of Luo as an immigrant, and therefore a native Hong Kong person, unlike the expatriate Western authors discussed in Chan's essay:

> Vis-à-vis foreigners, Hong Kong people are of course Chinese, but vis-à-vis the Chinese from the mainland or Taiwan, they seem to have the imprints of the West. A Hong Kong person who came from China after 1949 is obviously an 'outsider' or 'someone coming south'; but to those who 'came south' during the 1970s and 1980s, such a person is already a 'local' (Leung, cited in Chow, 1992: 155).

In Leung's definition of Hong Kong people, the distinctions between marginal and local are always fluid and in process, unlike the distinction between 'cosmopolitan' or 'expatriate' and 'local' explicated by Chan. Chow is interested in the 'emergent' character of Hong Kong culture, and the 'emergent', is defined as what 'is never only a matter of immediate practice; indeed it depends crucially on finding new forms or adaptations of form' (Raymond Williams, cited in Chow, 1992: 161).

The essays by Hong Kong creative writers included in this book gesture towards less stable categories than those provided by Abbas or Chow. English language writers represented here (Louise Ho, Agnes Lam, Nury Vittachi, Xu Xi) are cosmopolitan, if only by virtue of their deployment of that most cosmopolitan of modern languages, English. (I leave the discussion of Leung Ping-kwan's work, in English translation, till later.) However, 'English' is never one homogeneous language operating in their writing; instead, the varieties of English in these writers' collective repertoire range from standard international English, a cosmopolitan register, to national (British or American), local and even marginal registers.

In a recent essay on the history of Pidgin English, Bolton notes: 'In linguistics from the late nineteenth century onwards, the study of pidgin and creole languages has been situated within the discourse of a scientific enquiry into the nature and development of human languages ... "hybridization" is typically seen as an objective and neutral descriptor of processes of "language contact" or "mixed languages"' (2000: 36). The earliest accounts of Chinese pidgin English were written in the eighteenth and early nineteenth centuries in the context of the China trade. Such 'Canton-English', while appreciated for its utilitarian virtues, was often condemned for degrading or corrupting the English language. On the one hand, the use of pidgin English in Hong Kong has become associated with illiteracy, and continues to be represented in British and American literature as part of a stylistics of caricature. On the other hand, a utilitarian approach to the teaching of English in the colony, promulgated in the 1935 Burney Report, has received consistent official and government support. These dual positions have resulted in a complicated attitude towards the English language, the official language of colonial administration till 1997, and one of the two administrative languages today, whose vernacular varieties (labelled together with Cantonese-English code-switching as 'Chinglish') are held in contempt, even as their cultural use is discouraged.

The language debate after the 1997 Handover of Hong Kong to China remains as heated and perhaps even more complex. In September 1998, for example, despite protests by Hong Kong parents fearful that their children will be less competitive in an English language global society, more than 400 secondary schools were ordered to teach in Cantonese, with only 114 allowed to continue teaching in English (Tacey, 2000: 9). A fresh complication in the familiar decolonizing struggle between the maintenance of (colonial) English as an official language and the appeal to a mother tongue based on cultural nationalist and nativist ideologies (Cantonese, in the case of Hong Kong) is the emergence of Putonghua. Putonghua, the official state Chinese of the Mainland, is perceived as neither mother tongue for the majority Cantonese-speakers in Hong Kong nor necessary for participation in a global market. Indeed, as a Hong Kong academic observes, Putonghua, the national language for post-colonial Hong Kong, 'confers no status' in Hong Kong (Tacey, 2000: 9).

Hong Kong English language creative writers are inevitably embedded in this contentious language history, and their work is expressive of the tensions that saturate the tradition of English language creative writing in Hong Kong. The critical work on Hong Kong English language writing suggests that it is a relatively recent phenomenon particularly vulnerable to forces that undermine and subvert its claim to autonomy. English language creative writing at the University of Hong Kong, the only university in the territory until 1963, first appeared in the 1950s, under the tutelage of Edmund Blunden. Archival sources suggest that Hong Kong practitioners then reproduced (or mimicked) the British themes, settings and stylistics affected by Blunden. It was only in the 1970s and 1980s, when the return of Hong Kong to China in 1997, as stipulated under the second Convention of Peking in 1898, emerged as a political reality, that the concept of a Hong Kong identity (as differentiated from a British colonial or Chinese identity) began to be debated.

In 1975, Kwok and Chan, teaching creative writing at the University of Hong Kong, presented the problem of Hong Kong English language creative writing as 'the problem of saying [something new] in a language which is not [one's] own' (1975: 27). Their position implied that writing in a colonial language (as distinct from writing in an original language or a mother tongue) makes creativity difficult if not impossible. This position is different from that assumed in a number of other colonial territories where English language literature emerged to take on a national and elite position, as in Nigeria (Chinua Achebe), Ghana (Ama Ata Aidoo), Kenya (Ngugi Wa Thiong'o), and the Philippines (Nick Joaquin).

Kwok and Chan's pessimism is countered by the exuberance of literary production in Timothy Mo's *The Monkey King*, which appeared only three years after their essay was published. Mo, born in Hong Kong of a British mother and Cantonese father, was raised in Hong Kong till he left for Britain at age ten. *The Monkey King*, published when he was just 28, is a vividly imagined representation of Hong Kong social community in the 1950s. Encompassing major and minor Portuguese Eurasian Macanese, Cantonese, and British civil servants characters, the novel invents an oral pidgin approximating to a Cantonese and British English mix such as has never been heard in Hong Kong, but which is capable of advancing complex action, character and theme for sharply satirical ends. *The Monkey King*, arguably, may be said to inaugurate a new tradition and perspective on Hong Kong English language creative writing, one in which ethnic Chinese is no longer the locus for a Hong Kong culture. Instead, hybridity, of ethnicity, class, and language, reigns in full semiotic play.

Like Wallace Nolasco, the Eurasian hero in Mo's novel, who develops to become the patriarch of the extended urban Cantonese family and rural Chinese community, Nury Vittachi's position as one of Hong Kong's leading writers and editors interrogates Leung Ping-kwan's (and Chow's) definition of the local as composed of persons of Chinese descent. Born of Sri Lankan parents, Vittachi is both fluent in the Chinese vernacular, Cantonese, as well as in the semiotics of Hong Kong local culture. As a creative writer, he embodies Hong Kong as more than a Chinese social space. Rather, Vittachi writes Hong Kong as a multi-ethnic, multicultural world city, composed of multiple Asian and Western cultural practices and persons.

Ironically, it is this 'marginal' writer who is most concerned with teasing out, defining, reproducing, and legitimizing the specific contours of Hong Kong English. Vittachi distinguishes between the usual notion of this English as 'Chinglish', a form of Standard English riddled with errors in need of eradication, and 'Hong Kong English', with its unique usages that mark the English of the place. For Vittachi, the challenge for the creative writer is 'to capture something of the patterns of the community about which [he] is writing'. In this way, his work is complexly Hong Kong writing, for it is not merely about but constitutively, in grammatical and lexical expressiveness, uniquely out of Hong Kong. Such writing cannot be characterized as marginal, for in the HKSAR, Hong Kong English is central. Nor can it be said to be merely local, for its ironic play with multiple code-switching situates it in the range of the cosmopolitan, a category that encompasses diversity, difference and multiplicity of social worlds.

In contrast to Mo's invented Cantonese-English pidgin and Vittachi's sociologically drawn Hong Kong English linguistics, Louise Ho and Agnes Lam's poetry appeal to an international English language tradition. Ho's poems, for example, deploy allusions to Shakespearean dramas, Wordsworthian lyrics, and Metaphysical poetry in their outright claim to a British literary tradition, albeit within a local political imagination. Lam's poetry, in fact, is more insistent on staying within the bounds of a Hong Kong-identified setting, society and ethos. While *Woman to Woman*, her first book, covers her sojourn in Singapore, her new manuscript is fully faithful to portraying her Hong Kong life and community.

These two poets are unselfconscious about their use of the English language, perhaps because they have remained uncurious about what is possible outside the bounds of Standard English, which both perceive as 'global' rather than colonial or British national. Oddly enough, it is left to a novelist and to a putative Chinese language writer to illuminate the tensions in Hong Kong English language writing, tensions which need not be only unproductive, as Kwok and Chan had claimed, but also productive and stimulating in unexpectedly intercultural ways.

Xu Xi's chapter offers a complicated mapping of the growth of her English language fiction. A local writer born and raised in Hong Kong, she also identifies herself as a marginal Hong Kong person because of her part Indonesian identity and American education. Her early writing career careened between using English as a British and an American language. Divided between seeing Hong Kong as a local space, synonymous with Chinese ethnicity and Cantonese language, and as a global society, signifying multinational, multicultural, and English language elements, Xu Xi's anxieties rose out of her preconception that 'novelists tend to be defined ... by the reality of their national identity'. The disparity between her autobiographical experiences in a multi-ethnic multilingual community and the cultural nationalist ideology of Hong Kong as Chinese and Cantonese intensified those anxieties.

According to Xu Xi, she has found in the model of Maxine Hong Kingston's *The Woman Warrior* an English which is engaging because of its 'linguistic lack of self-consciousness'. To the contrary, Kingston's highly charged, entangled, nimble English, a mix of American and translated Cantonese phrases and idioms, is a very self-conscious linguistics project. Unlike Kingston's stylized American English, Xu Xi's own style, illustrated in the excerpt from her most recent novel, *The Unwalled City*, is composed of a straightforward Standard English stylistics with idiomatic American turns and punctuated by occasional Cantonese or non-English words.

Leung Ping-kwan's chapter begins: 'Growing up in Hong Kong, I have always written in Chinese. But there were exceptions.' Leung's 'exceptions' figure the exceptionalism of English in Hong Kong: its status shifting from a colonial language to a global language within a decade; its stature as a utilitarian language that is nonetheless associated with non-utilitarian values like freedom and pleasure; and, for Leung, the unparalleled access it offers to national literatures and international audiences via translation. The profound irony is that it takes a Chinese language writer to understand the manifold, subtle, and universalizing work that English serves for Hong Kong people. As Leung notes, it was through English translation that he read the masterworks of other language nations; instead of shaping a colonial hegemony, English language translation 'was a means to oppose the dominant trend, a kind of manifesto to promote alternate visions'. In negotiating the space between Chinese and English, translation permits a play of signifiers that speaks 'to new audiences' and itself creates new forms. Leung's 'Leaf of Passage' offers an intriguing example of what can happen in these interstices, when English and Chinese operate together in the composition of a poem. It represents one kind of creative writing in English that is emerging in Hong Kong, when the writer draws upon the resources of both language worlds, sometimes translating from Cantonese, sometimes playing with the traditional cadences and allusions of English literature, and composing on scenes, characters, social fragments, political themes, stories that are recognizably local yet not bounded to place.

Teaching creative writing to third-year English majors at the University of Hong Kong in 1999–2000, Lim has encouraged the emergence of an English contoured less on Standard British or American English and more on the usages featured in the English of the students' community. In this course, students are urged to observe their own surroundings, lives, and events, and to write with linguistic specificity, using names, lexical items, concrete references rather than generalities. Venus Tsang's poem, 'The Maid', for example, focuses on the thoughts of a Filipino maid employed by a Chinese Hong Kong family, whose domestic chores are contrasted to her longing for her son, left in the Philippines, her eagerness for a day off to be spent with thousands of other maids in Statue Square in Hong Kong's Central District, and her desire to return home to the Philippines.

The Maid
(By Venus Tsang Chiu-ying)

Under the same roof
Guarded by the left and right Men Shen:
Their stares shakes my legs
When I shut the door
To open the Bible in my soul.

Around the same table,
Among the pinching chopsticks,
My fork becomes a slingshot,
Rebounds when it shoots
At the Guangdong food.

On the upper deck,
The dragon boy crashes the plane above my head.
Seeing the same black hair,
The same brown eyes,
I hug my son in my dream.

A foam bath for the benz,
A cha-cha with the broom,
A massage for the windows:
I collect credits
For a Sunday ticket to Statue Square.

But when can I collect enough credits
For a ticket back to the Philippines?

Wong Ho-yin's 'Our Father' illustrates how the Hong Kong English language writer can deploy conventional literary rhythms and traditional forms (in this instance, a well-known prayer) to characterize and satirize a Hong Kong phenomenon, the minor civil servant.

> *Our Father*
> (By Wong Ho-yin)
>
> Our Father who art in office,
> Hallowed be thy post.
> Thy income come,
> Thy will be done,
> At work but not at home.
> Give us this day our daily cash;
> And forgive us for ignoring thee,
> As we also have forgiven thee for ignoring us;
> And lead us not into bankrupcy,
> But deliver us from proverty.
> For thine is the income, the money and the salary,
> For as long as thou art in the labour force –
> Poor man.

In contrast, Eliza Wong's poem, 'Market Hues', uses Chinese food images to evoke the colour, stimulus, and cultural vitality that makes a Hong Kong wet market an irresistable urban space. The hundred-year-old eggs with their black sooty carapaces are set against the purple aubergines; and then against the dark purple black albumin and yolk of the thousand-year-old eggs. This colour play can only be understood by readers familiar with these foods; but the poem's playful spirit and its visual and verbal puns (the waisted bottle gourd, the bare-chested winter melon, the bean sprouts' collectivism), calling upon local cultural knowledge, can also be enjoyed for their linguistic nimbleness.

> *Market Hues*
> (By Eliza Wong)
>
> Between scarlet chilies and
> tangerine persimmons,
> there is still room
> for aubergines' undertone.
> Purple fades out when
> heaps of hundred-year-
> old eggs dim the pallette.
> Bring them near to their
> thousand-year-old ancestors
> or fresh offspring aglow
> in beams from the overhead
> hemispheric lanterns.

Bitter gourds are hard
selling their life philosophy
while longans are napping.
The bottle gourd is bored
holding her waist erect
like a dumb guitar.
Bare-chested, mother
winter melon exposes
its seeds.

Angular silkgourds may
not be stiff if star fruits
don't twinkle at night.
In the margin of bean
sprouts' collectivism
lies a solitary taro.
Ginger – the older
the hotter?
Can I pick a garlic
segment which is
less tangy?

The work of these young Hong Kong writers, now published in a new journal of Hong Kong and international writing, *Yuan Yang*, gestures towards the possibility of an emergent body of Hong Kong English creative writing whose freshness and energy will be expressive of this cultural space that is both Hong Kong and global, Chinese and English language.

Note

1. We would like to thank Jennifer MacMahon for her generous help in the writing of this chapter.

References

Abbas, Ackbar (1997) *Hong Kong: Culture and the Politics of Disappearance*. Hong Kong: Hong Kong University Press. (Originally published by the University of Minnesota Press.)

Bacon-Shone, John and Bolton, Kingsley (1998) Charting multilingualism: Language censuses and language surveys in Hong Kong. In *Language in Hong Kong at Century's End*. Edited by M. Pennington. Hong Kong: Hong Kong University Press, pp. 43–90.

Bhabha, Homi (1994) *The Location of Culture*. London: Routledge.

Bolton, Kingsley (2000) Language and hybridization: Pidgin tales from the China Coast. *Interventions*, **2**(1), 35–52.

Boyle, Joseph (1997) Native speaker teachers of English in Hong Kong. *Language and Education,* **11**(3), 163–81.
Chan, Mimi (1988) Women in Hong Kong fiction written in English: The mixed liaison. *Renditions* **29** & **30**, 257–74.
Chang, Helen (1961) Tribute to Edmund Blunden. In *Edmund Blunden: Sixty-five.* Edited by W. C. Chan, K. M. Lo and K. K. Yung. Hong Kong: Hong Kong Cultural Enterprise Co.
Chow, Rey (1992) Between colonizers: Hong Kong's postcolonial self-writing in the 1990's. *Diaspora* 2, 151–70.
Gramsci, Antonio (1985) *Selections from Cultural Writings.* Edited by D. Forgacs and G. Nowell-Smith. Harvard: Harvard University Press.
Halliday, Michael A. K., MacIntosh, Angus and Strevens, Peter (1964) *The Linguistic Sciences and Language Teaching.* London: Longmans.
Harris, Roy (1989) The worst English in the world? *Supplement to the Gazette,* **36**(1). Hong Kong: The University of Hong Kong, pp. 37–46.
Johnson, Robert K. and Cheung Yat-shing (1995) *Reading Literacy in Hong Kong: An IEA World Literacy Project on the Reading Proficiency of Hong Kong Students in Chinese and English.* Hong Kong: Department of Chinese and Bilingual Studies, Hong Kong Polytechnic University.
Kachru, Braj B. (1976) Models of English for the third world: White man's linguistic burden or language pragmatics. *TESOL Quarterly,* **10**(2), 221–39.
King, Rex (1987) Why pupils are facing testing time. *South China Morning Post.* 24 February, 17.
Kwok, Helen and Chan, Mimi (1975) Creative writing in English: Problems faced by undergraduates in the English Department, The University of Hong Kong. *Topics in Culture Learning.* Vol. 3. Honolulu: East-West Center, University of Hawaii, pp. 27–38.
Lau, Chi-kuen (1986) Political excuse for poor studies. *South China Morning Post,* 16 December.
Lin, Angel Mei-yi (1997) Analyzing the 'language problem' discourses in Hong Kong: How official, academic, and media discourses construct and perpetuate dominant models of language, learning, and education. *Journal of Pragmatics,* **28**, 427–40.
McArthur, Tom (1992) New Englishes. In *The Oxford Companion to the English Language.* Edited by Tom McArthur. Oxford: Oxford University Press, pp. 688–9.
McGurn, William (1996). Money talks. *Far Eastern Economic Review.* 21 March, 40–4.
Prator, Clifford (1968) The British heresy in TESL. In *Language problems of developing nations.* Edited by J. A. Fishman, C. Ferguson and J. Das Gupta. New York: John Wiley and Sons, pp. 459–76.
Romaine, Suzanne (1994) *Language in Society: An Introduction to Sociolinguistics.* Oxford: Oxford University Press.
Romaine, Suzanne (1997) The British heresy in ESL revisited. In *Language and its Ecology: Essays in Memory of Einar Haugen.* Edited by S. Eliasson and E. H. Jahr. Berlin and New York: Mouton de Gruyter, pp. 417–32.
South China Morning Post (1986a) Language project deserves applause. Editorial. *South China Morning Post.* 1 November, 10.
South China Morning Post (1986b) Putonghua, not Cantonese in classes. Editorial. *South China Morning Post.* 22 July, 16.

South China Morning Post (1987) Need for far-sighted policy on languages. *South China Morning Post.* 25 January, 8.

South China Morning Post (1989) 'Worst' English tag should be eliminated. Editorial. *South China Morning Post.* 27 February, 18.

South China Morning Post (1996) Ignorant. *South China Morning Post.* 11 February, Letters page.

Tacey, Elizabeth (2000) Lessons of mother tongue learning. *Sunday Morning Post,* 9 April, 9.

T'sou, Benjamin (1983) Chinese and the cultural eunuch syndrome. In R. Lord and B. K. T'sou, *The Language Bomb.* Hong Kong: Longman (Far East), pp. 15–19.

Yee, Albert H. (1989) Cross-cultural perspectives on higher education in East Asia: Psychological effects upon Asian students. *Journal of Multilingual and Multicultural Devleopment,* **10**, 213–32.

Yu, Vivienne W. S. and Atkinson, Paul A. (1988). An investigation of the language difficulties experienced by Hong Kong secondary school students in English-medium schools: I the problems. *Journal of Multilingual and Multicultural Development,* **9**, 267–84.

Index

Abad, Germino 298
Abbas, Ackbar 29, 47–48, 176, 290, 303–305
accent, *see* Hong Kong English
acculturation 19, 30–31, 231
acts of identity 191–193
Adamson, Bob 285
Afendras, Evangelos A. 42, 43, 286
affricates in Hong Kong English 130, 139
Aidoo, Ama Ata 306
Alsagoff, Lubna 145, 146, 158
alveolar approximant in Hong Kong English 133, 136, 139
American English 19, 58, 67–68, 122, 163, 222–224, 227, 261, 308–309
Anglo-Chinese schools 5, 32, 34, 38
Apple Daily 11, 87, 90–93, 99, 104, 110
Asia 2000 184, 186, 290–291
Asia Inc. 105
Asian Englishes 19, 22, 31, 45, 59, 119, 153, 223, 241, 257, 266–268
Asian Values 214
Asiaweek 11, 105, 112, 185
Atkinson, Paul A. 41, 285, 300
attitudes, *see* language attitudes; language ideologies and myths
ATV (*Asia Television Limited*) 106
Austen, Jane 223
autonomy 1, 6, 13, 18–19, 22, 29, 31, 37, 39, 219–220, 258, 266, 295–303, 306
Axler, Maria 59, 287

B International 185
Back to the Wall 216
Bacon-Shone, John 2, 19, 42–43, 57, 158, 283, 286, 301
baihua 37
Baker, Barbara 184, 186, 190
Baker, Hugh D. 47
Balla, John 285
Bamgbose, Ayo 59
Basic Law 7, 35, 108–109, 114
Bauer, Robert S. 37, 79, 82
Bautista, M.L.A. 22
BBC (*British Broadcasting Corporation*) 46, 106, 109, 226, 266
Benedict, Paul K. 37
Benson, Phil 20, 45, 161–170, 257–258, 285, 289, 295
Bhabha, Homi 303
Bhatia, Vijay K. 288
Bickley, Gillian 287
Bilbow, Grahame T. 288
Bilingual Laws Project 9, 35–36
bilingualism 6, 9, 11, 13, 17, 19–20, 30–31, 34–35, 41, 43–45, 57–58, 79–80, 85–87, 90–95, 103, 191, 193, 260, 282–283, 303; *see also* monolingualism; multilingualism
Blair, Tony 6
Blanc, Haim 81
Bloomfield, Leonard 191
Blunden, Edmund 51, 189, 302, 306
Bolt, Philip 263, 289
Bolton, Kingsley 1–25, 29–55, 57, 95, 120,

122, 141, 158, 161–162, 241–264, 281–291, 295–313
Borges, Jorge Luis 199
Boyle, Joseph 17, 258, 284, 285, 287–288, 302
Boyle, Linda 258, 288
Branegan, Jay 35
British colonialism 2–3, 5–7, 13, 16, 19, 20, 29, 31–39, 44, 47–48, 58, 79, 101, 109–110, 113–114, 219, 222–224, 229, 231, 247, 266–267, 269, 296–297, 300, 302–308
British English 58, 67, 89, 143, 157, 224, 226, 228, 259–260, 302, 306
Bruce, Nigel 281–282, 291
Brunei English 59
Buck, Pearl S. 220
Budge, Carol 289
Bunton, David 20, 57–77, 258, 288, 295
Burney Report 305
Butalia, Kavita 184
Butler, Susan 22, 44–45, 47, 49

cable television 106, 111–112
Cameron 52
Candlin, Christopher N. 282, 291
Cannon, Garland 289
Canton English 5, 31
Cantonese: culture 11, 32, 216, 220–221, 226, 258; language 2–4, 8–13, 15, 20, 32, 35–43, 46, 50–52, 57–58, 79–99, 106–107, 126–129, 133, 138–154, 157–158, 161–163, 174–176, 208–230, 235–236, 254, 257, 266, 283, 298–299, 305–309; Putonghua and Cantonese in Hong Kong 35–37; written form 36, 42; *see also* code-mixing and code-switching in Cantonese and English
Carless, David R. 45, 162, 289
Carter, Ron 187
censorship 110–111, 165, 258
census results 2, 34, 42–43, 57, 76, 153, 158, 211, 302
Chako, Sussy, *see* Xu Xi
Chan, Brian Hok-shing 81, 286
Chan, E. P. 144
Chan, Felix 39, 42
Chan, Mimi 14–15, 45, 48, 162, 257, 286,

289, 290, 304, 306
Chan, Yuen-ying 10–11, 20, 101–115
Chang, Helen 302
Chen, Albert H. Y. 109
Chen, Juliette 189
Cheng, Christie 271, 280
Cheng, Helen N. L. 283–284, 286–287
Cheng, Kai-ming 10
Cheng, Tien-mu 36
Cheung, Anita 177
Cheung, Anne S. Y. 36, 110, 285
Cheung, Chi-fa 39
Cheung, Gary 10
Cheung, Martha P. 48, 202, 290
Cheung, Oi Ling 284
Cheung, Yat-shing 16–17, 284, 301
Chin, Wan-kan 37
China Daily 36, 102, 112
Chinese pidgin English 4–5, 31–32, 305–307
Chinese sovereignty 8, 15, 29, 32, 38, 58, 103, 108, 113–114, 299–300
Chinese speakers of English 4–6, 58, 130, 140, 157, 162, 192, 210
Chinese University of Hong Kong, The (CUHK) 32, 34, 184, 263, 283–284, 286–287, 290–291
Chinese writers 189–191, 220, 229, 304, 308
Chinese: communists 32, 37, 39, 103, 108, 110, 112; culture 21, 32, 41, 75, 174, 201–202, 229, 269, 274, 276; food 47, 84, 202, 210, 258, 271–272, 310; government 6, 8, 15–16, 35, 39, 101–103, 110, 112, 114, 162, 299; identity 13, 21, 41, 222, 230–231, 267, 306, 308; imaginary 5; language 2–4, 8–14, 17, 20–21, 32, 35–38, 40–43, 45, 49, 57, 59, 80–86, 88–95, 104, 106–107, 110–112, 145, 158, 174, 184, 186, 193, 199–205, 210, 212–213, 219, 221–222, 225, 227–228, 267–268, 281–282, 300–301, 306–308, 311; *see also* Cantonese; Putonghua; and Mandarin; literature 174, 184, 199–205, 220–221, 225, 228, 268; people 4–16, 21–22, 43–47, 51, 58, 76, 79–88, 94–95, 101, 108, 185, 188–189, 212–215, 220–224, 228–229, 251, 258, 266, 300, 304, 307–309; *see also* Hong Kong: Chinese

Index 317

Chinglish 21, 47, 59, 60, 207–218, 223, 305, 307
Chinoy, Mike 109
Chinua Achebe 306
Chiu, Annette 11
Chow, Rey 304–305, 307
Chu, Leonard 110
City at the End of Time 184, 200, 290
Clark, Julie 185
Clavell, James 214, 224, 304
Clyne, Michael 80, 82, 87
CNN (Cable News Network) 106, 112–113, 266
Coates, Austin 224
code-mixing and code-switching in Cantonese and English 3, 9, 11, 20, 38, 43, 49–52, 79–99, 282–283, 286–287, 295, 305, 307
colonialism, *see* British colonialism
complaint tradition, *see* Hong Kong English
Computerworld/InfoWorld 105
Comrie, Bernard 151
Conrad, Joseph 227
consonants in Hong Kong English 20, 120–121, 129–139, 159, 213, 257
Cook, Robin 6
Cortarzar, Julio 199
Cosmopolitan 105
Cox Report 103, 297
Cox, Ah Fong 282, 291
Craig, Kenneth 258, 289
creative writing: in Hong Kong 20–22, 48, 171–237, 242, 265–280, 283, 290, 303–313; by Hong Kong students 265–280, 309–311
Crismore, Avon 58–59
culture, *see* Chinese: culture; Hong Kong: culture

Davies, Stephen 162
Delbridge, Arthur 163, 169
democracy 108–109, 113–114, 219
Detaramani, Champa 287
dictionaries 22, 45, 48, 64–65, 72–73, 82, 85, 162, 228, 257
Dimsum 184, 186, 208, 291
diphthongs in Hong Kong English 127–129, 138

discourse analysis, *see* pragmatics and discourse analysis
discourse(s): of colonialism 113–114, 303; of teachers in Hong Kong 57–77; on Hong Kong English 14–18, 22, 40, 49, 52, 303; *see also* language ideologies and myths
Discovery Channel 112
distribution (phonological) 121, 129, 135, 137–138
Dream of the Red Chamber, The 221
Dryden, John 176, 181

Eckman, Fred R. 120
education 5–6, 17–18, 22, 30, 37, 57–77, 219, 266, 281–282, 297, 303, 305; *see also* medium of instruction issue
Elegant, Robert 304
Eliot, Thomas S. 176, 223
Elliot, Dorinda 4
error analysis and interlanguage studies 3, 30, 59–60, 119–120, 122, 133, 141, 150–151, 153, 157, 207, 258–259, 282–283, 288–289, 307
ESPN 106
Eurasians 43, 222
Evans, Stephen 284

Far Eastern Economic Review 105, 300
Fenby, Jonathan 104
fiction (Hong Kong) 21, 48, 208, 219–233, 267, 295, 304, 308
Filipino language 9
Filipinos in Hong Kong 3, 43, 76, 221, 224, 269, 274
Financial Times 105
Fitzpatrick, Liam 189
Flowerdew, John 283, 287, 288
Fok, Michelle Ka-ling 272, 280
Fong, Bernard 101–102
Foo, Rebecca 282, 291
Foodscape 202, 290
Forestier, Katherine 185
Forster, Edward M. 223
Fortune 105, 108
Fotouhi, Sanaz 279, 280
fricatives in Hong Kong English 130–133, 139

Fu, Gail Schaefer 41, 79, 286, 288

Galaxy Satellite Broadcasting Limited 107
Gautier, Theophile 176
Gibbons, John 14, 37, 79–81, 84, 95, 283, 285–287
Gibbs, Raymond W. 187
Giles, Howard 59
Gisborne, Nikolas 20, 141–161, 295
globalization 75, 86, 111, 113, 222, 266
Gould, Vanessa 18
grammar and usage books 61–63, 65–66, 68, 71–72, 74
grammar, *see* Hong Kong English
Gray, Lawrence 185–186
Green, Christopher F. 288
Green, Owen M. 5
Greenbaum, Sidney 72, 289
Gumperz, John 191
Guo, Zhongshi 106
Gupta, Anthea Fraser 40

Haida Gwaii 21, 203
Hall, Robert A. 5
Halliday, Michael A. K. 296
Hamlett, Tim 284
Hancock, Ian 29
Handover 4, 6, 108–110, 113, 183, 305
Hannah, Jean 141
Hardy, Thomas 223
Harris, Roy 3, 286, 289, 301
Henry, Gerard 185
Hirvela, Alan 59, 284
HKSAR Government (Hong Kong Special Administrative Region Government) 2, 8–9, 58, 94, 113; *see also* Hong Kong Government
Ho, Chee Lick 145–146, 158
Ho, Elaine Y. L. 290
Ho, Louise 21, 48, 173–182, 184, 189, 190, 290, 295, 307
Hollington, Michael 176
Holmes, Helen K. 283, 290
Hong Kong: accent, *see* Hong Kong English: accent; Cantonese and Putonghua in 35–37; *see also* Cantonese, Mandarin, Putonghua; Chinese 4, 9, 11, 22, 41, 44, 58, 81–83, 86–87, 89–95, 189, 212–214, 220–225, 230, 258, 304; civil service 2, 8–9, 35–36, 167, 223, 260, 280, 302; contemporary history 1–14; culture 2–4, 32, 36, 41, 46, 48, 173–175, 185, 188, 190, 193–194, 220, 224, 226, 229, 269, 295, 298, 303–307; English, *see* Hong Kong English; identity 2, 7, 13, 21, 39, 41, 47, 79, 108, 179, 181–183, 186, 191–193, 221–222, 230, 295, 300, 304, 306, 308; language planning and language policies 8–14, 35–37, 283–284, 297–298; law 2, 9, 35–36, 42, 216–217, 260; *see also* Basic Law, *Bilingual Laws Project*; literature, *see* Hong Kong English: literature; population 1–2, 6, 11, 33–35, 41–42, 57–58, 76, 153, 158, 301–302, *see also* census results; sociolinguistics of, *see* Hong Kong English: sociolinguistics
Hong Kong Baptist University (HKBU) 121
Hong Kong Cable Television Limited (HKCTV) 106
Hong Kong Commercial Daily 104
Hong Kong corpus of English, *see* International Corpus of English in Hong Kong (ICE-HK)
Hong Kong Daily News 104
Hong Kong Economic Times 90, 104
Hong Kong Economics Journal 104
Hong Kong English: accent (phonology) 20, 41, 44–45, 80, 119–140, 159, 161, 214, 222, 256–257, 266, 295–296; as a 'new English' 283, 289–290; attitudes, *see* language attitudes; autonomy 8–23, 295–303; complaint tradition 14–18; dictionary 48, 162; futures for 22, 295–313; grammar (and syntax) 141–160, 222, 228, 258–263; history of 44, 47–48; literary creativity, *see* creative writing, literary creativity in Hong Kong; literature 3, 21, 44, 189, 219–233, 303–304, 309; morphosyntax 153–156; origins of 4–6, 31–32; reference works 45–49; relative clauses 25, 141–160; sociolinguistics 13, 20, 29–55, 57–60, 141, 281; speech community

2, 4, 21, 41, 163, 169, 183, 191, 260, 298; standards of English 3, 8–9, 14–18, 40, 49–51, 58–59, 259, 268, 282, 297–303; vocabulary 19–20, 43–47, 49, 161–170, 204–218, 257–258
Hong Kong Examinations Authority (HKEA) 16, 68, 73, 301
Hong Kong Government 8–9, 33, 35, 37–38, 51–52, 76, 217; *see also* HKSAR Government
Hong Kong iMail 10
Hong Kong Rose 229, 291
Hong Kong Standard 104, 185, 208, 209
Hong Kong Telecom 58, 76
Hong Kong University (HKU); *see* University of Hong Kong, The
Hooper, Anthony G. 304
Huang, T. S. 288
Huckleberry Finn 221
Hudson, Richard 158, 191
Hui, Polly 9, 185, 186
human rights 114
Hung, Eva 186, 290
Hung, Joseph 263 289
Hung, Tony T. N. 20, 45, 49, 119–141, 256–257, 266, 295
Hunter, Duncan B. 14
Hutcheon, Robin 101
hybridity: cultural 4, 51, 307; linguistics 4, 49, 51, 210, 218, 269, 305, 307
Hyland, Ken 79
Hymes, Dell 81

identity, *see* Chinese: identity; Hong Kong: identity
imagination 21–22, 114, 265–280, 303, 307
India 32, 107, 112
Indian English 18–19, 29–32, 48, 57, 119, 127, 157, 168, 223–224, 241, 259, 266, 296
Indians in Hong Kong 3, 43, 76, 81, 210, 214, 222, 224
Ingham, Michael 22
interlanguage, *see* error analysis and interlanguage studies
International Corpus of English in Hong Kong (ICE-HK) 142, 157, 241–264

International Herald Tribune 105
Internet: explosion 4, 11–12, 111; ICQ 43, 49–51; usage 111–112, 185, 244, 268, 270, 282
Iyer, Pico 29

Jane Eyre 221
Janviroj, Pana 113
Jayawickrama, Nihal 114
Jefferies, Alan 184, 185
Jet TV 106
Joaquin, Nick 306
Johnson, Mark 187
Johnson, Robert K. 16–17, 38, 44, 95, 284–286, 301
Jones, Rodney 284
Joseph, John E. 290
Journey to the West 221

Kachru, Braj B. 18–19, 22, 29–31, 51, 58–74, 141, 191, 259, 265, 296, 303
Kachru, Yamuna 22
Kamwangamalu, Nkonko 286
Keenan, Edward L. 151
Kelen, Christopher 184, 185
Keobke, Ken 282, 291
Killingley, Siew-yue 149
King, Rex 16, 301
Kingman Report 297
Kingston, Maxine Hong 220, 226–227, 308
Klein, Richard 110
Knight, Alan 109
Kong, Kenneth C. C. 288
Kott, Jan 199
Kowloon Tong 228
Kraar, Louis 108
Kwo, Ora W. Y. 285
Kwok, Edmond S. T. 38
Kwok, Helen 14, 44–45, 120, 122, 141, 161–162, 256–257, 286, 289, 306, 308
Kwok, Shirley 9, 39

Ladefoged, Peter 139
Lai, Ellen 267, 269
Lai, Winnie Auyeung 285
Lakoff, George 158, 187

Lam, Agnes 21, 48, 183–197, 290, 295, 305, 307
Lam, William C. P. 258, 289
Lam, Wing-kwan 85
language attitudes 20, 57–77, 282, 287–288, 295–303; *see also* language ideologies and myths
language benchmarks 59, 267
language boundaries 83, 87, 202–205
Language Campaign 58
language community, *see* Hong Kong English: speech community
language ideologies and myths 2, 17–18, 30, 40–52, 295–303
language norms in Hong Kong 2, 12, 20, 44, 57–77, 82, 142, 153, 302
language planning and language policies, *see* Hong Kong: language planning and language policies; *see also* medium of instruction issue
lateral in Hong Kong English 133–136, 139
Lau, Chi-kuen 16, 35, 110, 300
Lau, Chunfat 139
Law, Eva 59
Law, Siu-lan 104
Lawrence, David Herbert 223
Le Page, Robert 45, 191
Lee Kwan Yew 38
Lee, Cher Leng 286
Lee, Ding Fai 304
Lee, Elbert S. P. 189
Lee, Keon Woong 270, 280
Lee, Micky 79, 83, 85, 95
Lee, Paul L. M. 286
Lee, Paul S. N. 110
Lee, Sik-yum 59
Lee, Wing-on 40
Leech, Geoffrey 157
Leland, Charles G. 5
Lessing, Doris 229
Leung, Benjamin K. P. 33
Leung, Mei Chun May 262
Leung, Ping-kwan 21, 48, 184, 189, 199, 201–202, 290, 295, 304–305, 307–308
Leung, Yin-bing 81
Li, Tsz-chiu 178
Li, Ching Chao 204
Li, David 300–301

Li, David C. S. 20, 43, 79–99, 283–284, 287–288, 295
Li, Peng 6
Li, Po 204
Lim, Shirley Geok-lin 21–22, 265–280, 295–313
Lin, Angel Mei Yi 15, 95, 285–288, 298
literary creativity in Hong Kong 20–22, 31, 44, 48, 173–37, 295, 302
Llamzon, Teodoro A. 19
localized words in Hong Kong English, *see* Hong Kong English: vocabulary
Lord, Robert 14, 283–284, 286–287
Lowenberg, Peter H. 59
Lui, Stephanie Po-man 276, 280
Luke, Kang-kwong 44, 58, 79, 82, 84–88, 95, 120, 161, 281, 284
Luo, Dayou 304

MacIntosh, Angus 296
MacLehose, Murray 1
MacMahon, Jennifer 311
Macquarie Dictionary 22, 45, 48, 257
Madden, Normandy 112
Malaysia 112, 168
Malaysian English 19, 29–32, 57–59, 126, 130, 153, 223–224
Malaysians in Hong Kong 3, 43, 221, 223
Man, Vicky 139
Mandarin 32, 37, 43, 85, 91, 107, 145, 158, 225–228, 255; *see also* Putonghua
Mansfield, Katherine 223
Marquez, Gabriel Garcia 199
Marsh, Jon 103
Mason, Richard 224
Matheson, Ruth 6–7
Matthews, Stephen 141–143, 147–153, 155, 157–158, 289
Maugham, Somerset 224
McArthur, Tom 22, 29, 163, 296
McCrum, Robert 29
McGowan, Joe 108
McGurn, William 300
McMahon, April 153
media: code-mixing and code-switching in 79–99; English media in Hong Kong 10–12, 20, 42, 67–68, 101–115, 185; radio and television 105–107

medium of instruction issue 10, 17, 37–41, 283–285, 296
Miller, Lindsay 287
Milroy, James 14
Milroy, Lesley 14, 191
Milton, John 258–259
Ming Pao Daily News 104
missionary schools 5, 32, 37
Mitchell, Robert Edward 102
mixed code, *see* code-mixing and code-switching in Cantonese and English
Mo, Timothy 306–307
Mohanan, K. P. 119, 139,142, 158
monolingualism 2–3, 41–43, 298
monophthongs in Hong Kong English 122–127, 138
Morley, David 107
morphosyntax of Hong Kong English 147, 153–156
morphosyntax of native varieties of English 154
Morrison, John R. 5
Moy, Joyce 39
multilingualism 2–3, 11, 19, 31, 34, 40–41, 43, 228, 282–283, 286, 308, *see also* bilingualism
Museum Pieces 202
Myers-Scotton, Carol 81

Nabokov, Vladimir 227, 229
Naipaul, Vidiadhar S. 227
Nakano, Yoshiko 109
Nanwani, Shalini 271
nasals in Hong Kong English 133–136, 138–139
National Geographic, 105
native speakers of English (NS) 30, 60–67, 70–71, 74, 125, 144, 151–152
Native-speaker English teachers (NET) 58, 67, 76
nativization 30, 151
Nelson, Cecil L. 259
Nelson, Gerald 21, 49, 241–264
New, Christopher 304
News Corporation 112
Newsbrook, Mark 141, 143–144, 146–148, 150–151, 156–157
Newsweek 105, 109

Ng, Addy 274, 280
Ng, Kang-chung 10
Ng, Margaret Ngoi-yee 13–14
Ngeow, Karen Yeok-hwa 58
Ngugi, Wa Thiong'o 306
Noble House 214
nomenclature 176–179
non-native speakers of English (NNS) 60–75
Norton, Teresa 216
novels (Hong Kong) 21, 48, 191, 214, 219–233, 243, 304

Oe, Kenzaburo 199
Ong, Timothy 105
Ong, Walter 173
Oriental Daily 104
Orwell, George 158, 199
Osing, Gordon 200, 290
Oxford Companion to the English Language 163, 296

Pakir, Anne 22
Palmer, Frank R. 191
Palmer, Gary B. 187
Pannu, Jasbir 81
Parker, Dorothy 223
Parkin, Andrew 48, 184, 202–204, 290
Paroles 185
Pasierbsky, Fritz 36
Patri, Mrudula 42, 81
Patten, Chris 252, 271, 280
Patten, Christopher 6, 33
PC World 105
Peking University 199
Peng, Long 120, 139
Pennington, Martha C. 4, 42, 59, 80–81, 95, 120, 283–288
Pennycook, Alastair 113
People's Republic of China (PRC) 6–7, 33, 36, 57, 108, 167, 258
Philippine Daily Inquirer 112, 298
Philippine English 3, 18–19, 29–32, 41, 48, 223, 241, 259, 267, 297–298, 306
Phoenix TV 112
phonology, *see* Hong Kong English: accent
Pidgin English, *see* Chinese pidgin English
Pierson, Herbert D. 59, 284, 287–288

Pierson-Smith, Anne 284
Pinter, Harold 280
Platt, John T. 161, 290
poetry (Hong Kong) 21–22, 48, 51, 177–178, 183–206, 262, 295, 307–308
Pollard, David E. 186
Pomery, Chris 167
Poon, Anita Y. K. 285
Poon, Wai Yi 95
Poplack, Shana 81
Postiglione, Gerald A. 40, 285, 287
postpositive modification in Hong Kong English 147
Potter, John 258, 289
Pound, Ezra 175
pragmatics and discourse analysis 82–85, 89, 93–94, 262, 283, 288
Prator, Clifford 296–298
Prince Charles 6
Putonghua 2, 6–10, 12, 15–16, 35–36, 38, 41, 43, 57, 91, 107, 228, 230, 255, 298–299, 306; *see also* Mandarin

Qian, Qichen 6
Quirk, Randolph 157

racism 5, 222
radio broadcasting in Hong Kong 20, 106–107, 185, 209, 249–251
Radio Television Hong Kong (RTHK) 67, 76, 106, 226, 249
Rao, Mani 184–186
Reader's Digest 105
recognition of Hong Kong English 3, 19–20, 29–31, 161–162, 298
reduced relatives 146–147, 152
reference works, *see* Hong Kong English
Regan, Mark 18
relative clauses, *see* Hong Kong English
Renditions: A Chinese-English Translation Magazine 174, 184, 186, 290
researching Hong Kong English 281–291
restrictive/non-restrictive constrasts in Hong Kong English 143, 151–153
resumptive pronouns in Hong Kong English 149–152
Richards, Jack C. 44, 58, 120, 161, 281, 284
Richards, Page 22

Richards, Stephen 185, 288
Roberts, Elfed 162
Robertson, Geoffrey 110
Robins, Devin 107
Roebuck, Derek 36
Romaine, Susanne 17, 143, 295–297, 302
Room of One's Own, A 219
RP (Received Pronunciation) 122
Running Dog 304
Rushdie, Salman 227
Rusmin, Ruru S. 284

Sankoff, David 81
Scollon, Ron 83, 87, 283, 288
Sebba, Mark 142
semantic oppositions in Hong Kong English vocabulary 163–167
Setter, Jane 120
Shakespeare, William 176, 249, 267, 270
Shimatsu, Yoichi Clarke 113
Shirk, Martha 111
short stories (Hong Kong) 21, 48, 184, 191, 221, 269, 276–280
Siegel, Jeff 81
Siegenthaler, Peter D. 108
Simpson, Robert K. M. 51
Sin Chew Jit Poh 112
Sin, King-sui 36
Sing Dao Daily 104
Sing Pao Newspaper 104
Singapore 11, 40, 112, 189, 307
Singaporean English 3, 18–19, 29–32, 38, 48, 57–59, 119, 126–127, 130, 141, 144–146, 153, 157, 161, 214, 219, 223–224, 241, 259, 266–267, 296
Singaporeans in Hong Kong 221
Singlish 266–267
Slavick, Madeleine 184, 186, 190
Smith, Carl T. 6, 32
Smith, Larry 22
Snell-Hornby, Mary 87
So, Daniel W. C. 32, 57, 285, 286
social class 12–14, 17, 33, 40, 43, 165, 219, 225–226, 300, 302
sociolinguistics, *see* Hong Kong English
sociology of language 282–284
Soo, Keng-soon 58
South China Morning Post (SCMP) 3, 7,

11, 15–17, 39–40, 42, 49, 67, 76, 99, 101–104, 113, 162, 165–167, 185, 208–209, 284, 289, 298–300
Souza, Jean D' 139
spectrographic analyses of Hong Kong English accent 122–123, 131–132, 136–137
speech community, *see* Hong Kong English
Spurr, David 109
Sri Lanka 119
Stambler, Peter 184, 186
Standard English 20, 58, 75, 141, 259, 307–308
standards of English, *see* Hong Kong English
Standing Committee on Language Education and Research (SCOLAR) 291
Star TV (Satellite Television Asian Region Ltd) 107, 112
Stevens, Trudy 287
Stewart, Sarah 113
stops in Hong Kong English 120, 130, 139, 257
Strasser, Steven 4
Strevens, Peter 296
substrate 145–146, 157–158
Sun, Andrew 185
superstrate 145–146, 157
Svartvik, Jan 157
Sweetser, Eve V. 158
syntax, *see* Hong Kong English: grammar

T'sou, Benjamin 14, 284, 298, 300
Tabouret-Keller, Andrée 45, 191
Tacey, Elisabeth 10, 305–306
Tam, Lawrence 282–291
taxonomies of Hong Kong English vocabulary 165–166, 259
Tay, Mary W. J. 44, 290
Taylor, Andrew 45, 162, 257, 290
teachers of English in Hong Kong 17, 20, 51, 57–77, 119, 223, 248, 282
text types in International Corpus of English project 242–255, 260
The Asian Wall Street Journal 105
The Economist 105

The Jakarta Post 112
The Korea Herald 112
The Monkey King 221, 306–307
The Nation 112
The Star 112
The Statesman 112
The Straits Times 112
The Sun 104
The Tatler 102
Theroux, Paul 228
Tiananmen 114, 176, 235, 300
Tien, Michael Puk-sun 10, 17
Tiger Standard 102
Time 105, 112
Time Warner 112
Tin Tin Daily News 104
Todd, Loreto 29
translation 48, 82–87, 95, 184, 191, 193, 199–205, 213, 305, 308
Trudgill, Peter 141, 154
Tsang, Venus Chiu-ying 272, 273, 280, 309
Tsang, Wai-king 83
Tse, S. K. 282, 291
Tsui, Amy B. M. 20, 57–77, 284, 295
Tsui, Sio-ming 105
Tsur, Reuven 187
Tung, Chee-hwa 4, 6, 8, 39, 51, 108, 113, 271, 280
Tung, Peter C.S. 285
TVB (Television Broadcasts Limited) 50, 93, 106, 112, 251
Twain, Mark 223

University of Hong Kong, The (HKU) 12, 14, 21, 32, 34, 48–19, 51, 60, 80, 166, 184, 189, 267–268, 280, 286, 289, 291, 300, 302, 306, 309
Unwalled City, The 21, 220, 229–230, 234–237, 291, 308
USA Today 105

Vagg, John 166
Vee, Louis 185, 186
Vietnam News 112
Vines, Stephen 104, 111
Vittachi, Nury 21, 48, 186, 207, 218, 291, 295, 305, 307
vocabulary, *see* Hong Kong English

vowels in Hong Kong English 20, 122–129, 138–139, 256–257
Vs: 12 Hong Kong Poets 184, 291

Waiting 229
Walcott, Derek 175, 227–228
Walters, Steve 285
Wanchai 216
Ward, Alan 258, 289
Webster, Michael 144, 152, 258, 289
Weir, Fred 87
WH-words and prepositions in Hong Kong English 145, 148–150
Wilkins, Karin G. 108
Williams, Raymond 305
Woman to Woman 184, 290, 307
Woman Warrior, The 226, 308
Wong, David T. K. 291
Wong, Eliza Fong-ting 271, 280, 310
Wong, Ho-yin 177, 310
Wong, Laurence 48, 184, 290
Wong, Nicholas Y. B. 274, 280
Wong, Nicole Chun-chi 276, 280
Wong, Sau-ling Cynthia 289
Woo, F. William 111
Woo, Ka Hei Michelle 22, 262
Woolf, Virginia 199, 219, 223
Workplace English Campaign 17–18
world Englishes 18–19, 29–31, 169, 219, 265–267, 282, 296
Wright, Susan 283

Xu, Xi (Sussy Chako/Komala) 21–22, 48, 174, 219–237, 290–291, 295, 305, 308

Yang, Anson 287
Yang, Xun 15, 299
Yano, Yasukata 22
Yau, Frances Man Siu 8, 41, 79, 284–285, 287
Yee, Albert H. 300–301
Yinglish 210–212
Yip, Virginia 141–143, 147–153, 155, 157–158, 289
Yow, Sophia 10
Yu, Vivenne W. S. 41, 285, 300
Yang Yung: A Journal of Hong Kong and International Writing 184, 269, 280, 311

Yue, Francis 59, 287
Yuen, Che Hung 189
Yung, Vicki 83

Zajc, Lydia 11
zero-subject relatives in Hong Kong English 143–146, 152–154, 158
Zhang, Wannian 6
Zuraidah, Ibrahim 113